THE PARISH PRIEST AT WORK

An Introduction to Systematic Pastoralia

BY

CHARLES R. FORDER

WITH A FOREWORD BY THE
RIGHT REV. A. W. F. BLUNT, D.D.
Bishop of Bradford

CONTENTS

FOREWORD

THE author of this book is one of our younger incumbents in the city of Bradford. He has had varied experience, some of it in the country, but most of it in town parishes; his brother-clergy know him as a parish priest of quiet effectiveness, and as a man with a real talent for organization, which has been proved by his work not only in his parishes, but also as secretary of a large and very active C.M.S. Association.

His book disclaims any special originality; but it covers the ground comprehensively, and is enriched by quotations from many sources; it ought to be of great service to any clergy (and especially to younger incumbents) who desire to familiarize themselves with the principles of pastoral work and to improve themselves in the technique of its practice.

We are living in unusual days; but whatever new ventures in Church work may have to be made, the staple of the Anglican parson's activity will always be pastoral; and the fundamentals of good pastoral work will always be the same. These fundamentals are, in my opinion, admirably set out in this book; I am glad to commend it to the notice of the clergy.

ALFRED BRADFORD.

PREFACE

THE purpose of this book is to give a comprehensive survey of the many subjects that comprise Pastoralia. There are, indeed, so many that only an introduction can be given to each, and only the dry bones can be presented. To make these dry bones live, every priest must come to his task with the inspiration of the Holy Spirit, and, unless he has the inner life of prayer and devotion, no study of the methods of pastoral work will help him. Many excellent books treat the all-important subjects of a priest's vocation and spiritual nourishment, but for the purpose of this book it must be assumed that all is well with the priest's own inner life.

This is perhaps a dangerous assumption. Canon Liddon has written:

> " It is a matter of just complaint with candidates for holy orders, that many books which profess to treat of pastoral work address themselves almost exclusively to the external duties of a Christian priest. They enter at length upon a consideration of sermons, visiting the sick, schools, ritual, and they continually insist upon the necessity of bringing the inward life to bear upon the discharge of such outward and visible ministries. The existence of an inward life is indeed assumed, but no attempt is made to determine its specific character, or the laws of its formation."[1]

Yet the subject of the priest's inner life demands many volumes to itself, and for the purpose in hand it must be assumed—even though the assumption is sometimes unjustified—to be part of the priest's preliminary concern before he approaches the practical problems.

Our object is to make a systematic approach to each department of Pastoralia, and to try to integrate the various departments into a planned unity. Many books on Pastoralia are concerned with certain sections of parochial work, such as preaching, Sunday schools, or evangelism, and some books give the impression that there is nothing else to do in the parish except the particular activity described. The various departments are, in fact, all interlocked.

---

[1] H. P. Liddon, *Clerical Life and Work*, 1895, p. 1.

The arrangement of the scheme of this survey is necessarily arti-
ficial, and so cross-references are frequently needed to keep the
unity of the work.

It would be presumptuous for anyone to pretend thorough
practical knowledge of every side of parochial life. So this work
attempts to build up its survey from the numerous books on Pastoralia, and also to codify or to compare various recommendations
from many authorities. For this reason numerous quotations
are given, some at length, since it is thought better to quote outright
than to try to say the same things in different words. Thus an
attempt is made to provide an introduction to the whole subject
of Pastoralia; and further lines of study and sources of information
are indicated either in the text, or in the footnotes, or in the bibliographies. Many books on Pastoralia give the personal experiences
of their writers, and this is very valuable, for pastoral work must be
personal if it is in any way to be effective, but it necessarily follows
that much is left unsaid. The curate or incumbent who is seeking
to learn more about his job has to read many different books, and
then may not discover the exact object of his quest. By correlating
the different books, a clearer picture of the full range of parochial
work can be secured, but the result is necessarily somewhat conventional, and may serve more as a guide-book or a reference-
book to the subject than as a complete study in itself.

This book is therefore designed to be useful for incumbents who
undertake the task of training deacons and priests ; for priests
whose training has for some reason been inadequate; and for young
incumbents in their first parishes. It is also hoped that it will be
valuable to those who enter the ministry at this time, and whose
curacies may consequently be shorter than usual. *Training for the
Ministry*, the Report of the Archbishops' Commission issued in
1944, recommends closer attention to post-ordination training,
and some suggestions are offered for this.

Preparing such a work as this in war-time and immediately afterwards, raises a number of difficulties. In order to describe ordinary
pastoral work the effects of the war have to be ignored. Some things
that are described as existing are actually in abeyance, and, owing
to evacuation or war damage, it is useless to give many addresses.
For this reason attention is drawn to the *Official Year Book of the Church
of England*, which is always up-to-date with addresses. Necessarily
no consideration is given to the immediate, and very important,
though only temporary, problems of the post-war period, such as
the return of the service men and women to the parishes.

In an essay of this kind we have to remember that no two parishes are alike, that every parish has its own unique problems, and that every kind of unique problem cannot be discussed. There are also the limitations that churchmanship and lack of wide experience are bound to impose upon anyone who tries to make a systematic and comprehensive survey of Pastoralia in the Church of England. My practical experience has been in the Industrial West Riding, though my early years were spent in the country. I am also aware that I fall far short of my own ideals, and that many things which I mention, I have not yet been able to do. I have tried to include those things that a priest in the Church of England should know, but this is not to say that it would be expedient to introduce into every parish everything herein described. Difficult questions of churchmanship arise on some points, so, as far as possible, an attempt has been made to give an idea of the Church of England as a whole, at the cost, in places, of the appearance of ' sitting on the fence '. In spite of the blemishes there must necessarily be, I hope that the general plan of this work will be of assistance to many parish priests. I owe a great debt to all those whose work I have so freely quoted or used. I hope that the readers of this book will in their turn follow the references in the footnotes, and read the various books for themselves.

My thanks are due to those who read through the manuscript, or parts of it, and made many suggestions. Especially I should thank Bishop Mackenzie, the Provost of Bradford, the Rev. R. D. Say of the Church of England Youth Council, Miss Bartlett of the National Society, Canon Perrett and Miss E. E. Peters. The Editorial Secretary of the S.P.C.K. rendered invaluable help and encouragement, and my greatest debt is due to him. For the final form of the book, and for all errors of taste or of judgement, I am alone responsible.

C. R. FORDER.

Dec. 1945.

Part I
THE PRIEST'S ADMINISTRATION

CHAPTER I

PAROCHIAL ADMINISTRATION

§ 1. The Need of an Orderly System

(a) *Necessity of Order in a Priest's Life.* At first sight it may appear that some apology is needed for the introduction of business methods into a parson's life, for a parson is, or should be, above all else, a man of prayer, a priest, a pastor, and a student. But order in a priest's life there must be, for it is necessary for self-discipline and for prayer. A man who does not order his life is not likely to order his prayers, though it does not follow that a man who *does* order his life will necessarily have prayers to arrange. In so ordering his life, the priest is doing no more than trying to do in his own life as God does in the world. God is a God of Order as well as a God of Love. " God is not a God of confusion." [1] The world is ordered, and yet there is room for individual initiative. A priest, then, in making himself a man of system, should always leave room for personal initiative in the needs of the moment.

In spite of the necessity for order, there is a deplorable lack of business efficiency among the clergy as a whole. It is not altogether their fault. On the one hand, many have never been properly trained, and, on the other hand, the duties and circumstances of clerical life make it very difficult to be systematic. The laity scarcely realize how much administration the clergy must do, and how very difficult it is to do it. [2]

(b) *General Reasons for Lack of System.* By the very nature of his office, a clergyman is master of his own time, and because of this he, being human, is in danger of allowing his life to be spent in a mere succession of trifles, just doing the congenial work rather than the uncongenial. [3]

Human nature has bigger snares for the parson even than this, for industrial psychology has demonstrated the ' tendency to minimum effort ' in all people, which hinders men from achieving their maximum efficiency. Thus the clergy are " only too prone

---

[1] I Cor. xiv. 33.
[2] C. E. Russell, *The Priest and Business*, pp. 5–6; Peter Green, *The Town Parson*, 1919, pp. 3–4; Peter Green, *The Man of God*, 1935, pp. 200–203.
[3] Peter Green, *The Town Parson*, pp. 2–4.

to remain contented with results which are hardly even ' fair '. How easy it is to be satisfied with a handful of weekly communicants in a large parish, or with an utterly inefficient Sunday School, or with a congregation in which men are conspicuous by their absence, or with the delivery of half-prepared sermons." [1]

In many spheres of industry applied psychology has considerably increased production by the elimination of ' unproductive working time '. Dewar and Hudson say that the clergy probably lose more by it than any other class of workers.

> " Our unbusinesslikeness is a by-word. To go into many clergy studies is to receive a severe shock. Books and papers lie about in a state of utter confusion. . . . The priest should regard shortcomings in these directions as sinful, for so they are. Nor are they by any means negligible factors in retarding the advance of the Kingdom of God." [2]

No doubt it is impossible to measure the productiveness of a parson's life, but it is clearly obvious that such results as can be, are bound to be improved by better business methods.

(c) *Present-Day Circumstances*. Human affairs in the world to-day are so complicated that parochial life must be infinitely more complex in its contact with the world. This complexity of life influences the laity in the parish for good or ill. The Church must move with the age, and it cannot speak to the world if its affairs are in a state of disorder. Probably the parochial system is proving to be unsatisfactory as a machine for pastoral and evangelistic endeavour. It appears to be breaking down. Perhaps all that is necessary to save it is efficient administration, for neither the parish nor the world can be evangelized through an inefficient machine. If anything like real efficiency is impossible with the present machinery, then certainly a new approach to pastoralia and evangelism must be found, and the present system abandoned, at least in town and city work. However, so long as the business side of the parish is not thoroughly efficient, it must not be concluded that modern ministerial life is entirely on the wrong lines.

(d) *The Laity and Parochial Business*. The laity are harsh judges of clerical failings, not so much in the spiritual sphere as in ordinary daily affairs. An inefficient preacher is tolerated as doing his best, but a priest slack in money matters is at once under suspicion. It is often said that the laity should manage the business side of the parish, and there is much truth in this. Yet the incumbent is always held

---

[1] L. Dewar and C. E. Hudson, *A Manual of Pastoral Psychology*, pp. 70, 71.
[2] *Ibid.*, p. 77.

responsible when there are financial difficulties, or when the Diocesan Quota is not paid. Though much of the administrative work must be done by the laity, only the parish priest can really take the full oversight of all parochial life. He is an exceptional layman who has the time or the ability for more than two or three sides of the work.

§ 2. PAROCHIAL ADMINISTRATION

(a) *Definition.* There must be a business side to the life of any priest, whether he likes it or not. This business side may conveniently be called 'Parochial Administration'. Its aim is to plan and organize the time and activities of the parochial clergy, and the various affairs of the parish, in such a way as to obtain in practice a maximum of efficiency, saving of time, and the elimination of friction. So only will the clergy be as free as possible for devotion, study and evangelism, and the laity be able to express a living, happy fellowship or family in the Body of Christ, both in its worship of God and in its witness to the world.

All parish work has its business side. It is a mistake to think that only the material interests can be made efficient, for the spiritual activities of the priest can also be made more effective by careful planning and business-like procedure behind the scenes. Parochial administration enters into all sides of the parson's work.

(b) *Its Values.* It is wrong to regard Parochial Administration as a regrettable necessity, for it can be a great power for good. " Business methods in the long run must lead to simplicity and the saving of time." [1] Memory lapses are reduced to a minimum, and worry and anxiety are much alleviated. True financial planning, for example, saves worry about money, and thus defeats one terrible enemy of true spiritual work. Spiritual intentions also become effective. " The object of organization is to provide an instrument by which energy can be made effective." [2]

Nor need it be feared that Parochial Administration is a bar to spiritual life. It is not true that the efficient priest necessarily lacks a real spiritual life, though he is often suspected of it, any more than it is true that he who lacks efficiency has thereby taken the first step to holiness.

(c) *Its Dangers.* True administration and planning are a power for Christ, though many fear to develop them because of a wrong impression that business methods accord ill with things of the spirit.

[1] C. E. Russell, *The Priest and Business*, p. 8.
[2] C. F. Rogers, *Principles of Parish Work*, p. 118.

These fears are not altogether groundless, and warnings are necessary.[1]

Planning is not sufficient in itself. Planned evangelism is no substitute for the living Word, but the living Word has more chance of being heard when preparations are made. It is the well-prepared soil that produces the most fruit.

Again, administration must be the servant, and not the master. It is possible to be so caught up in it that one lives for it. That is why many complain of being over-organized. There should always be a choice of organizations before any parish; no parish can have them all; and only those that can be mastered should be attempted. Over-organization comes about when organization is out of hand.

These dangers can be averted only by thoroughness. Only those things that can be done thoroughly should be attempted. If a priest, for example, acts as missionary-box secretary, he should see that the boxes are opened regularly and returned to their holders, and all the various amounts entered in a register. Often boxes lie about the study or the vestry, and the lay people complain that their boxes never come back.[2] There is no need to do all possible things, but those selected should be done thoroughly.

Although the dangers must never be ignored, they should never frighten any priest away from efficient parochial administration. The dangers of the absence of efficiency are far greater than the dangers of its presence. " Business-like methods, it is true, cannot create religion, but their absence may easily kill the life of the church." [3] Nor is it just a matter of the Church remaining alive; the Church has to capture the world, and its sources and powers must be used to the full to accomplish this.

> " If the small organism of the Church is to generate power to break the tyranny of the big machine and convert Britain again to Christ, it must have the best possible organization: no wasted power; no grit in the wheels." [4]

[1] Peter Green, *The Town Parson*, pp. 5, 6.   [2] Cf. Chapter XIX, § 2 (*c*).
[3] C. F. Rogers, *Principles of Parish Work*, 1905, p. 1. Cf. H. Latham, *Pastor Pastorum*, 1902, p. 397, also quoted in J. T. Inskip, *The Pastoral Idea*, 1905, p. 293.
[4] L. S. Hunter, *A Parson's Job*, 1931, p. 18.

SELECT BIBLIOGRAPHY

Peter Green, *The Town Parson*, 1919, Chapter I.
Peter Green, *The Man of God*, 1935, Chapter VI.
J. T. Inskip, *The Pastoral Idea*, 1905, Chapter IX.
C. F. Rogers, *Principles of Parish Work*, 1905.
C. E. Russell, *The Priest and Business*.
Lindsay Dewar and Cyril E. Hudson, *A Manual of Pastoral Psychology*, 1932, Part II.

CHAPTER II

THE STUDY AS AN OFFICE: RECORDS

§ 1. The Study and the Desk

(a) *The Administrative Centre,* the Whitehall of the Parish, is the study of the parish priest. It is not only a room for study, but it is also an office and, further, a consulting-room. Usually it is attached to the parsonage, indeed a room in it, and much ' unproductive working time ' [1] would be saved if it could be attached to the church or to the parochial buildings. Often there are three centres of work: the vestry at the church, an office at the school, and the study at the parsonage. If these three could always be one, administration would be much easier. If three there must be, the study will be the principal centre, with the vestry and school office as secondary places for interviews and administrative work. [2]

But this is not the only difficulty in the way of a parson making his study a business office. The records of the various departments of administration are scattered. Perhaps the account-books will be at a churchwarden's house, the minute book of the Church Council at the secretary's office, insurance policies will be (or should be) in the church safe, Sunday School registers in the hands of the superintendent, and various other records and documents in the hands of other church officials. The incumbent is indeed fortunate if the personnel of his voluntary staff are on the telephone, so that he can obtain information when required; otherwise time will be wasted going to the respective houses, or by trying to see the officials after services on Sundays.

The laity hardly realize that the parson has no clerical staff: he has no secretary, no office manager, no accountant, and so he has not only to supervise and plan the work but to do it all. The parish priest has to remember all that needs doing, he has to do his own typing and filing, he will perhaps do a certain amount of duplicating, count endless pennies, and lick his own stamps. While the telephone does save time, it also wastes much of it, because when the priest tries to reach somebody in an office he has to wait until

[1] See Chapter I, § 1 (*b*).
[2] Prof. Rogers in his books urges strongly that the vestry should be the principal office, but in actual practice few vestries are suitable.

7

the contact is made at the other end, while he is at the mercy of all wrong numbers. Not so the business man who has at least a staff of one.

For some of this work it is possible to use trained people in the parish; the more fortunate priest may obtain a leisured lady as a part-time secretary, while others can find office-girls willing to help some evenings with the duplicating, the addressing of envelopes and the postal service connected with appeals and general circulars. Notices of agenda can be given to the various secretaries to type and distribute, but at once the difficulty arises that they are not on the spot.

Consequently the need for efficiency is even more urgent than at first sight appears. The incumbent must have a careful, useful system, must realize the importance of habit in careful, quick checking, and must have a mind alert for the smallest details.

(b) *The Equipment of the Study.* If the study is to be this efficient centre of administration, it must be adequately equipped, and the equipment correctly used. The study must be carefully arranged and everything tidy. A desk littered with papers is worse than no desk at all. Tidiness cannot, however, be obtained if the study alone is tidy. A tidy bedroom, a tidy study, and a tidy life, are all connected. Yet tidiness is not a main characteristic of priest's studies—one incumbent, indeed, considered his own so bad that he never allowed his assistant to enter it. Certainly it would have revealed the man.

> "Few sidelights on personal character are more revealing than a private study. The choice of books, their arrangement on the shelves, their condition, and the aspect of the table where they are regularly studied—all yield trustworthy evidence to their owner's interest, habit, and method." [1]

The essential equipment of the study consists of a roll-top desk, or a large and workman-like writing-table,[2] according to choice; a typewriter and a duplicator; a filing cabinet or a set of box files; bookcases; a telephone (in spite of the danger of becoming its slave); and card-indexes, record books and index books of various kinds, for the different purposes to be described later.

The desk must be arranged on the principle of saving unproductive working time, and so planned that those things needed for ordinary desk work are near at hand. This is the value of the pigeon-holes and the little shelves in a roll-top desk; these should

---

[1] H. Hensley Henson, *Retrospect of an Unimportant Life*, 1942, Vol. I, p. 192.
[2] C. E. Russell, *The Priest and Business*, p. 19.

not be used for filing away papers, but used to keep, in a handy way, stationery of various shapes and sizes, some of which should have printed headings (for few can now write legibly enough for others to read their signatures); postcards, envelopes, handy plain cards for notices, scrap paper, sticky labels, missionary-box labels, receipt books. Such a desk will also have places for pens, pencils and ink of various colours; paste pot, stamps and stamp edgings; and a drawer or two for odds and ends like drawing-pins, scissors, paper clips, rubber bands, and the like.

Below the desk are drawers of varying depths, divided into compartments, which can be used for the various needs of administration, arranged in degrees of handiness and need—*e.g.*:

1. Diary, Administrative Sheet, Booking List, Future Plans.
2. Church Notices, Needs for next Sunday.
3. Notices, letters, information collected for various officials.
4. Notices received for Baptisms and Banns.
5. Current sermons and addresses in preparation.
6. Visiting needs, street book, lists and memoranda.
7. Various accounts, bank pass-books, paying-in books.
8. Correspondence of a temporary nature.
9. Drawers for matters of temporary interest, but which for a time demand considerable attention.

Some of these items will need more than one drawer. The purposes of the various items will become clear later.

(c) *The Diary and the Administrative Sheet.* The Diary [1] is the first item of importance for efficient parochial administration. It is best to have a big one kept in the desk and a small one for pocket use. The first contains all the details required, the second the main items for engagements for guidance when away from the study. When two diaries are used, care must be taken to see that engagements made away from the study are transferred from the pocket diary to the other. To avoid possible mistakes that might arise from the use of two diaries, some priests advise only one, but a busy man, away from his desk with no pocket diary, has been known to forget the place and purpose of his next engagement.

The first rule of the Diary is that all engagements should be entered promptly, as they are arranged. It is wise to insist on all engagements being confirmed by letter, especially when made on the telephone or at a casual meeting. It is handy to keep such

[1] Not to be confused with the Parish Diary advocated by Prof. Rogers in his *Principles of Parish Work*, 1905, p. 58. Cf. below, Chapter V, § 4 (*b*).

letters in the Diary for the days concerned, or in a separate file if convenient, and to keep them until the duty is fulfilled. The confirming of engagements avoids disputes about the day arranged, and prevents confusion between Sunday the 2nd of the month, or the 2nd Sunday in the month, or the 2nd Sunday in Lent.[1] Confirmatory letters will therefore specify the time of the service or meeting, its particular purpose, and where it is to take place.

Entries in the Diary about engagements are of no use unless the Diary is frequently consulted. Each evening the next day's engagements should be inspected, their obligations considered, preparations examined, and times to be spent travelling estimated, so that the next day's work will run smoothly and unpunctuality be avoided. Some time each day a glance forward over days approaching will ensure that preparations for events are begun in good time.

At the end of each day, or next morning, it is wise to check off the departing day, entering the duties done as well as marking engagements fulfilled, and adding the times for each. This helps in three ways. A permanent record is obtained of the way in which the day was spent—a very useful record if one is ever unfortunate enough to be involved for any reason in a court case. Secondly a glance over pages of the Diary helps to keep an adjusted and balanced time-table.[2] Thirdly, the record can act as a guide for prayers and thanksgivings for God's grace in the daily work.[3]

Besides the Diary, the administrative sheet is essential. This may take the form either of the top sheet of a small number of papers securely clipped together and resting in the same drawer as the Diary, or of a memorandum tablet on a frame on the top of the desk. An octavo sheet is a convenient size; urgent notes are entered at the head of the page, those requiring less immediate attention in the centre, and those concerned with distant events near the foot. On the sheet may be entered such diverse items as points demanding thought or action, material for the magazine, letters to be written, people to see, matters to follow up—indeed, anything of which a reminder is needed. When the matter in question is completed, the note should be deleted. Notes will be constantly crossed out and others added, so from time to time the sheet will need re-writing, perhaps fortnightly or once a month, according to need. The administrative sheet should be consulted several times a day, and its use made indispensable in parochial administration.

[1] Cf. Peter Green, *The Man of God*, p. 220.
[2] See below, Chapter III, § 1.
[3] Cf. T. W. Pym, *A Parson's Dilemmas*, 1930, p. 112.

In addition, a loose-leaf book or memorandum pad, similar to those carried by doctors, may be carried in the pocket when visiting or attending meetings. Information gathered should be noted, and eventually transferred to the administrative sheet, or to the correct place of record. It can also be used " to secure ideas which come suddenly and by the mental processes over which we have little control " [1]

§ 2. METHODS OF FILING, INDEXING AND RECORDING

It is already clear that we cannot get very far in efficient adminis-tration without an adequate system for making records and filing information. Lack of any such system is obvious when the desk is littered with papers of all kinds, and when any document or infor-mation wanted has to be sought for high and low. When he was preparing his Gifford Lectures, Bishop Henson lamented :

> " How deeply I regret my neglect of Common-place books, which, if carefully and intelligently kept and indexed, gather into convenient accessible form the reading of a life-time. I, having depended upon a memory which was never strong and accurate, and is now become wholly untrustworthy, don't know where to turn for the facts which I dimly recall, and am driven to laborious researches for that which should be ready to my hand." [2]

The purpose of filing is to secure that everything is immediately accessible when needed. At first sight filing seems to take up a vast amount of valuable time, but it prevents much more time being wasted in seeking for information. Indeed, in actual practice, filing can be done in the odd minutes, and often takes very little time at all. The parish priest would wish to file such things as these: Records of services, meetings and committees and events of all kinds; records of the results of study, reading and research; information gathered for any purpose; pamphlets and newspaper cuttings; catalogues, guides and Lenten lists; sermons, addresses, lectures and original papers on any subjects; correspondence, statistics, accounts and balance-sheets; and personal records of income tax, insurance and similar matters. [3]

It is a good rule that any work, once done, should not need to be done again, and filing preserves any research or preparation for any possible second occasion. Even a programme for a children's

---

[1] C. F. Rogers, *Principles of Parish Work*, 1905, pp. 57, 58.
[2] H. Hensley Henson, *Retrospect of an Unimportant Life*, Vol. II, 1943, p. 342.
[3] The old way was the keeping of a Parish Book, see J. T. Inskip, *The Pastoral Idea*, p. 269.

party, with notes on the games to be played, which has taken half-an-hour to prepare, is worth keeping for another occasion in the same or another parish, with further added notes on the success or failure of the items.

There are several possible methods of filing, and the priest will be well advised to take one that he can easily master, although even the apparently complicated system is very easily worked. One thing, however, must be avoided, and that is the keeping of papers and cuttings unfiled. Feats of memory sometimes enable the owner to discover his requirements, but usually such papers soon become mere litter.

(a) *A System of Box Files*. These can be purchased or easily made out of cardboard boxes, and labelled. Each box can be used for a subject or group of subjects, and some can have an alphabetical system of dividing leaves inside. These are certainly suitable for correspondence or receipts, and even for pamphlets and odd papers, but are not very helpful for notes on study. The more one desires to keep, the more complicated this system becomes, despite its apparent simplicity.

(b) *A Filing-Cabinet System*. This can be either wood or steel, upright, with four drawers for quarto or foolscap sizes. Sets of folders can be kept in the drawers, and they can be either simple meeting-sheets, or pockets with gussets for larger capacity, called document wallets. The folders can be of various colours, with tabs for marking their subject or number, and with stiff cards (alphabetical or plain) for dividing folders into sets. The cabinet can be used for filing in different ways.

(i) Alphabetical Arrangement.—Here each folder is given its subject name, according to the matter contained in it—*e.g.*, P.C.C., C.M.S., Dilapidations, Benefice Income, Hymns. The folders are arranged simply in order of the alphabet. This has the seeming merit of simplicity, but cross-references are difficult, and folders on like subjects are not always together. In practice it is convenient to have associated subjects grouped together. It is soon difficult to decide where to file subdivisions of a subject—*e.g.*, the King's Messengers of the S.P.G.; should this be under S or K? Whatever the decision made, there is no means of remembering it when the information is required.

(ii) Chronological Filing.—In this system each folder, irrespective of the subject it contains, is given the next vacant number as its subject is introduced. The first folder filed—say on Gambling—is given the number 1, the next—say on Mothers' Union—is given the number 2, and so on. Folders are added when a new subject is required, and numbers follow in the chronological order of filing. So that the folder may be found when required, an alphabetical index must be used, and this may be a loose-leaf book with alphabetical guides. In the instance given above, Mothers' Union would be placed under M, with the figure 2 placed next to it. This system has the big advantage of easy cross-reference, as the alphabetical entry can give the figures of any number of folders containing associated subjects. The disadvantage is that associated subjects are not together in the file and there is no real provision for reference to books.

(iii) Dewey Decimal System.—The Public Libraries have made most people familiar with the modern way of cataloguing books. In the Dewey system all possible subjects are divided into ten main classifications; these are subdivided into ten main divisions; these are further subdivided, and so on, and figures with decimals are used to indicate the subjects. This system can be adapted for the filing cabinet. Folders with the subject-title receive the appropriate index-number from the Dewey system, and are arranged in order of numbers; stiff-back cards with tabs can be used for the main divisions, to facilitate reference. To illustrate the method, the following are the numbers for these subjects likely to be found in a parish priest's cabinet: Apostolic Succession, 262·11; Resurrection, 232·5; Church Finance, 254; Thirty-nine Articles, 238·3; Franciscans, 271·3; Buddhism, 294·3; Sunday School Publicity, 268·145; St. Matthew, 236·2. A guide to the numbers can be consulted at the local Reference Library. Of course, as in the last system, an alphabetical index is needed, so that the folder for any subject can be quickly found.

In addition to the filing cabinet, in this system a card index can be very valuable. The cards have subject headings, just like the folders in the cabinet, and are arranged in order of their Dewey numbers, and any card can be found through the guidance of the same alphabetical index just mentioned. Whereas the folders are used for documents, letters, pamphlets and cuttings, the cards are used for short notes and references. Each card has a note about the material in the folder with the same number, and, in addition, references to books and other sources where the subject is mentioned.

The system is thus two-fold; it uses a filing cabinet and a card ndex, with the one alphabetical guide for each. Contrasted with ystems (i) and (ii) in this system, associated subjects have neighbouring folders or neighbouring cards; the Dewey method provides

c

for this. Further, the cards provide a handy and easy way of recording the results of systematic reading and quick references to casual quotations. A suitable card size is 6 × 4. An illustration of a card follows, on the subject of Betting and Gambling; this particular card would be filed under the number 174·6, and entered in the alphabetical index under both B and G.

BETTING AND GAMBLING   174·6

Pamphlets by Heywood, Mulliner.   In folder.
Newspaper Cuttings.   do.
Speaker's Bible. Minor Prophets, p. 172.
Mortimer in " Personal Ethics " (Kirk), p. 132.
C.O.P.E.C. Report V., " Leisure ", p. 65.
Senior Lessons Handbook, p. 304.

The main disadvantage of this system is that it was devised for another purpose and is not completely suitable for parish work. It is not balanced, as nearly all the required subjects will be in the 200 section, and many subjects must be added. Again, each group of sub-divisions is limited to ten, as it is a decimal system; the next system has a great advantage here.

(iv) The Mastrom Indexing System.[1]—This is a specialized system for clergy and ministers, and has all the advantages of the last system described, with a set of numbers of its own. All possible subjects of interest to the parish priest are intended to be included, divided into groups and divisions with wide range of extension, and there is a place provided for recording general reading and information. This is a copyright system, but it is worth the cost. The makers provide a key to the divisions, with explanations for working it, a prepared alphabetical index, a card-index system with special cards variously coloured and easily numbered to facilitate reference, and also material of a similar nature for use in a filing cabinet.

The advantages over system (iii), which it resembles in working, are fourfold. There is a ready-made key: if one knew the under-lying method, it would be possible to make up one's own key, but that would be a laborious process. It is not so complicated as it sounds, and can be used easily without actually understanding the method of classification; but it is better to know it, so that personal

---

[1] Made by Mastrom, Limited, 81 Holly Lane, Erdington, Birmingham.

additions can be made. The complete list is in itself valuable, as it reminds the parson of the many things he ought to study. Finally, everything of importance to the parish priest is contained in it— meetings, committees, study, sermons, and personal affairs. However, it could be improved in several ways. It has the appearance of being hastily constructed, and with more thought before its publication it could have been more balanced. Nevertheless, it can very easily be adapted to any man's requirements.

(c) *Box Containers.* In addition to a filing cabinet, box containers or drawers are also necessary. The cabinet file is not meant for bulky material, such as periodicals, papers—*e.g.*, reports of Societies, hymn-sheets, copies of plays. Necessary reference to periodicals for the subjects which they mention may be entered in the card index, giving the date and number of the periodical concerned. Any kind of cardboard boxes, box files or desk drawers may be used.

§ 3. Important Records

(a) *Correspondence.* Next to the Diary, correspondence looms large in the ordinary administration of the parish, and it is in this that the outside world usually discovers the inefficiency of the clergy.

> " The two commonest accusations against the clergy are that they never answer letters, and even when they do, you cannot read the reply. Recently a Bishop sent out a letter enclosing a very important recommendation to 300 incumbents. Enclosed was a stamped and addressed envelope for the reply which was essential to the scheme. Four of these envelopes were returned." [1]

Canon Green says wisely:—

> " As far as possible reply to letters by return of post. Where you are uncertain what answer to give send a postcard saying, ' Am unable to give you a definite answer to your letter of yesterday. I hope to be able to write fully by the end of the week.' " [2]

A tray or drawer can contain these letters waiting attention; it needs daily inspection. When the reply is sent it should be explicit in itself—that is to say, it should recapitulate enough of the letter received to make its meaning clear to anyone who may read it. This is particularly important in confirming dates.

The real problem in method is the way to meet the difficulties that arise when letters dispatched receive no reply. Correspondence

---

[1] C. E. Russell, *The Priest and Business*, p. 18.
[2] Peter Green, *The Man of God*, p. 219.

sent can be noted in a letter book, in the Diary, or on the administration sheet; a mark is made when the reply is received. If no
reply is received after a reasonable space of time, further enquiry
can be made. Usually once a letter is written, the writer feels that
the responsibility is on the correspondent, and the matter may be
forgotten.

Filing correspondence is not difficult, and, if the letters are typed,
carbon copies can be made and filed away also. The alphabetical
system is best for ordinary correspondence, with some convention
adopted for meeting double-barrelled names and other oddities of
nomenclature. Unimportant letters can be destroyed; those of
doubtful permanence can be placed in a " trial " file. Anonymous
letters should be destroyed.[1] It is sometimes advantageous to file
some correspondence under its appropriate subject-heads rather
than under the names of the senders; letters making or confirming
engagements may be placed, under the dates concerned, in the
Diary itself; about business for the Church, in the P.C.C. file with
notices of agenda; those relating to a special appeal, such as a
Centenary Fund, in a folder for that purpose; letters with rulings
from the Bishop, under the subjects to which they relate. In this
case cross-references will be useful. First they will secure that there
is in the alphabetical letter-file a list of all the letters received from
any one source (from the Bishop, for instance) with their place of
filing indicated; and, secondly, they will solve the problem of the
letter that deals with several subjects, which will be filed under one
subject, with cross-references in the others noting where it is to be
found.

Receipts belonging to personal accounts are conveniently kept in
a box file, with alphabetical guides. Receipts belonging to church
accounts should be placed in their own right place.[2] Other items
that reach a parish priest by post should not go immediately into the
waste-paper basket, although that will be the ultimate destination
of many of them. All should be inspected. All the appeals cannot
be given response, but some deserve more consideration, and should
be filed for reporting to the Church Council. Circulars are a source
of information; and many are suitable for filing. They may come
from church builders or cleaners, from makers of church furniture,
or suppliers of parochial requisites. They never come when they
are needed, but sometimes they are needed and cannot be found.
An expanding or concertina file (alphabetical) is useful for storing

[1] Hensley Henson, *Retrospect of an Unimportant Life*, Vol. 11, pp. 391–2.
[2] See below, Chapter X, § 3.

these, and cards should be placed in the card index under appropriate numbers for church cleaners, church furniture, and so on, and these cards will give the names of the firms whose catalogues have been filed.

(b) *Statistics.* The preservation of statistical information is most useful, although it is true that such records often stimulate the dangerous pursuit of record-breaking, or offer the snare of self-advertisement. Dr. Watts Ditchfield once pointed out how often numbers are mentioned in the Bible,[1] and Dr. Inskip hints why it is that some clergy do not trouble with numerical records:

> " Some clergymen talk glibly about leaving results to God, when no results of their work are apparent, or of not believing in statistics when there are none worth recording, or when they are too lazy to record them." [2]

Frequently a communication arrives through the post asking for information about the priest or his parish. Careful filing helps to provide the correct information, and the return forms can be accurately completed. It is unwise to guess at figures or to give impressions, for counting is not a strong point with many priests, and the way congregations are usually estimated in numbers is really amusing. It is quite easy to keep accurate statistics in the filing cabinet in folders under the appropriate subjects.

The Annual Parochial Return is sent at the beginning of the year, complete with instructional notes, by the Rural Dean. It looks much more complicated than it is. The instructions are that the second part should be filled in first by the Honorary Secretary of the P.C.C., and then the first part by the incumbent, but in many parishes the secretary will be glad of the incumbent's help. Of the statistical figures required, the number of the baptized, the confirmed, and the Easter communicants will be found in the vestry registers. Numbers in the Sunday School, Bible classes, fellowships and adult classes can be supplied by the secretaries concerned, but the priest is advised to have duplicate lists of the membership of all these bodies in his own files, and then he has only to turn to them for numbers. The Day School figures can only be supplied by the head-teachers. The church accounts, if printed in full every year, as they ought to be, will give all the details required for the completion of the financial details, and the minute-books will give the items required in the Church Council section. This last information will also be obtainable in the P.C.C. folder in the filing cabinet,

---

[1] J. E. Watts Ditchfield, *The Church in Action*, 1913, p. 32.
[2] J. T. Inskip, *The Pastoral Idea*, p. 290.

if the priest records a short note on each meeting. It is not a great matter to make this return, but Rural Deans do not find that they come in very readily. Some incumbents need several reminders, others return incomplete details, and neatness is not characteristic.

Diocesan and Deanery returns for assessment of quotas are sometimes required, and it is unfortunate that the Annual Parochial Return cannot suffice for all purposes. It is the *number* of the returns required that irritates, but local idiosyncrasies do not seem to be content with the figures on a Provincial plan. The Diocesan triennial returns are actually required to record the elections to the Diocesan Conference, and, as such, are necessary. The articles of enquiry sent out at the annual visitation are, fortunately, for the churchwardens to answer, though sometimes some figures may be required from the incumbent.[1]

Societies for Home and Overseas Missions also issue forms asking how the sums contributed to them are raised. These forms are very useful for the working of the societies, and the priest's goodwill will lead him to co-operate. Either he himself, or the parochial secretary for the societies concerned, should keep an accurate list of contributors, box-holders, collections; the completion of the form is elementary.[2]

The Bishop requires a list of Confirmation candidates when they are presented, giving the ages and dates of baptism.[3] Complaints are sometimes heard that these are badly written and untidy.

Two other annual return forms are personal and obligatory—the Income Tax and Clergy Pensions returns; these are considered later.[4]

Each year also a circular reaches all clergy from the Editor of *Crockford*. This famous Clerical Directory depends on the faithful co-operation of the clergy in returning the forms. It is useful for many people in all kinds of ways.

Other statistics the incumbent may keep for his own instruction or improvement, and sometimes they may be presented at his Annual Parochial Meeting. For example, the number of communicants for the year, of weddings and of funerals, the circulation of the magazine. It is good discipline, and sobering, to have an accurate count of the numbers present at different services, and also to keep a record of the number of visits paid in the course of the year, for these figures never reach those of guesses and estimates.

(c) *Books and Bookcases.* For the ordinary parson's library of

---

[1] See below, Chapter XX, § 5 (a) and (b). [2] Chapter XIX, § 2 (c).
[3] Chapter XXII, § 1 (c). [4] See below, Chapter XXVII, § 1 (b) and (c).

some thousand volumes there is no need to have an elaborate system of classification and arrangement. If desired, the Dewey or Mastrom system of numbers can be used, but it is best to group the books under a few general heads—Reference, Bible, Theology, Worship, Ethics, Sociology, Church History, Missions, popular works and sermon material, English and general books, with any other group of books on the priest's particular subject. Cataloguing is useful, as it shows at a glance which particular books are in the study on any subject. Either the card index or a loose-leaf book can be used in the Mastrom numbers, or with a small range of books a few selected subject headings will suffice.

It is necessary, however, to have cards in the index on which to enter books to buy, with a note for each on the publisher and price, and the review which recommended it; also some cards on which to enter books on loan to whom and when. A useful check on the progress of reading is a record of books read. This can be either a simple list with dates when they are begun and finished, or a more elaborate method which means a card for each book and a personal " review " recorded.

(d) *Sermon Indexing.* Some priests do not keep a sermon when once it has been preached, some keep them all, and others compromise by a complete destruction every ten years or so. It depends on the preacher's temperament, but old sermons can be useful, and the fruits of real research should not be destroyed; illustrations and facts are always of potential use. No sermon need be repeated as it stands, but some are the better for a second or third time of preaching. The wise householder brings from his treasure things new and things old. Ideas and opinions develop and change, and a preacher may well be surprised at the weakness of early efforts, though sometimes a good early sermon is the cause of renewed zeal. But if sermons are to be kept, they must be properly indexed.

Each sermon, whether written in full or preserved in note form, should be arranged on paper with space for indexing notes; the subject and text should be clear, and also the date and place of delivery. If it is used again, the further place and date should be added. The sources of information or illustrations used for the sermon are also worth recording. Sermons can be filed in envelopes of suitable size, either separately, or in groups. Each should be numbered in rotation as it is added to the file, 1, 2, 3, . . . and they must always be kept in order, and referred to by the number allotted.[1] To index sermons, a special section may be reserved in the

[1] See Chronological Filing, above, § 2 (*b*) ii.

card index; subjects are arranged under any convenient system, like that of Dewey or Mastrom, and entered in the general alphabetical guide, with the card number given some special mark to show that it is for sermons.

On each subject card the sermon can be mentioned by title and its chronological number in the sermon file, so that a glance will show how many sermons have been preached that bear directly or indirectly on the subject. A card will look like this, headed by the subject and its Dewey number with preface (S) indicating sermon section.

RESURRECTION   (S) 232·5

First Easter   18
Empty Tomb   50
Bereavement   289
Idle Tales   567

The advantage of this system is that any sermon can be found at once, if its subject is remembered. Again, if it is desired to preach on a certain subject, all old sermons on that subject may be consulted and partly used again, or a new line deliberately chosen. Also it can easily be seen if certain subjects have been neglected in preaching, and so a continual harping on a favourite theme can be avoided.

It is also possible for sermons to be entered by their numbers in the margin of a Bible kept for that purpose, against the text used; or, better still, on the reverse of the cards used for Bible study,[1] each card representing a chapter or shorter passage, as desired. A further record of sermons, if it is desired, can be made by entering the sermon in the Diary on the day of its preaching, with its number attached. A list of sermons in chronological order of preaching in the priest's own church is illuminating in showing which way his mind is working. Some priests may care to have cards for other churches, a card for each, on which to enter sermons preached away, to avoid preaching the same sermon twice at any one of them.

§ 4. FINAL COMMENTS ON FILING

Ways of filing other things will be mentioned as the different departments of administration are considered (though for reasons

---

[1] See below, Chapter IV, § 1 (b).

of space illustrations of method cannot be given for all), but enough has been said to indicate the general method. It certainly requires time to do it with any efficiency, but the system is well worth while, and saves much more time than is spent on it. A comprehensive system is a powerful asset to the parson; in different circumstances he will find himself using different parts of his system, but it is equally valuable in town or country parishes.

The system naturally has to grow and develop, and the plan takes two or three years to work before it becomes completely useful, its full usefulness becoming apparent only if information worth filing is filed away. Far from being a complicated machine, it becomes a personal affair, as the Mastrom publishers say of their system in the explanatory notes, " The whole system becomes at once a personal and intimate partner, growing daily with you and always ready for immediate service ". One difficulty is remembering that the information is there. This is overcome by habit in the use of material. When preparing an address, or sermon, or essay, the question must be asked, " What material have I already? ". When preparing for a committee or meeting, " Where are the notices of agenda, letters, records, statistics, and records of previous meetings? " When preparing for the next issue of the parish magazine, the incumbent simply turns up the folder for the current issue, in which has been placed any relevant information occurring since the last issue.[1] Habit in filing is equally essential. When the cabinet is consulted the priest will only find the material put in. A consistent habit of recording must be developed to give the system a fair test.

[1] See below, Chapter XVIII, § 4 (d).

BIBLIOGRAPHY

As for Chapter I.

CHAPTER III

THE STUDY AS AN OFFICE: PAROCHIAL PLANNING

§ 1. The Priest's Time-Table

BEFORE he can begin planning for the parish, the parson must be capable of planning for himself. Just because he is his own master he must be master of himself. A man can be very busy, and feel that he is working very hard, and yet may not be doing his full duty and making the best use of his time. He would be offended if he were told this. The fact is that a time-table is really necessary for guidance in the best use of time.[1]

In *A Manual of Pastoral Psychology*, in their chapter on " Clerical Applied Psychology," the authors demonstrate very clearly how a minister can be the victim of the pressure of business or physical necessity. The daily work in the sense of physical urgency could be ordered thus: " Conduct of Public Worship, surplice duty (weddings, funerals), correspondence, preparation of sermons and addresses, sick visiting, clubs and societies, committees and meetings, private prayer, study, visiting of the whole." [2] This does not in any way correspond with the needs of spiritual urgency, but without a time-table and self-discipline the line of least resistance will be taken. " In order to do his job efficiently, he must order and limit his work, so that, come what may, the order of spiritual urgency rules in his life, and not the order of physical necessity."[2]

The time-table needs a firm framework and yet must be elastic and adjustable for varying needs. To keep to it is good discipline and an essay in self-control, and it should not be replanned too often. The time-table needs a general structure for the day and a general structure for the week.

(a) *The Working Day*. The items in any ordinary working day will include: Prayer, Administration, Study, Parochial Activity and Parochial Organizations. These words are given a wide meaning for time-table purposes to cover a range of activity. Prayer is meant to cover the time set apart for Holy Communion, meditation or quiet time, and the daily Offices. Administration covers such diverse matters as attention to Diary, correspondence,

---

[1] Peter Green, *The Town Parson*, pp. 1–6; C. E. Russell, *The Priest and Business*, pp. 9–17; H. H. Henson, *Ad Clerum*, pp. 71–73. [2] Dewar and Hudson, p. 78.

staff meeting, forward planning, filing and indexing, business preparations and office hours. Study must cover not only serious reading, but also sermon preparation, clerical study circles and possible clergy chapters. Parochial Activity involves visiting, conduct of occasional services, attendance at meetings, private interviews and confessions. Parochial Organizations embraces clubs and meetings, Church Council, evening classes, preparation classes, choir practices and socials.

The sequence of these main points will be the same almost every day. Prayer in its wide sense will occupy the time from early rising (no priest who gets up late is likely to have a time-table) until 9 or 9.30 a.m., with a short interval for breakfast. After Day School an hour or more will be needed for administration, leaving two hours or more before lunch for study. A short rest with or without a book is wise after lunch,[1] and parochial activity occupies the afternoon. The type of parish will determine the time for tea, and Evensong and another short spell of administration (*i.e.*, filing visiting records, answering afternoon's post) can come before or after tea. The evening is devoted to parochial organizations, but sometimes there are opportunities for study and visiting.

(b) *The Weekly Time-Table*. The week is a succession of such days, but the five main points will vary in their main emphasis. Adjustments depend on individual requirements and capacity. A good plan is to have a general estimate of the number of hours to be devoted to each of the five sections each week, and to keep an approximate record daily in the Diary.[2] It is not wise to depend on impressions. Some might ask for a specimen time-table, such as is given by Mr. Russell,[3] but this has to be too simple to be of real help. There is no point in putting down visiting every afternoon, when funerals and weddings often occur, or the Bishop may call his clergy to meetings. But as soon as a time-table becomes personal it becomes complex, and is no help to another individual. The weekly time-table is a sequence of days, arranged on the daily sequence of the five points of activity.

But two days are different from the rest—Sunday, which is a day on its own, and the day-off. " On Sunday no ordinary business is done, and we are mercifully free from the necessity of dealing with correspondence." [4] But there is business in addition to the services of worship, as Sunday is often the only day when a priest

---

[1] See below, Chapter XXVII, § 2 (*a*).
[2] See above, Chapter II, § 1 (*c*).
[3] *The Priest and Business*, p. 17.
[4] C. E. Russell, *The Priest and Business*, p. 9.

can gather some kinds of information or give out notes to people he does not see during the week.[1] Sunday does lend itself to some recreation or light reading, and the evening is an opportunity for inviting parishioners to the vicarage for an hour or so. The free-day should be an equally fixed feature in every weekly programme.[2]

(c) *General Cautions*. The time-table needs revision from time to time in the light of experience, but not too often, or it will not have a fair trial. There is no need to be too anxious about booking up every moment of the week, for this would make life an intolerable burden. The things liked should not overshadow the rest of the programme, and in particular the temptation to follow the view of the world, that parochial activity constitutes the priest's real work,[3] should be overcome. The other things in the time-table may not be seen by the world, but they may be more vitally important.

Outside attractions, meetings and study circles, may easily be allowed to overbalance the time-table. It is quite inconsistent, and not helpful to others, for a priest to try to do much non-parochial work at one time, and then withdraw from it entirely. Similar consistency is necessary in the parish; once a thing is begun it has to be kept up, and one thing thoroughly done is worth five things scamped.[4]

It should not be forgotten that the time-table is adjustable in many different ways, and such variety helps to maintain it. It is good to emphasize the different parts from time to time, and to spend rather more time on one and rather less upon another. Study, for instance, can be increased in Lent, and visiting in the spring and autumn.

Yet even in the best-worked time-table interruptions are many and unavoidable. The doorbell or the telephone constantly calls the priest from his desk.[5] Sometimes it is possible to drill parishioners into certain hours, but beggars, not to mention organizing secretaries, come without warning. A good time-table can stand interruptions, but lack of system cannot cope with them. This raises the question of 'Office Hours', which is part of the daily administration section, but this subject is better considered later in its own place under 'consultations.'[6] However, interruptions at meals should be avoided if possible. It appears that experi-

---

[1] See below, Chapter XIII, § 5.
[2] See below, Chapter XXVII, § 2 (a).
[3] Dewar and Hudson, *A Manual of Pastoral Psychology*, p. 82.
[4] Peter Green, *The Town Parson*, p. 21.
[5] See below, Chapter XXIV, § 2 (b).
[6] *Ibid.*, § 2 (a).

mental psychology has shown, by means of vivisection of dogs, that even ' talking shop ' at meals is likely to arouse passions and emotions that prevent good digestion.[1]

§ 2. THE PRIEST'S PLANNING FOR THE PARISH

(a) *Importance of Planning.* In the study of Pastoralia not much thought has been given to planning, which, though obviously important, is a neglected side of parochial·administration. It is usually done in a casual way, perhaps while the parish priest is shaving, or over the breakfast coffee. Actually parochial efficiency depends more on planning than on filing, for the chief purpose of the second is to prepare the ground for the first. " Forethought is one of the marks of civilized life." [2]

Most parishes have routine, but not a planned programme. Routine is good in its way, even if it is developed haphazardly; in fact, routine is the backbone of effective work. It is essential as an individual's habits, and often is the expression in outward form of the traditions of the parish. But the danger of routine is that it makes it so easy to get into a rut, and then parish work in its various forms is afflicted with sameness or monotony, so that the parishioners speak of things being dead without knowing why.

Planning introduces variety, using routine as a basis. Its purpose is to provide the means for awakening people to a new life in Christ, and for the keeping alive and fresh those already awakened. All pastoral work provides for the impact upon people of Christian values, and the priest humbly offers himself and his work for use by the Holy Spirit, but the grace of God is much less hindered when the priest gives thought to his work. Old people need a variety of impact to keep them out of the rut, but this variety has to be planned so that it is not seen or realized by them. Young people need a variety of practice rather than of impact, as they need to be conscious of the variety to keep on the rails. There is further a rhythmic motion in parish life, for parishes have their moods and feelings, their depressions, their actions and reactions. No priest can keep his parish up to concert pitch all the time in the different spheres of activity, whether spiritual, social or financial. It only leads to disappointment to launch a campaign at an inopportune moment. True planning is the watching for the phases which move in waves, which rise or fall, and then merge or develop into

[1] Dewar and Hudson, *A Manual of Pastoral Psychology*, p. 82.
[2] C. F. Rogers, *Principles of Parish Work*, p. 71. Cf. pp. 70–72.

others. The Church Council often provides the pulse for testing such parochial feelings.

The priest must be on the watch, therefore, for new ideas, which he can gather by means of observation, reading, and clergy schools. But there is one big danger before the planning enthusiast. Just as it is possible to be so busy recording that there is no time to do anything worth recording, so, too, it is possible to be so busy planning that there is no time to carry out the things planned.

(b) *General Principles.* It is elementary to observe that the first thing in planning is the avoiding of clashes of events and the crowding of weeks. The different interests of different people should be well balanced. Planning future events should take into account diocesan and other outside events, but those in authority ought to help by announcing such dates as far ahead as possible. On the other hand, it is irritating to organizing secretaries and local organizers to find their circulars ignored, when they have tried to do this. A personal need in the planning of future dates is to see that meetings and addresses are so arranged as to leave time for adequate and necessary preparations. Scamped sermons are often a symptom that too much is being done one week and too little another.

Planning involves both a short-range and a long-range view, and the first requires more detail and consideration than the second. It could be made a habit that immediate work is planned as each monthly magazine is written, for then the next six weeks are under review, the ordinary routine is checked, and necessary variation considered. But it is also essential that sometimes, as part of the administration period, a general review of the next six months should be made. In the spring the next winter's programme, with its sessions for the various organizations, needs to be planned; and each Lent the summer sessions need similar consideration.

But how is the incumbent to remember those matters which must be planned? Once a yearly scheme is working in routine, the magazines of former years are most valuable as a guide. A whole set of bound issues from the foundation of the magazine is a great asset, but for handy reference the local matter each month should be detached and kept a year together in folders. In addition, a loose-leaf book, with a page for each month, or a card for each month in the card index in the appropriate section, can give the necessary guidance. Each card has on it such things as things to do this month; things to prepare this month in readiness for later events; things to have in mind for preliminary consideration. For example, the May card might mention: Dedication Festival, Summer Garden Party and Harvest preachers, as illustrating each type of note. Behind each monthly card, other cards could be filed, giving details of the special events of the month—as Harvest card behind September card. Cards can also be provided for each day of each month and for various reminder purposes. The cards for each Sunday in the year and those for the Christian Festivals must be kept in separate sequences, for the Christian year is independent of the months. The use of these cards is explained in the next section.

It is also useful if, after each event, be it service, meeting or social, any details that may guide future planning of similar events are filed away in a correctly numbered folder. Such information would include programmes, Lenten lists, printed matter, circulars, invitation cards, lists of names. The method of filing and indexing is the same as the procedure explained in the preceding chapter. Then, when an event has to be planned, the first thing to do is to turn up the appropriate folder; for example, for a Bring and Buy Sale, the organization of which often falls to the lot of the incumbent's wife, the folder will contain: a record of the quantities of provisions last obtained, their cost, and if enough or too many were purchased; who were invited, and how many came; when it was and how much was made. Nearly all the information for any event can be typed on a single sheet in very little time.

§ 3. PLANNING IN DETAIL

(a) *The Christian Year.* The calendar is already made for Christians, with its constant setting forth of the Christian Gospel, and it provides the background for all the spiritual work of the Church. But arrangements for the great Festivals must be made in advance, and this proves once again that planning is not concerned only with material matters. "Anticipation or foresight enters largely into the nature and performance of all priestly and pastoral work. . . . It is necessary, sometimes, to look a year ahead in arranging for a profitable Lent." [1]

(i) The principal seasons will involve preparations for worship in which due regard is given to the associated Christian doctrine. There are other points which need forethought and preparation. Advent and Lent give opportunities for special preaching schemes when definite Church teaching can be given. Visiting preachers

---

[1] Arthur W. Hopkinson, *Pastor's Progress,* 1942, p. 32.

can be invited to give independent addresses, or to give a course by arrangement; each, in turn, could take a clause from the Creed. Week-night services or meetings give a chance of planning a Missionary School, or a School of Bible Study, or an Evangelistic campaign, using the laity.[1] An Advent or Lenten leaflet (which should afterwards be filed),[2] gives an opportunity, not only to state the services, but also to send a message to the parishioners. Ways of emphasizing Lenten observances should be considered, and Passion Plays or choir works planned in conjunction with the Lenten theme.

Christmas involves arrangements for the decorations, carol services, Christmas cards, the Crib and Nativity plays. The parish may have some scheme for Christmas parcels or other poor relief. There will be parties for some organizations. Good Friday requires arrangements for Children's Services, the Three Hours' Service, or a Lantern Service. Perhaps the day will give opportunities for evangelistic work at factories, or for a Procession of Witness, or for united services with the Free Churchmen. Besides the joy of planning to present the wonderful message of Easter, there are details of less importance concerning the decorations, their cost, and those who decorate; the laundering of the surplices; and the planning of an Easter Garden. Of the other main seasons, Epiphany has missionary associations; Ascensiontide may mean a holiday for the Day School; and Whitsuntide, especially in the North, is the time for processions of the Sunday School children, hymn-singing, and perhaps an outing, a field-day or a ' bun-fight.'

The method of recording reminders was suggested in the preceding section; on the page or card for each Festival and Sunday in the year, filed in its chronological order, is entered each subject connected with the day or season, with the key to the places where the necessary information will be found. For example, the code number may indicate appropriate sermons, or the folder of Lenten leaflets, or of the sick and poor Christmas list, or the folder or box of Carol services, just as the particular season requires.

(ii) Special Sundays sometimes punctuate the Christian year, and depend on the monthly calendar; these, of course, need similar planning. The Harvest Thanksgiving needs much thought for the accepting of the gifts, the arrangement of the fruit and flowers, and, more especially, the subsequent distribution to the sick and needy. The latter often becomes an unholy scramble. A children's Gift service is a delight, but only when every detail is foreseen.

[1] Peter Green, *The Man of God*, p. 157.   [2] *Ibid.*, p. 224.

Such Sundays as the Dedication Festival, Choir Sunday, Sunday School Anniversary, Youth Sunday, Mothering Sunday, Hospital Sunday, are distinguished by the choice of hymns, the prayers and perhaps lessons, and certainly by the purpose of the collection.

A Diocesan Sunday offers an opportunity of reminding the congregation of its wider responsibilities; usually the Diocese has a fixed date for the purpose. Prayers for the Diocese, the Bishop and the cathedral should be prepared for the day.[1] There are also Society Sundays, for Overseas and Home Missions; prayers, hymns and lessons (by permission) can be appropriate. Preachers may be arranged by a local secretary, so all letters should be read carefully, and arrangements noted in the Diary; anything required in reply should be sent at once.[2] Each area usually has fixed annual dates for these Sundays.

A list of the special Sundays is best prepared each December for the following year, and presented to the Church Council as a part of routine for the approving of the ear-marking of the collections for specific objects. These Sundays chosen are best not too near together, and any undue increase in the number of ' specials ' is to be deprecated, as it obscures the Christian year.[3] A copy of this list will be of help to the choirmaster.

If it is intended to have visiting preachers, they should be invited in good time; the first choice may not be able to come, and it may then be too late to obtain an alternative. Yet some incumbents, when preparing the copy for the next magazine, begin ringing round on the telephone, to arrange for the preachers for one of the Sundays of the month concerned, and are surprised to find nearly everyone already engaged. It is wise to keep a list of the special occasions attached to the Administrative Sheet, with ideas for preachers jotted down on it. At the foot of this list the names of those who would sometime be welcome can be entered, and thus a variety in visitors can be secured and neighbours treated with courtesy. Again it must be stressed that engagements must be carefully entered in the Diary, and confirmations and reminders sent in due course. Some of these special occasions may be very big days, when the Lord Mayor and his retinue attend, or there is a parade of the British Legion, or of the parochial junior organizations. The churchwardens should be instructed to make the due reservation of seats.

---

[1] See below, Chapter XX, § 5 (a).
[2] See below, Chapter XIX, § 5.
[3] H. Hensley Henson, *Retrospect of an Unimportant Life*, Vol. II, p. 391.

D

Finally, on the page or card in the index for the event, which is filed in the monthly section, must be entered the useful information gleaned from previous years, just as cards are prepared for the Christian Festivals.

(iii) Sunday School events are planned with due regard to the Christian year and the big occasions, and Parents' Days, Open Afternoons, Project Schemes, and Nativity Plays, are all given their proper place.[1]

(iv) In a large parish, with several district churches or Sunday Schools, planning is more complicated, but some of it may be deputed to the responsible members of the staff. Certain occasions will be regarded as big parochial events with which nothing smaller must clash, but otherwise each district will devise its own programme.[2]

(b) *The Business of the Church.* The main business of the parish concerns the work of the Church Council and its various committees. There is real need for regular meetings, the frequency of which will depend on the parish. A regular scheme helps people to remember, and thus encourages attendance; it is also useful for the incumbent to have some general plan, so that things are not forgotten and left until too late or too much business has to be crowded into one meeting.[3] A draft outline scheme for a year can be attached to the Administrative Sheet. It should be elastic enough to allow for the incidence of movable Feasts. The Council can meet monthly, or every two months, and routine business can be allocated to each meeting—*e.g.*, in December allocations of collections and budget for the following year; in January or February the presentation of accounts ready for the Annual Meeting; in March or April the new Council elects officers and committees. Between the Council meetings the committees will meet, reporting at the Council following; the frequency of these meetings will depend on their usual business. For instance, the Youth Committee may meet in January, March, June, September and November; the Buildings Committee every two months; the Missionary Committee in March, June and November; the Standing Committee in May, September and December.

(c) *The Social Programme.* The incumbent may or may not be concerned with the organization and running of social events,[4] but he will be wise to approve all the dates selected for them. Any

---

[1] See below, Chapter XV, § 3 (c).   [2] See below, Chapter V, § 4.
[3] See below, Chapter IX, § 3 (a) and (c).
[4] See below, Chapter XII, § 3 (b).

casual booking with a parochial hall secretary causes confusion, and often dissatisfaction and disappointment among the organizations, even if the secretary is quite good with his diary.

Some social events are hardy annuals attached by custom to certain organizations—*e.g.*, Old Year's Night to the Young People, Shrovetide to the Sunday School teachers. Other events need to be varied and balanced—socials, concerts, dances, as the practice of the parish may be. Needless to say, weekday social events bear on the spiritual programme, and due regard to this should be paid in booking dates. The custom of having no social events in Lent is good both for the parish and for the clergy; for the parish because it is a timely reminder once a year of the higher things, even if the people go elsewhere for entertainment, and for the clergy since it gives relief from much serving of tables (especially as in a working-class parish these events are on Saturday evenings) and in Lent more time is needed for study and meditation. The summer should not be ignored in the yearly programme; a Garden Party can be a very pleasant social affair in the town, and in the country is often the gala day of the year. A list of the social programme for the year can be kept for convenient reference with the Administrative Sheet.

(d) *The Organizations*. The weekly programme of all the organizations is directly concerned with the use of the parochial buildings,[1] but once adjusted it ought to work like clockwork. The forward planning looks to the arrangements of special events for particular organizations, especially in the provision of speakers. Probably each organization will have its own official who is responsible for these arrangements, though often the planning for the Mothers' Union becomes the duty of the incumbent's wife, and that for the Young People is the concern of one of the clergy. In all circumstances the dates should be arranged by the officials with the clergy, so that clashes can be avoided; otherwise a speaker for the M.U. arrives during a Bazaar, or a lecturer for the Y.P.F. in the middle of a concert.

When the winter's planning is made, the dates for the different organizations can be chosen—carefully missing the holiday periods —and lists given to the officials. When they have made their plans for the dates, copies can be returned to the incumbent, so that he can keep with his Administrative Sheet the programmes for the organizations and information is always ready at hand for the magazine. Careful attention to such dates will lead to the best use

[1] See below, Chapter XII, § 2 (c).

being made of visitors—for example, a missionary deputation can be introduced to the M.U., the G.F.S., the Y.P.F., and perhaps to the Scouts and Guides, so that a visit is made well worth while.

(e) *Pastoral Work.* Some part of the administration period of the time-table must be devoted at times to the planning of ordinary pastoral work. Visiting, to be systematic, must be planned, and time can be set aside for the writing of personal letters to candidates for confirmation, backsliders, communicants, young people. Baptisms and weddings are planned to a certain extent and the times noted in the Diary; funerals come at very short notice, and must be fitted in as best may be.

Within the general framework of the yearly routine, extra features as short-term plans can be introduced for the furtherance of particular objectives: a series of lectures, meetings or classes for some educational purpose, a series of missionary conferences, or an evangelistic project. The introduction of such extra activities demands careful thought. The usual organizations must be informed, so that they can take their share in the scheme, or at least adjust their plans accordingly. The right time has to be chosen for any such campaign, just when the parish is ready for it, and much more advertisement is needed in the parish for the special event than for the ordinary routine affairs.

Many other things obviously come under the head of planning and arranging, and are considered in their own departments, but time spent upon such preparation can rightly be termed administration. Occasionally it is good to have a general review. What sort of things have not been done recently? What has been obviously overdone? Is there anything going on that is no longer useful and ought to be stopped? Is anything a discredit to Christ and His Church? Is the real purpose of the organizations being achieved? Is the cutting edge of the Gospel sharpened or blunted by any of the manifold activities under review? Without some such searching questions from time to time, planning merely becomes just another routine practice.

BIBLIOGRAPHY

As for Chapter I.

CHAPTER IV

THE STUDY AS A STUDY: PERSONAL PLANNING

§ 1. STUDY AND READING

(a) *A Priest must Study.* Study is undoubtedly an important item in the daily programme of the parson, but it is terribly easy to allow it to be neglected either because of too much serving of tables or through mere laziness. Even pastoral work should not steal the time allocated to study. In this case the issue is usually clear. Canon Green has quoted the first Archbishop Temple as saying, " If the time ever comes when you have to choose between study and visiting, and honestly cannot do both, choose study." [1] But, when laziness is in question, the issue is more complicated, for laziness is often concealed by such excuses as these—that the priest in question cannot concentrate, or is too tired and needs frequent rest, or just lacks interest.

" Clerical Applied Psychology " [2] lays equal stress upon the need for mental and for physical efficiency, and shows that a disciplined mind, a good memory and power of concentration are within the range of any parish priest. " If any clergyman, therefore, is tempted to think that he cannot concentrate because of unfavourable conditions, let him see to it that he becomes independent of them as quickly as possible." [3] In fact, study helps to prevent that tired feeling; it is only with a balanced time-table that many hours of work can be done. " Changing of occupation to study is a real rest, and does not lead to fatigue." [4]

So the daily time-table should be arranged to secure adequate time for study. In the scheme already given,[5] preparations and study are grouped under one heading, for the two are closely connected, but it is wise to prepare addresses at the beginning of the week, and to leave the periods towards the end of the week for study. A judicious use of odd minutes helps tremendously. New publications can often be tackled after meals, even during a ' rest '

[1] *The Town Parson*, p. 11. See also pp. 10–20; and Peter Green, *The Man of God*, pp. 67–79.
[2] Dewar and Hudson, *A Manual of Pastoral Psychology*, pp. 82–87.
[3] *Ibid.*, p. 87.
[4] *Ibid.*, p. 76.
[5] See above, Chapter III, § 1 (a).

period, but this applies to books that are read to keep abreast with the trend of modern thought rather than for the purpose of deeper study when notes need to be taken.

However, it is not enough merely to include reading in the time-table; so little time actually can be earmarked for this purpose that it must be used to the best advantage. Unless study is taken seriously, either very little will be done, or it will be done very casually. It may even cover a wide field, with small systematic result. There are obviously very many subjects of interest to the parson, and he cannot possibly be master of them all. He ought, nevertheless, to be aware of all the subjects connected with his vocation and the main outline of their processes. Works, usually composite, summarizing these various subjects, and bibliographies enabling further study of them, are normally available.[1] To these should be added the study of Pastoralia,[2] and of Overseas Missions.[3]

Each month something of the main themes of Bible Study, Theology, Pastoralia and Missions should be studied, and in addition a special section or department of the work should be developed for deeper study and research. It is a good plan to do this with the intention eventually of publishing the results, or submitting them in a thesis for a degree. Such objects will probably never be achieved, but it is a good discipline to try to achieve them.

(b) *Bible Study*. No priest who recollects his promises at ordination can neglect Bible study. The ideal is to read in turn each book of the Bible with a good commentary, so that eventually the whole is covered. A good system of indexing helps to preserve the results. One method is to have an inter-leaved Bible, but if full notes are written in, it soon fills up. The leaves should be used only for the making of signs or symbols indicating where notes or information can be found, or which sermons are on each text; or just the cream of the thinking can be entered, so that a personal commentary accompanies the Bible.

A more elaborate system can be developed in a loose-leaf book or in the card index, and for this one of the numbered systems is invaluable. Each book of the Bible has its appropriate number, and such numbers usually follow the ordinary Bible sequence. For each book, a card can be used for a chapter or a suitable shorter passage. No card, of course, need be inserted until it is wanted for a note. On each card can be entered the thoughts of private

---

[1] E.g., *The Priest as Student*, ed. by H. S. Box, and *A Study of Theology*, ed by K. E. Kirk.
[2] See below, Chapter XXIX, § 4 (*a*).   [3] See below, Chapter XIX, § 4.

meditation, the references to books which treat of the particular passage, or references to such publications as those of the Bible Reading Fellowship. The reverse side of the card can give references to any sermons filed which were preached on the passage.[1] More extensive notes can be written or typed on quarto sheets and kept in folders in the filing cabinet on the same numbered system. Any priest who develops his own Bible commentary in this way will have a most useful mine of material for future sermon preparation.

(c) *Theology*. A scheme of study can be followed according to choice or interest, or according to the questions of the hour. As fields of interest grow, and as the reader's capacity and ability are gradually discovered to himself, it may sometimes be necessary to abandon certain lines of reading. The results of study will be filed under the heading of the subjects in question, notes put in folders, the card index being used for references to sources not actually noted down or copied.[2] Cross references between subjects are even more useful. Any reference to a book, or any notes or quotations taken from it, should have the source clearly indicated, by author, title, date or edition, and page. There is thus a quick reference back if anything is uncertain, and not only so, but this information is important if the notes are subsequently used in any publication.

(d) *Books*.—The difficulty of obtaining books is one of the biggest hindrances to study, for the ordinary parson cannot afford to buy very many. Good use should be made of the various libraries available. In *The Teaching Church* by Archbishop Temple and others, Chapter VI, there is a valuable section on the various sources from which books may be borrowed. Particular attention may be drawn to the following:[3]

(i) County and Town Public Libraries.
(ii) The National Central Library. (Malet Place, W.C.1.)
(iii) Dr. Williams' Library. (14 Gordon Square, W.C.1.)
(iv) The Libraries of societies like the I.C.F. and the Missionary Societies, C.M.S., S.P.G., etc. The former has its main section devoted to industrial and social problems, and the latter are mainly devoted to missionary literature, but all have admirable general sections.

[1] See above, Chapter II, § 3 (*d*).
[2] *Ibid*., § 2 (*b*).
[3] See the General Notes at the end of each of the pamphlets issued by the *Way of Renewal* (S.P.C.K.).

(v) Dr. Bray's Library.   (15 Tufton Street, S.W.1.)
(vi) A list of Libraries is also given in the *Official Year Book of the Church of England*.   Cathedral Libraries are noted.

Some clergy study best with study circles, and these can be a very excellent stimulus to thought, but they can also be the means of frittering away much of the time allocated for study in the time-table. The leader of the study circle should know something of the subject discussed and be able to keep the members down to it; the syllabus should be closely followed, and the books recommended read and studied.[1]   Some syllabuses put out for group study can, in practice, be used by individuals; such, for instance, are those issued by the Archbishops' Advisory Committee on *A Way of Renewal*, and those published by the Society of Sacred Study.[2]

§ 2. SERMONS AND SERMON PLANNING

(a) *Preaching the Word.*   It is not the purpose of this book to develop specialized branches of Pastoralia, such as preaching, but it is necessary to emphasize the importance of the sermon, to discern its objectives, and to consider the details that go to the making of a good sermon, in order to see its place in pastoral work and also how planning and preparation can help the Ministry of the Word. Priests are ministers of the Word, as well as ministers of the Sacraments, and preaching must not be despised as unimportant.   " The importance of preaching is bound up with the importance of the Word of God, and we cannot despise the one without also despising the other." [3]

It might almost be said of some sermons that they are preached without any realization of the aims of preaching; they are preached simply because something of the kind is expected every Sunday. This has often been expressed in another way—that the good preacher has something to say, whereas the bad preacher has to say something; but even then the something to say should be the message of God, and not the message of a man.   " The real business of the preacher is to declare and minister the Word of God." [4] Why God's Word should be declared is summed up by Dr. Selwyn in his introduction to his own excellent sermons: " The importance

---

[1] *The Teaching Church at Work* (S.P.C.K.) contains a chapter on " Clerical Study Circles " by Canon Leonard Hodgson.
[2] For up-to-date information see the *Official Year Book of the Church of England.*
[3] H. L. Goudge, *Christian Teaching and the Christian Year*, 1937, p. 7.
[4] C. Smyth, *The Art of Preaching*, 1940, p. 8.

of preaching lies, then, primarily in the fact that it deals with man as a spiritual being, and thus illuminates his most important relationships, and the several obligations of each." [1]

Dr. Farmer investigates the meaning of preaching more deeply in the first chapter of his book, *The Servant of the Word*. Preaching is an instrument of salvation. He works out his theme on the relation of personalities, founded on Buber's *I and Thou*, and he declares:

"The necessity of preaching resides in the fact that when God saves a man through Christ He insists on a living, personal encounter with him here and now in the sphere of present personal relationships. Preaching is that divine, saving activity in history, which began two thousand years ago in the advent of Christ and in His personal relationships with men and women, and has continued throughout the ages in the sphere of redeemed personal relationships (which is the true Church), now focusing on me, confronting me, as a person indissolubly bound up with other persons at this present time." [2]

Again:

"It is God's great activity of redemption in history, in the world of persons, focusing itself in challenge and succour on 'these persons here present,' who listen to your words and look into your eyes." [3]

A grave responsibility rests upon all within the Church who undertake the task of preaching. Who can begrudge the time devoted to preparation? Who can refuse to learn the technique of preaching? "It should be every clergyman's aim to make himself, not certainly a great preacher, God forbid, but the most effective preacher possible." [4] Some men may think that, because preaching to them is not easy, trying to improve is not of much profit. Good preachers, like poets, may be born, but bad preachers have only themselves to blame. "Any man can preach, and preach effectively, who reads his Bible, says his prayers, and loves his people," [5] says Canon Charles Smyth in his *Art of Preaching*, but he then goes on to show how even such preaching can be improved. The art of preaching ought to be taken very much more seriously than it is; systematic training should come somewhere in the training of every priest. Indeed, the lack of training is a matter of some surprise

---

[1] E. G. Selwyn, *The White Horsemen*, p. 7.
[2] H. H. Farmer, *The Servant of the Word*, 1941, p. 27.
[3] *Ibid.*, p. 29. The whole book is very illuminating.
[4] Peter Green, *The Town Parson*, p. 116.
[5] C. Smyth, *The Art of Preaching*, p. 3.

to those who know how much training is given to practical matters in other professions.[1]

This is certainly in the minds of the members of the Archbishops' Commission on the Training of the Ministry. The *Final Report* speaks of it, and the *Interim Report* says:

> "We recommend that special attention should be systematically given to correct defects of speech and intonation, to impress on ordinands the importance of form as well as of matter, to train them to speak naturally and audibly in large buildings, and to develop in them the power of translating the technical language of theology into terms which can be understood by ordinary people." [2]

Yet the importance of preaching can be over-emphasized, and the sermon as the vehicle of God's Word may be losing its value in the world of today. A great preacher like Dr. Henson, who took infinite pains over his sermons, can look back on his life and say:

> "Yet I am bound to acknowledge that, as I review my career, I am sometimes disposed to think that I should have made a better use of my time if I had not devoted so much of it to the composition and delivery of sermons. The modern world seems to have outgrown preaching, and there is no sign that its tendency will alter." [3]

(b) *Planning the Individual Sermon.* The Sunday sermon does not suddenly come into the preacher's head on Saturday night; it must be well prepared and planned. Excellent books on preaching abound, and the advice and rules they give centre round these main heads.

(i) Choice of Subject.—Before a sermon can be prepared the subject must be chosen, and for many the making of a choice is more than half the battle.[4] If the sermon is one of a course, as it ought to be on the majority of Sundays, the choice is already made, but even the most diligent planner is sometimes faced with odd occasions that need a choice of sermon. He may feel himself impelled to take a particular subject, and this usually leads to an enthusiastic and sincere sermon. A particular text may appeal in a fresh way, during Bible-reading and meditation, and a fully-worked-out sermon is often visualized at once. Inspiration of this kind should be used as much as possible, as it springs from the spiritual life.

---

[1] Cf. E. G. Selwyn, *The White Horseman*, p. 13.
[2] *Interim Report*, 1942, p. 18.
[3] H. Hensley Henson, *Retrospect of an Unimportant Life*, Vol. I, 1942, p. 134.
[4] Cf. Peter Green, *The Town Parson*, pp. 133-140, and Paul Bull, *Preaching and Sermon Construction*, pp. 118-124.

Some would urge that the proper source of subject is to be found in the course of the Christian Year, in the Gospel, Epistle or Lessons; to others this is anathema, and they would look to visiting and other pastoral work to suggest the need of sermons on some aspects of life or of faith.[1]   A judicious preacher will use a variety of methods.

(ii) *Gathering Information.*—Once the choice is made, information is needed. Relevant commentaries and books should be consulted, but it is also obviously an advantage if there is material already collected on which one can call. Here lies part of the value of a well-kept index.[2]   Subject cards can give references to books, pamphlets, cuttings, Sunday School lesson books, novels, experiences personal or otherwise. Little books on religion published by various firms can, because they are simply expressed and popularly written, be a great help to those who cannot easily transpose textbook knowledge into intelligible language. The index to former sermons[3] is useful in discovering the preacher's earlier expressions on the subject. A warning should be given against sermon aids, which give numerous quotations from various sources; such sermons can always be recognized.[4]

Again, it is necessary to add that it is impossible to call upon the index, unless potentially useful information is constantly collected, although much of it may never be used. Father Paul Bull, who describes his own method of indexing material in his book *Preaching and Sermon Construction,*[5] also urges the importance of recording thoughts for sermons, ideas for schemes and courses, useful phrases, texts that are suggestive, and anything that may help for some future sermon.[6]   It is important to make immediate entries, for thoughts are very fleeting; and they must be made as full as possible, for things that were obvious when the entry was made are not always so clear when they are read later.

Perhaps the most useful things to index are illustrations, for it is very difficult to remember really apt illustrations when they are needed. It is the illustrations, or the *exempla*, that really bring a sermon home to the hearers. "The thought of the greater part of mankind is concrete and pictorial, and the most clearly reasoned conclusions are less impressive than some striking image from the

---

[1] J. B. Goodliffe, *The Parson and his Problems,* pp. 41–50.
[2] See above, Chapter II, § 2.
[3] *Ibid.,* § 3 (*d*).
[4] Cf. John Oman, *Concerning the Ministry,* p. 140; quoted in C. Smyth, *The Art of Preaching,* p. 188.
[5] p. 124.
[6] Paul Bull, *Preaching and Sermon Construction,* p. 275.

common circle of experience." [1]   However, illustrations, when used, must illustrate something; a string of illustrations and anecdotes is not a sermon.

> " It is a common fault of modern preachers to smother their message, when they have one, which is by no means commonly the case, with illustrations, not always well chosen, and too often taken at second-hand." [2]

(iii) Form and Matter.—When the material is gathered, it is necessary to remember that all collected material will not be needed and must not be pushed in somehow; it must be carefully selected in view of the purpose of the sermon. A sermon must not be without form and void. The various formal structures can be used, such as those that are well discussed in Canon Smyth's *Art of Preaching*,[3] or just a simple division according to the rule of three,[4] but a system must be adopted, since it will help both the preacher to remember what he has to say and those who listen to what has been said. There are various devices for making the divisions memorable, but alliteration should be used sparingly and with caution.[5] A study of the great preachers for their style is sure to have its influence.

A mistake made by many men is the using of the same kind of style for all occasions. There are various types of congregations, and their different capacities and circumstances need consideration. A logical argument in the open air or a simple breezy sermon to a well-educated congregation are equally out of place. The purpose of the sermon, as preaching, teaching or exhortation, will determine the style to be used. In this, help can be obtained from Father Paul Bull's book,[6] and some specimen types of addresses may be found in Mr. J. Ramsay McCallum's *A Short Method for Pulpit and Services*.[7]

A week is not really long enough for the preparation of a sermon. When the information has been collected, it should be allowed to simmer in the mind as long as possible, until it begins to crystallize out into its natural form.[8] Two or three sermons can thus be

---

[1] J. G. Simpson, *Preachers and Teachers*, 1901, p. 55, quoted in C. Smyth, *The Art of Preaching*, p. 75.
[2] H. H. Henson, *Retrospect of an Unimportant Life*, Vol. II, p. 213.
[3] Cf. Paul Bull, *Preaching and Sermon Construction*, pp. 132–158; Peter Green, *The Town Parson*, pp. 122–133.
[4] Clement Rogers, quoted in C. Smyth, *The Art of Preaching*, pp. 48–49.
[5] J. Oman, *Concerning the Ministry*, p. 212.
[6] Chapter VI.
[7] See pp. 70–96.
[8] Peter Green, *The Town Parson*, p. 141.

forming at the same time; either a drawer in the desk or a folder can be reserved for sermons in the making.[1]

Finally, attention should be given to language and style. This is best helped in preparation by writing out the sermon in full, often, if not every time, even though the sermon may be preached from notes or entirely from memory. While the language of the sermon should be kept simple, vigorous and forceful, the danger of slang or jargon should be avoided.

> " Of all the pitfalls which beset the preacher, the use of jargon in one form or another is perhaps the most insidious. All those who speak in public tend to become more dependent than they know upon favourite *clichés*." [2]

Some, indeed, come so frequently in sermons that they become a parish joke.

These aspects of matter, form and style may be regarded in the light of a sermon considered as a personal encounter in the ' I-Thou ' relationship. Dr. Farmer suggests that this relationship is hindered if a sermon is read, if it has too many adjectives and purple patches, if there are too many quotations, and if the speech is not direct. " The utterly flat, impersonal and insipid ' one ' should be avoided like the plague. ' We ' is almost as bad if used too often." [3] The way in which Dr. Farmer completes his theme in laying stress upon the need for concreteness in phraseology, content and presentation, and upon the necessity for understanding the contemporary mind, deserves close study by every preacher.[4]

(c) *Planning Courses of Sermons.*—Sermons should not be just weekly, independent affairs, though of course each should be complete in itself. While certain times and circumstances demand the isolated sermon, usually there should be in the preacher's mind a clear scheme involving a number of weeks, if not a complete year. Not only does this prevent the last-minute feverish hunting for a subject, but it enables the preacher to give consistent teaching over a series of subjects. A well-thought-out plan of teaching for a full year, or even a five-year plan, is a help to the preacher, and gives the congregation the things that they really need. Such a plan would cover all aspects of Christian Theology, Ethics, Worship, Missions and Biblical Teaching. The danger lies in making it too systematic—that is, taking the Creed all one year, the Command-

---

[1] See above, Chapter II, § 1 (*b*), 5.
[2] C. Smyth, *The Art of Preaching*, p. 141.
[3] H. H. Farmer, *The Servant of the Word*, pp. 58-65.
[4] *Ibid.*, pp. 93-149.

ments and ethics, say, for another year, and perhaps the New Testament in the third. One Diocesan scheme had the miracles of Christ on some twenty successive Sundays; if the congregation still believed in miracles after that, it would be singularly lacking in the rebel-complex.

The parish priest has the task of teaching his people, and there is no better way than a planned comprehensive scheme that is elastic enough to allow for the inspiration and the needs of the moment. By having future subjects ready chosen, there is ample time for sermons to simmer in the mind. In planning over a number of Sundays, provision can be made for a change of method. Straight expositions of Biblical passages, lectures on doctrine or practical demonstrations of meditation, are useful and helpful alternatives. If these are likely to take more time than the usual sermon, the congregation should be warned beforehand. The effective sermon in these days is not longer than twenty minutes, but, if they are warned, people will occasionally be ready for more. Visiting preachers, especially Organizing Secretaries, are the worst offenders; their zeal is to be commended, but they often hinder their own cause.

There are two valuable guides for systematic teaching, *Christian Teaching and the Christian Year*, by Dr. H. L. Goudge, 1937, and *A Five Year Plan of Teaching, as adopted in the Diocese of Ely*, 1939.

BIBLIOGRAPHY

Paul Bull, *Preaching and Sermon Construction*, 1922. The most systematic attempt to teach the art of preaching.

John Oman, *Concerning the Ministry*, 1936. Less systematic, but eminently readable.

Charles Smyth, *The Art of Preaching*, 1940. The approach from the historic point of view, full of suggestions, and urges due respect to preaching as an art.

H. H. Farmer, *The Servant of the Word*, 1942. The personal approach.

L. Dewar and C. Hudson, *A Manual of Pastoral Psychology*, 1932. Chapter VIII. An interesting psychological approach.

T. H. Hughes, *The Psychology of Preaching and Pastoral Work*, 1939, Chapters II, III, IV.

Peter Green, *The Town Parson*, Chapter IV.

J. T. Inskip, *The Pastoral Idea*, Chapter VI.

T. W. Pym, *A Parson's Dilemmas*, Chapter V.

A. L. Preston, *The Parish Priest in his Parish*, 1933, Chapter III.

Phillips Brooks, *Lectures on Preaching*, 1877.

R. W. Dale, *Nine Lectures on Preaching*, 1877.

J. Paterson Smyth, *The Preacher and his Sermon*, 1907.

W. C. E. Newbolt, *The Ministry of the Word*, 1913.

K. E. Kirk, *The Fourth River*, 1935.

E. G. Selwyn, *The White Horseman*.

E. C. Hoskyns, *Cambridge Sermons*, 1938.

F. D. Coggan, *The Ministry of the Word*, 1945.

A. E. Simpson, *The Post-War Preacher*, 1946.

§ 3. PLANNING FOR PRAYER

(a) *The Man of God.* It has already been said that without a time-table the priest is at the mercy of events, and in the order of physical urgency the place of private prayer is last but two.[1]   That prayer should be in such a position is wrong for the man of God. If he cannot put prayer first in his life, how can he hope to lead his people to prayer?   How, indeed, can he attempt to proclaim the Gospel and call his people to God?   For if he has no prayer-life, all the apparatus of a parson's life would be designed to bring others to the very thing that he neglects himself.

> " He may be exact and accurate, smart and up-to-date, capable and businesslike, true and just, courteous and considerate, energetic, hardworking, painstaking and self-denying. Yet he may lack spiritual life and power.   His training may be excellent, his scholarship may be quite good, his credentials may be unimpeachable, his orders may be unquestioned, yet he may not be capable of winning men to God, he may not even have the joy of the Lord in his own strength."[2]

The people themselves soon know if their minister is a man of God.

Perhaps the priest once had a true and great vision of God, which brought him to his vocation.   Like silver, which needs constant polishing to keep it bright, so that vision will grow dim if contact with Christ grows less instead of more.   His inner life must grow in grace as he threads his way through the stages of prayer.   Yet it is not given to every man to go far beyond the lower levels of prayer, for capacity in prayer is itself the gift of God.   However, just as geography can be learnt from a good atlas without travelling abroad, so the priest can know the country of prayer, even if he does not travel over all of it himself, or if, like Moses, he sees the Promised Land only from the distance.   To some men it is given to be great masters of prayer; others humbly and gratefully receive the little flashes of illumination granted to them; but all priests should strive to be acquainted with the art and the science of prayer.   On the other hand, the lower levels of prayer are not to be despised by those who see them from the mountain-top.

Every priest, therefore, has not only the duty of teaching himself to pray, but he has to prepare himself to be a director of souls to others.   His own prayer-life is his own best tutor in this.

> " That actual business of teaching prayer to others is not a text-book matter: it is not the passing on of a quantity of

[1] See above, Chapter III, § 1.
[2] J. T. Inskip, *The Pastoral Idea*, p. 44.

knowledge about knowledge of God; but the sharing of the knowledge of God." [1]

In this matter of prayer, the priest must pray with his Master, " For their sakes I consecrate myself." His own best method of prayer, however, may not be the most fitting for those whom he teaches, so he must make a full study of the subject, know the value of the classical Masters, and understand how others pray.

> " It would seem to be our business as teachers of prayer, be our own way of prayer and meditation never so simple, to know what the frightening words and phrases mean, and not to fear them. But the possibility has to be faced, and it amounts to a certainty for most of us, that we shall know ' on paper ' more than we practise in our own private prayers." [2]

The importance of prayer is not exhausted simply in the priest's own inner life and in his teaching of others to pray. His whole pastoral work depends upon it. Besides physical and mental efficiency, the priest needs spiritual efficiency, " the supreme requirement of the pastor." [3] Inspiration is of the Spirit, but inspiration does not always come without some struggle and effort. Without prayer and meditation there can be no spiritual efficiency, and without this all other efficiency in the priest is in vain.[4]

(b) *Finding Time.* It is not in the province of this book to do more than emphasize the importance of the priest's first task; as the Preface has already indicated, help for the nourishing of the inner life must be found elsewhere. Prayer, however, urgently demands a principal place in the daily and weekly programme. A rule of life embraces prayer; it can embrace the whole time-table of which prayer is the chief component and the keystone of the whole. The early hours are by tradition reserved for Mattins, Holy Communion and Prayer, though all priests do not find this part of the day the best for mental prayer. Some may reserve parts of the morning, afternoon and evening, others find the best time just before lunch.[5] He who would complain that there is no time must learn from Christ, Himself the Master of Time, how time can be used as a servant.[6]

Apart from the time set aside for actual prayer, some time is

---

[1] E. S. Abbott, " The Prayer of the Teacher of Prayer " (in *Training in Prayer*, edited by Lindsay Dewar, 1939), p. 194.
[2] *Ibid.,* p. 204.
[3] Dewar and Hudson, *A Manual of Pastoral Psychology*, 1932, p. 87.
[4] See also, Chapter XXVII, § 2 (*c*) for Retreats.
[5] Bede Frost, *Priesthood and Prayer*, 1939, p. 90. (See Chapter VI.)
[6] Cf. M. A. C. Warren, *The Master of Time*, 1943.

needed for the various preparations. A scheme of intercessions for weekly or longer periods can be planned, and a list of people for whom to pray needs to be set out and often revised. Thanksgiving can be noted: the Diary is often useful for this. Passages from the Bible must be selected, or subjects chosen, for meditation and contemplation. Constant Bible study gives the best way of preparation for the daily meditation.

Further, prayer should be part of the whole pastoral ministry. Brother Lawrence found the presence of God in his kitchen and about his work, and no aspect of ministerial work and administration is too trivial for dedication to God. It may be commonplace to say that sermon preparation and parochial visiting begin in prayer, but it needs to be urged also that personal letter-writing, or even the dispatch of circulars, need the spirit of prayer, and all planning and administration require a prayer for guidance from God.

(c) *The Apparatus of Prayer*. Some pray best with pen and ink; some like intercession papers in order to pray with understanding; others like set books of prayers, of which many excellent collections are published today; some like to pray over a map, for friends in other lands. Very little else is required for the prayer-time. Some like to keep a record of their meditations on Bible passages; either cards for an index (the 8″ × 5″ size is very convenient), or a looseleaf book can be used. They can be a fruitful source in sermon preparation, and sometimes of value in leading public meditation.

Both for private prayer and also for public use in meetings and services, a loose-leaf book, in which prayers from various sources are typed, can be extremely useful. With one subject, or subject sub-division, on each page, the pages can be arranged under an easy number scheme, which if desired can be part of the general number scheme of the general index. An alternative scheme is to have in the card index a set of cards indicating the sources of various prayers on particular subjects. This saves typing them out, but they are not then so convenient to handle at meetings. Typing out prayers involves time, but it can be done prayerfully, and can in itself be an act of prayer.

SELECT BIBLIOGRAPHY

J. T. Inskip, *The Pastoral Idea*, 1905, Chapters I and II.
Bede Frost, *Priesthood and Prayer*, 1939.
E. Seyzinger, *The Glory of Priesthood*, 1933.
C. P. Hankey, *The Young Priest*, 1933.
L. Dewar (Editor), *Training in Prayer*, 1939, Chapters V and VI.

G. S. Stewart, *Lower Levels of Prayer*, 1939.
Alan Richardson, *Preface to Bible-Study*, 1943.
Olive Wyon, *The School of Prayer*, 1943.*
Bede Frost, *The Art of Mental Prayer*.*
Evelyn Underhill, *Worship*, 1936.
Anon, *The Way, Following the Way, To Jerusalem*.
Phyllis Dent, *The Growth of Spiritual Life*, 1944.
P. Loyd, *The Way according to St. Mark*, 1935.
E. Milner-White and G. W. Briggs, *Daily Prayer*, 1941.

* These books contain excellent Bibliographies for further reading and Bede Frost especially is a good guide to the Classics.

CHAPTER V

STAFF WORK

§ 1. The Parish Priest and His Assistants

(a) *The Team.* When our Lord sent forth His disciples " two by two ", He knew the great value of spiritual work done by a team of two or more working together. There are dangers in being alone, although under our present parochial system to be so is unavoidable in nearly all country parishes, as well as in a large number of town parishes. Loneliness easily falls upon an educated and cultured man who can find no others of his standing in his neighbourhood, and clerical study circles are the only means of keeping his brain active if he is not a natural scholar. The single-handed town priest is overburdened, especially with occasional services that are not infrequent and with administrative duties; and there is no one with whom he can share his hopes and fears, for the best layman is no substitute for an assistant. Moreover, illness is a real source of fear to the lonely priest, who must often take a service or a funeral when he should be in bed.

The lonely priest will miss most the team spirit or community spirit of a group of men and women working together under a leader. They can meet together for regular worship at the Holy Communion, in the daily offices, and in other meetings for prayer; they can give the unique witness of a community; each can bring his own contribution and his own specialized gifts to the common work and to the regular business meetings and conferences. Such a group can consist of members who are ordained and others who are lay workers, both men and women, each with a defined department.

> " There are men who have worked on the staff of a big parish and later have accepted single-handed livings in a city, who say that they would gladly give up their independence as incumbents for the fellowship and stimulus of again working with brother priests in a larger area." [1]

The Archbishops' Commission on the Training of the Ministry confirms this for training purposes : " We do indeed think that there would be great gains from the training of deacons together in

[1] *Putting our House in Order*, 1941, p. 41.

large parishes, with large staffs under specially qualified men." [1]
While this team spirit is more obvious for a large staff, it is not
without meaning for two men working together, for they can form
a team, bringing to it complementary gifts, if not a wide variety.

(b) *The Choice of Assistants.* It is customary for some Principals
of Theological Colleges to advise each student to choose his first
vicar and parish with great care, since his first parish will leave a
lifelong mark upon his ministry. [2] A parish·priest needs to choose
his assistants with the same care, but in the present shortage of
clergy he has not much choice; often he has to choose between
one particular man and none at all. Perhaps it is better to be
alone than to take the wrong man, who would be a constant worry
and anxiety.

The relation between incumbent and assistant curate is peculiarly
personal, and so there should be common ground in thought and
outlook, especially in churchmanship, though at the same time an
incumbent may look to his curate for minor accomplishments
which he himself has not, such as music or sport, or an administrator may seek a preacher, or a preacher an administrator. A
curate cannot be appointed by correspondence; each prospective
curate must be interviewed, if possible more than once, and a
week-end visit is better still. His suitability for the parish can
then be better assessed, and his personality, charm and poten-
tialities gauged. It is not always what he is that is important,
but what he might be when developed and trained. What the
parish priest needs, therefore, is an assistant who is ready to be
loyal and to co-operate, ready to work and to study, and willing
to be trained. As for his spiritual life, sense of vocation and love
of his work, it is necessary to depend upon the recommendations
of his theological college and the Bishop who has suggested him,
though very often the Bishop is under an obligation to find the
man a title. The wise parish priest appointing an assistant priest
for his parish will naturally consult the man's last incumbent, if
only as a courtesy, though this is not always done. Regard should
be paid to the way he has already responded to training, and an
estimate made of his probable readiness to respond to another
man's methods. Curates are not inducted, as incumbents are, but
it adds to their status to give them a real welcome at their first
service, to seat them formally in the curate's stall, adding suitable
prayers for their ministry in the parish.

[1] *Training for the Ministry,* 1944, pp. 64, 65.
[2] Cf. C. F. Rogers, *Pastoral Theology in the Modern World,* 1920, pp. 145–53.

A special difficulty arises in a change of incumbency when a curate is already in office. That there is a difficulty is recognized by law, which allows for the curate to be asked to leave without the usual six months' notice. Generally speaking, it is better for both incumbent and curate that the curate should go. His loyalty to his old chief will inevitably conflict with his loyalty to the new, since a change of incumbency means a change of method or of emphasis if not of churchmanship. Moreover, every parish priest comes, in the course of a few years, to differentiate, mentally at least, between those parishioners who respond to his ministry and those who do not, and a loyal curate must necessarily observe the same alignment with caution. A new incumbent wants a completely clean sheet; his predecessor's quarrels or difficulties are nothing to him, and he wants an assistant who is not in any way committed. Nevertheless, there are many examples where a curate has served successive incumbents with distinction.

(c) *The Problem of Assistant Curates.* When the choice of a curate has been made, and the man well chosen, the art of working together has to be developed. Normally the relationship is that of teacher and disciple, rather than that of partners,[1] though the work of the ministry is shared. The assistant curate is not necessarily a ' prentice hand '—he may well be an able man and experienced priest—and then partnership guides the relationship. But if the parish priest has a young assistant, he should not treat him merely as a convenience. His curate is with him to be trained, to be instructed and sometimes reproved, and this has to be done with all delicacy, for the two men are brother ministers on sacred work together. Professor Rogers says of this relationship,

> " The pleasant personal relationship generally existing between him and his vicar make professional relationship the harder: every suggestion that he makes becomes a criticism, and every criticism a complaint. Differences of opinion are felt to be rude." [2]

The human factor, however, is uncertain, and " vicaritis " is not an unknown disease. The incumbent may fear to dominate his voluntary lay workers, but his paid subordinate is fair game, so the latter is treated as an office-boy rather than a clergyman, and not given a fair share of the parochial work. It is easy to be jealous of a curate's success, and of such accomplishments of his as the parish priest may lack; especially is this true if the curate is

---

[1] Cf. L. Hunter, *The Parson's Job*, 1931, p. 139.
[2] C. F. Rogers, *Pastoral Theology in the Modern World*, 1920, p. 46.

a good preacher and the parishioners say so. Few incumbents can say with sincerity, " I must decrease. . . ." On the other hand, a disloyal curate is a real problem, and his talkativeness can lead to serious trouble. Another curate's tactlessness and thoughtlessness can pain many good people, while his foolishness can bring the ministry to disrepute. One assistant can be really lazy, another only apparently so, because he suffers from constitutional slowness and sensitiveness. There is always the chance of a clash of temperaments. " An introvert thinking vicar is unlikely to be a hero to his extrovert feeling curate "; [1] or it may be a clash of youth and age. Curates are usually so full of life, enthusiasm and zeal, that they almost inevitably think they can do the job better than the parish priest, who is sure to have gained a mature cautiousness. This zeal of the curate is his main asset; they were young Christians who first turned the world upside-down. So the " unbeneficed clergy . . . often need protection ".[2]

All men have their idiosyncrasies, and real patience, much prayer, mutual respect, and devotion to the joint ministry are all needed to keep the staff working happily together. Rules and suggestions for the mutual relationship are not amiss, such as that given by Professor Rogers :

> " The clergy of a parish form one body; it is therefore the duty of the assistant priests to consult, and defer to, the wishes of the vicar, while a corresponding obligation lies on him to support their actions in public, even if he disagrees with it, and is obliged to remonstrate in private." [3]

Further suggestions from both angles may be useful.

(i) *Suggestions for a parish priest in relation to his assistant curate.*

Give him your friendship and be ready to advise in any matter if he desires help. Do not be too busy to see him or to talk to him about anything. Give praise when it is due, privately, and sometimes publicly.

Do not expect a pale imitation of yourself. Give scope for initiative. As far as possible, share the work with him. Do not ask him to do anything you would not do yourself. Do not expect him to be the office-boy or the vicarage gardener.

Give him plenty of warning of preachments and engagements. Do not tell him at 7.55 a.m. that he is celebrating at 8 a.m. that

---

[1] Dewar and Hudson, *A Manual of Pastoral Psychology*, p. 113.
[2] Joseph McCulloch, *We have our Orders*, p. 61.
[3] C. F. Rogers, *Principles in Parish Work*, p. 83.

day. Be clear in directions, and do not vaguely make half-intended promises, or, if you do, do not be annoyed if they are taken at their full value.

Help with guidance and criticisms when he is unsuccessful; do not merely take him off the job and suffer in silence. But do not correct, criticize, or order him about before parishioners. And do not correct him or make criticisms immediately before the beginning of a service, especially before Holy Communion. Do not write letters to him when there is a bone of contention between you; [1] talk it over and perhaps pray together.

Do not inspect every moment of his time. Do not leave him to find all his work for himself. See that he has a regular day-off.

Pay his stipend monthly, not quarterly, and on the due date. Give him the cheque yourself, even if the treasurers sign it.

Help him, when it is time, to find another suitable curacy; or, if he is ready for a full charge, make recommendations to suitable patrons. Do not selfishly keep a good man longer than for his own good.

(ii) *Suggestions for a curate in relation to his parish priest.* [2]

Be loyal, as is only proper in a junior partner. To this end, do not discuss your parish priest with parishioners. [3] Do not play for your own advantage or glory. Do not contradict the parish priest before others, especially before strangers. Support him when he has obviously forgotten something, and try to step into the breach if something has not been prepared.

Do not deliberately and consistently be different from the parish priest in services. The encouragement of initiative does not mean the development of the priest's use and the curate's use which the congregation can recognize and take sides upon; [4] so do not be offended if you are checked in this. " Do not burden your vicar with the necessity of telling you before the service what you are supposed to know or to find out for yourself." [5]

Do not misuse the time allowed at your own discretion for work and study. If you need extra time for theatres, make a point of asking for it; evenings are in the day's work of the clergy. Do not refuse to lend a hand with the manual work about the buildings—*e.g.*, moving chairs or curtains.

If you think you are in the wrong parish, think again. Perhaps

[1] Cf. H. H. Henson, *Ad Clerum*, p. 194.
[2] See also, J. T. Inskip, *The Pastoral Idea*, Chapter V.
[3] H. H. Henson, *Ad Clerum*, p. 194.
[4] See also, J. T. Inskip, *The Pastoral Idea*, p. 122.
[5] *Ibid.*, p. 121.

it is God's will for you to be where you are. If the circumstances are really difficult, consult a senior priest who knows you well. Be as loyal to your parish priest as you can in the circumstances.

If you make intimate friends of some of the parishioners—which is a natural thing to do—do not neglect others for them, but develop such friendships on off-days. When you leave the parish write only to such friends, and not to all and sundry. The value of a curate's work is not to be reckoned in terms of the number of people who write to him after he leaves, but in the number of people he adds to the congregation, and who remain in it after he has gone.

§ 2. THE TRAINING OF ASSISTANT CLERGY

(a) *Parochial Training.* It is not just enough for the parish priest to master the art of getting his staff to work in unison; he has the important task of training his assistant, especially the deacon, for his future ministry. To some extent the practical training has already begun, in ideal at least.

> " The right course seems to be that at the theological college men should study principles of pastoral work, and though the details of Pastoralia must largely be learned by the deacon during his diaconate, he should be given instruction before ordination in such matters as the preparation of candidates for confirmation, the conduct of worship, and ways of dealing with the difficulties of individuals. He should also learn the nature of his future responsibilities in the matter of private and parochial finance and correspondence: much harm is caused to the Church by carelessness in these things. The main object in all this should be to enable men to begin their work as clergymen with reasonable efficiency and confidence." [1]

But it should not be assumed either by the curate or the parish priest that the theological college has taught him all he ought to know.

> ". . . a large proportion of the difficulties [between incumbents and curates] arises from the assumption that a man has learnt his job during his time at a theological college . . . there are curates who refuse to learn, and, still more disastrous, there are vicars who refuse, or neglect, to teach. It is a strange frame of mind for a priest to think that he is too busy to give time to training and encouraging his younger brother in the ministry. . . . I do mean that he should consult him daily about everything that happens or should happen in the parish.

---

[1] *Training for the Ministry, Final Report*, p. 56.

It is the truest form of teaching to talk over all problems, plans, and difficulties, not only in parochial affairs, but also as they concern the devotional life or the affairs of the Church at large. . . . I know how hard it is for a curate to realize to the full extent of that sense of responsibility which presses upon any conscientious vicar. He cannot share it as he shares the work." [1]

Mr. Arthur Hopkinson gives us here the difficulty and the way to overcome it. By setting his assistant curate to work, the parish priest is preparing him for his future, but it must be done systematically. The younger man is there not simply to help the older, but to learn from him. He will learn by experience with gradually increasing responsibility, but really needs to be told what the purpose of each job is, and the correct, and in some circumstances the legal way of doing it. Talks are necessary as well as practice, and guidance should be given about the best books. A review of all pastoral work will help the curate to see that no parish comprehends every aspect of the ministry, and that there are other things to learn from other parishes. A deacon has his own studies to do in preparation for his priest's examination, but it is not beyond the wit of any priest to work out a scheme of training for a younger assistant which will begin during his diaconate and become more intensive during his third and fourth years in orders. This present book attempts to cover the ground of training which a man ought to receive before he takes full charge of a parish. [2]

If it is at all possible, a curate should be trained in his own churchmanship, and also with an understanding of the moderate variations of other sections of the Church, so that the young Evangelical knows how to wear vestments with ease, and the young Anglo-Catholic can take the North-End in all humility. A neighbouring incumbent can probably help in this, as in other aspects of this development of mutual training.

Young men should not at first be expected to take full charge of any department, but should be humble enough to learn their job under the parish priest's direction. This is brought out admirably by Mr. G. W. Clarkson in his *Reflections of a Post-War Ordinand.* [3]

"Deacons and junior priests should not be given 'practitioners' responsibilities' by being put in charge of organizations. Far too often are young men fresh from college given responsibility for 'Youth'. This is bad husbandry. It sets

[1] A. W. Hopkinson, *Pastor's Progress*, 1942, pp. 155, 156.
[2] See below, Chapter XXIX, § 3.
[3] In *Theology*, March 1943, p. 51.

fumblers to work where they can do most harm, it increases the exploitation of charm, and in view of the fact that young clergymen migrate sooner than they used to do, the continuation between junior and adult membership of the people they supervise is put in jeopardy at its unsafest period. This is a major cause of the leakage of adolescents, and England is crowded with curate's pets."

But responsibility should not be long delayed, and must be gradually increased.

"Though it is a commonplace of all training that you must give responsibility to students even at the risk of the work not being so well done, and that no one will continue to work his best unless he can gain some sort of recognized position by good work, the curate is seldom allowed to do anything on his own initiative." [1]

Nevertheless, a deacon should not be put in charge of a mission church, nor given too many funerals to conduct.

(b) *Diocesan Supervision.* In view of the importance of a clergyman's training, it is remarkable that men are still ordained to serve in parishes that happen to be lucky enough to afford a curate, without any regard being paid to the incumbent's capacity to train a deacon.[2] Some would urge that deacons should be licensed to the Bishop of the Diocese, and only posted to men who are "apt to teach and big enough in heart and mind to appreciate zeal and direct enthusiasm". But that they should be trained in the same parish for three years is essential. It is also true that "the parish where there is only one curate does not provide the best training for a newly ordained man ".[3] Insistence on this without some grouping of parishes would press very hardly upon many parishes that at present offer titles. Diocesan supervision would compensate for this, and this is now certain to develop, in view of the Report on *The Training for the Ministry.*[4] The *Interim Report* of the same Commission (1942) expresses the point excellently:

"Our aim is to bring the post-Ordination period, three or four years after Ordination, into more clearly coherent relation with the earlier training, to keep the period of the diaconate as free as possible from tests and examinations; to lighten the burden of the earlier training by the encouragement of more

[1] C. F. Rogers, *Pastoral Theology in the Modern World*, p. 46.
[2] Cf. Dewar and Hudson, *A Manual of Pastoral Psychology*, p. 79.
[3] *Putting our House in Order*, 1941, p. 66.
[4] See below, Chapter XXIX, § 2 (*b*).

systematic study and supervision after Ordination; to emphasize the need for discovering and developing special capacities; and to do all we can to correct the current if unconscious assumption that the parish and parochial activities have an exclusive and despotic claim upon a curate's interests." [1]

§ 3. THE PLACE OF THE PARSON'S WIFE

The critical importance of the wives of the clergy is indicated by Mr. Arthur Hopkinson when he introduces the problem of clergymen working together.

> "Why is it that two men (or more) working together in the highest cause of all, so often fail to hit it off? It would be cowardly not to answer frankly that it is so often not the fault of the men at all, but of their wives. A vicar's wife has an almost inevitable tendency to think that the curate is not doing his share, or is trying to steal the limelight. A curate's wife, on the other hand, is inclined to think that her husband is being put upon, or cheated of the credit for his share of the work. But unmarried vicars and curates get across one another; the problem cannot be solved by putting the blame on the wives." [2]

This last problem has already been considered; the other reflections of this paragraph raise several important considerations.

The incumbent's wife has an important place in the life of a parish,[3] although so far no ' pastoralia ' book has been written for her, no retreats and schools are planned for her, and she has, indeed, no recognized position. Yet though bachelors and celibates make excellent priests, parishes still demand a married parson, and this is not solely because the people are fearful of a bachelor's morals, but because they know the value of a good parson's wife. Her influence is inestimable, for though the parish priest can never reveal confidences reposed in him, she does share her husband's thoughts and ideals, his hopes and fears for the parish. She saves the single-handed priest from the worst aspects of loneliness. In addition, she often does valuable work among women and girls and in the Sunday School, and it is among the wives of the clergy that the Diocese finds most of its leaders for the Mothers' Union and the Girls' Friendly Society. Above all, she has her house and her family to administer so as to set the parish

---

[1] *Interim Report*, 1942, p. 21.
[2] A. W. Hopkinson, *Pastor's Progress*, 1942, p. 155. Cf. L. S. Hunter, *A Parson's Job*, 1931, p. 141.
[3] A. L. Preston, *The Parish Priest and his Parish*, 1933, pp. 87, 101, 102, 127.

an example of the Christian home as it should be. This last is, of course, the most important of her tasks. Dr. Henson, when asked if illiteracy in the wife should be a bar to her husband's preferment, replied:

> " The question of fitness or unfitness of the wife cannot be ignored, but it must not be given too great importance. If the lady be good, religious and sweet-tempered, able to keep her house Christianly, so that its cleanness and order are exemplary, then I think that her ' illiteracy ' and ' inability to take a leading part in the parish ' may be condoned: but if she be a slut or a scold nothing can be done but to keep her out of the vicarage at all hazards." [1]

This is altogether a terrible responsibility for any woman and no small wonder that Dr. Henson also wrote: " I used to say and I believe it to be roughly true, that ' fifty per cent of the married clergy were undone by their wives and fifty per cent were saved by them.' " So, in addition to her actual work, she has to be as discreet and tactful as the parish priest himself, in speaking or refraining from speaking she has to suppress her dislikes, bear with equanimity the jealous remarks and insinuations of the ladies of the parish, and take as many kicks as half-pence.

> " It is generally assumed . . . that the Church is to blame, and that it is the parson's fault that the world is frankly materialistic and indifferent to religion. . . . The parson's wife must meet the attack too, but generally her share of it is more personal and parochial. It may happen among her own flock that complaints about the choir, the heating arrangements, the choice of hymns, even the opinions of a visiting preacher, are brought to her in the hope that they may leak through her to vicar, rector or minister." [2]

She is thus an important member of the staff, yet she has no defined status and does not attend staff meetings. She must not even be seen too much in her husband's study.[3] This semi-official kind of position is most exacting and often uncomfortably trying. Even when she does her job well, she does not disarm criticism. Miss Margaret Watt writes of the end of the last century:

> " But it was an age of increasing specialization, and in all the growing appreciation and acknowledgement of her rights and powers, a new danger was in store for the parson's wife,

[1] H. Hensley Henson, *Retrospect of an Unimportant Life*, Vol. II, 1943, p. 114.
[2] Margaret Watt, *The History of the Parson's Wife*, 1943, p. 197.
[3] C. F. Rogers, *Pastoral Theology in the Modern World*, 1920, p. 151.

the danger of professionalism. The busybody, the managing parson's wife, became a well-known figure in satiric comment and popular comedy. By the end of the century there was but one limit set to her functions, to the amount of parish work she might undertake, the number and variety of the social and spiritual undertakings she might share in or promote. It is sometimes indeed a little hard on her that in an exacting congregation the idea that she is really a sort of curate may exist side by side with the suspicion that she is 'managing' or inclined to take too much upon herself. The one limit, of course, is that imposed by Holy Orders. She may not preach, nor officiate in church, nor administer the Sacraments, though she has been known to baptize infants in cases of emergency; and at sparsely attended services she may be seen modestly carrying round the alms-bag." [1]

It is an open question whether this should continue, whether she should simply help the parish priest at his desk more as a secretary, or receive definite appointment as a lady worker with proper status. Yet this would not do for all, as many have no flair for parish work. Whatever she does, the Income Tax authorities are loth to recognize that she helps her husband at all. This is not the end of her troubles; she usually has an unwieldy house to manage, and often this is the last straw.

"The Church of England allows and commends both the celibate and the married state for the clergy. It is not conspicuously successful in making the best use of either. Much has been written and said in praise of the parson's wife; too little has been done to make her lot more tolerable. Some of her difficulties are such as no economic adjustment can remove. To be a real helper of her husband's work, a servant of the parish, and at the same time the maker of a home, and the mother of a family, can never be anything less than an exacting task." [2]

To return to the particular difficulty of the curate and the incumbent's wife, it is easily seen that no man can serve two masters. Great tact and common sense are needed by the priest's wife in relation to her husband's assistants, when the human factor is so strong. She should be very guarded with her criticisms, even to her husband, though she may well be right, and often is. A married curate adds to the complications, but his lady might well best feel that her glory is yet to come. Altogether it may be said that the lot of the parson's wife is not an enviable one.

[1] Margaret Watt, *The History of the Parson's Wife*, pp. 99, 100.
[2] *Putting our House in Order*, 1941, p. 19.

§ 4. The Other Members of the Staff

(a) *Women Workers*. These give invaluable help in the work among women and girls, especially in visiting, and when properly trained in girls' club work, and in Sunday School work, they should be regarded as specialists on the staff. They need to be chosen with the same care as assistant curates, and with similar considerations. They are really essential for bachelor priests, but where the parish priest is married and the wife is capable and plays an active part, the sphere of work of each needs to be well defined. Generally speaking it is best if the woman worker is an ordained deaconess. She should be adequately paid.[1]

(b) *Lay Readers*. Church Army officers and stipendiary lay readers have a useful place on the parochial staff. They will be appointed with the same considerations as curates, but their work and training will be different. Voluntary lay readers are becoming increasingly useful as their sphere of usefulness is enlarged, though the difficulties that arise with voluntary workers are intensified with lay readers, for the work that they do is peculiarly subject to the direction of the parish priest. Preaching and the conduct of services are the incumbent's responsibility, and he can allow only those to help in whom he has full confidence. Tact, of course, is necessary. Some lay readers are worth their weight in gold, because of their Christian faith and energy; others seem impossible. Some take charge of mission halls and, with a false idea of their importance, act in an independent spirit, gain a following, and lay up trouble for future incumbents. The main problem arises when the new incumbent comes to a parish and finds a voluntary lay reader attached, with whom he finds it difficult to co-operate. It should be noticed that his licence, if parochial, is conditional upon the consent of any new incumbent for its continuation.

(c) *Ordinands*. It is here convenient to mention the need to be on the watch for young people with possible vocation for the ministry or overseas work. Encouragement and help can be given by way of suggestions for training and preparation, and by advice on financial aid and possible colleges for training. So far as their work allows, possible ordinands can be given opportunities for practical work in the parish, and they usually prove to be valuable helpers. Recruitment for the ministry is becoming increasingly important, and the parish priest should count this

[1] L. S. Hunter, *A Parson's Job*, 1931, p. 141.

part of his work.   However, some discernment is necessary: those unfit or unsuited for the ministry should not be encouraged.

" It is to be feared that at present there is often much mis-apprehension about the qualities of mind and character to be looked for in candidates for the ministry.   Precocious devotion to ecclesiastical observances is not seldom taken for more than it is really worth." [1]

§ 5. STAFF PLANNING

(a) *The Business Meeting.*   It is impossible to work with a large staff, or even with one assistant, unless there is planning together at regular business meetings.   On the day of the meeting, some time beforehand, it is desirable that the staff should meet together for corporate staff Communion.   The meeting itself should follow regular routine, beginning with brief prayers, and then with items in a usual order, so that everything is remembered.

For example, the routine could be:—

(i) *With the Diary.*—Consideration of the next few days, including two Sundays, for services, preaching, engagements; allocation of routine work of weddings, funerals and daily services; future preaching, covering the next three months, within a longer preaching scheme; future events and necessary preparations.

(ii) *People and their Problems.*—Arrangement of visiting; comparing records, removals, changes, lapsed; personal difficulties as noticed by the staff.

(iii) *Development.*—Constant consideration of procedure and the organizations, with suggestions for improvement and development.

The parish priest should have framework plans ready beforehand; the staff bring their reports and various questions produced by the week.   Part of the meeting from time to time can be a discussion of some aspect of parochial work, as part of the training for the younger men.   Various points for prayers in conclusion will arise during the meeting.

(b) *The Parish Diary.*   A scheme to save the passing of information by word of mouth is advocated by Professor Rogers, by which a Parish Diary is kept in the vestry, and in which are entered points of interest encountered by the various members of the staff.   By a system of headings, dates and cross-references, all the

[1] *Training for the Ministry, Final Report*, p. 18.   See pp. 12–24.

work is checked, overlapping is avoided, material is provided for agendas for committees, and a record is provided for the future.[1]

(c) *District Churches.* In a large parish there is often a mission room, or district church, perhaps more than one. They are justified only by geographical considerations—where the parish falls naturally into different parts, or where there is a centre of population at some distance from the parish church.[2] Where the mission-room is near the mother church, either there is a tendency for the poor to attend one and the rich the other, or there are divided loyalties and jealousies. The idea that the mission will gain new people who may be passed on to the parish church never seems to work. District churches in their own area do not present quite the same problems. They should be developed as young churches, creating their own life with full and proper church services and Church life, but, like the daughter churches in the Overseas field, they should look to the mother church for guidance and sympathy.

The danger of disloyalty arising in a district church can be overcome by staff meetings, so that all in charge of districts can plan together a common programme for mutual advantage. The staff meeting can arrange for changes of preaching, and otherwise make the men into a team, and not leave them merely as independent units. Far from being a number of competing churches, the daughter churches can form a real family centred round the mother. As a general rule district churches should be self-supporting. It is unnecessary for the parish to be burdened with a building that is used only by a few people. If the church is insufficiently attended, or otherwise shows its superfluity, it ought to be closed. There is far too much flogging of dead horses.

§ 6. THE BUSINESS SIDE

(a) *Necessary Records.* It will not be possible in every chapter to make exhaustive lists of the information that ought to be filed. It is done here in order to give an illustration of the method at work. In the filing cabinet there should be folders, under their appropriate numbers, for the following details: correspondence with each curate and with prospective curates, which make clear the arrangements under which the appointment is made, and the agreement about the stipend; correspondence with Societies, the

---

[1] C. F. Rogers, *Principles in Parish Work*, pp. 58–64. Sample page of such a Diary given in Appendix I.

[2] R. C. Joynt, *The Church's real Work*, 1934, pp. 89–91.

Ecclesiastical Commissioners, and the Diocesan Board of Finance, concerning grants towards the Curacy Fund of the parish; Curacy Fund account, if the incumbent is treasurer; correspondence or arrangements with lay readers, possible ordination candidates and women workers; information, Ember lists and appeals from theological colleges; information concerning the training for the ministry and possible sources of grants to Ordination candidates.

(b) *Necessary Information.* The regulations concerning Ordination and the employment of assistant curates are usually printed in the *Year Book* of the Diocese, and so also are the regulations for temporary clerical assistance, the syllabus for the Priest's Examinations, the regulations for lay readers, and the syllabus for the lay readers' examination. Information concerning the training of the ministry and possible sources for grants to Ordination candidates can be obtained from the Central Advisory Council of Training for the Ministry (the address can be found in the *Official Year-Book of the Church of England*). It is also important to read the *Training for the Ministry*, 1944, the Final Report of the Archbishops' Commission.

SELECT BIBLIOGRAPHY

C. F. Rogers, *Pastoral Theology in the Modern World*, 1920.
J. T. Inskip, *The Pastoral Idea*, 1905, Chapter V.
L. S. Hunter, *A Parson's Job*, 1931, Chapter IX.
Training for the Ministry, 1944.
Margaret Watt, *The History of the Parson's Wife*, 1943.
The Ministry of Women, Report of the Archbishops' Commission, 1935.
Women's Work in the Church, Report of an Archbishops' Committee, 1943.
H. S. Marshall (Editor), *Pastoralia for Women.*
Training for Service (Report of the Archbishops' Committee on the Training of Women for Work in the Church), 1945.
Serving the Church (The Central Councils of the Church), 1945.

F

BUSINESS AT THE CHURCH

§ 1. THE VESTRIES

(a) *Their Appearance.* " A parson's character is judged by the order or disorder of his vestry, his choir-stall and his church." [1] The vestry is the other office of the priest, yet many a parson with an orderly study is content with a small, uncomfortable, dirty and untidy vestry. It may be that he cannot help its smallness, and perhaps he has to share it with the choir as well as with the church-wardens; under such conditions, even a business man would find himself at a disadvantage. In more modern churches the architect's plan includes vestries, however small, but the ancient churches often have no such provision. Curtaining off parts of the church should be done with great discretion. One man will have in mind practical convenience—" it is better to have the curtained-off portion near the choir-stalls and altar, rather than in the west-end of the church " [2]—another will think of the appearance as the worshipper enters the church: " In most churches entered through a south door the least noticed place is the south-west corner of the building." [3]

(b) *The Clergy Vestry.* Where the clergy vestry is apart from the choir vestry, it is usually a small room which serves also as a sacristy, and some ingenuity is needed to put in the necessary fittings in the least possible space. The bare minimum is a table and chair, cupboards, a wardrobe or chest of drawers for altar linen, frontals, and vestments, and a shelf or side table for the preparing of vessels and vestments. Useful extra space can be gained for occasions when several clergymen are present, if the table is a folding one, bracketed to the wall. [4] A church with more elaborate ritual may require other furniture in the sacristy. Mr. C. E. Russell gives a useful list, ending with " a reliable clock, so that services may begin exactly on time ".[5]

The vestry table requires the necessary equipment of ink, pens

---

[1] Nevil Truman, *The Care of Churches*, 1935, p. 123.
[2] C. E. Russell, *The Priest and Business*, p. 36.
[3] Truman, p. 114.   [4] *Ibid.*
[5] *The Priest and Business*, pp. 38 f.

and blotting-paper, and not of the post-office variety. The drawers
of the table should contain the Service Register, the Banns Book,
and necessary forms and cards for the use of the clergy and wardens.
The Service Register should be neatly posted, clearly spaced,
well-written with correct and up-to-date entries. Neatness is
better maintained if it is one person's job. The book should
record the services and times, the celebrants and preachers (especially strange preachers), numbers of communicants, and the amounts
and objects of the collections. The last is for audit purposes, and
one of the duties of the auditors is to see that collections for special
objects duly reached their destinations. These records are all
useful for comparisons—churchwardens will often be looking back
to see if they are ' up ' or ' down '—and some of the facts are
required for statistical returns. The Banns Book must always be
carefully filled in, and no banns read from scraps of paper. Certificates of banns [1] can be obtained ready to fill in, or be printed
for the church, and should be completed at once after the third
reading, in readiness for the prospective bridegroom. With these
in the drawer there will be a supply of forms for notices of banns,
of baptism, baptism cards, and forms for the wardens for recording
collections and contributions through duplex envelopes.

On the vestry table, or. affixed to a wall, a diary memoranda
can give the information of times for weddings, funerals, baptisms,
and extra services, or even a complete list of all services with the
initials of the member of the staff responsible for each service and
sermon. The verger will need part of this information, and the
staff will have a reminder of staff-meeting arrangements.

The cupboards or drawers provide the secret of tidiness; not
only should there be proper places with adequate pegs and hangers
for robes, vestments, linen, frontals, with everything labelled for
quick access, but there should also be proper places for packets of
hymn-sheets and special services, old banns books and other
record books, cruets, bread box and collecting plates. On the
walls should be the Table of Fees, and the Table of Kindred and
Affinity, though no useful purpose for having this in the vestry
can now be discovered. It is a modern practice to adorn the
vestry walls with portraits of former incumbents or photographs
of various interest, while the vestries of some old churches are
veritable museums.

(c) *The Other Vestries*. The choir vestry can often compete with
the clergy vestry in untidiness. The greatest enemy is litter. " Old

[1] See below, Chapter XXIII, § 3 (a).

hassocks, old hymn books, torn and tattered copies of the music of the services, dirty surplices, unwound clocks, dirty vases and dead flowers, seem to be common." [1] For general tidiness the cleaners are responsible, but they cannot do their work if music-books are scattered everywhere. There should be good cupboards for music, so that all hymn-books have their right places, and all special music and anthems should be packed in stout envelopes and stored away. The choirmaster is responsible for this, and he can appoint a senior boy as librarian to see that everything is duly put away. The cupboards for robes need also to be kept in order and scrubbed out from time to time. Cassocks and surplices can hang on pegs, but, if hangers are provided for them, they can be arranged wardrobe-fashion on a rod, thus saving room and preventing collars being torn and tabs becoming unsightly. Collars or ruffs can be put in bags.

It is a fortunate church which has also a churchwarden's vestry; the wardens usually count the money where the clergy disrobe. Some suggest that the wardens should be in the choir vestry, for the better discipline of the boys, but generally it is before rather than after the service that such steadying influence is needed. It is, however, an advantage, if it can be secured, for the parish priest to be accessible after a service, and yet be able to see people alone. [2]

In one of the vestries a main article of furniture is the safe, which if possible should be built into the wall. In this are kept the Communion vessels, the registers and the various deeds and policies. The plate ought not to be kept at the vicarage, though sometimes this has to be done for better safety, but care should be taken to see that the incumbent does not take the plate away with him, inadvertently of course, when he leaves. Valuable old plate is both a treasure and a problem; business men dislike paying insurance on goods which cannot be used. This suggestion has been made: " Electrotype copies will be made by the Victoria and Albert Museum in exchange for original plate to be kept on loan. So the Church can see and use its rare plate in reproduction and the original can be seen by the public." [3]

This suggestion is not a good one; the plate was made for use, not to be shown in a museum. Every piece of plate ought to be used in church at least once a year. Better still, all the silver can be placed on the altar at the chief services at the great Festivals.

[1] C. E. Russell, *The Priest and Business*, p. 38.
[2] See below, Chapter XXIV, § 3 (a).
[3] N. Truman, *The Care of Churches*, p. 92.

It can make a fine show, it honours past benefactors, inspires future ones, and teaches the continuity of Church life.

Modern registers need little comment. They should be kept with care and written with clarity. Any ancient registers should be jealously preserved with any old documents, deeds, terriers, letters preserved from former years.[1] Ancient churches may possibly possess one or two terriers which are interesting as well as valuable possessions. The information about church lands may help to establish landmarks and boundaries, and charities of ancient standing are preserved from misuse by information handed down in this way. All these old documents are the foundation of parish histories,[2] and care should be taken to see that they are not lost; a list should be filed by the priest and copies kept by the wardens. An inventory [3] records the furniture of the church, and legally should be checked and signed at each change of office of incumbent or wardens. It ought to be the duty of the Rural Dean to check it in person once every five years, and it should contain also a list of deeds, faculties, and documents in the safe. Some deeds are best lodged at the office of the Diocesan Registrar.

(d) *Necessary Offices.* Very few churches, and those only modern buildings, are provided with sanitary accommodation. It is a strange omission when it is remembered how many consecutive hours the clergy must often spend in or near the church. It is a necessary convenience for the choir also. In addition, a water-tap and wash-basin are essential, though it is possible to provide for these in a corner of a vestry.

For the layout of a church with adequate vestry accommodation, see a plan in Dr. Percy Dearmer's, *The Parson's Handbook*, 1940, p. 79, with a description in pp. 167–178. An excellent attempt is also made in Miss Irene Caudwell's *The Care of God's House*, in Chapter III, to give a complete survey of the contents of vestries and to offer suggestions for keeping all tidy. She includes the suggestion for a drawer containing a work-basket and various other tools for the repair and cleaning of the various articles in the church.[4]

§ 2. THE PERMANENT LAY STAFF

(a) *The Verger.* The old-time parish clerk was both an important and a picturesque figure, with duties both statutory and

---

[1] N. Truman, *The Care of Churches*, p. 25.
[2] See below, Chapter XXVI, § 5 (a).
[3] Truman, p. 72. [4] p. 17.

customary, and enjoying the dignity of a freehold office.[1] The Parochial Church Councils (Powers) Measure, 1921, swept away the freehold, altering circumstances modified his duties, and now there is hardly any distinction between parish clerk and verger, except in name. The sexton has also lost his freehold, though his duties still appertain to the churchyard. The strict meaning of the title verger is that it applies to the official who carries a ' verge ' or mace before a dignitary. In common usage the term denotes the official who takes care of the interior of the church. He is the servant of the Parochial Church Council, and it is the Council that determines his duties, his hours, and his salary. The appointment or dismissal is made jointly by the incumbent and Council, and it is desirable that there should be a written contract defining terms of employment and conditions of termination.[2]

His duties are usually the general care of the building and its furniture, and he unlocks and locks up the church at stated times. He is in attendance at all services, and prepares for them; he probably rings the one bell, operates the lights, and fires the boilers. He may act as sacristan if thought desirable, and he may also be church cleaner, in which case his hours are much longer. In the ordinary parish church he is generally a part-time official, with undefined hours—a fact that frequently causes dissatisfaction. In the nature of the circumstances an older man is appointed, and if he is a devoted churchman his work is a labour of love and many hours are unrequited. If possible it is far better to have a full-time man who is both verger of the church and caretaker of the parochial buildings. His hours can then be better defined, and his work can be better supervised. A more satisfactory wage can be paid, as generally vergers appear to be badly paid.[3]

The main trouble for the verger is that he has too many masters, for the Church Council must have its wishes carried out, and, besides the wardens, any officious member of the Council may feel that he has the right, if not to interfere, at least to criticize. Even if the incumbent reserves to himself the right to issue instructions, criticisms will arise about the heat or cleanliness of the church, which somehow reach the verger's ears. It is not surprising that vergers and caretakers are often aggrieved men. A vivid description by Arnold Bennett [4] in a single phrase, " the chapel-keeper,

---

[1] Dr. Dearmer shows how the office can be used today. *The Parson's Handbook*, 1940, pp. 288–291.
[2] K. M. Macmorran, *Handbook for Churchwardens*, etc., 1933, pp. 43, 44.
[3] L. S. Hunter, *A Parson's Job*, p. 145.
[4] Arnold Bennett, *Anna of Five Towns*, Penguin Edition, p. 10.

who always had an injured expression . . .", speaks of the care-taker fraternity in general, and it is not all their fault.

A wise priest will treat his verger with respect; while he must obey orders, the verger is also a parishioner with a soul. The way he does his work will count much for the reverent atmosphere of the church. The incumbent should know the work the verger has to do, and even be ready to do some of it, as so many had to do in war-time; especially should he understand the efficient and scientific running of the heating apparatus.

Besides the verger there may be paid cleaners. They vary considerably in their ideas of cleanliness. Some keep the church like their own houses, while others are the sort who think that the church has done them a ' dirty trick ' if they are dismissed. Often they are met in the course of visiting. In addition to the regular cleaning, the church, like any other house, needs an annual spring clean.[1]

Proper regard should be given to the insurances of the paid permanent staff. The *Diocesan Year Book* probably gives particulars; otherwise they can be found in *Opinions of the Legal Board* (fourth edition): Health Insurance, pp. 158 ff.; Unemployment Insurance, pp. 165 ff.; Workmen's Compensation, pp. 166 ff.

(b) *Organist, Choirmaster and Choir.* Even in the churches where congregational singing is well developed, no one would minimize the importance of the choir. If it really leads the worship, and not merely sings, and if the members are keen Christian people, the choir is a very valuable asset for any church to have. So much depends on the leader of the choir—the choirmaster—who may be organist also. If there are two officials, it must be understood that the choirmaster is the head, but the organist has the rights of the organ. Every incumbent must be clear about the legal position. He is in absolute charge of the worship of the church and its services, and decides when and where there shall be singing and what shall be sung, but he will wisely co-operate with the choirmaster, who will generally know more about music than the incumbent.[2] The latter must have a veto, in order to control the length of the services and safeguard the interests of the congregation—not to mention those of theology. The selection of hymns must not be left to the choirmaster; this is best done by the parish priest and choirmaster together.[3]

[1] See below, Chapter XI, § 3.
[2] J. B. Goodliffe, *The Parson and his Problems*, 1933, pp. 108, 109.
[3] See below, Chapter XIII, § 4 (d).

The choirmaster and organist are appointed by the incumbent only, but as the Council provides the stipends, its co-operation should certainly be obtained. In making appointments it is a vital necessity that only churchmen who are good communicants should be chosen; no man should be appointed on a musical qualification only. A formal contract safeguards all parties, and defines the duties; without it, on an awkward occasion there might be some dispute. The right of the organist to holidays, pupils, use and care of the organ, wedding and funeral fees, should be observed. An excellent and clear statement of these rights and duties will be found in *Opinions of the Legal Board*,[1] and this has also been issued as a separate pamphlet by the Church Assembly Press and Publications Board.

A good choirmaster is not content merely with training the choir for the Sunday services, but will seek to develop a family spirit among the members. The choir can be a happy fellowship like any other parochial organization, and social activities, winter parties and summer trips are to be encouraged. For this reason, as well as in order to maintain a high standard of singing, admissions and dismissals should be made only by joint decision of the parish priest and the choirmaster. All adult members should be communicants. The wisdom of having ladies in the choir from a musical point of view is discussed by Sir Sydney Nicholson in his *Principles and Recommendations of the School of English Church Music*.[2]

The boys need special care and attention.[3] They are usually proud to be members of the choir and enjoy the singing, recalling all their lives that they were members of the parish church choir. But as they attend regularly at so many services during boyhood, they are very apt to break away afterwards, especially as they are not accustomed to sitting in the congregation. They need just as much ' after-care ' as the candidates for Confirmation, among whom they should be numbered. The gift of a Bible or Prayer Book when they leave, their appointment as servers, cross-bearers, or assistant vergers, or the formation of an old choirboys' association, are different ways of retaining their interest until they can be reckoned among the men. Boys to-day need more encouragement, as their companions outside the choir are freer than they

---

[1] Fourth Edition, pp. 180 ff.
[2] Pp. 54, 56. Now the " Royal School of Church Music ".
[3] J. B. Goodliffe, *The Parson and his Problems*, pp. 109–111, give interesting suggestions. Cf. the whole section in *A Parson's Job*, by L. S. Hunter, pp. 110–114; also P. M. Barry, *A Present for the Vicar*, 1945, Chapter IV.

used to be, and general discipline among children is much lower. A solemn admission to office impresses the boy with the importance of his position, and participation in such outside activities as football and cricket encourages fellowship. Summer outings and winter parties and prizes are taken for granted, not as bribes, but as rewards for work well done.

The closeness of the choir, both adults and boys, to holy things, always brings a danger of familiarity, and, if not of contempt, certainly of indifference. Much depends on reverence in the vestry beforehand, and a seemly dismissal afterwards. The members of the choir should use the vestry door, and not use the church before a service as a way into the vestry.[1] Rehearsals should not be in the chancel if alternative provision can be made.[2]

(c) *Servers and Sacristan.* Young communicants can be given a great interest in their church and its chief service if they are taught to be servers. The privilege of the position should be impressed upon them, and reverence, regularity and punctuality should be required. There is a danger of appointing them too young, as then the Holy Communion becomes something associated with childhood, but if choirboys whose voices have broken become servers, two problems are solved at once.[3]

A sacristan is a useful voluntary worker if he knows his job. He will attend to the altar furniture and the vestments, and superintend the keeping clean of the sanctuary and its equipment. A lady could possibly superintend behind the scenes when boys act as servers. A knowledge of the altar linen and vestments is required, and of how they should be kept clean.[4]

(d) *Bellringers.* A peal of bells is a pleasant adjunct to the church, especially in the country. A tradition of change-ringing is strong in some areas and in some families. The ringers are appointed by the incumbent alone; if they are paid by the Church Council, its concurrence should be invited. The ringers should not have uncontrolled access to the bells, but rehearse and ring at times prescribed by the parish priest. Better interest is secured if

---

[1] Sydney Nicholson, *Principles and Recommendations*, pp. 56–58.
[2] C. F. Rogers, *Principles of Parish Work*, pp. 160–163.
[3] Percy Dearmer, *The Server's Handbook*, 1932. The duties are mentioned also in various places under different names in the same writer's *The Parson's Handbook*.
[4] Percy Dearmer, *The Parson's Handbook*. Sacristan, Equipment and Duties (with cleaning hints), pp. 169–178: Altar Linen, pp. 78–84: Colours, Vestments and Ornaments, Chapter III.
Irene Caudwell, *Care of God's House*, Chapters IV and V. Description of Vestments and Linen, and duties explained.
See also below, Chapter XI, § 2 (b).

they are voluntary men, like the sidesmen and other church officials. The chief trouble attaching to bellringers is that usually, having called others to church, they do not worship themselves. Undoubtedly there is generally a bad tradition for this, which has to be overcome, but the practice is not surprising where no washing facilities are provided.[1]

§ 3. PUBLICITY

(a) *Notice-boards.* A notice-board is needed in the main porch, and each week a list of services and meetings for the week can be exhibited on it. Various church societies send posters of all kinds for exhibition, and the incumbent must decide with discretion which to use. They should be taken down immediately after the date they advertise. The legal notices of Annual Meetings and Church Council meetings, and the certified annual Balance Sheet should be displayed, and a special place provided for the Electoral Roll. Subscription lists and Church flower lists can also be posted, so that it is the fault of the people if these are not read. An outside poster board for special services and functions is read by many non-church people, so this is also the best display place for Church defence posters. A Church notice-board should give the dedication of the church, the times of the services, and the names and addresses of the clergy and the verger. It is convenient to have a special board for civic notices about income-tax and public-house licences.[2]

(b) *The Notices.* Besides the notices in the porch, another form of publicity to the church congregation is the announcing of notices during the services. There is a growing feeling against this, especially when the notices become a sermonette or degenerate into appeals for money. If the practice is adopted, the notices should be brief, clear and audible, real publicity and not self-advertisement. Routine services and meetings need not be included, though celebrations of the Holy Communion should be announced, and attention called to Saints' Days. Any changes of routine, especially alterations of time, must be announced. Special parochial functions or meetings of importance may be included. The notices should follow the same scheme week by week, and the chronological order is preferable—that is to say, not all the cele-

[1] Cf. C. F. Rogers, *Pastoral Theology and the Modern World*, p. 39; and L. S. Hunter, *A Parson's Job*, pp. 144, 145.
[2] *Opinions of the Legal Board*, 1939, pp. 179 ff.

brations first, and then other matters, as going backwards and forwards over the same days only confuses the people.[1] Notices should be precise, not giving vague details of place and time, but there is no need to waste words, as in " 8 a.m. in the morning " or " Evensong at 6 p.m." Circulars that ask for notices to be given out on two successive Sundays need not be obeyed.

The notices are usually announced after the Creed at Holy Communion, and after the State prayers at Mattins and Evensong.[2] Sometimes, at special services, the place for notices has not been carefully considered beforehand, and the preacher may find his sermon followed, disastrously, by a string of notices.

(c) *Publicity*. Apart from the Parish Magazine, the publicity methods of the ordinary parish church are limited to notices and notice-boards. The Church in general has little or no publicity methods. The Press and Publication Board of the Church Assembly makes some attempt to keep the world informed about the activities of the Church, but one Church scandal will receive far more publicity than anything the Board issues. To many people, publicity and propaganda are under suspicion, yet the Church exists as a Society meant to propagate its message, and in truth it has used a method which until recently was the most powerful method of propaganda—that of preaching. To-day the wireless, the cinema, and the Press are more powerful, but only the Press is available for use by the ordinary parish priest; the central Church authorities are making good use of the radio and to a less degree of the film. Press advertisements must be judged by the returns they bring, and used when likely to be of value, but this is not the only way of using the Press. Church news is now of interest to local papers, and it is worth while being on good terms with the local reporters and editors, not for the purpose of getting cheap advertisement for parish functions, but because it leads to the possibility of articles on all kinds of Christian subjects being printed in the local papers. " In short, Press and parson may become trusted allies in all that concerns the public interest in their localities." [3]

It is really necessary to let everyone know what the Church is doing and why it does it. " The man in the street knows more about certain brands of food, soap, and patent medicines than he

---

[1] Contrast, Peter Green, *The Town Parson*, p. 100.
[2] Cf. W. K. Lowther Clarke, *The Prayer Book of 1928 Reconsidered*, p. 57; also P. Dearmer, *The Parson's Handbook*, pp. 319-326.
[3] C. B. Mortlock, *Parson and Press* (Press and Publications Board).

knows about his Church." [1] It is more important that any campaign should be fully advertised, whether the aim be evangelistic
or teaching. Audiences are essential to any meeting, and must be
gathered by advertisement in the right places. If only churchpeople are wanted, announcements in church and a paragraph
in the Parish Magazine will reach them, but if those outside are
sought, then advertisements in newspapers, posters on hoardings,
handbills in shop-windows, announcements in trams and buses can
all be used. This should not be done in any haphazard way, for the
effectiveness of an advertisement depends on the way it catches the
public eye. "The printing must be judicious. There must be no
stinting, but effective printing is more important than wholesale." [2]

Various other propaganda devices may be used within a parish.
Circular letters are not without effect in working-class areas, both
for such events as Gift Days and for special services in church.
They may also be used, but sparingly, for rounding up slack
members of the various organizations, and as reminders, to young
people, of corporate Communion. Easter cards are really valuable
as publicity with a personal touch. The book-rack in church is a
means of propaganda in certain types of parishes, especially in
those that attract visitors, but not usually in working-class districts.
Most people buy few books of any kind, but might borrow and
read some, and a parochial library is better than a book-rack in
such parishes. Where book-racks are likely to be useful, they can
easily be stocked with many first-class little pamphlets, and the
S.P.C.K. has a special scheme for installing a complete folding-up
book and pamphlet rack.

Church publicity needs imagination, [3] or it will soon become
very ordinary advertisement; the evangelistic motive must be
paramount. In this, however, the finest publicity is undoubtedly
that given by the church people themselves. They can speak of
meetings and the affairs of the Church to their neighbours and
friends and bring them with them. This is true publicity and the
beginning of evangelism. [4]

[1] J. M. Swift, *The Parish Magazine*, 1939, p. 9.
[2] J. T. Inskip, *The Pastoral Idea*, p. 287.
[3] Cf. Cuthbert Cooper, *The Church and Publicity*; J. B. Goodliffe, *The Parson and
his Problems*, pp. 113–122; J. M. Swift, *The Parish Magazine*, pp. 7–10; *Special
Report on Evangelism*, C.A. 730, 1944, especially pp. 6–10.
[4] *Towards the Conversion of England*, 1945, Chapter V. Here is a full discussion
of the Church's use of modern publicity methods, particularly of advertisement,
especially in evangelism. The above section, which was written before the
publication of this Report, has in mind the ordinary parish church, and not nation-
wide publicity.

SELECT BIBLIOGRAPHY

C. E. Russell, *The Priest and Business*, Chapter VI.

Percy Dearmer, *The Parson's Handbook*, 1940, Chapter IV.

I. Caudwell, *The Care of God's House*, 1943, Chapter III.

N. Truman, *The Care of Churches*, 1935.

K. M. Macmorran, *Handbook for Churchwardens and Parochial Church Councillors*.

L. S. Hunter, *A Parson's Job*, 1931, Chapters VII, IX.

Sydney Nicholson, *Principles and Recommendations of the School of English Church Music*, 1941.

Opinions of the Legal Board, 1939.

J. M. Swift, *The Parish Magazine*, 1939, Chapter I.

J. B. Goodliffe, *The Parson and his Problems*, 1933, Chapters IX, X.

P. M. Barry, *A Present for the Vicar*, 1945, Chapter IV.

PART II
CO-OPERATIVE ADMINISTRATION

CHAPTER VII

WORKING TOGETHER

§ 1. THE PROBLEM STATED

(a) *Co-operation.* In the definition of the purpose and scope of Parochial Administration [1] it was said that its aim was " To plan and organize the time and activities of the parochial clergy, and the various affairs of the parish, in such a way as to obtain, in practice, a maximum of efficiency, saving of time, and the elimination of friction," for " so only will the clergy be as free as possible for devotion, study and evangelism, and the laity be able to express a living, happy fellowship or family in the Body of Christ, both in its worship of God and in its witness to the world ". This double-barrelled definition makes the results of parochial administration a means to an end; the aim of parochial administration is to achieve efficiency for a further purpose affecting both the clergy and the laity. In the foregoing chapters of Part I the main consideration has been how the clergy may be " as free as possible for devotion, study and evangelism ", and the next task is to see how the laity of the parish may " express a living, happy fellowship or family in the Body of Christ " both in worship and in witness.

This change of emphasis seems to be a turning from those things for which the incumbent is primarily responsible, to those things that depend on the co-operation between the parson and the people, and this introduces a harder problem. In one sense it could be called the turning from theory to practice, for there is a big difference between the planning and the achievement of what has been planned. ' The best-laid schemes ' have a habit of going a-gley when they concern human beings. It has already been hinted that the representatives of the laity must be consulted in any decision respecting the appointment of the paid officials of the Church. Indeed, much, if not all, of the activity in the parish needs the sincere co-operation of the priest and his people, if it is to proceed smoothly, and in fact many spheres of joint responsibility are defined by statute.

The parson must therefore know not only where the responsibility

---

[1] See above, Chapter I, § 2 (a).

lies in parochial affairs, but also how to handle the people who have that responsibility, and how to co-operate with them. Co-operation is the key-word. It is, accordingly, necessary to think a little about the art of working together before going on to examine those spheres of co-operative work with which Parts II and III are concerned. The parish is the world in miniature and contains wide varieties of people, and the difficulties of co-operation often lie not so much in the differences between the clergy and laity, as in the vast differences among the laity themselves. It often seems in the parish that the parson's main task is the keeping of all the people worshipping and working happily together. This is not always an easy task, but it is one that demands both tact and perseverance, and is eventually an art that depends on prudence, patience, and persuasion.

(b) *The Body of Christ*. But it is not just a matter of securing the co-operation of people in the sense that this is a way of overcoming an obstacle that prevents perfection in planning and administration; it is not a means to an end, but it is part of the end itself. The whole parochial machinery exists to provide means for the expression of the fellowship or family in the Body of Christ, and the co-operation of the laity is not just a matter of efficient machinery, but a matter of the real life and spirit of the whole fellowship. A parish is no totalitarian state whose parson is its dictator, but a living organism, part of the larger Body of Christ in which the members of Christ dwell together in unity.

God has given the Church, but the art of living together in unity has to be discovered by those called to be its members under the guidance of the Holy Spirit. There is much to be learned from the deeper study of the Scriptures, and the Christian doctrine of the Church as there defined, and on this subject many books have been written, including the exhaustive study by Dr. Thornton in his *Common Life in the Body of Christ*.[1] But other knowledge is also needed; " the children of this world are in their generation wiser than the children of light ", and there are many things in the wisdom of this world that Christians can learn to their profit in the matter of living and working together. The parish priest must be a tutor to his people in this very art; putting on one side all temptation to act as a dictator, he has to seek to be their leader and guide. " The ministers of Christ are to be specialists in two departments, (1) the knowledge of God, and (2) the knowledge of man ".[2] The parson

[1] 1942. Cf. *Towards the Conversion of England*, 1945, pp. 121–134.
[2] J. T. Inskip, *The Pastoral Idea*, p. 4.

must therefore learn to know people and discover how to keep people together in unity, so that this " togetherness " may be expressed in action.

§ 2. DIFFERENT TYPES OF PEOPLE

(a) *Different Kinds of People.* Psychology gives excellent guidance in the classification of the different types of people in the world. Each of the two main divisions of people, extraverts and introverts, is divided into four main types, with the chief characteristics of sensation, thinking, feeling, and intuition.[1] Although there are no hard-and-fast dividing lines between them, here are eight classes of individual types; and it is of great value in working with people to have some idea of the particular class of each individual. That it is necessary for pastors who wish to help people with individual advice is obvious,[2] but it is equally important to those who in parochial administration have many different types of people for partners.

Not only are there these different classes, but each individual has his own complexes and repressions, and very often the people who present a problem are the very ones that come into a church circle. The hardest lesson to learn in a parish is that people are not completely reasonable, logical and rational (neither is the priest, for that matter), and a simple recognition of this fact saves many tears and much heart-burning. All these different people are likely to be represented among the church officials, found on the Church Council, and are present at any meeting of parishioners, no matter for what purpose they are called together. The chairman can more easily handle his meeting if he can recognize his psychological types with some degree of approximation. It helps him to deduce the meaning of what is said, which otherwise is not clear, to give the right answers, and to sum up with general satisfaction to those present. Mistakes, of course, are always likely to happen, for human nature is very complex. Generally speaking, the parish priest must learn to recognize the danger of the dominating person, even when he supports the priest; to avoid feeling irritated at the long-winded, the noisy and the exhibitionist who must show-off; and not to depend too much on the ultimate votes of the ' yes-men ', though they usually represent the majority of the worshippers.

In addition to the various kinds of people, every parish has a group of the disgruntled (not necessarily in alliance), who have been offended for various reasons. Perhaps a challenging note from

---

[1] Dewar and Hudson, *A Manual of Pastoral Psychology*, p. 110.
[2] See below, Chapter XXIV, § 3.

the pulpit or a trivial change in the service has offended the more conservative, or, more often, a seeming slight from the clergy has given offence. Sometimes the reason as given is genuinely felt, even if there is no justification for it, but often the reason given is a rationalization of the real motive. Commonly it is due to removal from office for incompetence, and often it is due to the fact that the person concerned was much consulted by the previous incumbent, and so the actions of the new parson are resented.[1] It is sometimes better to lose the disgruntled rather than to have a feeling of suspicion and dislike constantly harming parochial work, though no true pastor will like to see any of the flock leaving the fold.

SELECT BIBLIOGRAPHY

L. Dewar and C. E. Hudson, *A Manual of Pastoral Psychology*, 1932.
W. Fearon Halliday, *Psychology and Religious Experience*, 1931.
L. W. Grensted, *Psychology and God*, 1930.
T. H. Hughes, *The Psychology of Preaching and Pastoral Work*, 1939.
E. S. Waterhouse, *Psychology and Pastoral Work*, 1939.

(b) *Different Groups of People.* The art of working together does not simply consist in keeping all the different individuals playing their part; in addition, it is necessary to prevent clashes between different groups. There is sometimes a difference of churchmanship, one group desiring a ' higher ' or ' lower ' type of ritual than another, but usually (not always) any such difference is not serious enough to cause a real rift. The difference between Youth and Age can sometimes cause tension, and this is often expressed as a cleavage of churchmanship;[2] such differences are susceptible to tactful handling and guidance.

Differences of the various social strata within the parish, like all class divisions, are much more pernicious. In villages this counts for little as far as worship is concerned, but in town parishes social interests are so different that mixing is almost impossible, and it is usually in such a parish that there is a marked distinction between the morning and the evening congregation. Canon Goodliffe advocates that an attempt should be made to interpret each class to the other,[3] and this should be done to foster greater Christian fellowship. The pastor must think out his approach to each class, according to its education. For example, his sermons may have to be differently constructed to suit the capacity of different congregations. But this must be the only difference. It goes without

[1] J. B. Goodliffe, *The Parson and his Problems*, p. 75.
[2] Peter Green, *The Man of God*, p. 108.
[3] J. B. Goodliffe, *The Parson and his Problems*, p. 70.

saying that it is abhorrent that there should be any suggestion of patronizing the poor and flattering the rich, but the tendency to do this is very deep in human nature. The opposite tendency is not unknown, and is, indeed, increasing—namely, that of snubbing the so-called 'upper classes' on the grounds that Christianity is 'democratic'. In some country parishes the 'squire' has been driven away from his own church.

In the past rich and poor have been treated as different categories, and the Church had some unworthy methods in its approach to the poor. Professor Rogers made a strong condemnation of this as long ago as 1905, and though passing years have made some changes, his analysis is well worth reading.[1] For many parishes these difficulties do not arise, for most slum parishes, artisan and suburban parishes are homogeneous, but some town areas do have both rich and poor, and church life is apt to be confined to one or the other of the classes, or made to run in parallel divisions, as in a Ladies' Sewing Class and a Women's Working Party. In the Christian Church neither class must be ignored, but both should be drawn together, and apart from worship and evangelism, committee work does this more effectively than the parish social. People's entertainment depends on their habits and standards of culture, but committee work puts all on an equal footing, though, owing to their more limited education, the poorer will be the slower thinkers and speakers. "On the common ground of action, of decision, of character, it is realized how essentially alike all men are, and how comparatively unimportant are social or even intellectual differences."[2]

But the worst divisions arise from parochial cliques, because they can develop the most uncharitable spirit. In a way they are unavoidable, for people have their likes and dislikes, their friends and their enemies, and a new parish priest is never very long discovering parochial feuds and jealousies. The incumbent, indeed, has to walk very warily, or he will increase instead of diminishing the divisions. The pillars of the church, the inner circle, tend to monopolize the priest, so that he can easily forget that there are other people whose advice is sound, or who need his ministry. Divisions of this kind frequently arise because of the wretched tendency to exclusiveness noticeable among church people. Those who have always come regard others as 'new', even though these are the more diligent worshippers, and some think that they are so important at the church that anybody not known to them cannot

[1] C. F. Rogers, *Principles of Parish Work*, Chapter VI.   [2] *Ibid.*, p. 205.

possibly belong. It is not easy to instil an evangelistic spirit into such a congregation. Nor is it easy to welcome new people and find them friends. Many poor lonely people come to church seeking friendship, finding none. On the other hand, some churches are so short of sufficient men for the official positions that new-comers are rushed into office before they have proved their worth.

It is easily seen how much rests upon the parish priest if all these various groups are to work happily together. In a village, or in a parish which is a self-contained community, the various groups are kept together at the church from age-long loyalty, but in a town parish the parson is often the corner-stone of the parochial edifice, since only his management keeps the different groups in unison. In these days the town parishes tend increasingly to be congregational in spirit.

(c) *The Priest's Attitude to his People.* So much, therefore, depends on the man at the head knowing something of the art of ' keeping people together ', but all the art and management in the world will be unavailing unless the priest shows in himself the right attitude to his flock. His own habits and example will themselves carry great weight with those among whom he works. Dr. Henson, speaking to his ordination candidates, says, " Don't underrate the importance of your example," [1] and again, " The clergyman's private life has an evident bearing on his personal influence, which indeed it may be said to determine ". [2] He stands in some ways at a disadvantage, especially in working-class districts, by reason of the house in which he has to live. This can create class consciousness, and many people cannot believe the cry of clerical poverty. [3] Often, again, the parsonage is an open house, the parson has no private life, his affairs are closely under the public eye, and his behaviour must be so much the more circumspect.

Yet this is but a negative argument; the parish priest must not merely set a good example, he must try to please, not for his own ends, but for the Gospel he has to commend. The salesman out for himself has complaisance, which is by definition " the action or habit of making oneself agreeable, desire or care to please, compliance with a deference to, the wishes of others, obligingness, courtesy, politeness ". Such complaisance in anyone helps to make the world run smoothly, but " the object of Christian complaisance is not merely to please, but so to please as by pleasing to predispose towards good those whom we please, not to strengthen and confirm

---

[1] H. H. Henson, *Ad Clerum*, p. 195.   [2] *Ibid.*, p. 132.
[3] L. S. Hunter, *A Parson's Job*, pp. 209–212.

them in error ".[1] St. Paul has this in mind when he says, " I am
become all things to all men, that I may by all means save some ".
Certainly the uncivil, rough and rude man will please none, and
none will listen to him, be his gospel true or false. No doubt there
is a time when plain, outspoken condemnation is required; this
will certainly not please, but it will be respected, especially from one
who is always gracious in manner and speech.[2]

Canon Green, in an excellent chapter, has illustrated how many-
sided this attitude of complaisance must be.[3] The priest must know
his people, and that can be done only by visiting them in their
homes and by being with them in their socials and meetings. Not
only must he know them, but he must understand them, the way
in which they think, and how they make their judgments. Further,
he must learn to love them, and for all their faults it is not really
difficult to be fond of them all. Dr. Herbert Gray would say that
this is the foundation of pastoral work. If the pastor loves his
people, he will soon seek to serve them, to please them in courtesy
and consideration, and yet be ready to rebuke when rebukes are
necessary. A priest who comes to his people in this way will win
their love and respect in return, and the foundations for working
together are then well and truly laid. Did not the Lord say, " I am
among you as he that serveth " ?

§ 3. DYNAMIC ADMINISTRATION

(a) *Leadership.* The priest has the task of being a leader to the
people. He can learn much from a study of modern psychology
as applied to business management and administration. *Dynamic
Administration* [4] is the title given to the collected papers of Mary
Parker Follett, who considers from various points of view how
production and profits can be increased by the right understanding
and treatment of human relationships. Without consciously
quoting a line of Scripture, she sets out principles that undoubtedly
give a Christian standard of co-operation in common life. This
subject has been studied and developed under the stimulus of the
profit motive; surely the same study could be made in some small
way for the higher motive of the love of Christ.

" What is the accepted *theory* of leadership? In general, we may

---

[1] H. H. Henson, *Ad Clerum*, p. 59.
[2] See below, Chapter XXVII, § 3 (d) and § 2 (c).
[3] Peter Green, *The Man of God*, pp. 88-126.
[4] Published by Management Publications Trust Limited, and Edited by Henry
C. Metcalfe and L. Urwick.

say that the leader is usually supposed to be one who has a compelling personality, who wields a personal power, who constrains others to his will." [1] It is found that in business the man with such ' ascendency traits ' is not always a success as a leader. Aggressiveness does not pay. Even paid employees do not like being ordered to do things, but do their work better when they see the reason for the orders. It is better that " orders come from action, and not action from orders ".[2] With the voluntary workers of the parish this is even more important; the priest cannot give orders, but he can describe the circumstances in which he and the parish are placed, and the necessity for action gives the orders to the workers. It was " the force of circumstances which seemed to make the demand " [3] can often be said by a Church Council as well as by a works committee.

" Don't exploit your personality; learn your job," [4] is a key instruction to business managers, and " Sincerity more than aggressiveness is a quality of leadership ".[5] People can be dominated for a time by a forceful personality, but not for ever, and eventually no common ground of action is left. Leadership is never the function of one alone, but he who leads and those who are led are part of a single unit. " Part of the task of the leader is to make others partake in leadership ",[6] and to do this " the leader must share their experiences ".[7] The true unity factor in the leader-led relationship is the common purpose,[8] and the Church has a far greater unifying factor of this nature than any business under the sun.

(b) *Orders and Control.* If it be granted that leadership is other than aggressive ascendency, how does control enter at all? " How can we avoid the two extremes: too great bossiness in giving orders, and practically no orders given? " The answer is : " To unite all concerned in the study of the situation, to discover the law of the situation and obey that." [9] This is nothing but a communal seeking for guidance, as a Christian company would seek the guidance of the Holy Spirit, though Christians would not speak of the law of the situation, but would rather say, " The love of Christ constraineth us ". As an example of the giving, or refraining from giving, of orders, the question of raffles may be cited.

" I am tired of hearing it said by indefatigable workers at bazaars and sales of work—' our vicar will not let us have

[1] *Dynamic Administration*, p. 270.   [2] *Ibid.*, p. 273.   [3] *Ibid.*, p. 276.
[4] *Ibid.*, p. 272.   [5] *Ibid.*, p. 276.   [6] *Ibid.*, p. 290.
[7] *Ibid.*, p. 285.   [8] *Ibid.*, p. 287.   [9] *Ibid.*, p. 58.

raffles '. All honour to the vicar, but it is time he shared his moral common sense with the inner circle of his laity." [1]

In one parish where raffles had always been allowed, the subject was discussed in debate at the Men's Society. The members were so convinced by the arguments that the subject was brought up at the Annual Parochial Meeting, and no more raffles were held in the parish. No orders were given at all.

But the business manager, though he does not give orders, nor try to persuade by cajolery—" in this factory they don't just try to persuade us, they try to convince us ",[2]—has to exercise control, for the main function of leadership is that of co-ordination.[3] Individuals doing different things are useless unless their efforts are co-ordinated, and this must be done by someone outside them, who not only grasps the idea of the whole, but conveys that idea to all who share in it.

> "While we think of the players in an orchestra as each knowing his part, and of the conductor as having an awareness of the total process as an integrative unity, we must remember also that the players play best when the conductor is able to make each share his inclusive awareness." [4]

Professor Whitehead has spoken of " the interplay of diverse values " which must be brought to some coherence, and the priest has something of that task to do in his parish.

> " The job of a parson in charge of a parish is to make of a medley of workers, officials and councillors, a united team that is keen, resourceful and trusting in his captaincy ".[5]

(c) *Constructive Conflict.* The good leader and administrator should not be disturbed by conflict; it is bound to happen, and in fact it should happen. The best Church Council is not one in which differences of opinion and conflict have been removed. " What people often mean by getting rid of conflict is getting rid of diversity," [6] whereas this diversity and conflict can be used. It is like the friction which a mechanical engineer will use, and on which much machinery depends.[7] But conflict is constructive only if it is encountered in the right way. There are three methods of dealing with conflict;[8] domination, compromise, and integration. By

---

[1] L. S. Hunter, *A Parson's Job*, p. 146.
[2] *Dynamic Administration*, p. 102.
[3] *Ibid.*, p. 206.
[4] *Ibid.*, p. 201.
[5] L. S. Hunter, *A Parson's Job*, p. 138. See also above, Chapter III, § 2 (a).
[6] *Dynamic Administration*, p. 31.
[7] *Ibid.*, p. 30.

domination one side gains the victory over the other; it is the easiest way out at any moment, but is not usually successful in the long run. Many business conflicts and more than one parish conflict has been terminated, but not settled, in this way. *Compromise* is the method most often used, and, in order to compromise, both sides begin by demanding more than they would, in fact, be prepared to accept. This is a method adopted by some incumbents, who ' step up ' their parishes by a series of compromises. Such men always leave an atmosphere of insincerity and lack of principle behind them. *Integration* is the true method; it tries to draw the best from all sides. Most modern attempts at union between the churches are founded on this principle, and not on compromise. Thus, through integration, conflict becomes constructive, but compromise can never create. " In dissensions between executives it is never merely peace that should be our aim, but progress "; [1] this is a rule which can apply to parishes as to business firms.

Integration is in itself a skilled way of working. Differences must first be brought into the open, so that the real issue can be faced and the conflict is uncovered. Usually the dramatic features in the differences of opinion are not the significant factors. Further, people tend to urge a whole proposition; often when it is resolved into its parts, some of these parts are acceptable to the opponents. The use of symbols often obscures ground for agreement, especially in ecclesiastical prejudices. Integration is also like a game of chess: there is much anticipation of response.

Integration must be the method by which committee work in the Church proceeds. A solution to differences must be that which is not a compromise. This is why committees are slow working, and often exasperating to busy people. " Committees at their best are not a way of speeding up executive action but of slowing it down." [2] But discussion is not only the way of finding a solution to difficulties; it is an education in itself. Much depends on the way in which people set their minds when they come to a committee meeting. " If you look back over your experience on any committee, I think you will find that it is the for-or-against attitude which makes conflict ".[3] Business should not be placed before people in two contrasting alternatives, " Shall this or that be done? ", but it should be approached from the angle of the desired result.

Miss Parker Follett [4] also sums up the common obstacles to inte-

---

[1] *Dynamic Administration*, p. 213.
[2] L. S. Hunter, *A Parson's Job*, p. 149.
[3] *Dynamic Administration*, p. 220.   [4] *Ibid.*, pp. 45–49.

gration. The chief is, when one side wants to fight and dominate; another, when the theoretical aspect of the problem attracts and there is no thought of putting it into practice. Wrong language can induce opposition by hetero-suggestion, but this usually comes from lack of training. In fact, lack of training in the method is given as a big hindrance to integration in business; much the same could be said of lack of training in the Church.

§ 4. The Fellowship of the Church

(a) *True Community.* A big responsibility rests on the parson in the exercise of true leadership of the people, but the laity are not without a responsibility of their own. There must be on the part of the people a response to the priest's efforts at integration, for the purpose of this is the formation of a community, and the true Christian community can only be such as the expression of the Holy Spirit through the hearts and minds of men and women. Integration is the work of man, the welding into the community of the work of the Holy Spirit; just as the setting of a fractured bone is the doctor's art, but the knitting of the bone together is the work of nature. This work of the Holy Spirit in cementing the Community is partly dependent on the people having a wish so to grow together.

So often the urge that every church feels for its own extension becomes a matter of trying to make individual conversions, and the spearhead of Christian attack is directed with this aim in view. But this is not enough. "The Gospel has got to have an unmistakable cosmic note about it; a note of community."[1] Sometimes evangelism fails because there is no adequate 'follow-up'; the newly-won—or, as they often are, the half-won—must be welded into the community and grafted into the Body of Christ. The need of the individual must not be overlooked; he must not be regarded as so much 'church fodder',[2] but must *for his own good* become completely and fully a member of the community. This is the crucial test of modern parochial work, especially in evangelism. Those who are attracted and partly won do not always find their real needs satisfied in the congregation they join. To them something seems to be missing, and it is that necessary fellowship, or the 'cosmic note'. In a church that has no community sense the members of the congregation are but individuals at worship; even when there is a 'fellowship of the parochial hall' (a characteristic

---

[1] H. H. Farmer, *The Servant of the Word*, p. 126.
[2] An expression the writer owes to Professor Hodgson.

of the North of England), it does not follow that this fellowship is fully expressive of the true Christian community, which finds its fullest expression in worship and in witness. It is this fellowship that the outsider is apt to find lacking when he feels drawn to the church, and his feelings are symbolized in the words " Nobody spoke to me ", which he uses after he has been. Nor is it just a handshake that has been missed, but a note of welcome expressed in the church and the service. Some people do not wish to be ' fussed ',[1] but even they can respond to the warmth that a fellowship that is truly a community at worship can give.

(b) *The Leaven.* How is that fellowship to be secured? A familiar way of approach is through the inner circle working as a leaven within the whole congregation. It is like a community within the community, with a special responsibility towards the wider body. The Church Council is a community of this kind, but it does not always form, as in theory it ought to do, the inner circle which is to be the leaven. The Apostles were such an inner circle, and were trained by the Master to lead His Church. So within the congregation the really keen, spiritually-alive people can form a Guild or Circle for prayer, Bible-reading, and fellowship. A priest who spends much of his time preparing such a circle is using his time wisely. It is impossible to influence personally everyone in the parish. It can be done only through an inner circle. Professor Rogers urged years ago that the parish priest should concentrate on his workers, and that they would influence the people.[2] The same truth applies to this leaven of the inner circle.[3]

However, the avowed aim of the ' circle ' must never be forgotten; it has to leaven the whole lump. The danger of a circle is that it may become an end in itself, a circle of spiritual experts who form yet one more division in the church and keep themselves to themselves, forgetful of their responsibility.

(c) *The Fellowship.* The leaven leavens the lump, the cells multiply together to form a living organism of a body, the end is the same. The whole congregation must become a fellowship and community alert in its own spiritual life, and alive to its responsibility to the world. The Church " cannot be content to keep alive a diffused sense of decency in the community through a congregation which in no degree is conscious of itself as a missionary body.

[1] C. F. Rogers, *Pastoral Theology and the Modern World,* pp. 161–164; an amusing essay on ' Letting People Alone '.
[2] C. F. Rogers, *Principles in Parish Work,* p. 210.
[3] *The Christian Cell and its Place in the Church,* 1943.

At present, in many parishes, the Church is trying to leaven society
with leaven that is merely bread, and however hard men work the
attempt is futile. A C3 ten per cent cannot change an indifferent
ninety per cent. The immediate task of the Church is to convert
existing congregations into leaven ".[1]

There are many who are experimenting to-day with attempts at
gathering the whole Church together in a fellowship for worship and
action. The fundamental idea is that the Church of the New
Testament was this kind of Church. The working of the leaven is
regarded as too slow; rather, a sudden leap forward is envisaged.
In fact, the magazine which is published by those who are like-
minded in this work is called *The Leap*,[2] after the words of the
psalmist, "With the Help of my God I shall leap over the Wall ".
In this scheme all and sundry are called to meet weekly for the discussion of church affairs, there is no hand-picking of the keen
people, and all matters affecting the church are thrashed out. To
some extent the legal authority of the Church Council is short-
circuited, though the fellowship has been described as the Church
Council in continual session. Such things as the times and the
conduct of services, the music and the choir, the finances and ways of
evangelism are made the concern of the whole church, as they rightly
are. Fellowship is fostered by meeting together in a large room
rather than in a school, with the usual refreshments, and a mutual
use of Christian names. Emphasis is laid upon the weekly parish
Communion, ideally only one celebration each Sunday, at which all
are present. The real difficulty is providing weekly meetings of
this kind with sufficient food for discussion and thought: on the
one hand the meetings can so easily become just another meeting
which the clergy address, or on the other hand degenerate into a
gossip circle with its attendant dangers. "There are few things
short of actual sin, that blunt the perceptions, and weaken the sense
of reality, or religion, more than the perpetual discussion of parish
gossip ".[3]

Nevertheless, the Fellowship need never be short of a programme
if it is built up on these four notes of activity. The Fellowship
of the Church must be a centre of supernatural vitality, from which
the members draw their life, just as the branches draw their life from
the vine. The members must feel that through their membership
they are brought into touch, and kept in touch, with God. It must

---

[1] L. S. Hunter, *A Parson's Job*, pp. 137 f.
[2] Obtainable from 5 Regent House, 72 Eversholt Street, N.W. 1.
[3] C. F. Rogers, *Principles of Parish Work*, p. 40.

be a centre of spiritual resistance to the low ideals of the world as they are so often expressed in the home and in the workshop; members can both individually and corporately resist the moral standards of the world with the high standards of the Church. The Fellowship of the Church must also be a centre of propaganda, expressing the Gospel of Christ as personally experienced within the Church, so that others may be drawn into it. Finally, the Fellowship of the Church must be a centre of real community life, as experienced in the early days of Christianity, with its outward expression embracing all aspects summed up in "And they continued steadfastly in the apostles' doctrine and fellowship, and in breaking of bread and in prayers." [1]

[1] Acts ii, 42. This last paragraph owes its contents to a paper read at a clergy chapter by the Provost of Bradford.

SELECT BIBLIOGRAPHY

Towards the Conversion of England, 1945, Chapter VI.

Metcalfe and Urwick, *Dynamic Administration*, 1941.   (The collected papers of M. Parker Follett.)

Joseph McCulloch, *We have our Orders*, 1943.

Joseph McCulloch, *The Trumpet shall Sound*, 1944.

L. S. Hunter, *A Parson's Job*, 1931, Chapter IX.

H. R. L. Sheppard, *The Human Parson.*

P. C. A. Carnegy, *Our Fellowship in the Gospel*, 1944.

The Christian Cell and its Place in the Church, 1943.   (The Advisory Group for Christian Cells, Townsend House, Greycoat Place, London, S.W. 1.)

Joseph McCulloch, *Medway Adventure*, 1946.

R. E. Parsons, *The Spirit of the Christian Cell*, 1946.

CHAPTER VIII

THE CHURCH MEMBERS AND OFFICIALS

§ 1. THE CHURCH PEOPLE

IT has already been noted [1] that in a town parish to-day the Church of England is in some ways more congregational than parochial, so much so that the so-called 'successful' parson is the one who gathers round him a good congregation either by his preaching or by his pastoral work; whether the congregation lives within the parish or not, or whatever may be the fate of the other parishioners, seems of little import. Modern conditions force these circumstances upon the priest, but he will endeavour to build up his congregation from the parish, and to care as far as possible for his other parishioners. Yet the fact remains that the priest is to a large extent concerned just with the church people, his own congregation.

(a) *The Constituents of the Congregation.* There is first that wonderful nucleus of active regular worshippers who gain their vision of God through their parish church, though they may not be able to explain why or how to others. These worshippers are of two kinds: the officials and helpers who realize that there is much to be done besides worship, and those who are just content to come. These last are by no means to be despised, though many are so difficult to get to know, just because they keep in the background. Though they have no desire to be drawn into parochial politics, they are often the best givers, and are, curiously enough, the parson's principal supporters in any unavoidable controversy. So often the priest has to use persuasion and tact with the vocal few that he forgets usually that if the worst comes to the worst and the vocal few desert him, then he still has his faithful, appreciative congregation.

Then there are the irregular worshippers—the people of the neighbourhood who know the church is theirs and claim membership of it. They come in times of joy and sorrow, as well as, of course, for baptisms, marriages, and funerals. They are church people, they are quite ready to give their support, and they expect their parish priest to know them. They are, many of them, Easter

---

[1] See above, Chapter VII, § 2 (*b*).

communicants, but they come so little at other times that they lower the spiritual level of the worship on Easter Day.[1] There are further the indirect members, the well-wishers, friends and parents of the children in the schools. They come to church as often as the last group, but do not claim actual membership. They give rather more readily to the work among children and young people, and to Sunday School funds. Many in this class have been brought up in nonconformity and find the Anglican services difficult. Here is a fruitful ground for developing keenness, and very often also for adult confirmation candidates. Finally there are the potential members—all the rest of the parishioners who are not attached to any other church. The empty seats in the church could be filled with these if only the Gospel message could be presented to them. The congregation is never complete without them.

(b) *Ministering to the Congregation.* The parish priest may be content to take the line of least resistance, and be content to find a congregation in his church. He will lead them in their worship and preach to them. In most parishes such an attitude would mean a steadily decreasing crowd, even if both the worship and the preaching were well expressed. It is necessary in addition to get to know the congregation, and various methods may be adopted. Many will be encountered in the parochial organizations, others will be met in their own homes if their names happen to be on the visiting list. Others must be known somehow. Slips of paper asking for names and addresses can be put in pews or given out at the door, but this does not bring in many fresh names as a rule. The only way is by doorway contacts, preferably after the service, but sometimes people can be met outside and welcomed. The ideal is for the priest to know everyone in church by name. In addition, the priest will seek to increase the congregation by the many ways of pastoral work and evangelism, and it is only by the continual addition of fresh blood that the congregation is kept alive. Notwithstanding, the priest who is anxious to have a big congregation in his church must be alive to the dangers of becoming narrowly congregationally-minded, and forgetful of his wider parochial charge.

§ 2. RECORDING MEMBERSHIP

(a) *The Electoral Roll.* The official basis of membership, the Electoral Roll, is not completely satisfactory, yet even so it is not usually worked quite as well as it might be. Ignorance of the

---

[1] Cf. J. B. Goodliffe, *The Parson and his Problems*, p. 74.

rules is a minor cause, indifference the major one. It is the legal basis of the lay representation in the Church of England, and yet few people trouble to apply for enrolment on their own accord, and many never apply at all. It is quite inadequate as a record of the members of the congregation, and the priest must keep a complete card index of his own pastoral work for visiting needs.

The Church Electoral Roll is described in the Representation of the Laity Measure, 1929, in the Schedule, section 3 : [1]

" (2) The persons entitled to have their names entered upon the Roll of a parish, shall be lay members of the Church of England of either sex, of eighteen years of age and upwards who :—

" (a) are baptized and declare that they are members of the Church of England and that they do not belong to any religious body which is not in communion with the Church of England ; and

" (b) are resident in the parish, or (whether or not so resident) have habitually attended public worship in the parish during a period of six months prior to enrolment ; and

" (c) have signed the form of application for enrolment."

There are obviously many people who can qualify under these conditions in any church, and the problem is how to bring them to apply for enrolment. In (4) of the same section above quoted, the Roll is to be " kept and revised by the Council." Anyone's job is nobody's job, and either the Council should find a keen layman to be Roll Official, or the clergy should be appointed to take charge of the Roll and report periodically to the Council. Strictly speaking, the representational affairs of the laity are best in their own hands, but actually the clergy are the best recruiters for the Roll.[2] They are the only people who know everybody (or if they do not, nobody does), including the shy members of the church, the new-comers, and the younger communicants as they reach the age of eighteen.[3] This last group should regularly be added to the Roll year by year, and the duties and the privileges explained to them.

In a country parish there is a difference. Often a lay person is best in a village, where a clergyman asking for signatures might be regarded with suspicion. In one country parish of sixty-five people of qualifying age, twenty-one were on the Roll, and all signed at the invitation of a lady.

[1] K. M. Macmorran, *Handbook for Churchwardens and Parochial Church Councillors*, 1933, p. 86; *Opinions of the Legal Board*, 1939, pp. 30–35.
[2] R. H. Malden, *This Church and Realm*, 1931, p. 16 n.
[3] The " Unicard System " (see below, Chapter XXI, § 2 (b)) provides for a method of bringing in the eighteens.

H

In almost every parish, if the Roll is examined not only will it be noticed that new names are surprisingly few, but also that the list usually includes many who are dead, many who have married, and many who have moved away. The section 3 of the Schedule provides rules for an annual revision that must take place at a stated time, when the names of such people should be removed. This procedure is not often observed. In some quite well-run parishes a five-yearly revision only seems to be undertaken, and then not quite according to statute. The clergy ought to visit all 'unknowns' on the Roll and report to the Council on their whereabouts or present churchmanship; the clergy visiting list should be compared with the Roll, and the people not on the latter should be asked to sign the form.[1] The best way to keep the Roll is on alphabetical loose sheets.

(b) *The Communicants' List.* Any baptized members of the congregation over the age of eighteen can apply to enrol on the Electoral Roll, though in most parishes only a small percentage of the members of the Roll are not confirmed. Many communicants, being under age or for other reasons, are not on the Roll, and it is most important in addition to have a Communicants' List. A card index that lends itself to easy revision is the best method of keeping the List. In some ways it is inconvenient to have two lists of members, and some incumbents confine their Roll to communicants and see that all communicants are on it; it is illegal to make the restriction.

In compiling a Communicants' List for the first time, or in revising a list in a parish where the priest is a new incumbent, the nucleus of the list is made from the officials, church councillors, and regular members. The Confirmation Register, if it has been kept, will provide the names of the younger members for the past few years. Other names will be gathered in the course of visiting and from discovering the names of all who come to the Communion services. A first Communion of the newly confirmed will frequently bring parents to a celebration for the first time for many years; their names can then be added. On Easter Day cards can be issued to all present, asking for names and addresses (several firms print such cards), and this method usually brings in some new names. All confirmed people, whether regular or not, should be on this list; there is always a hope that the lapsed may be recovered. In a large parish three years ought to be spent in con-

---

[1] The Unicard system provides a useful card for recording signatures of several parishioners.

structing the Communicants' List before it is used for working
purposes.

Once made, the Communicants' List can be used for invitations
to Communion services from time to time, or for letters about the
importance of regular Communion, or for any other means
designed to bring home to members their obligations. Easter
cards can be sent to all, and are much appreciated. The younger
communicants need much more attention—a subject connected
with the after-care of Confirmation candidates.[1]

Canon Peter Green urges the keeping of a Communicants'
attendance register.[2] This has obvious values, but the keeping of
such a record would seem to many hard-working priests a counsel of
perfection.

§ 3. THE OFFICIALS

(a) *Statutory Officials.* Though shorn of much of their previous
authority by the Parochial Church Councils (Powers) Act, 1921, the
churchwardens are still persons of importance. They have certain
legal rights connected with the church and its movable furniture,
the duty of maintaining order, allocating seats, providing registers
for Divine Service, and a voice in the disposal of the alms. During
a vacancy they are nearly always the Sequestrators, and, when the
appointment of an incumbent is proceeding, they have a legal status
as representing the Church Council. They are elected at a joint
meeting of the Vestry and Parochial Meeting held not later than
the week after Easter, and must be formally admitted into
office at the next Visitation. Every incumbent and churchwarden
should be conversant with the legal status and duties of wardens.[3]

The churchwardens should be carefully chosen; usually the
incumbent appoints one and the laity elect the other, but even for
the choice of People's Warden the parish priest should sometimes
see that there are two or three suitable candidates. The election
itself should be quite free. Because of their ancient office and
present legal status, though not so important as in former years,
the wardens should be real leaders of the laity while they are in
office. The incumbent will expect them to be loyal to him; he
should also be loyal to them. Their advice should be sought in
important matters, often before going to the Standing Committee,
and though anything like cut-and-dried business at a Committee

[1] See below, Chapter XXII, § 5.
[2] Peter Green, *The Town Parson*, pp. 212–215.
[3] K. M. Macmorran, *Handbook for Churchwardens and Parochial Church Councillors,* 1933, pp. 25–42.

is undesirable, the wardens can give valuable help from the lay point of view. There are two dangers, for on the one hand some lay people will feel jealous of the confidence which the parish priest must place in his wardens, and on the other a warden when he gives up office may still expect the confidences of the priest, not realizing that the previous privilege was due to his office and not to him personally. It is undesirable for any lay person not an official, though maybe a retired official, to be a power behind the throne. Wise words have been said by Chancellor Errington:

" The churchwardens doing their duty year in and year out, often to the great advantage of everyone concerned during many successive years, are the stabilising element in the parish. All incumbents do not see eye to eye with their church councils. The churchwardens have, so to speak, a foot in both camps, and with a little patience and perhaps a little humour can often bridge the gap." [1]

Next to the appointment of the churchwardens, the most important appointments are those of the secretary and the treasurer to the Church Council, who need to be able and capable men in their respective capacities. Their duties are more conveniently discussed later.[2] The sidesmen are not nearly so important as they appear. They are needed to help the Wardens in directing people to their places, in giving out and collecting up the Prayer Books, and in taking the collection. A very useful duty which they can perform is to welcome strangers, ask if they live near, and if they do, to take their names and addresses for the clergy. Sidesmen must be members on the Electoral Roll, and elected at the Annual Parochial Meeting in the way prescribed. If the incumbent and the meeting fail to agree on a joint election, each may appoint half the members.[3] If the priest does appoint some, he has an opportunity to bring in some new men. It is not a legal qualification, but a definite common-sense rule, to require all sidesmen to be confirmed. Formerly the sidesmen gained their importance by forming the priest's advisory committee, but in this respect they have been superseded by the Church Council. Under the new circumstances there is an opportunity to give a job to the young men, who should number at least half the sidesmen.

(b) *Other Officials.* Besides the statutory officials, it is an advantage to have as many others as possible. The chief appointments

[1] *Opinions of the Legal Board*, 1939, p. 224. Chancellor Errington's article is very useful pp. (214–224.) The Index to *Opinions* is a guide to other valuable information.
[2] See below, Chapter IX, § 3 (b).
[3] *Opinions of the Legal Board*, 1939, p. 38 and pp. 101 ff.

are those of the Sunday School superintendents and the various
secretaries and treasurers of the different committees and
organizations.

" My main job was to find jobs for everyone, which is much
more difficult than doing them oneself. But it is in doing something for the Church that a man comes to love the Church.
So long as everything is done for them by a devoted and over-
worked vicar, and paid for them by the liberality of their
ancestors, so long will the Church of England be an object of
criticism, rather than a focus of loyalty." [1]

Of course it is easier to do any particular job oneself, but in the long
run not a multitude of them. Yet in handing out the various jobs
it must be expected that many will be done badly and inefficiently,
and the parish priest will be blamed for it. Having many officials
creates interest, and though some prove to be inefficient, many
develop unexpected powers of organization and leadership.
Officials should always be regular attenders. Nominal but
wealthy churchmen are not desired.[2] For the great majority of
official positions, if not for all, the communicant rule is also essential,
and should operate for the officials of satellite bodies like cricket
clubs, whatever the membership rule may be.

Officials are apt to make the most of their own importance, to be
keen on their own piece of work, and often forget its position with
relation to the whole life of the Church. " Some may have so little
vision of the Church's purpose, that it becomes to them primarily
an institution which provides useful auspices and accommodation." [3]
And again, " Church workers, left to themselves, are liable to be
jealous of their autonomy and unwilling to co-operate with the
leaders of other clubs and classes." [3] The work of getting his
officials to co-operate is part of the priest's task of keeping all his
people living together in unity.

The inefficient official always presents a problem, and it often
happens that the least fitted man is always volunteering for jobs.
Such offers must sometimes be accepted and the man given a fair
trial. If he fails, the importance of the duty must be weighed
against his personal feelings. If his inefficiency is an offence, or a
hindrance to many of the congregation, he must be removed, and
when tact fails, as it usually does here, straight speaking must be
adopted.[4]

[1] A. W. Hopkinson, *Pastor's Progress*, p. 91.
[2] Cf. J. B. Goodliffe, *The Parson and his Problems*, pp. 107, 108.
[3] L. S. Hunter, *A Parson's Job*, p. 143.
[4] Cf. *Ibid.*, p. 144.

One other danger that sometimes presents itself is met in the parochial 'Pooh-Bah', the man who has too many jobs. This is unfair to other people, who often dislike him. He often falls in to the temptation of being the dictator both of the parish and of the priest, as he thinks he is indispensable. He is difficult to remove, as there are so many positions to fill in his place. Usually in removing an official the incumbent can always undertake the job himself, statutes permitting, until a suitable successor is found, and it is partly for this reason that the priest should understand all jobs.[1]

§ 4. THE ANNUAL PAROCHIAL CHURCH MEETING

The link between people, officials and parsons is provided in the Annual Parochial Church Meeting, which is now the foundation-stone of lay representation in the Church of England.[2] It should be the voice of the people, but in point of fact in most parishes attendance is very poor. Its importance is obvious, because it is both the means provided for the election of the Church Council and various officials, and also the legal opportunity for discussing the affairs of the parish and for bringing grievances out into the open. In the interests of the Church it is the duty of the clergy to cultivate and develop the Annual Parochial Church Meeting, but they can hardly be blamed for not doing the very obvious duty the laity should do for themselves. Nevertheless, both clergy and officials should be thoroughly acquainted with the legal procedure of the Annual Meeting and see that all is done in order.

(a) *Preliminaries*. There is no specified date for the Annual Parochial Church Meeting, except that it must not be later than the week after Easter week. Many parishes hold the meeting at the traditional time for the Easter Vestry, which is convenient for the election of churchwardens, but rather late for the presentation of the accounts for the period ending the previous December 31st. Other parishes hold their Annual Parochial Church Meeting in, or about, February, but, if the wardens are elected then, there is a disagreeable period until Easter, with the possibility of two pairs of wardens, the old and the new. The division of the meeting into two parts, one in February and the other after Easter, is inconvenient; the position is not at all satisfactory.

When the date has been fixed, the arrangements for the revision and the posting of the Electoral Roll can be made, and a final

---

[1] Cf. Chapter XXIX, § 1 (a).
[2] K. M. Macmorran, *Handbook for Churchwardens and Church Councillors*, pp. 89–91. *Opinions of the Legal Board*, pp. 41–45.

meeting held of the Church Council, so that the financial statement and other reports can be approved ready for presentation to the Annual Parochial Church Meeting. It is not correct for the treasurer to report direct to the Annual Parochial Church Meeting, for the treasurer is responsible to the Council, and the Council to the Annual Parochial Church Meeting. Statutory notice must be given of the Meeting at the principal door of the church for the stated period.

Before the meeting, a notice of agenda should be drawn up by the chairman and secretary, and, if possible, copies of this should be in the hands of all present at the meeting; it helps to keep the attention of the members and warns them against wasting time. Further, in readiness for the elections of the various lay representatives, nomination papers—printed ones are available—should be circulated for two or three weeks beforehand among the different organizations. This saves time in waiting for nominations at the meeting, and also secures the ' consent to stand ' beforehand from those unable to be present. The best candidates are found by this preliminary; often at the meeting itself fatuous nominations are made. Ballot-papers are a convenience for voters and can be printed beforehand; space should be left for the addition of any new names correctly proposed at the meeting, as it is not legal to insist on a closing date before the meeting is held.

(b) *The Meeting*. After the Vestry and Parochial Church Meeting, sitting jointly, have elected the churchwardens, these officials can be invited to support the Chairman at the table, and then there is an opportunity for a Chairman's address which reviews the spiritual work of the parish, and speaks of future prospects. This is the time to announce long-term policy. The statutory business follows, the presentation from the Council of the Electoral Roll, the Report of the proceedings of the Council by the secretary, the audited accounts by the treasurer, and a Report on the fabric of the church by the churchwardens. This is an opportunity to encourage the laymen to develop their speaking powers.

When the old Council has thus given an account of its stewardship, the election of a new Church Council takes place. It is good to have more names proposed than seats to fill; a ballot provokes interest, but those not elected sometimes become disgruntled. At stated periods Lay Representatives to the Diocesan Conferences, and to the Ruri-Decanal Conference (if any) must be elected. The election of sidesmen follows, and auditors appointed for the ensuing year. The appointment of these last officials is not required by the Act, but as accounts presented to the Annual Parochial Church Meeting must be audited, each Annual Parochial Church Meeting should appoint auditors for the following year, and not the Church Council.[1]

This fixed routine is followed by discussion of matters of parochial importance. In some parishes this discussion begins with the presentation of audited accounts from the various organizations. This is an excellent way of maintaining control of the financial affairs of all parochial groups, and also of stimulating a parochial interest in the organizations themselves. Further, " Any person entitled to attend the Annual Meeting may ask any questions about parochial church matters." In the final stage of the meeting there is a delightful unexpectedness about the questions which may be asked. The opportunity may be taken by one of the disgruntled to make himself unpleasant, or there may be a genuine desire to clear up some misunderstanding in the parish. Here is the real test of a chairman's tactfulness. It should be noticed that the Annual Parochial Church Meeting cannot make any decisions or settle any business, though it can " give any particular recommendations to the Council in relation to its duties." Due respect would no doubt be given to such a recommendation, but the Council is not bound by it. A dissatisfied Parochial Church Meeting should elect a Council that will fulfil its recommendations.

(c) *Development.* For an important annual event, the Annual Parochial Church Meeting as a rule is badly attended, and steps should be taken to popularize it. A circular with a notice of agenda can be sent to all the people on the Electoral Roll, reminding them of their duties as electors. Notes can be written in the Parish Magazine emphasizing its importance. Usually the meeting tends to be dull, there is so much formal business, but an election adds to the interest, and if the chairman can make some noteworthy statement (saved for this purpose) at each Annual Parochial Church Meeting, its importance would soon be recognized. The prospect of controversy creates excitement, though this is a dangerous method to use to encourage attendance. The meeting should begin with a hymn and prayers; a longer period of intercessions than is usually allowed would give the meeting a good atmosphere, but unfortunately the meeting is already too long. The laity ought to think of ways to improve their own meeting; it is really sad when it becomes necessary for the incumbent to ask various laymen if they will consent to nomination as representatives of the laity.

[1] Cf. *Opinions of the Legal Board*, pp. 96, 97.

SELECT BIBLIOGRAPHY

K. M. Macmorran, *Handbook for Churchwardens and Parochial Church Councillors*.
Opinions of the Legal Board, 1939.
The Official Year Book of the Church of England.
K. M. Macmorran, *Cripps on the Law Relating to the Church and Clergy*, Eighth Edition. 1937.
L. S. Hunter, *A Parson's Job*, 1931, Chapter IX.
J. B. Goodliffe, *The Parson and his Problems*, 1933, Chapter IX.
The Church Assembly and The Church, 1930, Chapters IV, VI.
A. E. Simpson, *Master Builders*, 1937, Chapter IX.

CHAPTER IX

THE PAROCHIAL CHURCH COUNCIL

§ 1. The Powers of the Church Council

A new factor was introduced into Parochial Administration by the Parochial Church Councils (Powers) Measure of 1921, and the time-honoured dictatorship of incumbent and churchwardens in many matters came to an end. The working of the Act is still in its experimental stage; some older incumbents still regret the intrusion of the laity into their affairs, and the laity themselves are not clear about their powers, and sometimes do encroach upon the privileges of the incumbent, to mutual irritation. But the Act definitely marked the beginning of a new order in the Church of England; more powers will be given to the Church Council as time passes, and both parsons and laity should by now be developing a practical procedure within the framework of the Act. Much ignorance about the powers of the Council still exists, and there is need for continual reference to the Act. Moreover, there is an even greater need that all new members of the Council, as they are elected, should be educated in their duties—and this is true also of the *ex-officio* clerical members on their institution or appointment.

The foundation powers of the Council are set out in the Act,[1] which should be carefully studied with the notes provided in the handbooks. The powers consist of certain powers transferred from the Vestry, from the churchwardens, and from Church Trustees, and of new powers created by the Act itself. In brief, subject to certain conditions, the powers of the Council are concerned with the material care and upkeep of the church and the raising and administering of money for the same. It is accordingly natural that a great deal of the Church Council's time is taken up with financial considerations, but this is not the sole intention of the Act, for in it is the oft-quoted definition of the general functions of the Church Council: " It shall be the primary duty of the Council in every parish to co-operate with the Incumbent in the initiation, conduct, and development of church work, both within the parish

[1] K. M. Macmorran, *Handbook for Churchwardens and Parochial Church Councillors*, 9th Ed., pp. 51–64.
Opinions of the Legal Board, 1939, pp. 77–109.

and outside." In point of fact the Act visualizes an ideal Church Council, and it is for every parish to try to make this ideal actual. The Council should be a fellowship or a community, with the priest at its head, working in happy co-operation, as the official and actual leaders of the family of church people. The Christian spirit should prevail, so that each is ready to learn from others in all humility, so that the Council is in no sense a dominating clique that dislikes the addition of new blood and younger members, and so that there is a discretion that prevents Council business from being discussed outside. A Church Council is not the same thing as a Parliament, where the party system is necessary for good government. Parties on the Church Council manœuvring for position, and seeking to humiliate other people, or members seeking to dominate by force of their own personality, or members who feel little sense of responsibility but appear to interpret their office as though they had been elected to put a ' spoke in the vicar's wheel ', are all alike intolerable.

Many priests feel that Councils fall far short of the ideal, and even of the hopes that were once held for their success. Many even fear their Councils and are often apprehensive before the meetings. They will appreciate these words of Mr. Arthur Hopkinson:

> " Even the Parochial Church Councils rouse little enthusiasm, and few of them can be pointed to as first-class examples of bodies carrying out their primary functions as laid down in the Act. . . . Many Councils are critical rather than constructive, or, at most, give themselves up to the question of how to raise money. They function as debating societies, often with a party in power, and a party in opposition, and fail to realize that they are executive bodies of workers meeting to consider how best they may do the work. My own experience is that Church Councils, if fairly treated, are of immense value, even though some of our hopes of them are disappointed, but frankly my feelings overrode my reason, for I dreaded every meeting of the Church Council, and spent many wakeful nights in anticipation of them." [1]

There is much here that is true, but it ought to be added that the system is yet young; in course of time the laity will come to appreciate their responsibilities.

§ 2. THE INCUMBENT AS CHAIRMAN

(a) *His Position.* The incumbent has certainly no easy task in co-operating with his Church Council. He is a permanent official, and his councillors are voluntary workers whose interest may cease

---

[1] A. W. Hopkinson, *Pastor's Progress*, pp. 90 ff.

at any time. So much depends in the parish on the incumbent's drive and initiative in Council work; he must have vision to prepare plans for long-term policy, though the laity can always make useful amendments to his suggestions. Sometimes the members of the Council are there for recreation, as an interesting way of filling leisure time until something more exciting diverts their attention, instead of being there because they feel the great importance of their office before God. Leadership therefore rests with the parish priest.

As well as being the leader, the incumbent has also to be chairman; he has to combine the functions of the ' Leader of the House ' and the ' Speaker '; he has to be fair in the conduct of discussions when different opinions are expressed, and yet give a lead in the way he thinks the Council should go. He certainly is not there just to conduct a debate, and then carry out the resolutions of the Council. He is not the executive officer of a Council in whose affairs he has no voice. Yet Councils often give no thought to the subsequent results of their debate.

> " At present councils contain too many arm-chair critics, who will talk happily through an evening, but devil a bit of real responsibility will they take or hand's turn of work will they do." [1]

It is possible to meet this situation by adopting dodges. One way is to put the important business at the end of the agenda, knowing that the councillors will go home at a certain time, and the business will be hurried through at the end. Another way is to throw a subject open for discussion without making any suggestive comments upon it, in order to leave the members to tie themselves up with arguments until in desperation they ask the chairman what ought to be done. This is perhaps permissible when a difficult corner has to be negotiated; it is nearly always better to adopt a more straightforward plan in fairness to the laity. Dodges of this kind do not solve conflict with integration. If the parson thinks that much depends on his own plan, he should go all out for it. " Have a plan drawn up, know your own mind, allow every possible criticism and amendment, and in nine cases out of ten the draft scheme will be passed." [2]   Where objections do arise, the priest may remember that he " has great power of silencing objectors by asking them to undertake the work of remedying the matter that they think at fault." [3]

[1] L. S. Hunter, *A Parson's Job*, p. 147.
[2] C. E. Russell, *The Priest and Business*, p. 43.
[3] C. F. Rogers, *Principles in Parish Work*, p. 86.

(b) *Smooth Running.* The incumbent should be quite clear on the extent of his own powers, and of those of the Council.

> " A great many matters are discussed in Church Councils which are strictly outside their scope, so that we must be thoroughly conversant with the law if we are to keep councils to their own business." [1]

Yet it is also wise to treat the Council in a consultative capacity in matters outside its actual power, for example in questions concerning the times of services and their conduct. Resolutions on such matters, if put to the vote, should then be worded as recommendations to the incumbent or to the congregation.

The chairman of the Council must realize that he is not presiding over a business directorate, a trade union or a parliament, but over a Christian organization in which everything is to a large measure personal and people are more important than business. [2] This ought to be explained to the members by the chairman, for the members also have a responsibility in this, since it is the tactless remarks of some members that do the most harm. Further, the Chairman must make every allowance for slowness in understanding; he has probably spent a long time thinking about the problem, and a resolution whose purport is luminous to him may not be so clear to the other members. Every allowance must also be made for the fact that the members do not always say what they mean, and their exact views should be elucidated by skilful questionings. The chairman uses his discretion about the time allowed for each speaker, but plenty of latitude should be given to the ordinary layman who is not good at making himself clear and takes a roundabout course to get to his point. All should be encouraged to express their views, and so enable the Council to reach a common mind. Yet " the first business of a chairman is to keep the business short and to the point. Without seeming to be impatient, or to hurry, he must exert himself to drive it through, and to bring it to a definite issue." [3]

Nevertheless, the desire to keep the right spirit should not override the observance of correct procedure. Resolutions should be clearly worded and put, or the secretary is liable to report his impressions of the proposition. Amendments should be taken in the correct order, which is often a puzzle to the layman not accustomed to business meetings. It is as well always to explain exactly the point of any vote that is taken.

[1] C. E. Russell, *The Priest and Business*, p. 40.
[2] Cf. J. B. Goodliffe, *The Parson and his Problems*, pp. 103 f.
[3] C. F. Rogers, *Principles in Parish Work*, p. 84.

(c) *The Members' Reactions.* Attention has already been called to the number of different kinds of people to be met in church circles, and the Church Council is no exception to the rule. There are usually some keen business men with not much idea of spiritual things, there are members to whom their church means much and the business little, there are always one or two awkward people who play a useful part, and there will be the specially talkative and the devotee of pet theories. The remainder will be quiet, seemingly indifferent folk, who are always ready to support the priest's proposals. But Church Councils are subject to crowd influences, and crowd psychology is unpredictable. It is, consequently, important to take nothing for granted with the Church Council, not even on the assurance of leading lay members. It should never be assumed beforehand that resolutions will go in a certain way; an incumbent can be placed in a humiliating position if it is. As far as possible, the priest should avoid putting a resolution that will bring an adverse vote to himself, but if that position comes about, he must keep an even temper. In fact he must never lose his temper even in the most provoking of circumstances—and some lay people can be very provoking at times.

The ventilation of new topics, or new plans and schemes, should be done slowly, so that the laity gradually get accustomed to the ideas. Few people like to vote finally on a subject just after they have heard of it for the first time. It is better for all, including the chairman, to keep an open mind, so that the subject can be thought out together. Proceeding with caution is not the same thing as safety first, and is the only way of reaching a common mind. In matters of serious controversy the Council can be asked to agree to the principle of no change, unless there is a two-thirds majority.[1] It is idealistic to expect unanimity on all questions, but action on a close division is unwise. In an important matter, " if there is any serious difference of opinion between the members, though [the chairman] may add his weight to one side, he must not bully or browbeat those with whom he disagrees, but must endeavour to convince them." [2]

The parson's duties as chairman are by no means easy, but he has to undertake them. An attitude of continual goodwill and friendliness, patience, prudence and persuasion, with a sense of humour even in difficult moments, will carry him a long way in his task.

[1] Peter Green, *The Man of God*, p. 108.
[2] C. F. Rogers, *Principles in Parish Work*, p. 85.

§ 3. MEETINGS AND PROCEDURE

(a) *Procedure for Meetings.* The Schedule attached to the Powers Measure gives the rules of procedure for the meetings of the Council. There should be at least four meetings a year, but more are advisable, with definite routine business for each.[1] Some parishes have monthly meetings, and regularity aids attendance; when the meeting is on a certain day each month it is easy to remember to keep it free. " If they [Church Councils] are to be of any use they must meet frequently and regularly, and (though this may surprise some people) it is only by having meetings frequently that members can be brought to attend regularly." [2] Provision is made for the calling of emergency meetings. A notice on the principal door of the church gives ten days notice, and a notice giving the agenda must be sent to all members seven days before. Notice of motions may be sent in writing to the secretary by members before the issue of the agenda. It is important to issue a notice of the agenda, as no business not mentioned on it can be discussed at any meeting except by the consent of three-quarters of the members present. Actually ' any other business ' is not in order in the agenda; anything really urgent that arises after the issue of the agenda should be presented in the form of a letter under correspondence. There are also pre-scribed rules concerning the quorum, voting, recording attendances, the minutes, and adjournments. It may be necessary to explain to the members that: " In case of an equal division of votes, the chairman of the meeting shall have a second or casting vote." So the chairman should always vote.

Each meeting should follow a regular plan. A hymn and the opening prayers,[3] which may take place beforehand in church, should be followed by the reading of the minutes, with brief references to business arising therefrom, and then the announcing of the apologies for absence (the courtesy of apologizing should be cultivated among the members). Reports of the various committees (Standing and Finance, School or Parochial Hall, Young People's, Missionary, Social, etc.) may follow, with discussion of the business they introduce. Reports may then be received from the repre-sentatives to the Diocesan and Ruri-decanal Conferences. These things must be done, but " most Church Council meetings are very dull and too much occupied with trivial details." [4] The remainder

---

[1] See above, Chapter III, § 3 (*b*).
[2] A. W. Hopkinson, *Pastor's Progress*, p. 91.
[3] *Evangelism* (S.P.C.K.), 1937, pp. 38–41. Some useful suggestions.
[4] J. B. Goodliffe, *The Parson and his Problems*, p. 105.

of the meeting must help to build up the fellowship of the Council. If the parish priest is " able to create a free and friendly atmosphere at its meetings and to lead it away from the petty details of church business to the larger issues of a church's life and witness, it will in turn be the best means of leavening the rank and file of the congregation." [1] The duties and authority of the Church Council can be studied, wider plans for evangelism, moral welfare, and missions can be discussed from time to time as part of the Council's primary duty, and under any of these heads outside speakers can be invited to come and address the members on some topic of importance to the Church as a whole.

In the wording and putting of resolutions there are two points to notice. First, the resolution must be given effectiveness, and somebody nominated to do the work specified.[2] It is not to be assumed that the chairman or secretary must perform anything about which the direction is not clear; use should be made of the various members of the Council, especially of those who have expert experience. The second point is that sometimes members vote without meaning to support the object of the resolution, for example, a proposal to clean the Church by voluntary labour. An affirmative vote with the mental resolution " Not I " is undesirable. Sometimes a Council passes a good resolution, and sets a bad example to the church people by not putting it into action itself.

(b) *The Officers.* The secretary of the Church Council (who also acts as secretary of the Annual Meeting) holds an important office. He should be a spiritually minded layman who can not only record the proceedings of the Council and issue notices of the agenda, but can also help the chairman on matters of procedure and speak with influence in discussions. The post can often, with advantage, be held by a woman; indeed, this is the executive office most obviously suitable for women. The full duties of the secretary become clear from a study of the Council procedure. The treasurers are appointed for their capacity in keeping accounts, and there can be as many as is desirable for the various funds. They can be, but need not be, the churchwardens; a man may make an excellent churchwarden and deserve the office, and yet not be suitable for keeping accounts.

(c) *Committees.* Provision for the appointment of committees is made in the Act, and actually without them it is not possible for the Council to tackle all tasks efficiently. The Council cannot

[1] L. S. Hunter, *A Parson's Job*, p. 149.
[2] C. F. Rogers, *An Introduction to Pastoral Theology*, 1912, p. 139.

delegate its authority, but it can give responsibility of a defined character to each committee. These committees can be given expert help, because persons not on the Council, and not even on the Roll, can be appointed direct to them, or co-opted to them by the committees themselves.

The Standing Committee, which is generally the Finance Committee, is important, and should consist of the principal officers and one or two ' elder statesmen ' who have the confidence of the Council. The Standing Committee is much smaller than the Council, and thus more private. It is possible to ventilate questions to the Standing Committee while avoiding full publicity; the Committee's reaction may lead the incumbent to decide not to go to the full Council with the suggestion.

Other possible committees will have obvious functions, such as the care of the parochial buildings, responsibility for Missions, Socials, Evangelism. Committees can be set up temporarily for special purposes—e.g., for the appointment of an organist. Committees can have their own procedure, but it is more satisfactory if it is modelled on that of the Church Council. A scheme for meetings has already been described.[1] It is not everyone, however, who likes working through committees; the Bishop of Sheffield's objection to them has already been stated;[2] further words of his can serve as a warning here. " Committees are not essential for good team-work. They should be as few as possible; they are usually more efficient when they are small."[3]

§ 4. DEVELOPMENT

Church Councils have come to stay, and so the councillors must be made to see the importance both of their responsibilities and privileges. In time each parish will develop a smooth-running procedure for its Council. Already additional powers have been given to the Councils since the original Act of 1921, and obviously others will be added from time to time, and the importance of the Council will be increased. The new powers [4] are concerned with the Union of Benefices, Transfer of Advowsons, Presentation to Benefices, Purchase of Advowsons, right of consultation in various matters such as the Sale of Parsonages, and the right, but not the obligation (except the moral obligation) to help the clergy with their Dilapidations and Pensions Payment.

[1] See above, Chapter III, § 3 (b).   [2] See above, Chapter VIII, § 3 (c).
[3] L. S. Hunter, *A Parson's Job*, p. 149.
[4] *Opinions of the Legal Board*, 1939, pp. 188–191.

I

The incumbent should help the Council to realize its importance. This can be done by training, especially in helping new members to understand their duties. The after-the-business-talks at Council meetings provide for this. Correct procedure can be used at the Young People's Committee to give potential church councillors preliminary training. The Church Assembly Press and Publications Board has published little pamphlets on the subject, which can be given to members. The Council should be made to feel its responsibility as well as to exercise its powers. Certain unpleasant duties that formerly fell on the shoulders of the incumbent can now be passed to the Council, though they are not always thankfully received. Any action taken by the police in regard to such a matter, for example, as the fact of crowded gangways at a concert, is the Council's concern, and should not be left to the incumbent alone.

To give the members of the Council that spiritual help which is the basis of all their work, a service of dedication can follow their election and all can share in an act of Communion. Use can be made of week-day Festivals, such as Ascension Day, when the congregation might not otherwise be very large, to invite the councillors, and, if desired, other church workers, to a corporate act of prayer and praise. In addition, at special parochial services, Council members should have places of honour, especially when admission is by ticket only (this is not, however, in practice easy, since their relatives all expect a seat as well). Little functions, such as a garden party at the vicarage, for the councillors and their wives (or husbands), can help to cultivate the spirit of fellowship among them and with the parish priest.

The right note was struck by the then Archbishop of York (Dr. Lang) in 1922, in his New Year Greeting to church councillors. " In the right spirit and in the right way magnify your office; you are the men and women to whom it is now given either to win or lose a great chance of enabling the old Church to renew its life, and to rise to the demands of a new age. Of course, it is not through any machinery, but through the Spirit of God that any renewal can come. But the Spirit works through a Body, and it is for you to open out a new channel through which the Spirit of God may quicken and inspire the Church—the Body of Christ." [1]

[1] F. A. T. Mossman, *The Powers Conferred upon Parochial Church Councils*, 1922, p. 14 (quoted).

BIBLIOGRAPHY

As for Chapter VIII.

CHAPTER X

CHURCH FINANCES

§ 1. THE RESPONSIBILITY

(a) *The Incumbent.* A chairman, who is also the leader, of the Church Council, cannot afford to be ignorant of a principal duty, even if it is not the primary function, of the Council. Much of the time of the Council must be spent on finance, and often the parish priest must play the chief part in it. It is certainly a big advantage, and a relief, to have competent treasurers, but it must not be forgotten that a church treasurer needs to be spiritually minded as well as a good book-keeper. There is also the opposite danger:

> " Business men judge spiritual work by its material effects. It pays its way, or it does not. There is a real prospect, if all the parochial finances are handled only by the business men, that the mission field will soon be forgotten." [1]

However, the incumbent cannot always count upon the help of a good accountant. Sometimes a supposedly good business man is elected, an excellent fellow enough, who is surprisingly lax in keeping accounts. The incumbent, when he discovers it, must both watch and help him, to avoid possible scandal, and get him changed as soon as is tactfully possible.

> " It is a mistake, too, to suppose that the business man is necessarily quicker at figures, or can grasp a financial situation more readily than the parson. The reverse is often the truth." [2]

The fact is that the big business man is quite unused to keeping accounts.

In an artisan parish it may well be that most of the money must be handled by the clergy; workmen cannot always get to the bank, and are not always capable of handling banking accounts. In almost every parish the incumbent will have the care of some minor funds, which are often more trouble than the larger accounts. Every parson should know something about accounts, and an hour or two at the theological college could well be spent by every

[1] J. B. Goodliffe, *The Parson and his Problems*, p. 103.
[2] *Ibid.*, p. 105.

ordinand learning the rudiments of a system. Even with good
treasurers, the priest's initiative is nearly always necessary for
missionary and charitable giving, and he should have a general
idea of the needs of the parish, and insist on a proper way of working. An overdraft on the ordinary working account, as distinct
from debts incurred for unexpected heavy repairs, is a distraction
both to incumbent and Council, and might even be described as
immoral. The efficient incumbent meets an unexpected danger.
It is not always realized by his people that an insistence upon a
straight way of working is a preliminary to more spiritual work.[1]
So the parish priest is sometimes regarded simply as wishing to
make the parish pay like a financial concern, and therefore as always
thinking of money. The reaction of people to different procedure
is always an incalculable phenomenon.

(b) *The Finance Committee.* Whatever the incumbent's interest,
in theory the Church Council is in charge of the finances. Methods
differ in parishes as much in finance as in other matters, and
more uniform methods would be useful both to the clergy as they
move about, and also to those who are concerned with the assessment of quotas of various kinds. It lightens the work if there is a
finance committee to prepare the details for the Council. The
Standing Committee [2] usually undertakes this task. It is recommended by the Legal Board [3] that the incumbent should be chairman of the Standing Committee, although he is not so *ex officio.*
If there is a separate finance committee, whose function is to
investigate rather than to administer, the chairman could with
advantage be a layman.

The usual procedure is for the Finance Committee to prepare
for the Council by drawing up interim financial reports, allocating
possible expenditure and income, and giving warning of immediate
needs. It should prepare the Budget for the ensuing year, make
possible estimates of future heavy expenses, and, when necessary,
examine tenders and make recommendations about them to the
Council. If possible, a lay member of the committee should
present the committee's argument to the Council, as this is much
better than all explanations being made from the Chair. The
Council has, of course, the power to accept or reject proposals
made by the committee; generally it will do no more than amend
them; in any case the committee's preparatory work is never
wasted.

[1] Cf. C. F. Rogers, *Principles in Parish Work,* Chapter I.
[2] See above, Chapter IX, § 3 (c).
[3] *Opinions of the Legal Board,* 1939, p. 98.

§ 2. The Scope of Church Finances

(a) *Expenses.* If there were no expenses, there would be no subject of Church Finances. Both the poor parish and the rich parish have unavoidable expenses, and, as the need for the maintenance of a building is independent of the wealth of the congregation that uses it, their expenses are very much alike. The richer parish can have more luxuries, such as a higher-paid organist, more expensive music, and extra curates. The main divisions of Church Expenses are Maintenance and Extension, and these may be further subdivided. Maintenance includes: (i) The church—lighting, heating, cleaning, insurances, ordinary repairs, and workpeople's salaries; (ii) The Services—music, laundry, Communion requisites, choir grants, and salaries of choir officials; (iii) The Staff—benefice augmentations, curates' stipends, and vicarage dilapidations; (iv) Office—administration, printing, stationery, and postages; (v) The Buildings—schools, parochial halls, parish rooms; (vi) The Diocese; and (vii) Repair reserve for big repairs, restoration and decorations.[1] Extension includes: (i) Home Missions; (ii) Overseas Missions; (iii) Charities; and (iv) Ordination Candidates' Training.

These items are all self-explanatory; the only item under maintenance that calls for further comment is the Diocesan Quota. This is estimated for the parish by the method adopted by the Diocese in which the parish is situated. Comparisons in the same Diocese between different parishes can give rise to heart-burnings, and when parishes that are in different dioceses are compared the sense of unfairness is increased. Much depends on how much the Diocese itself pays of its own quota to the Central Board of Finance. Undoubtedly the method of quotas has been an inestimable boon to the Church of England as a whole. Every parish should try to meet its Diocesan obligations, and explanations of the purpose of the payment should from time to time be made to the Council.

"In many parishes the diocesan quota is paid reluctantly and is looked upon as a tax paid to officials in the cathedral city or at the Church House in Westminster, to be spent by them in ambitious schemes. Everything should be done to educate the parish out of such notions."[2]

There are Reports of the Diocesan Board of Finance, which can e put in the hands of the chief officials of the Church, and the

[1] See below, Chapter XI, § 1 (c).
[2] W. K. Lowther Clarke, *Almsgiving*, 1936, pp. 115 f.

details of the Central Board can be obtained from the current *Official Year Book*.[1]

The items under Extension are of moral obligation only. There is no need for any parish to give to any of them, but the strength of the parochial financial system will be seen in the high amounts that can be devoted to these important objects. More often than not these items depend on the zeal and enthusiasm of the parish priest, especially for the missionary causes.[2] Much more could be given than at present for the training of ordination candidates.[3]

The Powers Measure[4] gives the Council power to frame an Annual Budget, and this should be done in November or December for the ensuing year. All the expenses listed above should be taken into account, based on the actual experiences of the previous year, bearing in mind the cardinal principle, " Expenditure to be regulated by receipts." [5] People will give more readily when they know how much is needed, and why. When the Budget is prepared, the collections in church on certain Sundays for the next twelve months can be allocated to special objects,[6] all the rest presumably being allocated to church expenses. The incumbent has an equal voice with the Council in allocations.[7]

(b) *Income*. To meet the various expenses mentioned, an income of some kind is needed. The compulsory Church Rate was abolished some time ago, and the principal source of income now available is the collection taken in church. In itself this is a very haphazard method, when the size of the congregation depends on the weather, and people are not so regular as they used to be. There is no doubt that the collections are considerably improved by the introduction of an envelope Free-Will Offering Scheme, or the Duplex method, or the Church Duty Money Movement. Everywhere collections are increased by the introduction of such schemes, no matter what people who are not in the Scheme may say about making it up to the Church for the times they are absent. Many people are against it because they feel that they are being compelled to give something every week whether they can afford it or not, and others have a strong dislike

---

[1] See also below, Chapter XX, § 5 (*a*).
[2] See below, Chapter XIX.
[3] Report of Archbishops' Commission, *Training for the Ministry*, 1944, Appendix " D ".
[4] Section 6 (i).
[5] C. F. Rogers, *Principles in Parish Work*, p. 15.
[6] See above, Chapter III, § 3 (*a*) ii.
[7] *Opinions of the Legal Board*, p. 187.

to anyone knowing how much they give. Usually people do not mind the priest being secretary, so long as only he knows the numbers; this at once brings him into the financial system, for as only he knows the members, it falls to his lot to do the recruiting for new members. Such recruiting is always necessary. The Scheme begins well, but real work is needed both to keep pace with inevitable losses, and to increase the actual membership. The inclusion of the young people in the scheme teaches them when young the obligations of giving.

In the average parish, even the introduction of the envelope method will not secure sufficient income to meet all the expenses of the church, the schools, and the Diocesan Quota, so, in addition, some special efforts are needed. These are of two kinds, the direct giving and the indirect sale of work or social effort. In theory the argument for direct giving is very strong. It is the easiest way for all concerned, especially for the clergy, who are saved much time. If the spirit of Christian stewardship [1] is really developed, lay people would see that most of the money they give is for their own comfort, but this cannot be pressed too closely. [2] Regarded solely as a hobby or a recreation, as many do regard church attendance, it is very inexpensive. A good budget well explained should bring in sufficient by direct giving.

Nevertheless, the indirect method is not to be despised, and in many parishes is really necessary. People can often give work when they cannot give money—money, after all, is only work in tabloid form—and this is the origin of sales of work and bazaars. As far as concerts and socials are concerned, they are genuinely enjoyed in certain types of parishes, and the money thus raised is often all the recreation-money the people have to spend. It may even be argued that the church is actually helping them by providing them with recreation in which they often take an active part, and that this is better than the " spoon-feeding " cinemas where the people just watch passively, but this argument is unfortunately rapidly becoming less valid.

There is another point worthy of deep consideration. Many people would rather give goods than money, although it costs as much or maybe more. Whatever may be said about the sacramental value of money, there is a deep instinct in people to give of their store. This is part of the attraction of the Harvest Festival. The bazaar helps people to feel that they are really giving. How-

[1] See Church Assembly Report, *Christian Stewardship*, 1929.
[2] W. K. Lowther Clarke, *Almsgiving*, 1936, pp. 83–87.

ever, it is said that " bazaars are going out of fashion; a *man* who likes them has yet to be found, but, if they do good by uniting the ladies of a congregation in Christian fellowship, they are not to be despised ".[1]   As is so often claimed in the North, the indirect method of socials and bazaars really does keep people together. It provides a social side of church life, and encourages the co-operative and community spirit.   In this way people make friends, and new people can be introduced to the family circle in a way that is impossible on Sundays.   The completely " direct-method " church can offer a very dull kind of church life, though of course it is possible to have socials that have no pecuniary purpose.   On the other hand, the indirect method, curiously enough, presents the danger that the means may become the end; if so, the whole parish revolves round the annual bazaar, which is the chief festival in the calendar, and the church becomes a useful way of expending the money so raised.

When the envelope scheme has proved insufficient, the principal direct method of raising money is the Gift Day.   Gifts can be invited at certain Sunday services, or a week-day can be used when the clergy sit for certain hours at the church to receive gifts. The whole affair can be arranged, circulars issued to members, and saving boxes issued, months beforehand, when such aids are necessary.   The day itself can be marked with services and periods of prayer.   A Gift Day is generally successful the first time it is tried, but tends to be a diminishing source of income.

Bazaars need more organization.   Usually when a priest goes to a parish there is an elaborate system already in existence, and this he has to understand and guide.   Much of the parish politics is concerned with the right balance between the different sets of workers, ' the stall-holders ', who are entitled to certain annual dates for functions and who at the bazaar itself have rights and privileges of position, precedence, and classes of goods.   Meetings of bazaar workers are very happy affairs when spent in joint planning.   The decoration of bazaar rooms often calls forth artistic ability and taste.   Besides the general oversight, the parish priest's main task is to secure a speaker to open the bazaar.

So far the raising of the income to meet the ordinary church expenses has been discussed.   Money has also to be found for the extension of the Church.   Some of this is raised by direct giving, in the duplex envelopes, and in the collections allocated for the purpose, and also by the indirect method by such means as grants

1 W. K. Lowther Clarke, *Almsgiving*, p. 115.

from the annual bazaar. Further ways of raising money for work
of this kind are considered separately.[1]

Mention should be made of the disposal of the alms taken at
the Communion Services. The Council has no voice in this
matter, for by rubric it is allocated by the incumbent and churchwardens.[2] In many parishes at the early Sunday and the week-
day celebrations the alms are simply earmarked 'Sick and Poor
Fund', or 'Vicar's Discretion Fund', but in these days of public
assistance there is not the same call upon the Church for such
purposes, so part of the alms can be devoted to various good
causes, as the Waifs and Strays Society, Missions and Medical
Missions, Clergy Widows and Orphans' Fund, and Ordination
Candidates' Funds. When the Communion is the principal service,
the alms usually go to Church Expenses.

§ 3. KEEPING ACCOUNTS

(a) *Church Accounts*. "It might be considered superfluous to
insist on the necessity of absolute soundness in the financial affairs
of a parish. Unfortunately, however, confused methods are
frequently adopted."[3] It is not the turn-over but the number
of special objects and the giving of allocated collections and
donations that complicate the Church Accounts. Several people
may be involved, and a change of treasurer may come at any
time, so a clear method must be used for recording even the smallest
item of expenditure. Avoiding the issue of a cheque for the small
account is not the cheapest way in the long run.

The Church Council should open an account, or as many
accounts as it desires, at a bank, and appoint officers to sign
cheques, and two should always sign. Church money should
never be kept at home or in a private account. All income should
be paid into the bank and everything paid by cheque, though one
cheque can be drawn for petty cash and the various items for
which it is used marked on the counterfoil. When the signatures
of two people are needed for a cheque, one should never sign
blank cheques for the convenience of the other. It is often done.
Honest treasurers should not be affronted by such precautions,
which are meant to guard against the one dishonest treasurer in a
thousand, who does the Church so much harm.[4]

[1] See below, Chapter XIX, § 2 (c) and (d).
[2] *Opinions of the Legal Board*, pp. 141 ff.
[3] C. F. Rogers, *Principles in Parish Work*, 1905, p. 6.
[4] Cf. Peter Green, *The Man of God*, pp. 206–218.

The analysis type of book-keeping is the best to use, so that additions of like items for the purposes of statements are easy. This method is even more useful for special objects, since it ensures that no money so ear-marked can possibly be overlooked.[1] Such funds ought to be paid into a separate account, a ' Trust Account ', and should never be used to bolster up a Church overdraft. Amounts subscribed should be paid over regularly to the right people. This financial honesty should also be observed within the parish: " Deficits from one fund must never be made up from another." [2]

The Church Council, or its Finance Committee, should have direct control over the Church money. Ideally, nothing should be ordered without a resolution duly recorded in the Minute Book, and, if this is the rule, the official giving an order without authority should be made to pay the expense of it. The treasurer should be authorized to pay routine accounts, as those for electricity, unless there is some query about them, but the other accounts should be passed for payment by the proper authority. The efficient working of this depends on the frequency of the meetings of the Council or its committee. On the whole, there is need for general improvement in the financial procedure of most parishes.

The accounts should be properly audited every year, if possible by a professional auditor, but at any rate by someone who is competent. Members of the Church Council can be appointed auditors, but this is by some thought undesirable.[3] The same auditors should act for all parochial accounts, so that they can ascertain if all are in line. Particularly they should make sure that all sums ear-marked for special objects have reached their destination, and for this reason some consider that Diocesan or Deanery auditors should be appointed by authority. Since everything should be done to help the auditors, ' paying-in ' books and cheque counterfoils must be so marked that every item of income and expenditure can be clearly traced. When the accounts [4] have been audited they should be presented for examination to the Church Council, and, if accepted, signed by the chairman and printed for the Annual Meeting. The printing of accounts is very desirable; everyone at the meeting can then follow the discussion. Printing, moreover, facilitates the preservation of accounts among the church records, and enables returns of statistics to be made

[1] See the sample page at the end of this chapter.
[2] C. F. Rogers, *Principles of Parish Work*, p. 14.
[3] *Opinions of the Legal Board*, pp. 96 f.
[4] *Ibid.*, pp. 184–187.

to the appropriate authorities as occasion demands. If an author-ized method of keeping and printing accounts could be adopted in all parishes, various problems connected with the Diocesan Quota could be solved.

There is sometimes a discussion about the advantages of one account over against several. One comprehensive account under one competent treasurer certainly saves time and simplifies the work of the auditor. On the other hand, separate accounts for separate entities with separate treasurers create more jobs, and keep more men interested. The possession of a fund that may be in difficulties will often make a group of people work for it, and keep it in a more satisfactory condition. It must, however, be insisted that all accounts of parochial organizations not directly under the Church Council should be audited and presented to the Annual Meeting.

(b) *The Clergy Accounts.* Whatever may be his feelings about finance, some money is certain to come the way of the parson. At times he may even be treasurer for various church accounts, such as the School Managers' Accounts, or the Magazine Fund, and in this case all the foregoing recommendations will apply to him. In fact, a clergyman must, if anything, be more careful in money matters than a layman, since any scandal arising from slackness in keeping of accounts is so much the worse for the Church when a clergyman is involved. In particular, he should never pay church money into his own account and will, if he is wise, keep the latter at a different bank from that at which the church accounts are kept.[1]

Even if the parson has no particular post as treasurer, odd sums will certainly be sent to him, and he must see that they reach the right accounts. People love to give direct to the clergy, and subscriptions for all sorts of funds are pressed upon them at all sorts of inconvenient times, usually with the request that nothing should be said about it. It is the easiest thing in the world for such sums to be put into the pocket and completely forgotten. The only way is to insist on giving a receipt for every sum received, filling in the counterfoil, and, if so requested, marking it " anon ".[2] If the incumbent is likely to have several odd sums in his possession for long, his best plan is to have a ' Discretion Fund ' account at the bank through which he can pass all such funds. This money is all ' allocated ' already, so, in addition, the parish priest generally

---

[1] C. E. Russell, *The Priest and Business*, p. 26.
[2] Peter Green, *The Man of God*, pp. 206–218.

needs other money to spend at his own discretion; some of the alms could be devoted to this purpose, or the offerings at Churchings and Baptisms. Baptism cards, Confirmation Manuals, sundry printing and postages, can be financed from this source, and contributions can often be made in addition to the lesser missionary and charitable societies. The clergy should never pay even small sums out of their own pockets; it places a poorer successor in a difficult position. Whatever the clergy can afford to give should be given direct to the church, and all expenses paid from the appropriate funds.

SELECT BIBLIOGRAPHY

W. K. L. Clarke, *Almsgiving*, 1936.
Christian Stewardship, Church Assembly Report, C.A. 381. (Contains an Appendix with useful bibliography.)
The Gospel of Giving, Anon., S.P.C.K., 1919.
E. S. G. Wickham, *Parson and People*, 1931, Chapter X.
C. F. Rogers, *Principles of Parish Work*, 1905, Chapter I.
C. E. Russell, *The Priest and Business*, p. 27. Sample account.
A. E. Simpson, *Master Builders*, 1937, Chapter VIII.
G. R. Y. Radcliffe, *Seven Year Covenants* (Church of England Newspaper).

Date.	Details.	Cash. (1)			Bank. (2)			Cheques. (3)			Duplex. (4)			Alms. (5)			C.M.S. (6)			A.C.S. (7)			Waifs and Strays. (8)		
		£	s.	d.	£	s.	d.	£	s.	d.	£	s.	d.	£	s.	d.	£	s.	d.	£	s.	d.	£	s.	d.
May 18	Forward (*Receipts*)	160	1	8	151	19	8	60	11	10	61	16	1		19	5	49	11	6	19	2	4	10	6	3
	Do. (*Payments*)	*151*	*19*	*8*													*41*	*9*	*6*	*19*	*2*	*4*			
19	Alms		5	6											5	6									
21	Duplex		10	0							1	0	0												
	Waifs and Strays Collection.		15	3																				15	3
	Boxes, C.M.S.	1	0	6													1	0	6						
22	M.U. for A.C.S.		10	6																	10	6			
23	Cash Banked	*11*	*3*	*9*	*11*	*3*	*9*																		
24	Cheque, Waifs and Strays							*11*	*1*	*6*													*11*	*1*	*6*
	Duplex. Allocated										*30*	*0*	*0*				*30*	*0*	*0*						
	Cheque, C.M.S.							*39*	*2*	*6*							*39*	*2*	*6*						

NOTES.

1. Each figure is entered twice so a constant check is possible.
2. Payments are entered in the book in **red**, printed above in italics.
3. As many other columns as necessary can be used.
4. Duplex and Alms can be allocated and carried to appropriate columns.
5. In any column by adding black and **red** figures separately, it can be seen if any allocated money is in hand.
6. The total of both receipts and payments are Carried Forward page by page to the year end, and the preparation of a statement of accounts is then very easy.

Notice that this page is not completed.

CHAPTER XI

THE CARE OF THE CHURCH

§ 1. A Necessary Duty

(a) *A Valuable Charge.*

" The Country Parson hath a special care of his Church, that all things there be decent and befitting his name by which it is called. Therefore, first, he takes order, that all things be in good repair; as walls plastered, windows glazed, floors paved, seats whole, firm and uniform, especially that the pulpit, and desk, and communion table, and font, be as they ought, for those great duties that are performed in them. Secondly that the Church be swept, kept clean, without dust or cobwebs . . ." [1]

George Herbert's advice to the country parson applies equally well to the town parson, though the latter is not always burdened with the care of an ancient church. It is to be feared that many incumbents, excellent men in other ways, are lax in their care of the fabric and indolent in demanding cleanliness. Others again make it an important part of their work to see that the building is kept as it should be, and probably find it necessary to raise large sums of money in order to do so, in a succession of parishes. [2]

The difficulty is that so many incumbents have little knowledge of the needs of a building, and know even less about the care of ancient churches. The latest ideas about training for the Ministry would make the ordinand a better pastor, preacher and teacher, with a knowledge of some psychology and sociology; none of these things will help the town-trained curate to care for an ancient country church. Perhaps it is necessary for every country parson to have an instinctive love for church architecture, enough to find the styles of different periods worthy of study, and a desire to preserve in the right way the treasures committed to him. At any rate, in all churches, general tidiness, cleanness, and careful preservation should come before the piling up of furniture and ornaments.

A hundred years ago there was much enthusiasm for restoration and care of churches, with very little knowledge, and plaster was

---

[1] George Herbert, *A Priest to the Temple*, Chapter XIII (quoted in A. W. Hopkinson, *Pastor's Progress*, p. 115).
[2] For example, see G. H. Harris, *Vernon Faithful Storr*, p. 20.

stripped off the walls, unnecessary steps added in the chancel, not to mention the amateur touching up of screen paintings. But there is no excuse for lack of knowledge to-day. There is much useful information for the restoration and the preservation of ancient buildings, and the parson needs to know where it can be found. Much good work has been done by the Society for the Protection of Ancient Buildings, and any of its reports are worthy of respect. More for the help of incumbents and Church Councils are the Reports of the Central Council for the Care of Churches, which not only describe the work of the various Diocesan Committees, supplying excellent illustrations, but also give many useful directions, the accumulation of the knowledge and experience of experts. It would be even more helpful if the various recommendations were reprinted in one volume without the diocesan reports. As it is, throughout this chapter the references to the various reports must be given.[1] Another useful guide is *The Care of Churches*, 1935, by Nevil Truman, and for general cleaning, *The Care of God's House*, 1943, by Irene Caudwell, and a brief note in *The Parson's Handbook*, 1940, by Percy Dearmer, pp. 66–74.

(b) *The Responsible Officers.* Each Church Council is charged by statute with the " care, maintenance, preservation and insurance of the fabric of the Church," [2] and also with the presentation to the Annual Parochial Meeting of " a report upon the fabric . . . of the church (or churches) of the Parish ".[3] A yearly survey by the church officials could only be given in general terms, but the fabric and furniture should be conscientiously inspected regularly and expert help called when needed. There is something to be said for employing an architect to make a survey of dilapidations every five years on similar lines to the vicarage survey, for this would certainly prevent serious decay from going too far, and would also encourage the parish to set aside, each year, money for future repairs, on the advice of the architect.

The ordinary jobbing work of plumbing, mending loose tiles and broken windows, gutter cleaning and repair, are well within the capacity of the Council to supervise through its officers, but anything more important should be referred to the Diocesan Advisory Board. That is to say, any major repairs, alterations or restorations, introduction or alterations of furniture, seating, organs, bells, heating and lighting systems, and also decoration schemes, are all

---

[1] *First Report*, 1923; *Second*, 1925; *Third*, 1928; *Fourth*, 1930; *Fifth*, 1932; *Sixth*, 1934; *Seventh*, 1937; *Eighth*, 1940.
[2] *The Parochial Church Council (Powers) Measure*, 1921, § 4, ii (*b*).
[3] *Representation of the Laity Measure*, 1929, *Schedule*, § 8 (i) *d*.

matters on which expert advice is needed. Under the Faculty Jurisdiction Measure [1] of 1938 the procedure is regularized, and the Advisory Board can be consulted before plans are prepared or the final form of the projected work decided. The Board's approval having been obtained, application can be made for an Archdeacon's Certificate or a Faculty, according to the nature of the work, in the prescribed form and with stated fees; otherwise no work should be done.

A resolution passed by the Church Council is an important part of the procedure, and it is open for dissatisfied or aggrieved parishioners to contest the application for the Faculty in the Consistory Court. Most Church Councils regard Faculties as an unnecessary expense and an unwarrantable limitation of their rights. The incumbent has an important, though not always pleasant duty, of explaining the position.

> " If some people are disposed to say, ' Why shouldn't we have what we like? ', the answer is that the Church of England, as the guardian of her great inheritance of artistic treasures, is bound in honour to deal with it on certain definite lines. The circumstances to-day are such that if there is repeated local resistance, there will be danger of a renewed agitation to secure some kind of state control over ancient churches." [2]

The church of the parish is not just the private property of the Church Council, it is in their trust and care. It belongs to all ages, and the Church Council has a public responsibility.

For similar reasons many Church Councillors do not like to employ architects, because it is considered expensive to do so. They prefer to rely on the advice of local tradespeople and business men, often excellent people with no expert knowledge, but capable of repairing any house but God's House.

> " This is a very short-sighted policy, and one that is attended with considerable danger. . . . It is necessary to emphasize the fact that the amount of the architect's fee is nearly always covered by the savings due to his control of the expenditure." [3]

Local pride can raise further difficulties, even after a Faculty has been obtained. Some councillors may consider that local firms should be given the work, but undoubtedly it is best to invite tenders, and, on the advice of the architect, to take the best possible firm,

---

[1] An excellent explanation is given in the *Eighth Report*, pp. 70 ff.; Cf. a note in Truman, pp. 51 ff. The Year Book of each Diocese should explain procedure under the measure and also the working of the Consistory Courts.

[2] *Seventh Report*, p. 21.

[3] *Ibid.*, p. 23.

and not always the cheapest. If as a consequence some aggrieved tradesmen cease to attend Church, it cannot be helped.

The incumbent has an important part to play in the delicate task of steering the Church Council through these various difficulties. He must always insist on the legal requirements, and on the disinterestedness of all in voting for tenders. He must bring his general knowledge of the care of churches to the guidance of his Council, and, if the opportunity presents itself, learn something about tenders and builders' quantities. He will need to know something about them for the vicarage dilapidations.[1] If the parish priest finds himself in disagreement with his Council on the need for a Faculty, he should seek the advice of the Rural Dean or the Archdeacon.

(c) *Insurances.* The Council is charged not only with the care, maintenance and preservation, but also with the insurance, of the church. Adequate insurance must be taken in the names of the right officials, for fire, burglary, housebreaking and larceny, employers' liability, third-party risks, voluntary workers' accidents, as well for the parochial buildings as for the Church. Details and advice can be found in *Opinions of the Legal Board*, 1939, pp. 157–172.

It has already been stated that Fabric and Repair Funds offer a good way of providing for future extraordinary repairs from time to time. The prevalent method of waiting until the worst happens is dangerous, uneconomical and unfair, as a heavy cost falls on one generation alone. A policy can be taken out with an insurance company, whereby a contribution is paid yearly and interest accumulates, not so much to guard against risk, as to endow the church with reserves to meet the cost of maintenance. "A payment of £14 10s. annually for forty years (£580 in all) would secure that £1,000 would be available at the end of that period."[2] A sum like this is needed for an ancient church every fifty years, and this is the best way to secure it.

§ 2. General Guidance

The difficulty with most incumbents is that they do not realize that there is a correct way of attending to certain things, and thus they do not think of looking up specialized information. It is true that any matter could be at once referred to the Advisory Board, but it does save the time of the members if the preliminary investigation has already been done, and, besides that, there is the ordinary work

---

[1] See below, Chapter XXV, § 3 (*b*).
[2] *Eighth Report*, p. 89. Cf. Truman, pp. 49 ff.

K

of cleaning and preserving. The object of this section is to indicate
the different matters that need care, and the source of specialized
information.

(a) *Fabric and Structure.* The following are the most important
items:

(i) External Walls and Draining. It is necessary to notice
several things connected with the preservation of stonework, correct
drainage, pointing, iron-work in stone. Damp is the chief enemy:
so lean-to huts, neighbouring trees and ivy are dangerous.
See *Seventh*,[1] pp. 37 ff., Truman, pp. 45 ff.; For protection of
stonework and iron, *Seventh*, p. 39, Truman, pp. 99 f.; Pointing,
Truman, pp. 93 f.; White limewash, Truman, pp. 117 ff.

(ii) Internal Walls and Roof Surfaces. The Victorians made a
big mistake about plaster, and also about colouring. People still
" repeat like parrots the old tags:

1. That you must not colour oak,
2. That you must not whitewash stone,
3. That you must strip plaster to show bare stone." [2]

Wall surfaces generally should be plastered and decorated in white,
the woodwork, stone bosses and textile hangings coloured for
contrast.
See *Seventh*, pp. 39 f. and p. 25; Plaster, Truman, pp. 90 ff.;
Colouring wood and stone, Truman, pp. 42 ff.; Wall paintings,
Seventh, p. 40; White limewash, Truman, pp. 117 ff.

(iii) Roofs. These must be weather-proof and watched for
beetles.
See *Seventh*, p. 41; Truman, pp. 100 ff.; Tiled roofs, *Seventh*, pp.
57 ff.; Beetles, Truman, p. 28.

(iv) Arrangements of Fittings and Seatings. There is no need
to have every space occupied by seats and fittings; open spaces add
to dignity and reverence. Seats are often so close that kneeling is
impossible.[3] Chancels are often overcrowded; it is not really the
place for the choir, and some ancient buildings have been spoilt
by the addition of too many steps. All woodwork needs proper
care, and voluntary workers look after it, when how to do so is
explained to them.
See *Seventh*, pp. 42 f.; Value of open spaces, Truman, p. 102;
Chancels, Truman, pp. 36 ff. *Parson's Handbook*, pp. 46 ff.; Levels

[1] This is a convenient way of referring to the Reports of the Central Council
for the Care of Churches.
[2] N. Truman, *The Care of Churches*, p. 117.
[3] C. F. Rogers, *Principles of Parish Work*, p. 129.

nd steps, Truman, pp. 74 ff.; Woodwork, *Eighth*, pp. 92 f., Truman, p. 84 ff.; Victorian Furniture, Truman, pp. 115 f.; Preservatives, Truman, pp. 120 ff.; Box Pews, *Fifth*, pp. 89 ff.

(v) Style of New Work. New additions need not be in imitation of the style of the church, but should harmonize with it; here expert advice is needed.

See *Seventh*, pp. 35 ff., Truman, pp. 16 ff. and 95 ff.

(vi) Monuments and Tablets. Those already in must be preserved, and kept clean. Suggestions for adding to them must be received very cautiously.

See *Seventh*, pp. 47 ff., Truman, pp. 77 ff.

(vii) Lighting and Heating. Installations have spoilt the beauty of many a church. The regulations about electric light should be carefully followed.

See *Eighth*, pp. 79 ff., especially, and also *Seventh*, pp. 60 ff. and Truman, pp. 76 f.; Suggestions for heating, *Fourth*, pp. 88 ff.; Lightning Conductors, *Seventh*, pp. 65 ff.

(b) *Ornaments of the Church and of the Ministers.* A bare list of references must here suffice.

(i) The Altar and its Furniture,[1] Truman, pp. 21 ff., Dearmer,[2] pp. 74–80, *Handbook*,[3] pp. 75–102; Altar Linen, *Handbook*, pp. 78–84, Caudwell,[4] Chapter V; Vestments, *Handbook*, pp. 117–150, Caudwell, Chapter V; Ornaments of Sacristy, *Handbook*, pp. 150–166.

(ii) Fonts, Truman, pp. 58 ff. *Handbook*, pp. 60–61; Lecterns, Dearmer, p. 73, *Handbook*, pp. 57–60; Pulpits, Dearmer, p. 73, *Handbook*, pp. 52–57.

(iii) Organs,[1] *Fourth*, pp. 83 ff., Truman, pp. 83 f.; Bells, *Fourth*, pp. 77 ff., *Seventh*, p. 42, Truman, p. 33; Stained Glass, *Seventh*, pp. 44 f., Truman, pp. 60 ff. Church Flag, *Eighth*, p. 91.

(iv) Chapels. Both useful and beautiful additions to the church, chapels can be devoted to specific purposes, for children's worship rather than for a mere children's corner, for missionary intercessions, when properly fitted. They may be more convenient for week-day celebrations of Holy Communion, and for the daily Office, if it is really impracticable to say this in the Choir, and, of course, for other more informal services.

(c) *Decorating Schemes.* With the general principles in mind for

---

[1] See also above, Chapter VI, § 2 (*c*).
[2] P. Dearmer, *A Short Handbook of Public Worship*, 1931.
[3] P. Dearmer, *The Parson's Handbook*, 1940.
[4] I. Caudwell, *The Care of God's House*, 1943.

the various parts and furniture of the church, a comprehensive
scheme for the church should be adopted and gradually introduced.
The care of the fabric comes first, and then decoration. There is
no need for the introduction of all kinds of ornaments. " The
bareness of so many churches is not due to the absence of accessories,
but to the dismal brick walls, bad proportions, shapeless form, dirty
colour, and the mechanical application of a dull heartlessness in the
ornaments." [1] The right colouring of the walls is thus the next
step after the care of the fabric, and then the addition of the textiles
in keeping. " In textiles the standard of colour in many churches is
still far behind that of the modest homes of educated people." [2]
It is essential to consult qualified architects in planning the decoration of a Church.

It is not the high cost of the material that makes it suitable for the
church, but its good colour and shape. " The catch phrase ' nothing
but the best ' has been misinterpreted to mean ' nothing but the
most costly,' which is by no means the same thing." [3] A church
can be beautifully decorated by true artists at very little outlay, and
the textiles, if properly cared for, can be useful for many years.[4]
The same principles apply to ornaments, and these should be made
by competent people. Names can be obtained from the Diocesan
Advisory Committee. Church furnishers, however, are continually
improving their standards, and it is worth while to file and index
their catalogues for reference.[5]

A general principle of decoration will make it easier to handle the
question of gifts to the church. People are always willing to give,
especially in memory of some relative, and the desire to give can be
cultivated at times of Jubilee or Centenary Celebrations, but all
gifts should be part of a comprehensive scheme. A working rule is
to insist that nothing must be obtained for presentation for use in
church before the incumbent has been consulted. " Such a rule
will prevent duplication and the receipt of items in bad taste or not
fitting from a Church point of view." [6] The possible necessity for a
faculty can always be given as the reason for the rule. Generally
people not only ask the priest for suggestions, but ask him to make
the purchase, though the opposite sometimes happens, as when a
churchwarden presented a quantity of hymn books because he

[1] P. Dearmer, *A Short Handbook to Public Worship*, 1931, p. 72.
[2] *Ibid.*, p. 73.
[3] N. Truman, *The Care of Churches*, p. 113.
[4] *Ibid.*, pp. 111 ff.
[5] See above, Chapter II, § 3 (a).
[6] N. Truman, *The Care of Churches*, pp. 108 ff. Cf. P. Dearmer, *The Parson's Handbook*, pp. 117 f.

thought the church was in short supply, just when the parish priest was contemplating a change in the hymn book used.

In the removal of undesirable fittings due regard should be given to the original donors' wishes, as an act of courtesy and also an act of wisdom, for the contrary practice is apt to dry up the sources of future gifts. Nevertheless, it should be made clear that when anything is given to the church, the donor has no further personal right in it. Loans of furniture and fittings, except for special temporary needs, should not be accepted.

§ 3. CLEANING

(a) *Church and Furniture.* The country parson of George Herbert, after that he has seen that all things are in good repair, is to see that the church " be swept, kept clean ". All churches need an annual spring clean,[1] and volunteers can be found to help. Woodwork should be cared for, stonework brushed down, cobwebs removed, windows cleaned; mats, carpets, hassocks beaten and all hangings shaken. This is also an opportunity to clean out cupboards and remove old notices and papers, dilapidated hymn books, and attend to the linen and robes in the vestries. Miss Irene Caudwell [2] gives many very useful hints and suggestions for the cleaning of the church and its furniture, cleaning of all metals, glass and other articles, care and washing of church linen, and general needlework, mending of fabrics and removal of stains. Her book is a good one to put into the hands of the leader of the Sanctuary Guild, and every incumbent can learn much from it. It needs to be compared with the warnings of Mr. Truman, especially in the use of linseed oil on wood, and also for the cleaning of silver. Mr. Truman [3] urges the use only of soap and water for silver, and the wiping regularly with a soft cloth, an opinion also expressed in the Seventh Report.[4] Dearmer also gives useful hints on cleaning.[5]

The annual " clean " does not dispense with the weekly attention the church should have to keep it free from dust; special attention should be given to floral decorations, when used at Easter or Harvest, and precautions taken against the possible effect of vegetation on wood and stone. Rules about such decorations are not amiss.[6]

[1] N. Truman, *The Care of Churches*, pp. 105 f. and pp. 123 f.
[2] *The Care of God's House*, 1943.
[3] *The Care of Churches*, p. 92.
[4] *Seventh Report*, p. 44, and pp. 48 f.
[5] *The Parson's Handbook*, pp. 176–178.
[6] *Fourth Report*, p. 7. *Truman*, pp. 56 f.

(b) *Altar and Linen.* Flowers on altars are beloved by the people, just as sixty years ago they were suspected as improper. Fashions change, and now the movement is to ban flowers in front of a reredos.[1] They can be put near the altar, or on a window-sill, but they must not be put in the way of the clergy, or accidents will happen. In many churches flowers will still be placed on the altar. Some woman should be in charge of them, so that they can be removed before they fade or fall. The same woman can be in charge of a flower fund or flower list of donors, so that there is an adequate supply. There is a real personal link with the Church when flowers are given on a personal anniversary of gladness or of sorrow.[2]

If the church has no sacristan, the verger or clergy will do some of his duties, but a Sanctuary Guild gives a number of girls something to do for their church, and they will love to do it. They can care for the sanctuary and clergy vestry and keep them clean, attend to the vessels, and to the laundering of the linen. A rota for services will provide someone to attend to the Table, and put everything away—a useful courtesy when provided for a visiting priest in the incumbent's absence.[3]

§ 4. The Care of Churchyards

" Our Churchyards are a great possession, and their importance is only second to that of the priceless buildings within them. Their beauty and order is indispensable from that of the churches they contain; the finest building loses much of its charm if its surroundings are unworthy." [4]

Owing to the legal position connected with the freehold of the churchyard and the customary control he has of the introduction of monuments, the incumbent has an important place in the care of the churchyard, but he shares his oversight with the Church Council, which has " The care and maintenance of the churchyard (including a closed churchyard) with all the rights now possessed by the Churchwardens to recover from the overseers the cost of maintaining a closed churchyard." [5]

For the guidance of those who wish to fulfil their duties faithfully,

[1] P. Dearmer, *A Short Handbook to Public Worship*, p. 78.
[2] Irene Caudwell, *The Care of God's House*, pp. 37 ff. (For flowers on the altar and general floral decoration.) See also P. Dearmer, *The Parson's Handbook*, pp. 94 f.
[3] See above, Chapter VI, § 2 (c).
[4] *The Care of Churchyards*, Report of Central Council (The Preface).
[5] Parochial Church Councils (Powers) Measure, 1921, § 4 (ii), (c).

a very helpful report has been issued by the Central Council for the Care of Churches, *The Care of Churchyards* [1] (Third Edition, 1936). Reference can also be made with profit to *Concerning Churchyards* by A. Laurence Harriss, 1938, more briefly in *The Care of Churches* by Nevil Truman, 1935; *The Parson's Handbook* by Percy Dearmer, 1940; and for legal questions in *Opinions of the Legal Board*, 1939. [2]

(a) *Surroundings.* The lych gate, where it exists, is a characteristic and striking feature, but it does not follow that all churchyards should have one. Where they are they should be faithfully preserved with all picturesque adjuncts (*Report*, Chapter I). The walls and fences must be kept in repair, ancient work preserved, and the new work done in keeping with traditions of the neighbourhood (*Report*, Chapter II). It should not be forgotten that such things as sundials, notice-boards and the lighting of the church exterior, can all add or detract from the beauty of the churchyard (*Report*, Chapters VII and IX). The lay-out needs care; paths, drainage, grass and mounds are troublesome features, and call for careful planning, and often for voluntary workers. Mounds should be levelled, the grass cut (Report, Chapters VIII, X, XI; Harriss, pp. 34 ff.; Truman, pp. 40 ff.; *Opinions*, pp. 134 f.). As for flowers, shrubs and trees, they should be suited to the district. Trees should not be allowed to grow near the church. No timber trees may be cut down in any churchyard without the permission of the Dilapidations Board of the Diocese (*Report*, Chapters XII, XIII; Opinions, pp. 209–213; *Handbook*, pp. 42 ff.). But the best lay-out can be spoilt by the unsightliness of such things as sheds and rubbish-places, when a little commonsense would meet the situation (*Report*, Chapter XIV; Harriss, pp. 37 ff.).

(b) *Monuments.* In the churchyard of old the most important feature was the churchyard Cross, and ancient examples need expert attention for preservation. Recommendations have been made about the conditions for erecting new Crosses; ideally there should be no other cross in the churchyard (*Report*, Chapter III). Old churchyards are certain to have ancient and valuable monuments; different types and their ages can be noted, and dilapidated ones restored under direction. Some headstones can be re-set, but it is an advantage to have them flat. Iron railings were not originally a sign of social distinctions, but a necessary protection against sacrilege; they are now obsolete and are best removed. [3] Decaying and

[1] Quoted in the following references as ' Report '.
[2] These quoted respectively as ' Harriss ', ' Truman ', ' *Handbook* ' and ' *Opinions* '.
[3] Many were removed during the Second World War.

splitting, useless monuments should be removed,[1] but a record of their inscriptions and sites ought to be preserved in a register kept for the purpose (Report, Chapters IV, V). New monuments can be introduced only at the discretion of the incumbent, and they should conform to the standard of the churchyard, and have sensible lettering. " If application is made for the setting up of an unusual monument it is the duty of the incumbent to reply that a faculty is required." [2] Many churchyards have already been spoilt by the ostentation of some stones and the unsuitability of others. Monumental masions of repute are ready to co-operate, but some place the parish priest in a difficult position with his flock. A central authority for an area, if one could be established, might perhaps more easily exercise jurisdiction; incumbents change too rapidly for a long-term policy to be followed. (*Report*, Chapter VI, Harriss, pp. 26 ff.; Truman, p. 39; *Handbook*, pp. 438 ff.)

(c) *Closed Churchyards*. When a churchyard is no longer needed for burials it can be closed either by Order in Council or by Act of Parliament. The Order so closing it may refer only to new gravespaces, and may permit further burials in old graves. The action for closing it may come from the local authorities if they consider that its continued use for burials is detrimental to the health of the district. An incumbent who wishes to have the churchyard closed should apply to the Minister of Health, whose duty it is to set the procedure in action, but it is advisable to discuss the matter beforehand with the local Medical Officer of Health.

If the churchyard is closed (or partially closed, thus allowing the use of old graves) by Order in Council, the responsibility and expense of the maintenance of the churchyard can be transferred to the local rating authority, but this cannot be done if it is closed by Act of Parliament. Maintenance covers the upkeep of the paths and fences, and the duty of keeping the churchyard generally in good order. The procedure of transference is quite simple.

> " When once the Parochial Church Council have given a certificate in order to recover the costs of upkeep from the local authority, their powers, duties and liabilities so far as they relate to the repair and maintenance of the closed churchyard pass automatically to the local authority, whether municipal or parish council." [3]

---

[1] Monuments can be removed only be faculty.
[2] Report, *The Care of Churchyards*, 1932, p. 24.
[3] *The Care of Churchyards* (Diocese of York, Report of the Committee), 1936 (S.P.C.K.), p. 7.

Once the transference has been made, the Church Council should not make further contracts for such work.

The rights of the incumbent and the Church Council are not affected by any such transference. It is most desirable that claims for maintenance should be made in order that parishes may gain the benefit of an enactment which relieves the church of an expense without depriving it of any privilege (*Opinions*, pp. 136–141).

The matters connected with burials and grave-spaces in the churchyard are discussed in a later chapter.[1]

[1] See below, Chapter XXIII, § 4 (*a*).

BRIEF BIBLIOGRAPHY

The Reports of the Central Council, 1923–1940.
Nevil Truman, *The Care of Churches*, 1935.
Irene Caudwell, *The Care of God's House*, 1943.
Percy Dearmer, *The Parson's Handbook*, 1940.
A. R. Powys, *The Repair of Ancient Buildings*.
The Care of Churchyards, Report of the Central Council: Third Edition, 1936.
The Care of Churchyards (Diocese of York, Report of the Committee on the Care of Churchyards), S.P.C.K., 1936.
A. L. Harriss, *Concerning Churchyards*, 1938.
L. S. Hunter, *A Parson's Job*, 1931, Chapter VIII.
The *Eighth Report* of the Central Council, 1940, gives an excellent list of inexpensive but reliable publications on a variety of matters, with some notes on available lantern slides.
The *Ninth Report*, 1945, has articles on:— (1) Repair of plaster ceilings; (2) Loudspeakers and acoustics; (3) Wall surfaces. The main Report is on War Damage.

CHAPTER XII

THE PAROCHIAL BUILDINGS

§ 1. The Buildings

(a) *Their Necessity.* In addition to the church, every parish needs some kind of parochial hall, or a building which can be used as such. It might be a large, well-equipped building, or the Day School, or, in a small parish, a parish room. Its primary use is for religious education, especially in the Sunday School, for which the buildings are principally required, but it also has tremendous value for the development of the family fellowship outside the corporate worship in church. It is here that the different groups will come for their meetings—the women of the Mothers' Union, the members of sewing meetings, the men for their Institute and Fellowship, and the young people and children for their Youth Centre or various organizations. It is here that all will come together for the family socials, whatever forms these may take. Adequate parochial buildings add much to the life and activity of the parish; they also add to the work of the clergy and the Church Council, and often add a large item to the parochial expenses. So much is this so that sometimes all that can happen in the buildings are the functions necessary to raise the cost of the upkeep, and then the whole purpose of the hall is defeated.

(b) *Their Equipment.* The Sunday School and the religious meetings must take the place of honour in the parochial hall, so it should be planned with ample space for a well-graded Sunday School, and space for all the weekday activity. In a large parish with many children this means four rooms, each with ample accommodation for a Sunday School department. One room can be the large hall, for socials and dances, and be fitted with a stage for concerts. The stage can sometimes be made to shut off as a separate room. Several smaller rooms round make useful class-rooms and committee rooms, and a kitchen is a convenient amenity. Cloakrooms and lavatories are essential, and in parochial buildings are generally inadequate.

The chief furnishings will be forms, or chairs, for seating; chairs that fold or are otherwise easy to stack are the best. A good many cupboards are needed so that all Sunday School necessities can be put away decently, and so that each organization can keep its equipment under lock and key. Pianos are necessary for each Sunday School department. The stage requires curtains, good lighting effects and some decent scenery, and a place for storing the same. The kitchen needs the customary effects—crockery, wash-basins, geyser, and gas cooker.

One room should be reserved for the use of the clergy as an office, and all Sunday School records and stores can be kept in it. This can also be the Committee Room and furnished more comfortably than is usual in school buildings.

§ 2. MANAGEMENT

(a) *The Committee.* As a general rule the parochial hall is under the care of the Church Council, and the best method of administration is through a Hall Management Committee, responsible to the Council. The Committee may consist of appointed members of the Council, who are practical people in matters of property, with representatives of the teachers from the Sunday School departments. The Committee will have its own chairman, secretary and treasurer; minutes of the meetings will be recorded, and it will have its own accounts.

The Committee will be concerned with the cleanliness and ordinary repairs of the building and its general maintenance. No faculties are required for the repair or alteration of the building, but it should be, like the church, regarded as a responsibility for which the committee at the time are the temporary trustees. Often the buildings are dull, dingy, dirty and uninspiring, with a depressing effect upon all who come, especially upon the Sunday School children, so cleanliness and bright decoration must be a main concern of the committee. The Management Committee should be empowered to make small expenditure, and for larger schemes make recommendations to the Church Council. Previous comments made about tenders and local firms apply equally to parochial buildings as to churches.[1]

A caretaker-cleaner is required for the building. The best is one who is a full-time worker for both church and hall.[2] The caretaker has no easy task—too many children use the school, and even adults are not always considerate. Like the verger, he is apt to suffer from too many bosses. One member of the committee should direct his activities: this is preferably a task for the secretary. Often the

[1] See above, Chapter XI, § 1 (b).   [2] See above, Chapter VI, § 2 (a).

incumbent is the only member of the committee who can and does visit the hall daily, but it is too much to assume that every priest is good at directing the cleaners in their routine work. A conscientious worker and a clear programme of work to be done are essentials if a building is to be well kept. No amount of directing will make a lazy caretaker clean. There are many things that a caretaker cannot be expected to do, and the movement of chairs about the parish and similar manual work call for voluntary aid. The clergy should be ready to lend a hand at this kind of work, as it helps to kindle a friendly spirit, but the clergy should certainly go on strike if all such activity is just left to them.

The expenses that the Committee must meet are obvious: the upkeep of the buildings, repairs, lighting and heating, payment of caretaker, insurances, and perhaps the provision of Sunday School requisites. The income is provided from church expenses, though it may include the collection in the Sunday School, donations from the parochial organizations using the building, and the income from lettings of various descriptions. Usually some grant is needed from the annual effort, be it Bazaar or Gift Day, to balance the budget of the Hall Management Committee.

(b) *Church Day Schools*. In a great many parishes, especially in the country, the Church Day School serves also as the parochial hall. The Day School Managers are appointed under a separate trust, and have generally no connection with the Church Council, though most of the Managers are Church officials. Apart from the educational duties,[1] the Managers have charge of the upkeep of the school, and the care of the building involves much the same duties as the care of a parochial hall.

For maintenance of heat and light and cleaning the Local Education Authority pays its shares, so actually a Day School costs less to run in proportion than a parochial hall. But the fabric has to be kept up to a higher standard of repair, and so many schools are antiquated in design that it often costs a great deal to modernize the building. The caretaker is appointed by the Managers, but paid for work done in Day School hours by the L.E.A., and the parish has only to find the payment for the work done for the parish affairs, especially for the use of the school for Sunday School purposes. The caretaker has to reach the L.E.A. standard of cleanliness—a standard which the ordinary parochial hall does not often attain.

The use of the Day School as a hall has both advantages and disadvantages. For a Sunday School the equipment is better than

---

[1] See below, Chapter XV, § 2.

the ordinary hall provides, but for other purposes there is a restriction of hours; the women cannot meet in an afternoon, and in the evening the school furniture is in the way, and the seating accommodation is often not suitable for adults. Many of the administration problems of the parochial buildings apply also to the Day Schools when used for the same purpose.

(c) *Administration.* When there is much activity in the parochial hall and many organizations are attached to the parish, there must be careful planning, usually on the part of the incumbent, for the use of the hall. Certain days, hours and rooms must be allocated to the organizations, and none should be allowed to change its times without consultation with the incumbent or secretary. Extra activities, such as rehearsals and concerts, not to mention the annual upheaval of the Bazaar, must be fitted into the weekly programme. In each parish almost every group seems to think itself the only group entitled to the use of the rooms just when it pleases, and members walk in for that extra rehearsal without any courtesy to others. Careful planning and warning of groups of any changes would avoid such unhappy incidents. A good scheme is to issue a weekly plan,[1] posted on the main notice-board of the hall. This plan can be prepared with the main regular items printed, and the special engagements or alterations added in ink. A copy may be posted in the caretaker's kitchen, as he, poor man, is often unaware of any special arrangements. Usually nobody remembers to tell him.

The social functions organized by the different groups are best planned for a session at a time. These dates also should be entered on the weekly plan as they occur, for the guidance of the users of the hall and the caretaker. Parochial halls are sometimes ' let ' for outside purposes, such as concerts organized by other than church people, for funeral teas and wedding receptions, for Horticultural Shows, for political meetings and polling-booths. The school secretary can do the bookings for these lettings, but care must be taken to avoid clashes with internal functions. The incumbent has nearly always to be consulted, and often has so many inquiries by letter or telephone, that it is quite the wisest plan for him to do all the booking. How the hall should be let, how often, and for what fee, should be subject to a settled policy.

In the filing cabinet, in connection with the Hall Management Committee, the priest will need folders for the business of the Committee, for the list of the caretaker's duties, and for the list of

[1] See example at the end of this chapter.

fees for the letting of the hall, and the hire of crockery and other equipment.

(d) *Legal Matters.* A few legal points arise in connection with the parochial buildings.

(i) Rates.—" Parish Halls have a rateable value, and legislation would be needed to exempt them." [1] There is no common practice even in the same town in the matter of rating of halls. One may be rated, whereas in the next parish, which makes exactly the same kind of use of its hall, it may not be rated. The position is unsatisfactory.

(ii) Licences.—Application should be made to the police for direction about licences for the hall for singing, dancing, concerts and dramatics, and films. Certain regulations must be observed.

(iii) Entertainment Tax.—Application for exemption must always be made for all concerts and performances for which tax is payable, if the proceeds are for religious and charitable objects. Exemption is granted if no expenses are taken from the gross proceeds, or, in certain circumstances, if the expenses are taken from the proceeds. The form proper to the particular claim must be used, and information may be obtained from the local customs and excise office.

(iv) Royalties are payable for all performances of songs and music in the hall. Arrangements can be made with the Performing Rights Society, at the cost of an annual subscription, to cover liabilities in this respect. Licences are also required for the public performances of gramophone records—*e.g.*, by radiogram at dances—and these may be obtained from the Phonographic Performance, Limited. Royalties must also be paid for public theatrical performances to the representatives of the author. It is only just that authors should receive the due reward for their work and talent.

§ 3. Social Activities

(a) *Nature and Purpose.* Apart from the religious and educational purposes of the hall, which are discussed in later chapters,[2] the hall is used mainly for social activities of various kinds. It then becomes a community centre to the neighbourhood. The relation of the social to the raising of funds has already been considered in connection with church finance.[3] There is certainly a place for the social side in a church's activities, whether it is used as a source of income or not. " Social life is not a necessary evil, but a necessity

[1] *Opinions of the Legal Board*, pp. 199–201.
[2] See below, Chapters XV, XVI, and XVII.
[3] See above, Chapter X, § 2 (*b*).

of life, a real part of that kingdom of the world which needs re-demption and conversion into the kindgom of God." [1] The social function provides a happy meeting-place for young and old, definitely helps to build up the fellowship of the family of the church, encourages friendship, gives opportunities for work and self-expression to many people, and was in the past, and still is in the country, the only means of bringing colour into the drabness of people's lives.

> " Christianity cannot be divorced from any side of a person's life. Every part of life should be brought under the sway of Christ the King. If that is so, the Church is bound to have a message to give concerning the amusements of the people which, frequently, are to the tired and weary worker a recrea-tion and refreshment." [2]

The Church has traditionally been associated with the amuse-ments of the people, as indeed it was associated in the Middle Ages with the whole of life.

> " More directly under the patronage of the clergy were the ' Church ales ', forerunners of the religious tea and phil-anthropic bazaar. Men and women sold and drank ale in the Church itself or the churchyard, to raise funds for the fabric or for some other good purpose. Church ales were very common in the Fifteenth Century though they had been, frowned upon by the more ascetic churchmen of earlier times. The nave of the church was the ' village hall ' for most com-munal purposes." [3]

A difficulty turns on the question whether the socials are ' open ' or ' closed '; while there is a good argument for the Christian family enjoying good fellowship, should the outsider be permitted to come? Socials have very little value for evangelism; indeed, " they may—just in proportion as they attract the outsider—give him a false impression of the Church's objective ".[4] In money-making affairs numbers are welcomed, but this danger should be watched; some if not all of such functions should be limited only to church folk. Something of this sort can be done by issuing a kind of season ticket.[5]

The kind of programme of socials to be provided requires thought. It must not be all of one kind. The old-time social would bore the young people of to-day, but too many dances would give the place

---

[1] E. S. G. Wickham, *Parson and People*, 1931, p. 68.
[2] J. C. Watts-Ditchfield, *The Church in Action*, p. 84.
[3] G. M. Trevelyan, *English Social History*, 1944, p. 90.
[4] E. S. G. Wickham, *Parson and People*, p. 66.
[5] *Ibid.*, p. 67.

the character of a dance-hall. A place for concerts and dramatics is essential, as these encourage people to entertain themselves. However, dances and whist drives form the main element in the programme of many parishes to-day, and modern opinion sees no harm in them. The Methodist Conference changed its policy on this subject in 1943. But both dances and whist drives must be properly organized. The undesirable element should not be allowed at dances, and the hall and its entrances and passages should be stewarded. Whist drives should be run for entertainment and costly prizes forbidden.

The clergy should not be afraid to share in the social side,[1] but if possible should not run the functions; they come rather to meet the people and to talk to them. In an artisan parish it is often necessary for the clergy to organize these affairs, there being no other capable persons. The principal difficulty for the clergy is that in industrial areas they are often held on Saturday evenings. This cannot be avoided, although it is not the best preparation for Sunday, either for the people or the parson. The people to-day will have their Saturday night out, if not in the parochial hall, then in one of the town's cinemas or dance-halls.

In some parishes certain functions are great annual events, the Annual Tea, for instance, and of course the Annual Bazaar. They provide for the annual reunion of old parishioners and friends, and have a ritual and ceremony of their own.

(b) *Necessary Planning.* Obviously if such social activities are to be well planned and conducted, there must be machinery for it. The incumbent will naturally wish to be concerned with as little of this as possible, and the Church Council should also be only indirectly associated. It is necessary for the Council to lay down rules and regulations for the conduct of all affairs in the parochial buildings, but the prospect of much of the time of the Council being taken up with a discussion of ham and buns, and knives and forks, is much to be deprecated. When the Council is actually directly concerned, as, for example, with an Annual Tea, the work of its preparation is better done through a Social Committee or a Ladies' Committee. Some parishes arrange for all their social activities to be in the hands of a Social Committee of the Church Council, or the responsibility can be given to the Hall Committee or the Young People's Committee. In other parishes the different organizations run their own functions guided by the regulations of the Church Council.

[1] Cf. E. Seyzinger, *The Glory of Priesthood*, 1933, p. 143.

In parishes where there are many organizations it is helpful to have an Organizations' Council, to which should be invited the Leaders of the junior organizations and the secretaries of the adult groups. It is an advantage if members of the Hall Management Committee are present. This Organizations' Council can meet once or twice a year, and can not only make plans for social activities, so that all have their share in the programme and allocation of dates, but can also use the occasion to make complaints or representations to the Hall Committee concerning the general management of the buildings, to mutual advantage.

SELECT BIBLIOGRAPHY

E. S. G. Wickham, *Parson and People*, 1931, Chapter IX.
L. S. Hunter, *A Parson's Job*, 1931, Chapter X.
A. L. Preston, *A Parish Priest in his Parish*, 1933, Chapter VII.

L

ST. JOHN'S CHURCH—PAROCHIAL PROGRAMME

	Church Services.	Hall.	Room A.	Room B.	Com'tee Room.	Class Rooms.
Sunday *Oct. 8th*	8.00 H.C. 9.00 H.C. 10.30 M.P. 2.00 Guild 6.30 E.P.	2.00 Junior S.S.	2.00 Senior S.S. 7.45 Y.P.F.	2.00 Kindergarten		2.00 Classes
Monday	9.30 H.C. 8.00 M.P. 6.30 E.P. 7.30 Intercessions		7.00 Cubs	7.30 *P.C.C.*		7.00 Y.P.F. handicrafts
Tuesday	7.30 H.C. 8.00 M.P. 3.00 *Funeral* 6.30 E.P.	7.00 *Rehearsal*	2.30 Sewing class 7.00 G.F.S.		7.00 Prep. class	7.00 *Scout's First Aid*
Wednesday	6.00 H.C. 8.00 M.P. 6.30 E.P.	7.00 Y.P.F. dance	2.45 M.U.			

Thursday	9.30 H.C. 8.00 M.P.	7.30 Choir 6.30 E.P.			7.00 Brownies	7.00 Prep. class	7.00 Y.P.U.
Friday	7.00 H.C. 8.00 M.P.	7.30 Intercessions 6.30 E.P.		7.00 Scouts	7.00 Guides		
Saturday	7.00 H.C. 8.00 M.P. 2.00 *Wedding*	6.30 E.P.	7.00 *G.F.S. social*	2.30 *Wedding party*			
Sunday *Oct. 15th*	8.00 H.C. 9.00 H.C. 10.30 M.P. 2.00 Guild	6.30 E.P.	2.00 Junior S.S.	2.00 Senior S.S. 7.45 Y.P.F.	2.00 Kinder-garten		2.00 Classes

NOTE. The main programme is printed, and additional notes (illustrations in italics) added in ink when required.

Part III

THE MINISTRY TO THE BODY CORPORATE

CHAPTER XIII

THE DETAILS OF WORSHIP

§ 1. The Importance of Worship

(a) *The Revival of Worship*. Worship obviously plays an important part in the life and work of the priest. " Everything that a minister of religion may be called upon to do is subordinate to the function of leading a congregation in worship." [1] At first sight there seems to be little to add to the fact that the priest has his guide to worship provided in the Book of Common Prayer, and if it be said, as it can truly be said, that the Book of 1662 is in need of revision, there are for the time being the variations permitted by the Bishops within the limits of the Book of 1928. There are extremists in different directions, who are disloyal, but, as well as these, too many are just complacent, content with dullness and drabness, so that their loyalty is only in the letter, not in the spirit.

The present century has seen a steady decline in attendance at worship, and many reasons could be given for this, but it is more important to ask how there can be a revival of worship. This, said Dr. Underhill, no mean authority on the subject, is " the most important practical question at present before the Church ".[2] If there is to be any revival, worship must be well prepared. It is not sufficient merely to walk into church to take a service with only the sermon ready. The simplest service of the regular routine of services must be prepared in all its details.[3] So the parish priest must know not only how to take the services, but how to plan them, indeed the two go together. Once again the definition of parochial administration already given may be recalled, for it gives as part of the aim, " that the laity of the parish may express a living, happy fellowship or family in the Body of Christ . . . in its worship . . .",[4] and again it is clear that planning is not just a matter of raising money, but enters into the most important sides of a parson's job.

" Nothing requires more careful planning beforehand than the public worship of the Church. Nothing repays it better.

[1] L. S. Hunter, *A Parson's Job*, 1931, p. 64.
[2] Francis Underhill, *The Revival of Worship*, 1938, p. 9.
[3] L. S. Hunter, *A Parson's Job*, 1931, p. 67.   [4] See above, Chapter I, § 2 (a).

I have known processions in Church reduced to a farce by the banners being caught in unforeseen chandeliers, or two streams of choir boys encircling the font getting entangled because it was not realized that the passage would prove too narrow." [1]

It can be said at once that planning is not sufficient to make a service an act of worship, nor to create that revival of worship so much desired, but, given the spirit and nature of worship, planning can give it more effectiveness than a slack, disorderly, come-what-may service.

(b) *Liturgical Principles.* Besides those obvious practical details which, if not prepared beforehand, will spoil a service, there must be present in the preparation a true knowledge of the nature of Christian worship, and thus a sense of liturgical proprieties which can be gained only by a study of liturgiology in the works of competent masters. Christian worship is not the same as worship in other religions; nor is it achieved by arranging a collection of hymns, prayers and lessons, to bring in the elements of praise, intercessions and meditation, but each of the liturgical services is an entity in itself and has its own purpose. Matins and Evensong are services of the Word, setting forth the theme of the Incarnation, with *Te Deum* as the focus point of one, and *Magnificat* as the focus point of the other,[2] the climax of each service being the second Lord's Prayer.[3] Then the Holy Communion is the great act of Christian worship to which the other services are subsidiary, because it sets forth the Divine Drama of Redemption.

" The Church teaches that in the Eucharist the worshippers commemorate, present, and claim their part in the sacrifice made once for all upon the Cross. For this reason the Church claims that the Eucharist is the climax of Christian worship. In it the whole society consciously approaches the throne of God, and in it becomes sensitively aware of His Presence, realizing that the barrier between man and God is finally removed by the Sacrifice which the Eucharist commemorates." [4]

However, different schools of thought within the Church have their different places of emphasis, and the variations in worship between differing churches are somewhat chaotic. The Anglican Church is comprehensive and there is room for all, so there is

[1] A. W. Hopkinson, *Pastor's Progress*, 1942, pp. 32 f.
[2] G. W. Ireson, *Church Worship and the Non-Churchgoer*, 1944, p. 119, suggests the interchange of *Te Deum* and *Benedictus* to bring the theme more into line.
[3] H. de Candole, *The Church's Prayers*, 1939, p. 82.
[4] Report of the Lambeth Conference, 1930, p. 82.

need for each section of the Church to have both knowledge and appreciation of the ways of worship of other sections. This is a necessary preliminary to the fulfilment of the hope of a development of a new English. use, with recognized variations, arising from the present chaos.[1]

(c) *The Laity and Worship.* Lay people generally desire that such development should be in the direction of simplicity (that is, simplicity as opposed to over-elaborateness), not in the direction of neglect of liturgical principles. Many people have a respect for ceremonial and a love for beauty, but they dislike fussiness and " for ordinary Sunday by Sunday prayer and praise, most people prefer a simplicity which is far from being incompatible with beauty or mystery." [1] Yet even more are the laity conservative. " I have found over and over again that nothing scatters a congregation so much as divergences from the forms of service to which they and their forefathers have been accustomed "; [2] again, " men are very conservative in their religious customs; and indeed the strength of religion in human history has been largely due to this tenacity ".[3] However, there must be some development, otherwise there is dullness and stagnation, and then for these reasons people do not come to worship. " The emptiest churches seem to be those which have not changed since 1900; the next emptiest those which have changed too much." [4]

The clergy often fail to observe the difference between the clerical and lay attitude to worship. Most lay people have very little sense of liturgy, they fail to understand most of the service, and have no idea of meditation; the clergy are obliged to make a deep study of these very matters. Consequently " the average churchgoer loves sentimental hymns, dislikes creeds and abhors psalms ".[6] Progress and development must necessarily be slow. The great task to-day is the training of the laity in worship, explaining the services and developing an understanding and appreciation of the liturgy. This has to be done for those inside the church, and valuable suggestions for this have been made by Mr. Gordon Ireson, who outlines teaching sermons explaining the different parts of the services of Holy Communion and Morning and Evening Prayer within the structure of the whole service, the sermon itself

---

[1] Cf. L. S. Hunter, *A Parson's Job*, p. 75.
[2] Francis Underhill, *The Revival of Worship*, 1938, p. 37.
[3] *Ibid.*, p. 38.
[4] Percy Dearmer, *A Short Handbook of Public Worship*, 1931, p. 24.
[5] *Ibid.*, p. 24.
[6] J. B. Goodliffe, *The Parson and his Problems*, 1933, p. 51.

occurring at different points each Sunday.[1] Those outside the
the church need far more careful preparation for admission to
Christian worship than is thought necessary to-day. In fact, the
general practice is for each church to provide the services, open
to anyone and explained to none. To remedy this, a Catechu-
menate, worked on the principle of cells, is suggested, in which
training in worship is given, to prepare for admission to the Christian liturgical services. The idea is carefully thought out and
guidance for experiments in this is given.[2]

Such training is far more likely to create a deeper sense of
worship among the laity than any drastic changes. Each priest
should have a sense of the ideals of Christian worship, and he
ought to be able to make one or two changes in the right direction,
which is quite independent of any preferences of churchmanship, but
the services such as they are in the tradition of his church can
always be improved by attention to details, and by the cultivation
of a reverent, worshipful spirit in the congregation.

§ 2. GENERAL PRELIMINARIES

(a) *Suitable Hours.* The traditional hours of 8 a.m., 10.30 or
11 a.m., and 6.30 p.m. are being challenged. " Sunday must be
re-thought ",[3] said Dr. Underhill, and he has in mind the needs
of the young people for recreation on the Sunday. To attend early
service every week is beyond people in the industrial areas, who
rise early every day of the week. The widespread movement
among all types of churchmanship for a Parish Communion [4] at 9
or 9.30 a.m., with an instructional address, has much to commend
it as a substitute for the two morning services. The people are
not up too soon, they are free then until evening, and the housewife
is away in time to cook the Sunday dinner. Sunday School at
11.30 a.m. would free the afternoon for children, for in the next
generation children will join increasingly with their parents in the
Sunday afternoon outing. Evensong could be much later than
6.30 p.m., especially in the summer, or the day might end with
compline or an " epilogue " form of service.

In the morning scheme there ought to be a place for Matins,
and its liturgical place is before Holy Communion. Matins is

---

[1] G. W. Ireson, *Church Worship and the Non-Churchgoer*, 1944, Chapters IV, V.
[2] *Ibid.*, Chapters I, II, and III. See also, *Towards the Conversion of England*,
1945, pp. 140–142.
[3] Francis Underhill, *The Revival of Worship*, p. 14.
[4] *The Parish Communion*, S.P.C.K., Edited by A. G. Hebert.

dear to the heart of many devout Anglicans, and its disappearance
would alienate more than is usually thought. The discovery of
the right times for services is complicated by the teaching on
fasting Communion, which a large number of church people regard
as important, as the Church at present has no suitable alternative
form of preparatory ' discipline ' to recommend to its members.
Other church people, however, think that this has been wrongly
emphasized, and that if the Eucharist is to be held when most
people can come, then the evening is the right place for it.

Within the limits of order, each priest and his parish must decide
for themselves. This is a time of transition, and it will be many
years before there is an agreed policy about the hours of service.
Each priest must proceed carefully, having due regard to the
traditions of the parish and local circumstances. It is no use
disturbing strong congregations for the sake of hypothetical members
who might come.[1] " The method of approach . . . must be by
addition, and not by subtraction." [2]

Weekday services should be arranged for hours when people
are most likely to be able to come. This would seem an
obvious precaution, but Canon Green says that it is usually
ignored, and urges further thought on the best times for the daily
services.[3]

(b) *Regularity and Punctuality*. Services, both daily and weekly,
should be regular, in order that people can feel certain that they
can attend at the stated times and find a service.[4] Alterations of
times for the convenience of the priest are to be deprecated, even
if a notice is put in the Magazine and announced the previous
Sunday. This was made clear in war-time, when black-out circumstances forced alterations of times; such was the confusion
that some came early and others late, although the times were
clearly stated in the Magazine. A similar difficulty is found in
parishes where the services vary according to the Sunday in the
month; people do not find it easy to remember which is the
Sunday for this or that, and in a month with five Sundays, complications are increased. This is unavoidable in certain town
parishes in this period of transition; it is certainly unavoidable
in the country, where one priest has two or more churches and
wishes to give them equal opportunities for worship.

[1] Percy Dearmer, *A Short Handbook of Public Worship*, pp. 23–25; cf. *The Parson's Handbook*, 1940, pp. 181–185.
[2] G. W. Ireson, *Church Worship and the Non-Churchgoer*, 1944, p. 118.
[3] Peter Green, *The Town Parson*, pp. 93 f.
[4] *Ibid.*, pp. 86–89.

" Unpunctuality is regarded by some as little more than an amiable weakness; in reality it can be both irritating and selfish, especially where, as in divine service, many persons besides the minister are involved." [1] There is no need to labour this point, which applies to all meetings as well as to services. It is useless to pander to the unpunctuality of the people; the priest's unpunctuality only makes them worse. [2]

(c) *Reverence and Audibility.* The most necessary condition for a service is the most difficult to achieve. Regularity and punctuality can be achieved by habit, but habit is the enemy of reverence. Just because the clergy are so accustomed to the services of the Church, they tend to gabble and go too fast. This is especially so at the daily offices, and is too common on Sundays. The very fact that the service is printed demands a greater care in this need for reverence. It is so easy to develop mannerisms, affectations and dronings, that a parson can hardly believe his candid friends when they do venture to speak. It is essential to be natural and audible. [3]

It is as easy to be slipshod in actions as in speaking. Lazy lolling on the desk or in the pulpit is not inspiring, nor is the constant gazing down the church. Although lay people like their parson to know they are in church, they do not like him constantly looking at them. All movements about the church should be deliberate and natural. The priest should not only be reverent because reverence is due to God, but also because his reverence will guide and inspire his people. " The parson who has most to say about his people being indifferent to religion, is usually one who is himself most slipshod in church." [4] The clergy are not the only people who can destroy an atmosphere of reverence in a church. A verger who rattles his keys immediately after the Blessing, [5] members of the choir who laze over their seats, and churchwardens and sidesmen who chatter at the back are all equally culpable.

The worst enemy of reverence is the clerical voice, and an untrained voice spoils many services and sermons. The use of the voice is an art that has to be learnt and practised, and the professional teacher of voice production is the best person to help; yet this is an art that any man can attain.

[1] Francis Underhill, *The Revival of Worship*, p. 36.
[2] Peter Green, *The Town Parson*, p. 89.
[3] *Ibid.*, pp. 89–93. Cf. L. S. Hunter, *A Parson's Job*, Chapter V.
[4] G. W. Clarkson in *Theology*, March 1943, p. 51.
[5] C. F. Rogers, *Principles of Parish Work*, p. 129.

" Everyone can, if he will, pronounce his final consonants, raise his voice slightly at the end of a sentence, make reasonable pauses, and never allow himself to get breathless. If he observes these rules, and one or two others, which he can discover for himself, *and perseveres in their observance*, his congregation will have little cause for complaint." [1]

§ 3. THE SERVICES OF THE CHURCH

(a) *Liturgical Services.* The study of Christian Worship is included in the curriculum of the Theological Colleges, and the knowledge of the Book of Common Prayer is for Anglican ordinands an essential part of that study, though much of the ritual and ceremonial is learnt only by practical assistance at services. A description of the details of the technique of the liturgical services can only be given by an expert liturgiologist, for it depends on an exact knowledge both of historical precedence and modern customs. To enter into such details is thus beyond the scope of this book, and space would certainly not allow an exposition of even the simplest ritual and ceremonial of Matins and Evensong and of the Holy Communion.

It must, however, be stressed again that there are correct liturgical methods, which admit of many variations. To ignore them does not only mean offending the susceptibilities of those who appreciate such things, for they are very few, if any, in the average congregation, but it may mean the presentation of a travesty of Christian worship. This is true both of the simplest ' Evangelical Low Church ' services and of the ' Anglo-Catholic High Church ' services. All such things as the beginning and ending of the services, [2] actions, initial phrases, standing and kneeling, necessary ornaments and vestments, processions, have to be considered and a consistent method adopted. The structure of Divine Service and of the Communion Service must be thoroughly understood. " Orderly and disciplined movement makes for reverence and beauty." [3]

It has already been said that worship and its meaning must be

---

[1] A. W. Hopkinson, *Pastor's Psychology*, 1944, p. 105. For advice in reading the lessons and speaking in conduct of services, a useful book is R. S. T. Haslehurst, *How to Read the Bible Aloud*, 1938. For use of the voice in preaching, reference should be made to Paul Bull, *Preaching and Sermon Construction*. For the general ordering of services, a small book is P. M. Barry, *A Present for the Vicar*, 1945; see especially Chapters I and II.

[2] G. W. Ireson, *Church Worship and the Non-Churchgoer*, 1944, pp. 156–158.

[3] Peter Green, *The Town Parson*, p. 99.

expounded to the people, and it must be emphasized that ceremonies need explanations, especially when first introduced.[1] As
the Anglican services are all congregational, great pains should
be taken to teach the congregation to take its share in the services
and do it correctly. In particular, the newly confirmed ought to
be taught how to communicate; many in the past have not been
properly taught, and should be properly instructed.[2]

Attention is called to the use of good books, such as those mentioned in the Bibliography to this chapter. Particularly Dr.
Dearmer in *The Parson's Handbook* considers the subject exhaustively,
though he gives a very strong warning against over-elaboration.[3]
To those unversed in the subject the study of the following chapters
gives a good introduction. Matins and Evensong, Chapter VI;
The Litany, Chapter VII; Processions, Chapter VIII; Holy
Communion, Chapters IX, X, XI, XII; Position of the Minister,
pp. 195–198; Turning, kneeling, standing, sitting, pp. 198–201;
Bowing and the Sign of the Cross, pp. 201–214; Priest and Servers,
pp. 214–216; Lights and Incense, pp. 216–227.

(b) *Special Services.* Certain occasions require special services,
but there should not be too many, nor should they be introduced
merely as stunts. Many people will come to special services, even
if they do not attend at other times. The really special service is
both an occasion of the rejoicing of the parochial family and an
opportunity for evangelism. The parish family naturally wishes to
rejoice at the Jubilee or Centenary of the church, to share in the
occasional dedication of new gifts and ornaments, and to show
respect when an honoured Church leader is called to the Church
Expectant. There are also State and civic occasions when the
Lord Mayor may come to the church.[4] The war has increased the
special parades of various organizations, and there are industrial
occasions when the local factories come to confess that all good
things are of God.

On Sundays these special services will naturally have the liturgical
basis with suitable hymns, special psalms and lessons by permission
of the Ordinary. On weekdays, services after the manner of
National Days of Prayer and Thanksgiving can be devised or
copied. They must be built upon liturgical principles, and never
be just a collection of hymns, lessons and prayers put together

[1] See below, Chapter XXVI, § 3.
[2] P. Dearmer, *The Parson's Handbook*, 1940, " Suggestions for Communicants ",
pp. 272, 273. Cf. below Chapter XXII, § 2 (b).
[3] Page 355. These references are to the Twelfth Edition (1932 and 1940).
[4] See below, Chapter XX, § 2 (b).

haphazard.[1] Not every priest has a genius for such construction, and not every church takes readily to them. It has been suggested that experiments should only be allowed in certain churches.[2] It is best if each of these services could be printed, if possible with a brief note about its aims and purpose, which might otherwise be misunderstood by an uninstructed crowd.[3]

Other preparatory details of a business nature must not be overlooked: seats must be correctly counted and allocated to visitors, necessary invitations or circulars written and dispatched, posters and advertisements arranged. If these things are to be done, they must be well done.

(c) *Weekday Services.* In addition to the daily offices, or in conjunction with them, various other types of services are often required. A regular scheme of intercessions after Evensong,[4] prayer meetings in which the laity can join, missionary intercessions, mid-week Bible Classes for members of the Bible Reading Fellowship, are all possible needs, and are best discussed under other heads.[5]

§ 4. THE PLANNING OF SERVICES

(a) *The Planned Service.* The clergy are often reminded that the services should be as carefully prepared as the sermons. The variable parts of the service are in the hands of the priest, and he can so arrange them as to give them direction. This is obvious at the Festivals, when naturally all hymns, lessons, psalms, prayers and sermon have one theme, but it can be so more often, from the Opening Sentence [6] to the prayer before the Blessing.[7]

> "Unity in conception and structure, the subordination of parts to one whole, are among the obvious qualities of good art. By contrast, what is often the worst failure in the worship of God as we know it, is its distracted, episodic character." [8]

[1] Cf. L. S. Hunter, *A Parson's Job*, 1931, Appendix of Services; G. W. Ireson, *Church Worship and the Non-Churchgoer*, 1944, Appendix C for various suggestions; and P. M. Barry, *A Present for the Vicar*, 1945, Chapter VII. Also, P. Dearmer and F. R. Barry, *Westminster Prayers*, 1936.
A discussion of the subject in L. S. Hunter, *A Parson's Job*, pp. 52–62; and F. R. Barry, *The Relevance of the Church*, 1935, pp. 142–150.
[2] W. K. Lowther Clarke, *The Prayer Book of 1928 Reconsidered*, 1943, p. 85.
[3] J. B. Goodliffe, *A Parson and his Problems*, p. 61.
[4] Peter Green, *The Town Parson*, p. 96.
[5] See below, Chapter XVII, § 4 (*b*).
[6] In spite of the new sentences proposed in the 1928 Book, the Opening Sentence is really concerned with penitence.
[7] J. B. Goodliffe, *The Parson and his Problems*, p. 53. (Theme, The God of Beauty.)
[8] F. R. Barry, *The Relevance of the Church*, p. 146.

Dr. Underhill compares the service to a jigsaw puzzle,[1] and also points out that it is a mistake to follow up an address with a hymn which does not keep the thought of the sermon in the minds of the people; the two may sometimes, even, be ludicrously contradictory.

To make a completely planned service involves choosing lessons and psalms other than those provided in the Lectionary and Table of Proper Psalms. This is certainly justified at times, and is, indeed, done by authority on National occasions, but otherwise, quite apart from its impropriety, it is unwise to mutilate the Lectionary, which aims at continuous readings throughout the year. It is very easy to revolve round a few favourite lessons.[2] The liturgical way is to find the thought that ties the lessons, or the Collect, Epistle and Gospel together, and to make that the subject of the hymns and address. A revision of the Lectionary for an experimental period has been provided by Convocations, which should go some way to meet the difficulties of the times.[3]

The one-theme service is both impressive and effective, but it must not be overdone, or the laity will become so used to the method as to find it tedious. In such a service there can also be a bareness of thought; much richer is that which has its associated themes partly developed, without liturgical improprieties, by bringing into the prayers the themes raised earlier in the different parts of the service.

One practical point of difficulty lies in the choice of hymns to harmonize with the subject of the address. Sermons are not always ready so long ahead that the choice of hymns can be made in time for the choir rehearsals. A planned scheme of sermons over a period will allow for a general choice of hymns, but it is sometimes necessary to modify the selection at the last minute; even planning must be subject to second thoughts.

One other variation that can be made is the position of the sermon, the place of which, except in the Holy Communion Service, is not fixed by the Prayer Book. For teaching purposes, the sermon might be at any time during the service—after one of the lessons, for example—(after the second lesson is the right place for catechizing), or for devotional purposes it should be before the 'second Prayers' and naturally introduce them. Teaching on some aspect of prayer can thus be illustrated at once. The usual place

---

[1] Francis Underhill, *The Revival of Worship*, p. 29.
[2] C. S. Lewis, *The Screwtape Letters*, 1942, p. 83. (An oft-quoted passage.)
[3] *The Amended Lectionary for Sundays and Certain Holy Days*, 1944.

of the sermon is much too late to gain the whole attention of the people, yet it can be argued that when the sermon is strictly 'preaching' the declaration of the Word and the evangelistic message, then it fittingly forms the climax of the service.

(b) *Psalms and Lessons*. There is a movement for a return to the singing of all the set psalms for the day. The monthly recitation of the psalms at the daily offices is excellent, but on Sundays psalms suitable for the day are a more likely aid to devotion.[1] The fact that the day is Rogation Sunday is surely more important than the fact that it is the 29th day of May.[2] The psalms are certainly not popular among the laity as a whole.

For the lessons, the Lectionary should be followed, but often those provided are too long.[3] The experience of broadcasting has shown that people's minds are not capable of sustained attention, and if services are made too long they will be badly attended. Difficult lessons require introductions, which should be very brief; to guard against verbosity, a short, succinct sentence should be written down beforehand. A loose-leaf book, or a set of cards in the index, with these sentences entered, can be a perpetual commentary on the lessons, which can be revised, from time to time, in the light of further meditation. The book or card can be taken to church with the sermon. The cards, if used, should be filed behind the appropriate cards for the Sundays of the Year.[4] There are books that provide introductions.[5] Psalms can also be introduced in a similar way, but there is a danger of turning the service into a running commentary; it can be done occasionally and with discretion. All introductions can be banned for a period with profit.

(c) *Prayers*. Perhaps more attention is needed in preparing for the prayers than for any other of the variable parts of the service. The priest can so easily forget that he has a congregation. People like prayer to be real, spontaneous and related to life, but "few people catch the full meaning of a new prayer for the first time".[6]

---

[1] G. W. Ireson, *Church Worship and the Non-Churchgoer*, 1944, p. 115.

[2] P. Dearmer, *The Parson's Handbook*, 1940, p. 229. The oldest custom is to have special psalms.

[3] W. K. Lowther Clarke, *The Prayer Book of 1928 Reconsidered*, 1943, p. 6.

[4] See above, Chapter III, § 2 (*b*) and § 3 (*a*).

[5] W. K. Lowther Clarke, *The Prayer Book of 1928 Reconsidered*, 1943, p. 7. In a footnote he says, " Dr. Hunkin is primarily academic and scholarly; Dr. Hardman reduces the words to the barest minimum; Dr. Chavasse introduces an evangelistic and devotional touch. The two latter include summaries of the Psalms ". H. F. D. Sparks, *The Old Testament in the Christian Church*, 1944, p. 110, arguments against such introductions.

[6] J. B. Goodliffe, *A Parson and his Problems*, p. 57.

M

On the other hand, time-honoured phrases in the well-known prayers have in the minds of the laity associations of much inspiration and force. So the priest must combine the old and the new, and the new must be repeated until it become familiar and old.[1] Four warnings by Dr. Dearmer are well worth quoting:

"(1) The familiar prayers should often be used as well as new ones; (2) The intercessions should not be too long; the time occupied by four (or five) collects is a good limit; (3) Care must be taken that new prayers especially are everywhere audible; (4) The congregation can follow much better if there is a bidding before each prayer (as is provided in the [1928] Book)." [2]

Sometimes a short litany with a response in which the congregation can join is appreciated and a slightly longer time allowed. A very short period of silence can come in the prayers; one minute to the laity seems like five, but the silence is really liked and used by them. These 'prayers after the Third Collect' can be taken from the back of the nave, a position that helps the people to feel the corporateness of the prayers and that, incidentally, is a good and justifiable place for the Litany-desk. They should be read standing up, the wisest thing to do when reading prayers, even in the chancel, except when ordered otherwise.[3]

The choice of prayers must be made before the service, otherwise they will be unbalanced, unrelated to the service, too long, or a repetition of those used a week before. The lack of preparation will be obvious to the congregation when there is a long gap between, "Let us pray for . . ." and the subject chosen. A loose-leaf book of prayers from various sources, compiled by the priest, is most useful here.[4] In it he can enter suitable litanies, and any of his own best efforts of writing collects or prayers. The various prayers issued by societies for use on their special Sundays are also conveniently filed or entered in this book.[5]

(d) *Music and Hymns.* The music, as much as anything may be said to do so, will make or mar a service, and though the choirmaster is the incumbent's deputy in this department, the parish

[1] G. W. Ireson, *Church Worship and the Non-Churchgoer*, p. 11. A comparison of some new prayers with those of the Prayer Book.

[2] P. Dearmer, *A Short Handbook of Public Worship*, p. 18.

[3] *Ibid.*, p. 18. Cf. *The Parson's Handbook*, p. 236; A. L. Preston, *The Parish Priest in his Parish*, 1933, pp. 22, 23.

[4] See above, Chapter IV, § 3.

[5] The various compilations of prayers are too numerous and well-known to require mention here; *Daily Prayer*, Edited by E. Milner-White and G. W. Briggs (Oxford, 1941), is specially commended.

priest must always give it due consideration, and, of course, has complete control.[1] Cathedrals are the home of English Church Music, but the services suitable for a cathedral are not always suitable for a parish church. The church services should always be congregational, and the first task of the choir is to render the services perfectly in leading the people, before anything elaborate is performed.

"Our congregations will sit happily while occasional anthems are sung and find their hearts really raised to God. But few of them seem to enjoy standing, with or without books in their hands, while elaborate Creed, *Gloria, Te Deum, Magnificat,* or *Nunc Dimittis* is being sung."[2]

But whatever music is sung, it must be of the best, and the people who can hear the best sung on the wireless will become very critical judges.[3]

In the music of the service the choirmaster can have no better guide than the "Royal School of Church Music". The Principles and Recommendations are admirable, although they cannot all be achieved at once. Several of the Recommendations are concerned with the actual arrangement of the service, and help in the development of a uniform English use. The *Notes and Comments on the Principles and Recommendations,* by Sir Sydney Nicholson, published in book form by the School in 1941, is indispensable. Other suggestions are to be found in the Report of the Archbishops' Committee on *Music in Worship,* 1922; in Percy Dearmer, *The Parson's Handbook,* 1940, pp. 189–195; and in L. S. Hunter, *A Parson's Job,* 1931, Chapter VII.

If there is a monthly conference between parish priest and choirmaster the programme of hymns can be so planned that new ones are introduced from time to time and are repeated often enough to allow the congregation to learn them. If people were more regular at services it would be easier to do this. Many new hymns from the best hymn-books can be introduced over the course of a few years, without dropping old and familiar favourites, though some must without comment disappear completely.[4] Controversy over new hymns does arise from time to time, and tact and sympathy are needed for progress. In the North of England

[1] See above, Chapter VI, § 2 (*b*).
[2] Francis Underhill, *The Revival of Worship,* pp. 37 f.
[3] "If we cannot sing in tune, and many excellent parish priests cannot, then for mercy's sake do not let us try to sing the priest's part in the service."—A. L. Preston, *The Parish Priest in his Parish,* 1933, p. 20.
[4] See P. M. Barry, *A Present for the Vicar,* 1945, Chapter VI.

the publication of Whitsuntide hymn-sheets is a welcomed aid to the provision of new hymns and tunes. Needless to say, the closest co-operation is necessary between the priest and the choirmaster, who cannot be expected to put on a new tune when warned only just before the service. A danger is the repeating of the favourite hymns of the priest or the choirmaster to the exclusion of the people's favourites. A wide range of hymns should be allowed. To help to attain this, all choir-lists should be kept for two years for reference. But it is better still—and easier—to make a record in an exercise book, noting each hymn, its tune as sung in church, whether known, to be learnt, or never to be sung; and adding columns for each year, in which to enter the dates when it is sung. Three minutes on Monday will keep it up to date; later inspection reveals many surprises.

(e) *Several Ministers.* A single priest can arrange the service to his heart's content to obtain a single theme, and make all parts of the service in keeping with the address. When more than one share in the service, the planning is not so simple. Yet a service is much more inspiring when two or three voices take a part in it.[1] The different parts of the service can be allocated at a weekly staff meeting, but the entities of the service should be observed. At Matins or Evensong, the Introduction could be by one, the ' sung part ', the lessons, the second prayers, and the sermon, by others, or in various combinations. Everyone's part must be quite clear, " though too often it is quite obvious that none of them has given a moment's thought to it till the last minute in the vestry, and the ministrants are all at cross purposes ".[2] One priest should set the general theme of the service. A warning is needed because each ministrant tends to make the most of his part if he has free choice, and though this is natural, the balance of the service is upset. If all a minister has to do is to take the prayers or read the lesson, he will make them, unconsciously, twice as long as he should.

§ 5. Summary of Preparation

At the Staff Meeting beforehand the share of each minister in the service is arranged.[3] The choirmaster has already been provided with the list of hymns and psalms for rehearsal.[4] On

---

[1] P. Dearmer, *A Short Handbook to Public Worship,* pp. 13 ff. Cf. *The Parson's Handbook,* p. 239.
[2] F. R. Barry, *The Relevance of the Church,* 1935, p. 149.
[3] See above, § 4 (*e*) and Chapter V, § 5.
[4] See above, § 4 (*d*).

Saturday morning each member of the staff will review his work for the next day. (If the Staff Meeting is on Saturday, this work will be done together.) Sermons should by now be prepared and need only revision. When the Service of Communion is of elaborate form, any details for Sunday must be considered; certainly the Collect, Epistle and Gospel must be read,[1] and might well be the basis of devotional preparation. Biddings for the Holy Communion will be prepared in view of special intentions or topical events. The lessons [2] will be read over, and introductory notes prepared where necessary, and the prayers for Matins and Evensong selected. The Notices [3] will be written, the Service Register Prepared, and the Banns entered.[4] The official responsible will prepare the Holy Table, and any vestments, according to the ecclesiastical season.[5]

It is also necessary, unfortunately, for the incumbent to make notes·for the people he wishes to see on the Sunday, and to sort out messages or letters that may have arrived for various officials. Sunday is often the only day when these officials can easily be seen.

On devotional and disciplinary grounds, a wise priest will be at church at least fifteen minutes before every Sunday service—and the weekday celebration—in order to say his prayers. If he is, he will immediately perceive when an unforeseen hitch has occurred, and there will be time to cope with it. Sometimes voluntary officials are missing without warning, and then the priest must make arrangements to meet the situation.

Afterwards, perhaps on Monday, records, such as any special service-sheet, notes prepared for lessons, special prayers, sermons, can be filed or card indexed, the hymn register completed,[6] and any other notes of hints for future services recorded.[7]

[1] See above, § 4 (a).   [2] See above, § 4 (b).
[3] See above, Chapter VI, § 3 (b).   [4] Ibid., § 1 (b).
[5] Ibid., § 2 (d).   [6] See above, § 4 (d).
[7] According to the methods described in Part I.

SELECT BIBLIOGRAPHY

Proctor and Frere, *A New History of the Book of Common Prayer*, 1905.
W. K. Lowther Clarke (Ed.), *Liturgy and Worship*, 1932.
J. P. Hodges, *The Riches of Our Prayer Book*, 1941.
Henry De Candole, *The Church's Offering*.
Henry De Candole, *The Church's Prayers*, 1939.
Evelyn Underhill, *Worship*, 1936.
Towards the Conversion of England, 1945, pp. 134–143.
Percy Dearmer, *The Parson's Handbook*, 1940.
Percy Dearmer, *A Short Handbook to Public Worship*, 1931.
Percy Dearmer, *The Art of Public Worship*, 1920.

W. H. Frere, *The Principles of Religious Ceremonial*, 1928.
Oxford Diocesan Service Book, 1920.
P. M. Barry, *A Present for the Vicar*, 1945.
W. K. Lowther Clarke, *The Prayer Book of 1928 Reconsidered*, 1943.
R. S. T. Haslehurst, *How to Read the Bible Aloud*, 1938.
W. G. Ireson, *Church Worship and the Non-Churchgoer*, 1944.
L. S. Hunter, *A Parson's Job*, 1931, Chapters III, IV, V, and VII.
Sydney Nicholson, *Principles and Recommendations of the School of English Church Music*, 1941.
Archbishops' Committee, *Music in Worship*, 1922.
D. E. W. Harrison, *The Book of Common Prayer*, 1946.
M. A. C. Warren, *Strange Victory*, 1946.

CHAPTER XIV

PAROCHIAL EVANGELISM

§ 1. The Necessity of Evangelism

(a) *The Danger of Efficiency.* Referring yet once again to the definition of parochial administration, its aim is, in part, to secure that the laity of the parish may " express a living, happy fellowship or family in the Body of Christ, both in its worship of God and in its witness to the world." [1] The business of worship should naturally lead to witness, but the final objective often seems to lie out of reach, and indeed is often forgotten altogether. Parochial administration, concerned as it is with all aspects of parish work, can be destroyed by its own efficiency. The parish can become like a machine, the running of which is an end in itself. The working of the Church Council, the burden of finances, the care of the church and hall, and even the maintenance of worship, are all complex enough to occupy the time of a busy parish priest and the energies of busy laymen. Says Archbishop Temple, ". . . we are greatly absorbed, perhaps inevitably, in maintaining the life of a congregation that is already secure, and not thinking very much about those who are completely detached." [2] If a parish pays its diocesan quota, if its missionary contributions are considerable, and if acts of Communion are many, then that parish is high in the estimation of the powers that be. The missionary test is not a bad one, but even then it must be remembered that the organization which can make a parish ' pay ' can easily provide for an item for missions without being particularly missionary-hearted.

Parochial administration must be tested not so much in the efficiency of the machinery as in the results that follow from it, and these must be found in the fellowship of the community, the worthiness of the worship, and the spread of the Kingdom.

(b) *The Nature of Evangelism.* The spread of the Kingdom is achieved by Evangelism. The words of Archbishop Temple already quoted indicate the direction in which the Kingdom must spread— to " those who are completely detached." In the same context the Archbishop strengthens his theme by asserting: " The preoccupa-

[1] See above, Chapter I, § 2 (a).   [2] *Evangelism* (S.P.C.K.), 1937, p. 2.

tion of the Church should be with those outside." [1] Evangelism
is definitely concerned with those outside, and is thus one of the
main duties of the Church. Before the War, Evangelism was the
subject of the hour, and probably it was more talked about than
performed. Nevertheless much of the research done cleared
Evangelism of the accusation of being vague. The definition given
by the Archbishops' Commission that reported in 1918 on the
subject, can be the basis of the theory and practice of Evangelism. [2]

> " To evangelize is so to present Christ Jesus in the power
> of the Holy Spirit, that men shall come to put their trust in
> God through Him; to accept Him as their Saviour, and to
> serve Him as their King in the fellowship of His Church."

Here it is clear that the message of Evangelism is Christ and his
Gospel. Most books on Evangelism recognize this, and begin by
asking, " What is the Gospel? " [3] If the Gospel is anything, it is
certainly the proclamation of a revelation by God which demands a
response, but which is independent of that response. Dr. Max
Warren writes, [4]

> " To sum up, then, the Gospel is essentially a proclamation
> by God Himself of Himself. It is in itself a message of good
> news apart from any response man may choose to make, it is
> the offer of forgiveness or restoration to fellowship. *It is a word
> spoken* in a language that even a child could understand.
> Once the nature of the Evangel is seen to be just that, nothing
> less and nothing more, we can begin to see what Evangelism is.
> It is the effective mediation of the Evangel by the Society of
> the Divine Forgiveness which exists for the two-fold purpose of
> responding to the love of God and diffusing the knowledge of it."

The beginning of the definition also makes clear that Evangelism
is something that must be done in the power of the Holy Spirit.
No amount of planning, and no experiments with methods, will
succeed unless they are approached in the spirit of prayer and with a
sense of guidance. The danger of Evangelism becoming just another
stunt is always present.

The message of Evangelism is presented with a purpose—that of
securing for all men four things in succession: faith in God,
acceptance of a Saviour, service to a King, and a joining in fellowship. These four things correspond to the traditional four stages
in the conversion of an outsider: the response, crossing the line,

[1] *Evangelism* (S.P.C.K.), 1937, p. 2.
[2] Quoted in *Evangelism, Way of Renewal Paper*, No. 22, p. 5.
[3] Cf. H. A. Jones, *Evangelism and the Laity*, 1937, pp. 29 ff. A good exposition
is given in *Towards the Conversion of England*, 1945, Chapter II.
[4] M. A. C. Warren, *Interpreters*, 1936, p. 12.

declaratory acts, entry into the fellowship.[1] Some people, however, are drawn first into the fellowship and serve the King before they are brought to accept the Saviour, and for that reason it is always necessary to bring the church congregation within the scope of Evangelism. But conversion is different for different people; for some it is a sharp break in life, for others it is a continual, wonderful experience all through life. So Evangelism must recognize the different types that need conversion.[2]

When the message and purpose of Evangelism are grasped, the possible methods can be considered, and here the difficulties begin. In the definition the methods are implied in the word " so," " So to present," and much of the discussion about Evangelism has turned on the question of the suitability of age-long methods for use in the world as it is to-day. The difficulties of preaching Christ to-day lie in the circumstances of the times in which we live. Most people are hardened to the Gospel because they have received a weak version of Christianity diffused through the day schools, and perhaps through the Sunday schools, and it has acted as inoculation against a disease would act. Those outside the Church imagine that they are familiar with Christianity, and are not so much hostile as indifferent. Life is very full in these days, and many things compete with the Gospel for a claim on the attention of the people, who in addition live in an atmosphere created by the prevalent Humanism and the New Morality, and into whose minds the " acids of modernity " have eaten deep. When human thought is mass-produced, the presentation of a Gospel to individuals begins at a disadvantage.

Archbishop Temple held that the Church should be concerned with the state not only of men's minds but also of their bodies. Evangelism must begin with things which people can understand, and the only thing that many of them can understand is their bread and butter, or the lack of it. The Social Gospel is therefore an important part of the evangelistic approach.

" For I am convinced that in this period of history social witness is an indispensable instrument of Evangelism. We cannot obtain a hearing for our primary message if with regard to the evils of which men are chiefly conscious we have to say that for these it contains no remedy. We must first find where men are, and then, taking them by the hand, lead them to the true source of power and peace." [3]

[1] Cf. *Evangelism* (S.P.C.K.), 1937, pp. 15, 24–30.
[2] *Way of Renewal* Pamphlet, No. 22, pp. 21, 17–18.
[3] William Temple, *Social Witness and Evangelism*, 1943, p. 7.

This is the whole argument of the Archbishop's Beckly Lecture, and the summary of his argument at the end of the lecture [1] is very cogent.

Another approach to the problem of Evangelism is discussed by Dr. Welch in his ' Foreword ' to *The Man Born to be King*, in which he speaks of the difficulties of religious broadcasting. Apart from those who approve of religious broadcasts, the others—double their number—

> " were unmoved and usually unreached by this conventional presentation. Of them, in general, we felt we could say (a) the dimension we call ' God ' has largely vanished from their lives; they had discovered that it was possible and easy to live without any vital belief in God; God was no longer a factor to be reckoned with in making decisions; He did not count at all: (b) the language of religion had lost most, and for some people all, its meaning: especially was this true of the language of the Authorised Version: (c) everywhere there was great ignorance of the Christian faith: . . . (d) there was a widespread dissatisfaction with materialism, a feeling after a spiritual interpretation of life and an almost unanimous consensus of opinion that in the man Jesus lay the key to many of the riddles of life." [2]

This analysis, though still pointing out the difficulties, brings in a note of hope by saying that people are ready for a spiritual interpretation of life. This is a new and welcome note, and it was lacking in the similar analyses of a decade ago.[3] Here, however, it is necessary to notice that Dorothy Sayers' play was an attempt, and a very good attempt, at Evangelism in a way that was both modern and mass-produced. Such new methods must be the concern of the leaders of the Church;[4] the ordinary parish priest has little except the old weapons for use in his parish against the difficulties of a new age, but such weapons are by no means to be despised.

But besides the winning of souls to Christ, it must be realized that the Church must be prepared to receive them. Evangelism is a high responsibility: only those who are fit can undertake the task.

---

[1] William Temple, *Social Witness and Evangelism*, 1943, p. 17.
[2] Dorothy Sayers, *The Man Born to be King*, 1943, p. 11.
[3] Cf. A. E. J. Rawlinson, *The Church and the Challenge of To-day*, 1937, Chapter II; T. W. Pym, *A Parson's Dilemmas*, 1930, Chapters I and II; and G. K. A. Bell, *The Modern Parson*, 1928, Chapters I and II. See also, F. R. Barry, *The Relevance of Christianity*, 1931, Chapters I and II. For an analysis of the present time, see *Towards the Conversion of England*, 1945, Chapter I.
[4] *Special Report on Evangelism*, 1944, pp. 6–10, for suggestions of methods from ' above '.

The Church must be a happy fellowship in the Body of Christ, so that those newly-won members of the Body may feel at home in it.[1] Further, the preparation of the newly-won in Christian worship is an important part in their reception.[2]

At this juncture it is necessary to notice the connection between Evangelism and education. Education is the handmaid of Evangelism. The instruction of the children, and of adults, in the faith must always continue; it both prepares the ground for the evangelistic appeal and provides the best method of the ' follow-up '— a process robbed of its importance by the lack of a suitable name. Educational methods are the subject of later chapters; here it must be said that they are no substitute for Evangelism.[3]

(c) *The Evangelists*. Upon whom lies the task of Evangelism? It is beginning to be recognized that this is no longer merely the concern of the clergy, but that the laity are also vitally implicated. But it is still the great concern of the clergy. The Ordinal of the Church of England teaches that every priest has not only " to teach and premonish, to feed and provide for the Lord's family ", but also " to seek for Christ's sheep that are dispersed abroad and for His children who are in the midst of this naughty world that they may be saved through Christ for ever ". Some priests certainly have the gifts of an evangelist above others, and the expert is needed to guide and counsel others, and sometimes to lead special evangelistic campaigns. But every parson should know something of the aim, the theory and the methods of Evangelism, and should make it a recurrent study.[4]

But it is right that the laity should be called to aid in the task of Evangelism. Some parishioners will have a natural bent in that way, and an enthusiasm for souls, but it must be shown that the duty of Evangelism, like the duty of worship, is to be shared by all the laity. The Church Councils Powers Act makes this clear in the celebrated clause:[5]

" It is the primary duty of the parochial church council in every parish to co-operate with the incumbent in the initiation,

---

[1] See above, Chapter VII.
[2] See above, Chapter XIII, § 1 (c); and G. W. Ireson, *Church Worship and the Non-Churchgoer*, 1944.
[3] Cf. A. E. J. Rawlinson, *The Church and the Challenge of To-day*, 1937, pp. 40–58; M. A. C. Warren, *Interpreters*, 1936, pp. 84–98; and H. A. Jones, *Evangelism and the Laity*, 1937, pp. 80–94.
[4] Much help can be found in the *Way of Renewal Paper* No. 22, and in *Evangelism* (S.P.C.K.), 1937, pp. 21–22. A more thorough exposition is given in *Towards the Conversion of England*, Chapters II and IV. See especially, " The Training of the Clergy in Evangelism ", pp. 45–48.
[5] See above, Chapter IX, § 1.

conduct and development of the work of the Church, both within the parish and outside."

In some Dioceses, notably in the Diocese of Leicester, the Church Councillors have been brought to face their responsibilities. In Leicester a series of conferences was held which produced valuable findings and led to much good work. But, generally speaking, members of the Church Council do not seem to be concerned that so many parishioners do not come to church, and would probably stare very hard at them if they did.[1] Canon Peter Green insists that if a parish is to have a Mission, the Church Council must be ready for it, or it will fail. He mentions a Church Council at which, at the suggestion of a Mission, everyone said it would be unnecessary if everybody else did their work better. " No one wanted to do anything. Everyone was sure that the fault lay elsewhere." [2]

This is the kind of response that many incumbents receive if they mention a Mission to the Church Council. Nevertheless the Council must be taught gradually that Evangelism is one of the main reasons for its existence. The work of training can be begun by having an Evangelistic Committee as well as Committees for Finance and Schools. This can be formed from the keenest members of the Council, with other keen laymen co-opted, and it should report to the Council from time to time to remind the parent body of its obligations. Such a committee can give invaluable help to the priest both with advice and in the active sharing of evangelistic work.[3]

§ 2. EVANGELISM THROUGH ROUTINE WORK

A Mission, or some other special campaign, is not the only weapon of Evangelism, but much of the best Evangelism is done in the routine work of the parish. Even a mission needs both preparation and ' follow-up ' in conjunction with parochial routine. Indeed, it is a mistake to think of Evangelism as consisting in method, for " Evangelism is not a list of certain things to be done, but the spirit in which they are done. . . . It is . . . an attitude of mind towards God and the world." [4] The evangelistic spirit is the right basis for all parochial work, the desire to win souls for Christ, and to train them in the fellowship, although it is true, as Professor Rogers

---

[1] Cf. H. A. Jones, *Evangelism and the Laity*, 1937, pp. 72–75; and *Evangelism* (S.P.C.K.), pp. 37–43.

[2] Peter Green, *The Man of God*, p. 198.

[3] *Towards the Conversion of England*, pp. 50–63, " The Part of the Laity in Evangelism ".

[4] *Evangelism* (S.P.C.K.), p. 8; *Towards the Conversion of England*, p. 41.

taught long ago, that there is a distinction within parochial work between the pastoral and the evangelistic elements, which must not be confused.[1]

It is convenient to mention here the various aspects of parochial work, to indicate their evangelistic use, and to give references to various books in which the subjects are more fully discussed.

(a) *Within the Church.* The evangelistic note should always be present in the services of the Church.

(i) Worship.—The Gospel message of the Incarnation and the Atonement is portrayed in the services, particularly in the Eucharist. See above, Chapter XIII; Warren,[2] pp. 23-38; Jones,[3] pp. 109-119; C.A., 773,[4] pp. 134-142, 42.

(ii) Preaching.—Here is the supreme method of Evangelism. The pulpit should be used both for preaching and teaching, and in this distinction Professor Dodd has helped many during the last decade with his analysis of Apostolic Preaching.[5] Definite Church teaching and instruction is needed from the pulpit, but so is also the proclamation of the Gospel message issued as a challenge to souls. See Warren,[2] pp. 39-53; Jones,[3] pp. 32-34; C.A. 773,[4] pp. 42-43; and below § 3 (a).

(iii) Occasional Services.—People are more than half ready to listen at weddings, baptisms and funerals. See *Evangelism* (S.P.C.K.), p. 108; C.A. 773, pp. 43-45; and below, Chapter XXIII.

(b) *Within the Parish.* But Evangelism is directed more towards the outsiders, beyond the immediate range of the congregation.

(i) Pastoral Visits.—The original purpose of visiting was to help people with their spiritual lives, but to-day most people are in a much more elementary stage. Visits to those with an indefinite connection with a church should be evangelistic in purpose, though it might be necessary to make several visits to prepare the ground. See below, Chapter XXI, and C.A. 773, p. 43.

(ii) The Organizations.—In the Mothers' Union, the Men's Society and the Youth Organizations are often many who come very little or not at all to church. Their programmes should include from time to time talks leading to a challenge. In Confirmation the young people should definitely be given the Challenge of Christ. Youth work lends itself to Evangelism, and young people

[1] C. F. Rogers, *Principles of Parish Work*, 1905, p. 121.
[2] M. A. C. Warren, *Interpreters*.
[3] H. A. Jones, *Evangelism and the Laity*.
[4] *Towards the Conversion of England*, 1945.
[5] C. H. Dodd, *The Apostolic Preaching and its Development*, 1936.

will respond to the call to help in the work, but adolescence should not be exploited. See *Evangelism* (S.P.C.K.), pp. 61–73; and below Chapters XVI, XVII, and XXII. Also C.A. 773, pp. 92–96.

(iii) Cells.—Many urge that the method of the ' leaven ' or the ' cell ' is the only way to see the Kingdom grow, and they would suggest the formation of small groups for prayer, or for Bible study. Such cells can be the mainspring of Evangelism within the parish. See above, Chapter VII, § 4; compare Chapter XVII, § 4 (b), and C.A. 773, pp. 69–72.

(c) *Specialized Directions.* Just on the borders of parochial routine are special methods that may be adopted for shorter or longer periods.

(i) Local Contacts.—Routine work in the mills, factories, hotels, hospitals, barracks, transport departments and the like is a fruitful sphere for finding souls in need of the Gospel. The people in such places need more than mere pastoral care; dinner-hour talks may open up possibilities of study circles and more direct Evangelism. An I.C.F. Crusade will often prepare the way for work of this nature. See below, Chapter XX, § 4 (d), and C.A. 773, pp. 64–65.

(ii) Religious Drama.—The presentation of a Passion Play in Lent can be the means of proclaiming the Gospel in pictorial form to those who come to see their relatives on the stage. It can also have a profound impression upon the members of the caste, who are brought into a living contact with the Gospel in this way. For practical suggestions, see Irene Caudwell, *The Care of God's House*, 1943, pp. 59–60; G. W. Ireson, *Church Worship and the Non-Church-goer*, 1944. Chapter VI; and see below, Chapter XVI, § 4 (d).

(iii) Educational Methods.—The various means adopted for the instruction of the flock all have their evangelistic side, such as the Parish Magazine, Religious Films, Lantern Lectures. The Church Bookrack can also be considered from this point of view. A Sunday lecture with no service is recommended by Canon Pym. See T. W. Pym, *A Parson's Dilemmas*, 1930, pp. 76–80; and below, Chapters XVII and XVIII.

§ 3. EVANGELISTIC CAMPAIGNS

In addition to the routine work, special campaigns can have an important place in the parochial programme, and if the time for them is well chosen, a good man or a good team secured, and real preparation is made, then such campaigns are a source of infinite blessings.

(a) *Parochial Missions.* This time-honoured method of Evangelism is often the one most stigmatized as being out of date. The technique needs revision every decade, but as a method it is without equal. It has been used by men of all varieties of churchmanship. Canon Peter Green,[1] a well-known missioner of long experience, who has often urged the importance of many more men undertaking work of this kind, points out that there are two good reasons for missions. The first is quite simply that there are very many people in this country who are not converted, and only a mission will reach them. The second is that missions are a great stimulus to the clergy, both to those who are missioners and to those in whose parishes the missions are held. It is a real tonic to see the spiritual power of God in action.

Dr. Max Warren sets out three principles for Evangelism—namely, conviction, co-operation, and careful ' follow-up.' [2] These three principles are made by Canon Green into rules for Parochial Missions; the missioner must know his message and lead to decision, the mission must be congregational, and the mission should be followed up. That the missioner should know his message is obvious, for otherwise he cannot declare the Gospel, the necessity of Evangelism. The mission must be congregational, on the one hand because it is wrong and futile to thrust a mission on an unwilling congregation, and on the other hand because team work and co-operation add to the strength of the mission. Christianity demands team-work because it is a fellowship. The congregation fellowship must be expressed in any mission. Finally, ' follow-up ' as a necessary principle could be taken for granted if it were not so often overlooked. The mission is a beginning, not an end, and the decision of a convert is his beginning in the Christian life.

> " The end of the Society is not evangelism but worship. To train men for the activity of worship is not part of the work of an evangelist, but it is most certainly part of the work of the Church. The follow-up of the evangelistic task is training in worship, without which evangelism is simply abortive." [3]

Plans for ' follow-up ' work must be in the programme from the beginning of the preparations, and not left to chance ideas when the mission is over.

Very much work and preparation go to the making of a successful

[1] Peter Green, *The Man of God*, pp. 165–200.
[2] M. A. C. Warren, *Interpreters*, pp. 127–142.
[3] *Ibid.*, p. 140.

mission, and those who undertake it should understand very clearly the nature of their task.[1]

(b) *Open-Air Work*. Though enumerated under special campaigns, open-air work could be made part of the routine of every summer. There are different types of outside work which can be undertaken—the Christian Evidence type, the Christian Worship type, and the Christian Witness type—and each type has its own technique. The right times and pitches must be selected for all these. The worship type is sometimes called extended ' evensong,' and the clergy robed with the choir lead the congregation out to witness in worship.[2]

A Good Friday " Procession of Witness " can, especially when a co-operative effort of several churches, be very effective. The procession stops at various pitches for a hymn and a short talk, and ends with a United Service in one of the churches.

(c) *The Work of the Laity*. In examining the necessity of Evangelism, stress was laid upon the importance of the laity's share in this great task. Indeed, without the laity evangelistic campaigns are likely to fail. Canon Green, who has thoroughly faced this problem, says that it is the weakness of the Church of England that she has not made full use of the lay people. " The job of the clergy is first to collect a congregation of converts, instructed, and missionary-hearted people. Secondly, to set the congregation to work." [3] He goes on to say in a celebrated sentence, " Until you have got a man down on his knees and up on his feet to speak, you have got nowhere in using him." [4]

How are the laity to be used? In the first place comes the creation of the right atmosphere in the Church Council, so that the whole Council is keen to fulfil its primary purpose. Much depends on the incumbent inviting the co-operation of the Council, and on his taking the members into his confidence about his plans for the spiritual welfare of the parishioners. But there is much hard work for any parish priest who would share his spiritual work with his Church Council.[5]

It is, however, quite within the capabilities of most lay people to undertake the various types of visitation, although they are usually shy of it. In town parishes the task of adequate visitation is quite

---

[1] Cf. *Evangelism* (S.P.C.K.), pp. 51–60; *Towards the Conversion of England*, pp. 72–81.

[2] T. W. Pym, *A Parson's Dilemmas*, 1930, pp. 71–76. Cf. *Evangelism* (S.P.C.K.), pp. 74–88.

[3] *Evangelism* (S.P.C.K.), p. 34.

[4] *Ibid.*, p. 34.   [5] *Ibid.*, pp. 37–43.

beyond the most energetic clergy. The administrative side only involves the division of the parish into suitable areas of streets,[1] over which could be a 'divisional' officer. The first stage is visiting for information, sick cases, Sunday School scholars and the names of church people not already on the church's lists, and sometimes obtaining magazine customers. The next stage is more definitely evangelistic—trying to get people to church or special services, or seeking opportunities of talking to them with a view to leading up to real subjects. During the War our towns were divided up into areas and sectors for Civil Defence purposes, and A.R.P. Wardens visited houses for all kinds of purposes, testing gas masks, gathering information, and organizing street fire-fighting parties. It was all very natural; the purpose was clear and understood. Those same wardens would, many of them, make good Church visitors.[2]

A further stage is getting the lay people to speak, and for this there are many varied opportunities. News teams, giving simple personal witness, have been sponsored successfully by the Church Army, and in the Teams lay people can speak in halls, churches or in the open air. The lay people work better in teams, and, in visiting, two are better working together. Two or three can form little teams for cottage meetings, which can be held where a hostess can be found to invite in a few of her neighbours. Some lay people can certainly be trained for more direct speaking for evangelistic purposes. An excellent use of the team spirit, begun by Canon Green,[3] but used with great success in many places,[4] can be adopted in Lent. Each week subjects following a certain theme are given by the different parochial organizations, each adopting its own method of presentation. Many people are thus actively brought into direct contact with evangelism.

But for all these evangelistic methods the lay people must be trained, and the parish priest can do no better work than preparing the keen lay people for their evangelistic task. Various methods may be adopted to suit the particular circumstances; some must be with individuals, but the team spirit can be cultivated from the beginning. Weekly meetings, or week-end conferences, to discuss the purpose of the work and the technique of the methods, and above all for the sharing in the fellowship of prayer, are essential parts of the training programme.[5] This work can be linked up with the

[1] See below, Chapter XXI, § 2 (a).   [2] Evangelism, pp. 45, 46.
[3] Peter Green, The Man of God, pp. 157–163.
[4] Evangelism, pp. 35, 50.
[5] Ibid., pp. 47–49; C.A. 773, pp. 50–63; H. A. Jones, Evangelism and the Laity, pp. 77–79.

N

parochial educational programme,[1] and on the devotional side can be the beginning of a real spiritual ' cell.',

(d) *Interdenominational Work and Crusades.* There is much to be said on either side about the value of co-operation among denominations in Evangelism. The co-operative witness of all the churches has a big appeal, and in a self-contained area a procession of witness is best as a united affair. United missions need careful handling, for conversions must lead to church fellowship, and on a united platform it is meaningless to invite converts to join the Church. The only way in a united mission is for a preliminary meeting to divide up in denominations for meetings at the various pitches so that the appeal to join the church can be made.[2] For the proclamation of the social aspect of the Gospel interdenominational work is more profitable, as the ' Religion and Life Weeks ' showed. This is important work for the Church to undertake, as Dr. Temple has urged.[3] Those outside the Church are shown the meaning which Christianity has for life, and it has the effect of making people ask more about the Church which has such a splendid message.

The Crusades of the Industrial Christian Fellowship, inasmuch as they are denominational, combine the social message more effectively with Evangelism, since the whole can be presented with a sacramental view of life. Such campaigns are for a wider area than a parish; but they do give the parish priest an opportunity, not to say an excuse, for real, deep preparation in his own parish, and for sincere co-operation with his neighbours in a combined attack on the forces of evil.[4]

§ 4. The Place of Planning

Evangelistic efforts can easily fail for lack of adequate preparation and ' follow-up.' Nothing can be more fatal. Many lay people are ready to say that these things have been tried before and failed terribly. There is no detail too small to be carefully planned by those responsible.

For special campaigns the choice of a date is of first importance. It has to be considered in connection with the routine time-table, and with the local circumstances of holidays, wakes, feasts and elections. After the date has been fixed, the choice of missioner must be made, and he must be booked in good time. The details of the meetings

---

[1] See below, Chapter XVII.
[2] William Temple, *The Church Looks Forward*, 1944, p. 11.
[3] See above, § 1 (*b*).
[4] C.A. 773, pp. 80, 81, 96–99.

will be decided by the missioner in consultation with the incumbent. The preliminary visiting needs a careful survey of the streets, arrangements in suitable areas, the appointment of the lay visitors and the printing in good time of the necessary literature. For open-air work suitable sites must be selected with a view to the busyness of the spots and the absence of noise. Stewards, speakers, singers and possibly hand-organs are detailed for the right place at the right time on the right days. Hymn-sheets are liable to be forgotten; it can be somebody's special and only job.

Plans for the follow-up must be made before the campaign. If they are left to the end, ' to see what happens ', then there is no sign-post to direct the way to the future. Decision cards can be used, indicating different things that people can do, and care taken to see that all offers are recorded and used. Dates must be ready for the adult confirmation class which should be necessary. Bible and Prayer circles must be ready in embryo for the influx of members. Converts must be drafted into the different organizations, and not left to vague membership of the church at this critical stage in their lives. After a children's mission, Sunday Schools must be ready with facilities for new classes with teachers ready for them. Lack of preparation for a ' follow-up ' would indicate an expectation that the campaign will produce no results, and such would be the inevitable end.

Because it is a campaign of Evangelism, it is not necessary that it should be unbusinesslike. Dr. Warren quotes from John Foster's *The Chinese Church in Action*:

" In one great city of the coast all the churches recently co-operated in a special mission. The leaders in its organization were laymen, business men who had felt that Evangelism had never yet been businesslike enough. They had three hundred thousand handbills printed. One was delivered to every house and to every crowded tenement. . . ." [1]

The Western Church can learn its business ways from its Eastern sisters.

[1] M. A. C. Warren, *Interpreters*, p. 51 (Foster, p. 104).

SELECT BIBLIOGRAPHY

Evangelism, S.P.C.K., 1937.
Evangelism, Way of Renewal Paper, No. 22.
H. A. Jones, *Evangelism and the Laity*, 1937.
M. A. C. Warren, *Interpreters*, 1936.
William Temple, *Social Witness and Evangelism*, 1943.

A. E. J. Rawlinson, *The Church and the Challenge of Today*, 1937, Chapter II.
T. W. Pym, *A Parson's Dilemmas*, 1930, Chapters I, II, and IV.
G. K. A. Bell, *The Modern Parson*, 1928, Chapters I and II.
F. R. Barry, *The Relevance of Christianity*, 1931, Chapters I and II.
G. W. Ireson, *Church Worship and the Non-Churchgoer*, 1944.
Special Report on Evangelism, 1944. C.A. 730.
Peter Green, *The Man of God*, 1935, Chapter V.
Peter Green, *The Town Parson*, 1919, Chapter VI.
Peter Green, *Parochial Missions Today*.
P. C. A. Carnegy, *Our Fellowship in the Gospel*, 1944.
A. L. Preston, *The Parish Priest in his Parish*, 1933, Chapter V.
Towards the Conversion of England, C.A. 773, Archbishops' Commission Report, 1945.

This Report was published after the above chapter was written, so footnotes are used to indicate the sections of the Report relevant to the subject matter of the chapter. The Report is an excellent exposition of Evangelism and every student of Pastoralia should give it careful attention.

Evangelism and Youth, C.E.Y.C., 1945.

CHAPTER XV

PASTORAL WORK AMONG CHILDREN

§ 1. The Children

To every parish priest the care of the children in the parish is both a responsibility and a prized privilege. It is a delightful sphere of work, and often one of the most encouraging, for there is never any doubt about the response of the children. There are wide possibilities in pastoral work among the children, and it is primarily educational. But there is also the care of each child, individually and personally, and the true pastor will know them all by name and watch over the particular needs of each. The parson has to lead every one from Baptism to Confirmation, helping each tender soul to develop in its spiritual life, and to increase ' in wisdom and stature and in favour with God and man '.

The after-care of baptized infants and the preparation of the Confirmation candidates are subjects for other chapters.[1] In this chapter educational work through the Day and Sunday Schools claims chief attention, but it is also necessary to discuss the relation of the children to the Church, their missionary education, and also the provision that must be made for their recreation through secular activity connected with the schools and the church.

As in the leading of worship and in preaching, so in teaching the children, the parish priest has a unique position and responsibility. In such things as the syllabus of teaching and the grading the children in the Sunday School he has dictatorial powers, though of course, since he has to work through voluntary teachers, it will be wise for him to exercise these powers with tact and discretion. The Church Council has no authority to interfere; it is, however, a tremendous help to the incumbent when the Council takes an active interest in the work of the Day and Sunday schools, and makes it its duty to see that there are no hindrances from lack of financial support.

§ 2. The Day Schools

(a) *The Dual System.* Though it increases the work of an incumbent, a Church Day School in the parish is a valuable asset, but to

[1] See below, Chapters XXII and XXIII.

make full use of it involves far more than just visiting the school for teaching two or three times a week. It is essential that the incumbent should understand his part in the complicated control of the school under the Dual System.[1] In the Church Day Schools there is joint control of the education of the children. Whereas the County Schools are completely under the Local Education Authority, the Voluntary Schools, or Church Schools, are for certain purposes under the control of the Church managers. In these latter schools the Local Education Authority directs the secular work, but the managers appoint the teachers and caretakers, though the L.E.A. pays them, and the managers direct the religious instruction through the teachers. The school normally belongs to the parish, under a Trust which is responsible for the structure, though the cost of internal maintenance is shared with the L.E.A.

This brief statement is not intended to be exhaustive, but simply to indicate the complicated state of affairs. Unfortunately, the complications tend to increase rather than to diminish, and, whereas under the Education Act of 1921 all voluntary schools had the same rules, under the subsequent Acts of 1936 and 1944 such schools are placed in different classes according to the financial aid received in reconstruction and the methods of appointments are considerably modified. Every incumbent must have exact knowledge of powers and procedure under the various Acts, and therefore it is absolutely essential that he should keep up-to-date. Not all parishes have Day Schools, and a junior priest in such a parish should not wait until he is an incumbent in charge of a Day School before he begins to learn about the details of Day School management. He should at least have some idea of the duties of the chairman of the Managers, and know where to find the necessary information when any particular need arises.

(b) *The School Managers.* To quote the Education Act of 1921: " The expression ' managers ' in relation to an elementary school includes all persons who have the management of the school, whether the legal interest in the schoolhouse is or is not vested in them."[2] The managers are not necessarily the same as the trustees of the building, who are appointed according to the Trust

[1] See E. F. Braley, *A Policy in Religious Education*, 1941. The first chapter gives a good summary of the background history.

[2] The Education Act, 1921, 170 (10). Quoted in G. D. Barker, *A Guide for Church School Managers*, 1936. This or some other such book in the latest edition (after 1944) is indispensable for the incumbent, and should be carefully studied. See also, G. D. Barker, *The Education Act* 1944 (National Society).

Deed, but are people who are appointed or elected according to the Final Order of the Board of Education concerning that School. (The Final Order is only made where the Trust Deed makes inadequate provision for the management.) Usually the incumbent is *ex officio* a manager and often *ex officio* the chairman; two Managers are elected by the subscribers, and a fourth is co-opted. These four are the foundation members and should be churchmen. The L.E.A. further appoints other managers, in numbers according to the classification of the school.

There are proper regulations for the procedure of the managers' meetings, for the election of a correspondent (who is the link with the L.E.A.), and a treasurer, and rules for the elections annually by the subscribers of managers.[1] Most school managers seem to be very lax in their procedure, especially in the matter of elections, but it is often very difficult for a new incumbent to discover the correct methods for his parish, and so he has to be content to carry on as has always been done. The duties of the managers are, briefly, to appoint the head-teacher and assistant teachers, and also caretakers when required; to visit the school, and approve the time-table and the requisitions list of the head-teacher; to arrange for the Diocesan Inspection; to care for the building and secure adequate insurances; and to work for the welfare of the school and its scholars in every possible way in conjunction with the L.E.A. and the Diocesan Education Committee.

Some of these duties require further explanation. The appointment of teachers is a crucial point. The whole school turns on the kind of staff it has, and it is essential in a Church School that all the members of the staff should be keen Christians and churchmen. The teachers are in the employ of the managers, not of the L.E.A., and though the consent of the L.E.A. is required for any appointment, it can only be withheld on educational grounds. Most Trust deeds require the appointment of a churchman as head-teacher. Managers have power to inquire into the religious beliefs of candidates for assistant posts, and can appoint church members only, if they wish. It is wise to co-operate with the L.E.A., and to consult the headmaster in the choice of assistants, but the rule of churchmanship should be unvaried. Under the more recent Acts this power is modified in schools that have accepted grants under certain conditions; in Local Agreement Schools and Controlled Schools the managers have only a limited voice in appointments, but in the Aided Schools the previous rights of the managers con-

[1] G. D. Barker, *A Guide or Church School Managers*, 1936, Chapter III.

tinue. Every incumbent must be clear about the circumstances of
his own school.[1]

The managers have the duty of maintaining the school as a
building; the L.E.A. has to provide for the maintenance of the
school as an institution. Thus the L.E.A. should provide all the
furniture and equipment needed in the work of education, both
religious and secular. The managers are responsible for the external
repairs, or what are usually termed landlord's repairs, but the cost of
internal repairs arising from fair wear and tear, the internal decorations, the cost of light and heat, are the responsibility of the L.E.A.
As the school is more often than not used out of Day School hours
for parochial purposes, an agreed figure proportions the cost of such
internal upkeep between the L.E.A. and the parish, as *e.g.*, five-
sevenths to two-sevenths. The wording of the various Acts adds
complications to this somewhat simple statement, and the circumstances of each item of expenditure may demand different treatment.
Under former Acts the phrase ' fair wear and tear ' occasioned
different interpretations in different areas, but under the 1944
Act the matter is made simpler, and more favourable to the
managers.

The present difficulties in the dual system arise chiefly over the
cost of reconstruction and improving school buildings, which,
according to modern requirements, involve a heavier cost than the
ordinary parish can afford.[2] The Board of Education makes
grants under certain conditions towards the cost of such recon-
structions, but the giving of these grants determines the class of the
school, which affects the appointment of teachers in the way already
described. Since the 1944 Act, the building standards have been
set out in the *Regulations Prescribing Standards for School Premises*,
published by H.M. Stationery Office.

The financial responsibilities of the managers are defined in the
work they must do, and for this expenditure the income which they
receive is of a variable nature. Sometimes there is an endowment;
often there is a house which, if not used by the head-teacher, can
otherwise be let; the buildings may be let for various purposes
outside school hours; those responsible for the Sunday School, if
it is held in the Day School, may make a contribution; and the
parish, through the Church Council or otherwise, will subscribe in

[1] E. F. Braley, *A Policy in Religious Education*, 1941, pp. 56–69; on the difficulties
of staffing Church Schools.
[2] Ibid., pp. 54–55; 70–74; on Church School buildings.

return for the use of the building as a parochial hall. There should be subscription lists, the ' qualified ' subscribers having the right to vote for the election of the managers. This varied income usually suffices for the ordinary running expenses; for heavy expenditure upon reconstruction a special appeal is generally necessary.

The way in which a Day School can be used as a parochial hall, and the attendant advantages and disadvantages have already been discussed, as has also the position of the Day School caretaker in regard to parochial affairs.[1]

Apart from the ordinary management of the school, special circumstances sometimes arise, which involve responsibilities too heavy for independent action by the managers. When reconstruction or improvements are required by the L.E.A., or when new buildings are under discussion, or if plans are proposed for educational reorganizations, especially any that involve the possible closing of a Church School, the Diocesan Education Committee must be consulted, and the Association of Day School Managers, which has a branch in most Dioceses, may be asked for advice. Independent action by local managers has often proved disastrous. Should it be necessary to close a Church Day School, legal help should be obtained to secure the use of the building for future church purposes, if possible. It may be that the building must be sold and the proceeds used by the Diocesan Education Committee for educational work in the Diocese.

(c) *Religious Instruction.* The whole purpose of the Church Day School is to secure that the children will be taught by Christian teachers, and that adequate religious instruction will be given, including the denominational teaching of the Church of England through the Catechism. For this reason the Church continues to struggle under the disadvantages of the dual system, although full use is not made by all the clergy of the privilege they have of directing the religious instruction in their schools. The parish priest, if he has the qualifications, should take his share in the actual teaching. It is part of his primary duty, but it is more than that, because it is a wonderful experience in which he will learn as much as he teaches. It will give him a splendid opportunity of getting to know the children of his parish, and will certainly help him to plan the religious instruction that must be given through the Sunday School.

The key to success lies in the co-operation with the head-teacher and his staff. It is not by any means sufficient to portion out the

---

[1] See above, Chapter XII, § 2 (b).

different parts of the Diocesan Syllabus or the Agreed Syllabus [1] which will be followed, but, if possible, the parish priest should hold joint conferences with the teachers about the religious instruction and the best ways of teaching it.   The teachers can bring practical experience to such discussions and can suggest the best expression work, but often their knowledge, even of the Bible, is limited, and the priest should be ready to suggest books that can help them. Generally in the actual teaching the clergy will give the doctrinal instruction, using the catechism for this purpose.   There is no space here to set out detailed suggestions for preparing the programme, and planning the lessons, but this has been done in Canon J. R. Lumb's excellent manual, *Religious Instruction in the Elementary School.* There are chapters not only on teaching the Old Testament, the New Testament, and the Catechism, but a useful and necessary chapter on Missionary lessons, and another on new methods in religious instruction.   For Bible lessons there is a very good book by Dr. Helen Wodehouse, *The Scripture Lesson in the Elementary School.* Books published for Sunday School work are often helpful in the Day Schools.[2]

Canon Lumb has also a chapter on the School at Prayer, for the daily worship of the school does need very great care.   It is so often formal and stereotyped, without variety and without imagination, merely a religious exercise that will never inspire the children to come in later life to worship.   The hymns taught and sung are usually better, though sometimes only those learnt by heart are sung, and are sung too often.   The parish priest could surely exercise his prerogative in the introduction of a better standard of worship.[3] Sometimes the act of worship could take place in the church, if near to the school, especially in Lent or Advent, or on Saints' Days, or during a Children's Mission.   The teachers cannot be compelled to come; they usually will, but care must be taken not to encroach upon the secular time-table.

The Diocesan Inspection is often a bugbear to teachers.   It has not always been conducted in the best possible ways, and reports have often been expressed in stereotyped phrases.   Yet these inspections can be extremely useful—as all external examinations can be—for assessing the work the teachers have done and giving

[1] E. F. Braley, *A Policy in Religious Education*, 1941, pp. 76–85; for arguments in favour of Agreed Syllabuses.

[2] Many are published by the National Society in conjunction with the S.P.C.K. See also: *The Cambridgeshire Syllabus of Religious Education*, 1939; *Handbook of Christian Teaching for use with Agreed Syllabuses*, 1939.

[3] Useful books are: *The Leicestershire Book of Prayers for Schools*; and more for secondary schools, *A Book of Prayers for Schools*, S.C.M.

advice and suggestions for future work. An inspection ending with
a teachers' conference can be most useful.[1]

(d) *Children in the Council Schools*. Not all children of the church
people attend the Church Schools—in fact the number of those that
do is diminishing, and this process is being accelerated. The
clergy have a responsibility towards these children who are not in
their schools, and in this lies much of the controversy connected
with the recent Education Act. While the standard of undenominational teaching and worship in the Council Schools has been
raised and improved, by the Cowper-Temple clause, denominational
teaching is forbidden in them, though children can be withdrawn
for denominational teaching under the Anson By-law and section
13 of the Education Act, 1936.

The best way of taking advantage of this rule is for a group of
parishes to work together. The room chosen should be near the
school, teachers must be capable and exercise good discipline, and
strict punctuality should be observed. Due care should be given to
grading, and continuity under a good syllabus must be observed.[2]
This is not easy to operate. It may be noticed that parents of nonconformist children attending Church Schools can require that their
children shall receive teaching to their liking from an agreed syllabus
on the *school premises*. In addition to the withdrawing for religious
instruction, since the Act of 1870 parents have had the right to
withdraw their children from school attendance on any day
especially set apart for religious observance, such as Ascension Day.
When it is intended to use this privilege, courtesy demands that
notice should be given to the head-teacher beforehand.

This book is concerned with things as they are, rather than with
matters concerning future policy. The end of the controversy is
not yet. An equitable solution would be to allow church children
to be instructed with denominational teaching on Council School
premises, and not to be put to the difficulties connected with withdrawal. Another important approach to the whole problem is
given by Dr. Braley in his book, *A Policy in Religious Education*, in
which he urges that denominational instruction should be confined
to the Sunday School organization. It is doubtful if that organization could bear so great a burden.

[1] J. R. Lumb, *Religious Instruction in the Elementary School,* 1934, pp. 182–187;
compare E. F. Braley, *A Policy in Religious Education,* 1941, pp. 67–69; and L. S.
Hunter, *A Parson's Job,* 1931, pp. 172–174.
[2] G. D. Barker, *A Guide for Church School Managers,* 1936, Chapter VI. Cf. E. F.
Braley, *A Policy in Religious Education,* 1941, pp. 96–101; Phyllis Dent, *A New
Approach to the Church's Work with her Growing Boys and Girls,* 1938, pp. 139 f.

§ 3. THE SUNDAY SCHOOL

(a) *Principles.* Every parish does not possess a Day School, but every parish should have a Sunday School, or some good alternative. This form of religious education is the direct concern of the parish priest, and while it can often be a problem, it can always be a joy. It does mean that he should know something about teaching methods and therefore something about child study, upon which those methods are founded.[1] These subjects should be included in the preparations of all ordinands, and further instruction should be obligatory during the first two years in the ministry. The Church owes much to the pioneer work in this direction of St. Christopher's College, and the old Church of England Sunday School Institute, now part of the National Society.

> " The object of all religious education is that through it the child may be brought into close union with God, and that he may be so trained and developed in every part of his being as to be gradually progressing along that approach to God." [2]

In the fulfilment of this object in Sunday School work there are three principles to follow:[3] (i) Every point in room arrangements, seating accommodation, surroundings, music, programme, hymns, worship, movement, subject-matter, expression work, etc., must be adapted to suit the bodily, mental and spiritual stages of development which the child has reached. (ii) No methods and arrangements may be used but those through which the natural instincts of the child at each period of growth can find expression. (iii) It is not always a wise plan to begin with what seems the ideal.

In the course of the past twenty-five years many Sunday Schools have been influenced by these principles, not only through the work of the clergy who know their job, but also through the good work of the Sunday School Organizers. Yet many others are far from the ideal, and bad discipline and teaching, useless lesson books, dead worship, and poor grading, are still features of some of the schools. Sunday School reform is still in its infancy, and an incumbent needs to know not only how to conduct a good school, but also how to reform a poor one.[4]

(b) *Methods.* Correct grading is the foundation of good method.

---

[1] C. R. Newby, *An Introduction to Child Study*; J. B. Goodliffe, *Child Study in the Sunday School*; E. W. Sara, *Teaching Method in the Sunday School*; A. R. Browne-Wilkinson, *Pastoral Work Among Children*, Chapter II.

[2] Phyllis and Doris Dent, *Principles in Practice*, p. 9.

[3] *Ibid.*, p. 8.

[4] P. and D. Dent, *Principles in Practice*, pp. 11–19; A. R. Browne-Wilkinson, *Pastoral Work among Children*, Chapter VI.

The grading should correspond wherever possible to that in the Day School,—*i.e.*, nursery, infant and junior for the children of Primary age, and some completely separate organization for those over eleven who are going to secondary schools. This should be followed by further instruction in Fellowships or Bible Classes.

The ideal is that each should have its own room, and that each department should be by itself for its appropriate worship and teaching. The difficulty is usually the lack of sufficient suitable rooms in the parochial buildings for four separate departments. It is true that the Fellowship could be in the church, but this does not always foster the development of a spirit of reverence in the young people, it does not encourage discussion, and if the young people are to be encouraged to attend the services of the Church they are better out of the church in the afternoon. A little ingenuity is necessary to make the most of the space in a small school. Different times for different departments, or at least different times for worship, with a little use of curtaining can work wonders. The very minimum is that the Kindergarten and the Fellowship ages are separate from the others.[1]

The worship and the teaching in each department must be appropriate to that grade. The hymn-and-collect type of worship for all ages is almost, if not already, dead; and most schools try to create a real sense of atmosphere in worship with the use of music, pictures, carefully prepared prayers and litanies, and in the Kindergarten especially, actions, walking, and movements. The danger is that the new method becomes formal in its turn, getting stiff and lifeless when it should be variable, living, and imaginative. From time to time Worship must be examined and overhauled, while enough similarity is preserved for the children not to feel lost. New hymns should be learnt, and for older children the canticles and new prayers also. The room itself should promote a sense of worship by being clean and tidy and furnished with pictures and flowers.[2]

Lesson books are published annually by the S.P.C.K. and the National Society, and these follow a carefully-thought-out plan and are properly graded, but they can only be used by those who understand something of the teaching methods for the various grades. They ought not to be in the hands of the teachers unless they come regularly to preparation classes. The lesson should be carefully

[1] P. and D. Dent, *Principles in Practice*, pp. 20–28; P. Dent, *Country Sunday Schools.* Very useful on making the best of inadequate conditions.
[2] *Ibid.*, pp. 66–80; A. R. Browne-Wilkinson, *Pastoral Work Among Children*, Chapters III and IV.

related to the rest of the session, the programme for which should
be well balanced.[1]   For effective teaching there should be suitable
equipment, blackboards, hand-blackboards, large pictures, small
pictures for classes, diagrams and models, Bibles and Prayer Books.
The chairs, desks or other furniture should be suitable for the ages
of the children.[2]

Lessons have not really been successful until they have created a
response in the minds of the scholars, and expression work is the
outcome of a good lesson.   Further equipment is needed for any
expression work done inside school—sandtrays, paper and crayons
in the Kindergarten, notebooks and pencils in the Junior and
Senior, or facilities for making models or private prayer books.
Dramatic expression is possible for all ages, drawing for the younger
ages, and discussions and debates for the seniors.[3]

Generally speaking, expression work among the younger ages is
comparatively easy, but the task of teaching the 11 + is becoming
more difficult, yet adequate expression for them, too, is a necessity.
The reorganization of the Day Schools, with the creation first of the
Modern or Senior Schools, now all to be called Secondary Schools,
means that the children in them must be given a similar status in the
Sunday School. All this is still in the experimental stage. An
account of some of these experiments is to be found in *A New Approach to the Church's Work with her growing Boys and Girls* (1938), by
Phyllis Dent.   Under this ' new approach ', instruction is given by a
method called *Plans, Propositions and Projects*. The lessons are
usually in short courses, leading up to some plan or project. It
might be a series of missionary lessons leading up to a pageant, play
or exhibition.   Or a series of lessons on the Church leading up to a
visit there, or a series on Church history leading up to a visit to a
Cathedral. The summer ramble receives new life as the project
of a lesson on God and Nature, and the subject of Christ and Work
can lead to visits to factories, printing-works or public libraries.
Or the lessons can be expressed in model-making, missionary maps,
Christ's newspapers, personal prayer books; other lessons can be
built up round group study and discussion, leading up to the conduct
of services with addresses in church by the young people, with the
Bishop's permission. The main problem is keeping up a succession
of plans and projects and building them into a coherent scheme of
instruction that may give an adequate syllabus for a period of two

[1] P. and D. Dent, *Principles in Practice*, pp. 54–65.
[2] *Ibid.*, pp. 29–53.
[3] E. W. Sara, *Teaching Method in the Sunday School*, 1928, pp. 96–106.

or three years.[1] Miss Dent works out in some detail the subject-matter for teaching in this way.[2] It may further be said that for the over-elevens it is not strictly necessary that the instruction should be given on Sundays, and even when it is, it can with profit be connected with week-day activity, and be made part of a wider scheme of social activity, or club or guild work.[3]

Much of the success of the modern methods in Sunday School work will depend on the teachers. Faithful souls have done good hard work in days gone by, and their influence has been excellent. But the circumstances of to-day demand teachers with some training and a readiness to go on learning new methods. A well-graded school needs a large staff, and there is a place both for young adolescents and for older men and women. By themselves the young are apt to be unstable and the older people to stagnate. The parish priest has sometimes a difficult task in persuading teachers to retire when their usefulness is over.

With such high standards of teaching in the Day School, it is more than ever necessary that Sunday School teachers should be trained. Too often young people are called from the Bible Class and asked to take a class of youngsters, and many a time volunteers for teaching are given a class without more ado. A little simple training by the clergy in child study and teaching methods is well worth the time spent on it. Ideally a whole series of lessons should be given to them before they begin to teach, but often an attempt at teaching soon shows them how much they themselves must learn. A very useful book for a priest attempting this training is *Training Future Teachers* by Phyllis Dent and others.

Even when teachers have received some such preliminary training, preparation classes each week are a vital part of modern Sunday School method. Only those who attend the class should be allowed to teach on Sunday. Features of such classes include worship together, preparation of the lesson and programme for the following Sunday, and some instruction of background or theology, or some further talks on teaching method.

It is not always possible for the clergy to take the preparation classes for all departments, and in any case it is better for those in

---

[1] P. Dent, *A New Approach*, pp. 51–27. For a good lesson book of this type, see *The Church in Action* (Muriel Breary and Phyllis Dent); see also the series of booklets, published by S.P.C.K., on *Plans, Propositions and Projects*. An alternative method for the over-elevens is the Confirmation School method, see *The Confirmation School*, 1930, by A. R. Browne-Wilkinson.

[2] P. Dent, *A New Approach*, pp. 80–101.

[3] *Ibid.*, 143–149.

charge of the departments to take a large share in planning the lessons and programmes.[1] Sometimes the assistance of Day School teachers can be obtained, but although their help is valuable for training the teachers in teaching method, they are not always the best people to help in the actual preparation of lessons for Sunday School purposes.

An incumbent need not feel that he is left to tackle this vital problem of teachers by himself. The Diocesan Organizer is always willing to help, and frequently there is a special night school for teachers at which they are prepared for their next Sunday's lesson, as well as given some training. Through this method teachers can be encouraged to enter for certificates. Diocesan Summer Schools and Conferences are splendid for those who can attend them, and combine profit with pleasure. For those who cannot attend classes or conferences the St. Christopher's College Correspondence School provides useful courses on various subjects and of varying degrees of difficulty. Such courses are also useful for group work, and are integrated with the majority of Diocesan Training Schemes for Sunday School teachers.

(c) *Special Events.* Open afternoons are features of Day Schools, and they both interest the parents and encourage the children. They are worth introducing into the Sunday School, but must be well planned for date and season, and the programme very carefully prepared. There is no doubt that parents will come, and they may be shown a typical afternoon's Opening, see some practical expression work in pageant or dramatics, a Nativity Play, for example, and paper expression work can be displayed. There is opportunity to stress the place of the home in religious education.[2]

In some parts of the country, more especially perhaps in the North, the Sunday School Anniversary and the Whitsuntide procession are big features, and may be regarded as elaborate open afternoons. For both events, special hymns are taught (selected from the various "Whitsuntide Hymns" offered by different towns), and this is a good way of introducing something new, but often tends to spoil ordinary work in the practices involved. The Anniversary is an occasion for having special preachers, and a good collection is expected, but it should be made a real children's day, with the scholars taking part in the various services not only with the hymns, but also by acting as readers and sidesmen and carrying banners.

[1] P. and D. Dent, *Principles in Practice*, pp. 100–122; P. Dent, *A New Approach*, pp. 150–165; A. R. Browne-Wilkinson, *Pastoral Work among Children*, Chapter VII.
[2] P. and D. Dent, *Principles in Practice*, pp. 81–88.

A gathering of all the little ones with their parents becomes a real family service. The Whitsuntide procession is connected both with hymn-singing and a jolly outdoor treat. The procession may be on the Sunday or Monday or Tuesday; it is an effective act of witness, and finishes with a service in the church. It must be added, however, that many parish priests do not think that these anniversaries are worth preserving, and that the special services of a family character such as on Mothering Sunday or the Patronal Festival are better.

(d) *Administration.* Even modern Sunday School methods require an effective administrative side—for instance, grading is impossible if the children's ages are not known. The basis of administration here is a simple record of every child. Every new scholar should be given a form for the parents to complete. It should give the child's full name, address, date of birth (not age), place of baptism, and it is a good idea to ask the parents to sign that the child will be sent regularly. These particulars should be entered into the School Secretary's record book, with the date of admission, and the class then assigned.

The departments and classes are made up according to the ages of the children. Each class should have a register, and the superintendent should have in addition a complete record kept up-to-date from the class register. All these should be kept with meticulous care.[1]

These Sunday School records are invaluable for ordinary pastoral visiting for the clergy, especially for a new incumbent. They should be used by the teachers themselves for visiting their scholars. Sickness can be followed up and other absenteeism investigated. The registers can also be used for sending out invitations to the open afternoons, and thus further the co-operation with parents.[2]

The children should be taught to give through the Sunday School, and the collection is essentially an act of worship. The children love to collect, and soon learn to do it reverently. Plates, or little bags for each class, may be employed. A prayer of offering ought always to be used. The purpose to which the collection will be allocated will depend on parochial circumstances, but at least once a month it should be for overseas missions and connected with the teaching on missions in the school. Contact with definite mission fields can be effected through missionary societies.[3]

[1] P. and D. Dent, *Principles in Practice*, pp. 97–99. (Some sample register pages are shown.)
[2] *Ibid.*, pp. 81–88.
[3] See below, Chapter XIX, § 3 (a).

O

Prizes are out of fashion in modern Sunday School methods, and the arguments against them are fairly conclusive.[1] But the abolition of prizes is the most difficult reform to undertake. Parents who have a shelf full of prizes want their children to have the same, and many of the best teachers have unexpected prejudices in this matter. No prize system is ever fair, but on the other hand prizes for attendance may count for more in a child's mind than adults can always understand. Modern schools that have not abolished prizes must plead principle (iii) in the first paragraph of this section.

§ 4. THE CHILDREN IN THE CHURCH

Although the subject-matter of many of the published books contains excellent lessons on the Church and its worship, there is always a danger of the Sunday School being divorced from the Church, and this is especially true where geographical circumstances require a Sunday School at some distance from the church. There must be some occasions when the children are brought to church for services, and, in spite of all that has been said about grading and ages, there is a place and time for all children to be together for children's services. They are not easy to conduct, and even less easy to address, yet they do cultivate a corporate spirit, and lead the way to worship. These services should certainly be held at the great Festivals, and perhaps also on special Sundays for Missions, Harvest, Mothering Sunday, and Sunday School Anniversary. A monthly service is not so necessary, though it is not without justification if there is more than one school in the parish. Monthly services break the continuity of teaching, unless they are graded, when the normal lesson can be used and adapted to suit the occasion.

Many parishes still have Sunday School in the afternoon, but new customs will more and more necessitate the principal session being after morning church.[2] In some parishes Sunday School children come into church and leave before the sermon. This certainly helps them to learn to follow the worship of the Church, but ideally parents and children should come together for morning worship. In some churches a children's talk is given after the second lesson, before the children leave, but this is apt to prolong the service unduly.

Two methods of training children to know and love their church and its worship call for special mention.

[1] P. and D. Dent, *Principles in Practice*, pp. 89–92.
[2] See above, Chapter XIII, § 2 (a).

(a) *The Children's Church.* The children may have a special service of their own either before morning service in the Church, or at the same time as morning service in some separate place. This can be in addition to Sunday School, sometimes it must take the place of it. There is endless possible elaboration to the Children's Church, and some suggestions are given by Canon Goodliffe.[1] A principal idea is to invite the co-operation of the children, for choir, wardens, sidesmen, and by instruction to teach them something of the worship of the Church. The danger is that it may separate them from the parents and the services of the Church, although the whole idea of the method is to train the children in preparation for this very thing.

(b) *The Children's Corner.* It is hard to say whether the Children's Corners have been introduced more because the adults love to see them than because the children are likely to use them. Mr. Nevil Truman says that they " have been over-done. In many cases they seem rarely to be used by the children and are the untidiest and shabbiest parts of the church ".[2] On the whole, children cannot be left unsupervised to use them: the aisles are too long and too tempting for races. But the idea is good in itself. A child loves to have a little piece of daddy's garden for his own, and why should he not have a little part of his Father's House? Mr. Truman would urge that the corner should be a chapel with an altar, but the other type of corner, when arranged by an expert, can encourage the children to read and to pray. An adult ought to be in attendance to explain things to them. Canon Goodliffe suggests that each article in the Corner should have some personal associations.[3]

§ 5. WEEKDAY ACTIVITY

Pastoral Work among children must not be confined to Sunday; week-day activities will supplement and build up the Sunday instructions. These activities are of two kinds, regular work done through means of organizations, and spasmodic activity of a recreational type.

(a) *Organizations.* The younger children will find all they need in the well-known organizations like Brownies, Cubs, Life Brigade, Church Lads Training Corps and Candidates of the Girls' Friendly

---

[1] J. B. Goodliffe, *The Parson and his Problems*, 1933, pp. 1–11; W. M. Silcock, *The Children's Church.*

[2] Nevil Truman, *The Care of Churches*, p. 38.

[3] J. B. Goodliffe, *The Parson and his Problems*, pp. 8–10. For a fuller consideration of the Corner, F. Lillie, *The Children's Corner in the Parish Church.* Cf. I. Caudwell, *The Care of God's House*, pp. 54–55.

Society. They all have their own specified programmes, have the advantage of being linked up with the world beyond the parish, and provide certain facilities for training and approving leaders. Their rules vary widely, and the incumbent must be acquainted generally with their schemes. He must have the appointment or final approval of leaders, who should be practising church men and women. The weekly programme should include prayers, but the religious instruction is left to the Sunday School, though some moral instruction is usually implied in the rules of the organizations.

The senior children are drawn into the older organizations, under consideration in the next chapter. For some of them extra provision is often necessary, and the new way of teaching the over-elevens provides the very thing they need. Clubs or organizations under the title of ' Companions of the Church ' or ' The Guild of St. Peter ' can provide for simple rules of life, some religious instruction when it is inconvenient for this on Sundays, and the beginnings of a social club.[1]

There should also be room for missionary organizations for juniors and seniors, either linked with the other organizations or as completely separate entities. Either the King's Messengers or the C.M.S. Discoverers can provide the necessary over-the-parish-boundary link, and the Headquarters of these societies can supply the needed information for prayers, teaching material and practical methods.[2]

(b) *Recreation.* It is usual in connection with the Sunday School to arrange for Christmas parties and summer treats. These are greatly valued by the children, and are very jolly, but exacting, events. Like all other children's activities, they need careful planning and preparation.

The Christmas parties should be organized in age groups. Some teachers will prepare the catering needs, others with capacities that way should organize the games. The children must be given something to do immediately on their arrival; a prepared programme is essential, and the ' props ' for every game secured in readiness. Children can soon be out of hand, but they enjoy themselves more if games are well organized. It is an expert's job.

The Summer Treat is often a bigger undertaking. A visit to the seaside requires a special train, and meals arranged; a visit to the country requires in addition a field secured, adequate shelter available, races organized and food prepared and transported.

---

[1] P. Dent, *A New Approach*, pp. 127–128; 184–189.
[2] See below, Chapter XIX, § 3 (*a*).

Concerts are a joy to children and are always well patronized by their parents. Endless patience is needed by the producer, but the happiness of the children makes it worth while, and financial results can be very good.

SELECT BIBLIOGRAPHY

G. D. Barker, *A Guide for Church School Managers.*
E. F. Braley, *A Policy in Religious Education*, 1941.
J. R. Lumb, *Religious Instruction in the Elementary School*, 1934.
Helen Wodehouse, *The Scripture Lesson in the Elementary School*, 1926.
The Cambridgeshire Syllabus of Religious Education, 1939.
Handbook of Christian Teaching for use with Agreed Syllabuses, 1939.
The Leicestershire Book of Prayers for Schools.
A Book of School Prayers (S.C.M.), 1936.
L. S. Hunter, *A Parson's Job*, 1931, Chapter II.
C. R. Newby, *An Introduction to Child Study.*
J. B. Goodliffe, *Child Study in the Sunday School.*
E. W. Sara, *Teaching Method in the Sunday School.*
Phyllis and Doris Dent, *Principles in Practice.*
Phyllis Dent, *A New Approach to the Church's Work with her growing Boys and Girls*, 1938.
A. R. Browne-Wilkinson, *The Confirmation School*, 1930.
Phyllis Dent and others, *Training Future Teachers.*
J. B. Goodliffe, *The Parson and his Problems*, 1933, Chapter I.
F. Lillie, *The Children's Corner in the Parish Church.*
W. M. Silcock, *The Children's Church.*
J. R. Lumb, *Tomorrow's Teaching*, 1946. This is concerned with the Education Act of 1944.
Handbook to the Scheme of Training for Church Children (National Society), 1946.
The Church; and Secondary and Further Education (National Society), 1946.
The Church; and Voluntary Religious Education (National Society), 1946.

To these must be added the important book, *Pastoral Work among Children*, by A. R. Browne-Wilkinson, 1934. In addition to the chapters already mentioned in the footnotes, there are also valuable chapters on " The Moral Training of Children ", and " Children's Missions, Confessions, and Retreats ". Excellent bibliographies form an important feature of the book.

Towards the Conversion of England, 1945, pp. 87–92, gives a good section on " Evangelism and Children ".

CHAPTER XVI

IN THE SERVICE OF YOUTH

§ 1. THE YOUNG MEN AND WOMEN OF THE CHURCH

(a) *The Scope of Parochial Youth Work.* The Church has had an honoured place in the history of youth work. The present-day emphasis on the needs of youth should not obscure the fact that the Church has long had its own ways of teaching and training young people between fourteen and twenty-five years of age. The method of the Catechism and other preparation for Confirmation helped boys and girls of the past, as to-day, to begin their journey through adolescence.[1] The Church was the pioneer of education, and the Universities were part of the Church's method of youth service in an earlier age. Nearer to modern times the churches were pioneers in the uniformed organizations which sprang from Christian work, and Boys' Clubs and Girls' Clubs have long been part of the work of the Church in industrial areas. Canon Peter Green first published his book *How to Deal with Lads* in 1910, and it is worth reading to-day, for though the whole social and economic background has changed, and equipment has improved, the lads have just the same human nature as they always had. The youth work of the Church has been limited only by the resources in leaders and equipment. It is worth noting that at the Lambeth Conference of 1930 a committee met to consider the problem of Youth and a report was submitted.[2]

Youth work is still a valuable part of the parochial programme, and demands much thought from the parish priest. It cannot be described as easy, but the parish priest neglects it at his peril. Not only are the young people the basis of his future congregation; he has a pastoral responsibility and duty towards them as individuals. Their deepest needs are paramount. To quote *A New Generation for Christ*, a statement of the *Task and Policy of the Church of England Youth Council*:[3]

" In these times of unparalleled difficulty and opportunity in youth welfare, the young people of our land have a right to

[1] Confirmation is not considered in this chapter, but in Chapter XXII.
[2] *Report of the Lambeth Conference*, 1930, pp. 188–200.
[3] Page 3.

be brought effectively to a knowledge of the Catholic Faith, to be challenged to give themselves in loyal service to Christ and His Church, and to be trained to take their part in the daily offering to God of the worship of the world wide Church, in sacrament and in the life of personal devotion. Only so can each generation of Christians begin to live the life for which God made them, to pass on to their contemporaries the Truth which He reveals, and to win their fellows for that Life which alone is eternal."

Youth work in the Church of England is, then, to equip young men and women " to go forth into the world to serve God faithfully in the fellowship of His Church," and it should aim particularly at " enabling young people to assume their responsibilities and duties in Church, community and State, as members of the World-Wide Church of Jesus Christ." [1]

This youth work will not be content with helping only those within the membership of the Church, but it will be directed also to those outside, and who are not attached to any branch of the Christian Church. The work should be ' extensive ', to bring as many as possible into the influence of the Church, so that they can grow up into the Christian Faith, and it should also be ' intensive ', to meet the needs of those whose development is faster and who respond more readily to the challenge of Christ.

A warning ought to be given that there are no hard-and-fast rules for Church youth work. It is very easy to be dogmatic on this subject, but it must be remembered that parishes and areas differ widely, and methods in one parish may not be at all suitable in another. There is, for instance, the vast difference between town and country work.[2] Yet there is a general direction along which the work should go. " The statements of policy are not meant in any sense as decrees, but rather as signposts on a road which still needs for the greater part to be mapped out." [3] The suggestions advanced in this chapter are offered in the same spirit.

(b) *Understanding the Adolescent.* Good youth work depends on a knowledge of the subject. In order that the deepest needs of young people may be met, it is necessary to understand what those needs are. Those in charge of youth work must have a knowledge of the main characteristics of adolescence, the physical and psychological changes of that period of the lives of boys and girls, and the effect of these changes on the spiritual life of the young people.

---

[1] Page 3.　　　　[2] See Chapter XXVIII, § 3 (c).
[3] *A New Generation for Christ*, p. 2.

It is part of the object of youth work to help the adolescents to adjust themselves to these changes and to develop normal adult life. The environment of the young people, their home-life and working conditions, are factors which must be considered, in order that the young people may be helped in their personal relationships with each other and with other people, and also in their moral and ethical difficulties. This is not the place to set out that knowledge, but there is a wide range of books in which the necessary information may be found.[1]

It is because of this lack of understanding that so much youth work fails. Some parish priests fail in the work, and regard it as something for their assistants to do. Advertisements for curates in the Church papers usually require that applicants should be ' good with youth ', but youth leadership requires something more than that, for it is work for an expert.

Fortunately there are opportunities for attending courses of training in youth leadership; some are arranged by the local education authorities, the Ministry of Education, the Universities and the Voluntary Organizations; others are arranged by different dioceses or by the Church of England Youth Council, and others by such bodies in conjunction. The wise priest will attend some such course of training if he can, and will also try to find among his young people those with a talent for leadership which would be developed by training. Courses are provided for the training not only of those who wish to become full-time paid youth leaders, but also those who wish to take up part-time voluntary work in their spare time. There is a very great need for more trained youth leaders of every kind.[2]

(c) *The Aims of Youth Work.* Before the different organizations for youth work are considered, it is convenient here to consider the aims by which the youth work in the Church of England should be guided. The Church of England Youth Council offers the following aims, which should be expressed in programmes and activities, for the guidance of youth work, if it is to help the young people to find

[1] See A. P. Jephcott, *Girls Growing Up*, 1942; J. MacAlister Brew, *In the Service of Youth*, 1943, Chapters I, X–XVII; D. Edwards-Rees, *The Service of Youth Book*, 1943, Chapters VIII and IX; A. E. Morgan, *The Needs of Youth*; *Advance in Understanding the Adolescent* (Home and School Council); *Spiritual Well-being through Boys' Clubs*, N.A.B.C., *Christian Leadership in the Service of Youth*, S.C.M., 1942. The St. Christopher's College Correspondence Course in Youth Leadership includes the study of this subject; and excellent book-list is provided with the notes for the course.

[2] See *Christian Youth Leadership*, 1944, issued by the Church of England Youth Council. The Council has also issued syllabuses for the study of Christian Doctrine by Youth Leaders.

true fellowship in and through the life of the Church in loyalty to Jesus Christ.[1]

Worship—to provide opportunities both for the understanding of, and progress in, corporate worship and private prayer.

Thought—to enable young people to learn together the meaning of the Christian Faith, and of its relevance to the life of their generation.

Service—to lead young people to offer their work and their leisure to God as members of His Church—in local, national and international life.

Witness—to prepare young people for Christian witness by life, word and action.

Recreation—to give due recognition to the importance of fitness of body and mind, and to the provision of suitable varied forms of recreation in all youth organizations and groups.

§ 2. METHODS OF WORK

(a) *Different Possibilities.* In many churches much of the work among young people is achieved through the organizations specially devoted to this purpose. Most of them have been working for many years and have been successful in their own spheres. They are similar in character and in objective, but there are wide differences in their theory and practice. As a rule they provide for younger children as well as for the different ages in adolescence, and the dividing ages are founded on psychological considerations. Nearly all profess to be striving for the spiritual, mental and physical needs of young people. Most societies have admission ceremonies and rites of some description, and it should be possible for the clergy to take an active part in these. Information about the various societies is given below,[2] and every parish priest should seek to be familiar with the Rules and Regulations of those he has in his own parish.

Generally, when a priest takes charge of a parish, he finds one or more organizations already at work. If they are functioning well, he will naturally work through them. If they are functioning indifferently, or if there are no methods of work at all, he will be under the necessity of deciding how he will continue the youth work in the parish. One of the first big decisions he must make is whether he

---

[1] *A New Generation for Christ*, pp. 5, 6. These aims are considered in more detail in § 4 below.
[2] See § 3.

will work through the nationally organized associations, or through a parochially organized group. A nationally organized association will bring to him a vast wealth of experience accumulated over many years, and will offer, if it can, trained leaders to help him—at any rate there will be the official hand-books laying down the line of work. A parochially organized group will depend more on the priest's own initiative and imagination, and it may be very successful if he is a natural youth leader. A parochial group, however, may become very narrow in its views, whereas a nation-wide or world-wide society gives a valuable sense of a wider community and fellowship. On the other hand, societies with a national basis demand a loyalty from its members, and unless care is exercised, this loyalty to the societies may clash with loyalty to the Church. Successful youth work will help young people to balance the loyalties which life brings to them, and to give the prior place to loyalty to God, but the possible conflict of loyalties must be recognized.[1] The choice of the method of youth work will depend also on the numbers which will be touched—some of the national voluntary associations work best when handling a limited number—and a related problem again is whether the parish is in the town or in the country.

In a large town parish there is no need to have a clear-cut division between the nationally and parochially organized groups, as there is usually room for more than one organization. Age divisions and the different needs of boys and girls should be taken into consideration. A parish may have the Church Lads' Brigade and the Girls' Friendly Society, or the Boy Scouts and Girl Guides, and in addition may have a Boys' Club and a Girls' Club. The national societies might be part of the club activities. It is also necessary to provide for mixed activity, specially for the boys and girls over sixteen years of age, so that they can have a common meeting-ground when they begin to have interest in each other. Mixed clubs can be successful when the age limit is lower, though many experts would dispute this. In rural parishes one organization may be sufficient, or it may be advisable to join with another parish. In any case, it is essential that provision should be made wherever necessary for all three types of activity—boys', girls' and mixed.

The parochial Youth Fellowship is well suited to meet the personal and social needs of young people over sixteen, and to prepare them for the responsibilities of home and community and for Church

[1] This is recognized in *Scouting, Religion and the Churches*, 1944, pp. 15–23.

membership. Moreover, it provides a common meeting-place for members of all the other organizations as well as for those untouched by other activities. The adolescents attached to a church are within the family of the Church a block on their own, and it is good to cultivate a corporate spirit amongst them. And again, whatever the other organizations may teach, the Fellowship can help them to complete a well-balanced programme of youth activities which fulfil all the aims of youth work described above.

There are infinite possibilities in the planning of the programme for a Youth Fellowship, and usually only limited time. The range of work will therefore depend on the number of meeting nights. It is important to keep a well-balanced programme, so that all the deepest needs of the members are met. For many parishes most of the indoor activities have to be concentrated on one night a week, perhaps on Sunday evening after service. Such an evening would devote an hour to the set programme, with intervals before and after for social intercourse, finally ending with an Epilogue, which can be taken by the members in turn. A canteen adds to the enjoyment of the evening. The set programme can follow a four-weekly sequence—for example, Discussion, Mental Training, Missionary, Social or Amusing.[1] Outdoor activity will depend on the number of members and the provision already made by other organizations in the parish.

Another big decision the parish priest must make is whether his organizations will be open or closed. Whatever rule he makes will depend on his parish, and the nature of the organization concerned. It seems to be now generally recognized that most organizations should be open to those who are not already members of the church. The intention is that they should be won into membership: the policy of the Scout Organization, for instance, requires such membership. " It is expected that every *Scout* shall belong to some religious denomination and attend its services." [2] Some organizations have the object at least of giving those who otherwise would not be touched by Christianity a better ideal of life and citizenship. An ' open ' club is also good for the young church people themselves; it gives them the opportunity of being the leaven in the club, and may prevent them from being too priggish in their religion. Dr. MacAlister Brew is very definite. " Until the churches open their clubs to the unconverted, until that monstrous thing

[1] Suggestions for programmes, see § 4 below. See also, H. C. Warner, *Christian Advance*, 1943, pp. 63–70.
[2] *Policy, Organization and Rules*, 10, (1).

known as a ' closed ' club dies the death, a marvellous opportunity is being thrown away." [1]

In the ' open ' club the Church is ' extensive ' in its work; it must also be ' intensive ' for some of its members. Some are ready to be called to a higher standard of Christian life, and are willing to accept a definite rule of life for prayer, communion and service. There are some societies—*e.g.*, the A.Y.P.A.,[2] which provide such a rule of life, and some Diocesan Youth Fellowships also give such a rule. An inner circle may be suspected of exclusiveness just as much among young people as among their elders, but it can be the real leaven of the youth work of the parish, setting its tone and supplying the leaders. Some parishes have been successful in promoting a background circle of keen young people with almost no organization, and thus no obtrusiveness, and yet with all the members pledged to lives of Christian witness.

(b) *The Parochial Youth Council.* The young people should have a say in the control of their own activities, although they need guidance and cannot be given a completely free hand. This is best achieved through a Parochial Youth Council,[3] which can be formed in various ways, including all or some of these representatives : (i) Four or five appointed by the Parochial Church Council. This gives the Youth Council a standing, and maintains a contact with the parent Council, to which reports should be given. Those appointed should be the younger members of the Church Council, say those under thirty. (ii) Members elected by the Parochial Youth Fellowship. (iii) Representatives of the Rovers, Rangers, G.F.S., etc. (iv) Co-opted members, or members nominated by the clergy. This is a useful reservation, as sometimes valuable workers are forgotten in elections. The clergy should be members, the parish priest or his assistant acting as chairman.

The Council should have a regular routine of meetings, with well-ordered business, minutes kept, notices of agenda issued and resolutions correctly put and carried. This is excellent training for future Church Councillors. The Council can run events, concerts, work for bazaars or missionary sales and, by votes, make grants to parochial and charitable objectives; it has to plan the youth activities, the Youth week-ends, Summer events, rambles and sports; it can also arrange for one or more Youth Sundays each

---

[1] J. MacAlister Brew, *In the Service of Youth*, 1943, p. 55.
[2] See below, § 3 (*g*).
[3] See *Youth's Job in the Parish*, pp. 13–18. Cf. L. S. Hunter, *A Parson's Job*, p. 149. Here they are not commended, but the last decade has seen another swing of the pendulum.

year, electing sidesmen, suggesting hymns, providing readers; it can promote missionary interest by supporting an ' own ' missionary; and it can appoint its own representatives to such things as Diocesan Youth Councils and Deanery Missionary Committees.

The Council can be responsible for issuing a Young People's News Letter, giving details of programme, reminders of special services, suitable study notes, missionary notes and devotional help. Preferably it should be edited and duplicated by the young people themselves, but it will not always be possible to begin in this way. It can be circulated by hand, or by post, to members and possible members.

(c) *Youth's Place in the Parish.* The work with the young people should not be conducted in complete independence from the rest of pastoral work. There should be a definite connection on the one hand with the Sunday School, and on the other hand with adult activities. The junior organizations usually keep a link with the Sunday School, and some parishes will have young people's classes on Sunday afternoon. More thought is required to introduce youth to age, and age to youth. The age-long conflict of youth and age finds its place somewhere in the parish, and may be shown in complaints that the clergy spend too much time with the young people and not enough with their elders, or in complaints about the behaviour of young people in church and school. The jealousies of the older folk can be forestalled if they are taken into the confidence of the clergy and their co-operation sought. Some of them are needed as leaders, some will be invited to help financially, some can be asked to help with the training of youth in worship; and all may be informed of the aims, purposes and activities of the youth organizations, and made aware of the importance of this work. There is also the opposite duty of interpreting age to youth, and the teaching that patience and co-operation are necessary in the corporate venture of the Church family.

The older people can help the younger by their presence at corporate Communion services for young people or at the weekly family Communion. A place should be found for the older young people on the Church Council, and a good opportunity for the young and old to mix together is in the Congregational or Church Fellowship.[1]

It is convenient to mention here the need of machinery to keep the various parochial organizations dwelling together in unity.

[1] See above, Chapter VII, § 4 (c).

An Organizations' Council on which the Leaders can serve and do useful co-operative work has already been described.[1] The task of planning the use of the halls for the different groups has also been mentioned.[2] Leaders should be asked annually to supply a list of members, so that names can be entered on the clergy visiting lists. For some organizations a Parents' Committee is definitely helpful; its function is not to interfere with the work of the officers, but to unite parents and leaders in their common concern for the welfare of the young people.

§ 3. THE PRINCIPAL YOUTH ORGANIZATIONS

It is proposed to give here an indication of the aims and methods of the principal youth organizations which are to be found in parish work. Such summaries as these cannot be complete. Youth organizations which do not normally take an important part in parish life are not mentioned. Further information can be obtained from the Headquarters of the organization concerned.[3]

(a) *Church Lads' Brigade*. The object of the Brigade is ' to extend the Kingdom of Christ among lads and to make them faithful members of the Church of England or other Episcopal Church in communion with the Church of England '. The Brigade method includes instruction in the doctrine and practice of the Church, religious, educational, physical and recreative agencies, and the symbolic use of such military organization, training and equipment as promotes the object of the Brigade. Thus through drill, games, physical training and competitions, the lads are trained in self-respect and self-reliance, a team spirit and a sense of responsibility are cultivated. The incumbent has control of the company in his parish, and all officers are nominated by him, and must be communicants. The incumbent or his assistant curate is the chaplain, and is responsible for the regular weekly instruction and attendance at Church of all his boys. In some dioceses there is a Church Girls' Brigade, organized on similar lines.

(b) *The Girls' Friendly Society*. This is a Church Society, and its object is " to unite girls and women in a fellowship of prayer, service and purity of life, for the glory of God." The G.F.S. works in closest co-operation with the clergy. Without the consent of the incumbent a branch cannot be opened, and he is the patron of the branch. Girls of all denominations may be admitted. The method is founded on the personal friendship between Associates (Leaders) and members. Encouragement is given to handicrafts, dramatic work and physical training, and inter-Diocesan competitions provide a good stimulus to endeavour. The activities are spiritual, educational and recreational, and much has been done in recent years to make the programme up-to-date. Membership of the G.F.S. is until marriage (unless members become Associates or Helpers), or for life, thus making this society unique as a youth organization. Some parishes find that this leads to the difficulty of having a branch, consisting chiefly of older women, that the adolescent will not join. Perhaps it would be better if a different organization were provided for older single women who wish to have, and ought to have, a friendly society.

(c) *The Boys' Brigade.* Its object is " the Advancement of Christ's Kingdom among Boys, and the promotion of habits of Obedience, Reverence, Discipline, Self-respect and all that tends towards a true Christian manliness." The B.B. is an inter-denominational organization, but it has the Church of England Council of the Boys' Brigade as a separate entity within the organization. The B.B. follows the brigade method, and is very similar in character to the C.L.B., though the weekly Bible Class is, if anything, more emphasized. The Girls' Life Brigade is the feminine counterpart of the B.B.

(d) *Boy Scouts' Association.* Baden-Powell, the Founder of the Boy Scouts, summed up the purpose and method of Scouting as " a School of Citizenship through Woodcraft." The Scout programme is admirable. Boys are taught to educate themselves through woodcraft and open-air activity. Character, service, observation and self-reliance are the keynotes, and the Scout law sets a fine ideal. The text-books of the movement written by Baden-Powell are fine works for any boy to read; the other organizations have nothing to compare to them. Scouting tends to lack discipline, but it does cultivate self-reliance. The Scout promise imposes a pledge of loyalty to God, and the Association tries to help the members to fulfil their obligations. An important booklet, *Scouting, Religion, and the Churches* (1944), makes some practical suggestions, and offers the guiding principle of partnership between the Scouter and the Parson.

" The Scouter, who should be a member of the Church concerned, must recognize that the Parson has to ensure that the boys receive proper instruction in the faith of the Church and that they attend its services. The Parson must recognize the Scouter's duty to carry out the training of the boys by the characteristic methods of the Movement." [1]

This book faces in a realistic manner the possibilities of a mis-understanding between Parson and Scouter, and makes excellent suggestions to overcome it.

The demands of a troop are really too great for one of the clergy to act as Scoutmaster, especially if he is single-handed, although the parish priest sometimes assumes the post of Group Scoutmaster. One of the clergy ought to act as chaplain to the parish group. A priest can also give useful service as a Rover Leader. The senior division of the Scout Movement gives much scope for keen young men, though Rover nights can become mere talking shops effecting little. But the Rovers do respond to the appeal of service, and they are apt pupils for training in Christian citizenship. [2]

(e) *Girl Guides' Association.* The aim of the Girl Guides' Association is the promotion of good citizenship, through individual character training which will help the girl to develop physically, mentally and spiritually. This is a parallel movement to that of the Scouts, and it is similar in its strength, and in its problems. The Movement has considered its religious policy in *The Girl Guide Movement and the Churches,* and the foundation stone of Guiding is true and practised loyalty to God.

(f) *National Association of Boys' Clubs* and *The National Association of Girls' Clubs and Mixed Clubs.* These Associations have similar objects, to promote the spiritual, educational, physical and industrial welfare of boys and girls. The club method creates a community wherein each member learns to practise the art of human relation-ships. The members share in the management and responsibility of the club, and they are helped to develop self-discipline. The interests of each individual are studied, but the whole group has to learn to co-operate for the happiness of all. A good club pro-gramme has wide activities intended to meet the needs and desires of the members and to help them to develop physically, mentally and spiritually. Naturally the activities provided will depend partly on whether the club is for boys, or for girls, or if it is mixed. The Club can be a small, one-night-a-week club with a dozen members, or a big club open every night of the week. A good leader is essential. The clergy can act as chaplains, and can possibly help with some of the activities. Some suggestions for those sides of

---

[1] Page 16.   [2] For Church parades, see below, § 4 (a).

the programme which the clergy will more especially watch are given below.[1] It is through such an open club that some clergy find that they can do their most extensive work among young people.[2]

(g) *Anglican Young People's Association.* The object of the Association is to promote youth work in individual parishes and to provide fellowship between parishes and different parts of the Anglican Communion. The work is planned on four principles: Worship, Work, Fellowship and Edification. The members are trained to bear witness in their daily work and in youth activities. The branch in the parish is under the ultimate control of the incumbent, but it is actually organized by an executive committee consisting of the Chaplain and elected lay officers. The movement is specially designed to bring young people into the full life of the Church and to provide for a real fellowship in which they will learn the Christian faith. Some excellent books of study have been issued under the auspices of this Association.[3]

(h) *The Christian Workers' Union.* This is a fellowship of working lads and girls from the factories, mines, workshops and shops of England. All members must be between the ages of sixteen and thirty, and must be willing to put themselves under a course of instruction in the Faith and Principles of the Church of England with a view to full membership of the Church.

> " Our aims are to teach young people to see that their *work* is the contribution they are making to divine worship and human service, and that it must be done in such spirit and under such decent conditions that it may be a worthy offering to God." [4]

Sections of the fellowship are attached to a parish church, and are under the instruction of a Priest Adviser.

§ 4. Aspects of Youth Activities

The five Aims of Youth work have been stated above,[5] and the wise priest will try to see that the members of his organizations have an opportunity of sharing in each type of activity. The Youth Fellowship especially will try to provide for all five aims.

[1] See below, § 4.
[2] See below, § 5 (b) and its concluding list of books to which should be added: *Approach to Religion in the Club,* N.A.G.C. and M.C.; *Spiritual Well-being through Boys' Clubs,* N.A.B.C.
[3] The volumes of the series entitled, *Unto a Full-grown Man.*
[4] See Douglas Cooke, *Youth Organizations of Great Britain,* 1944–45, p. 209.
[5] See above, § 1 (a).

P

(a) *Worship.* Different types of parishes will have different rules for the guidance of its members in worship. Some may have a regular communicant rule, either a monthly corporate Communion or weekly attendance at the parish Communion. Various methods may be adopted to help the young people to become intelligent and practising worshippers: Youth Sunday evenings, corporate intercessions, epilogues at meetings, devotional and instructional evenings at regular intervals, debates on religious subjects, hymn or carol evenings; outdoor witness and religious drama help indirectly. Training in worship is essential.[1] The private prayer life of the individual members needs much encouragement; a Rule of Life is good and the Bible-Reading Fellowship leaflets are very valuable.

Some parishes have a monthly parade of their uniformed organizations, and find it of value as a demonstration to the other members of the Church that the youth organizations are part of the family; but the parade should never be merely a show, for it is an act of worship, and there is a need that the presence of the young people in the church should be recognized in the service, at least by the choice of hymns, prayers and by the address.[2] Many priests and youth leaders take the opposite view—that monthly parades tend to suggest infrequent attendance, though it may be regular, as the norm—and set a standard of regular weekly worship, for which they train their members. It is not, however, impossible to train members for weekly worship, even if they attend monthly parades.

Sunday outings and week-end trips and camps raise other problems of worship. The wise priest can make use of camps for training in worship, and some clergy arrange for youth week-end conferences, which can help to fulfil more than the first aim of youth work.

Useful references are:

H. C. Warner, *Youth in Action*, 1939, pp. 1–34, 163–170.
Youth's Job in the Parish, A.Y.P.A., 1939, pp. 19–33.
Youth in the Church, S.P.C.K., 1937, pp. 9–15.
J. Singleton, *Epilogues for Youth*, 1943.
Programme Possibilities for Church Youth Groups, 1945, pp. 9–15.
G. Ireson, *Learning to Worship*, C.E.Y.C.
G. Ireson, *Church Worship and the Non-Churchgoer*, 1944.

[1] See above, Chapter XIII, § 1 (c).
[2] See *Scouting, Religion, and the Churches*, 1944, p. 19.

Other books are recommended in:

H. C. Warner, *Christian Youth Leadership*, 1942, p. 96.
D. Edwards-Rees, *The Service of Youth Book*, 1943, pp. 55, 153.

(b) *Thought.* Study and mental training introduce many methods. Introductory talks can lead to group discussions on questions. This is good training for young leaders and encourages self-expression and thinking. This is a useful method for the Sunday afternoon Guild or Fellowship. Smaller groups can operate as study circles and go more deeply into the various subjects. There is a wide range of possibilities, including Biblical and theological subjects, Missions, Sociology, international problems and ethical questions. Many other things help in informal religious education—films, drama, music, visual aids,[1] etc.—and mental training methods can use observation tests, memory contests, questionnaires (run with opposing sides), snap speaking, hobby nights, debates, mock parliament and mock trials, and brains trusts.

> *Youth's Job in the Parish*, A.Y.P.A., pp. 33–50.
> *Youth in the Church*, S.P.C.K., pp. 16–23.
> H. C. Warner, *Youth in Action*, pp. 99–116.
> H. C. Warner, *Christian Youth Leadership*, 1942, pp. 99–103.
> *Christian Leadership in the Service of Youth*, S.C.M., 1943, pp. 36–39.
> *Programme Possibilities for Church Youth Groups*, 1944, pp. 15–38.
> G. Fallows and S. Lord, *Youth Fellowship Programmes*, 1945, pp. 7–30.
> A. Richardson, *Preface to Bible Study*, 1943, pp. 112–126.
> *Senior Lessons Handbook* (Discussion Topics for Youth). Edited by G. S. Pain and E. H. Hayes.
> *Talking Things Over.* Edited by R. G. Martin, 1942.
> *Teaching for Lads*, Peter Green, 1923.
> Percy Dearmer, *Lessons on the Way*, 5 vols., 1921–25.
> *Unto a Full Grown Man*, series issued by the A.Y.P.A.
> H. C. Warner, *Christian Advance*, 1943, pp. 71–79.

(c) *Service.* If young people are to be led to offer their work and their leisure to God as members of His Church in local, national and international life, a very bold programme must be put before them. In the *Statement on the Training of Youth in the Churches* (agreed upon by the Youth Committees of Churches associated in

---

[1] See also below, Chapter XVII, § 4 (a).

the British Council of Churches), section 2 on *The Christian Life*,[1]
reads:—

"Young people should receive guidance in the Christian
understanding of:—

"(a) Personal relationships, including sex, marriage and
family life; [2]
"(b) The use of their powers of body and mind, their
time and possessions in the service of God's purpose, both
at work and in leisure;
"(c) Their duties as workers within the community
with some knowledge of the structure of modern society
and the changes that are taking place in it;
"(d) Their duties as citizens in respect of local and
national politics;
"(e) Their duties as world citizens and their share of
responsibility for public policy in international affairs and
for contact with people of other nations."

There is much material here for wide vision, but the objectives
must not be lost in vague talk. The Leader should try to find
active ways of service for the Church and Community, and hum-
drum parochial jobs are not to be despised when put in their right
perspective.

Youth's Job in the Parish, A.Y.P.A., pp. 51–66.

H. C. Warner, *Youth in Action*, pp. 117–135.

H. C. Warner, *Christian Youth Leadership*, pp. 65–79.

G. Fallows and S. Lord, *Youth Fellowship Programmes*, 1945,
pp. 55–60.

Programme Possibilities for Church Youth Groups, 1944, pp. 31–38,
43, 44.

Serving the Church, 1945 (Central Co-ordinating Committee).

See also publications of the Christian Workers' Union, and of the
Industrial Christian Fellowship, such as:

God and My Neighbour, and *Christ the Lord of All Life*.

(d) *Witness*. Some of the most useful work the young people can
do is in the sphere of witness, and this can be the most effective of
evangelistic work.[3] Study, discussion and speaking practice can
all lead up to this. Youth News Teams can be the spearhead of
evangelistic witness, whether operating in the open air, in schools
or in church. The value of religious drama and of religious films

---

[1] See *Programme Possibilities for Church Youth Groups*, 1944, p. 54.
[2] See also below, Chapter XXII, § 2 (c).
[3] See above, Chapter XIV, § 2 and § 3.

for effective witness must not be overlooked. The wider field of Church life brings an interest in missionary work which can become very keen. Missionary evenings can take the form either of discussions about its necessity and purpose, or of lantern lectures and films on the work. Practical support can be gained by the usual methods.[1]

> *Towards the Conversion of England*, 1945, pp. 92–96.
> *Youth's Job in the Parish*, A.Y.P.A., pp. 54–58, 65–66.
> *Youth in the Church*, S.P.C.K., pp. 24–53.
> H. C. Warner, *Youth in Action*, The Gospel, pp. 35–46; The Films, pp. 47–60; The Drama, pp. 61–79; The Spoken Word, pp. 80–98.
> *Programme Possibilities for Church Youth Groups*, 1945, pp. 39–42.
> *Evangelism and Youth*, C.E.Y.C., 1945.

(e) *Recreation.* Healthy young Christians will want to play games and have physical exercise and excitement together. Outdoor programmes must be provided involving the different sports and games and such activity as swimming, cycling and hiking. All these things not only develop the body, but they are also splendid ways of creating fellowship. Indoor physical training is an important part of the usual club programme embracing both drill and games. In addition to physical training, other forms of recreation help to create an atmosphere of friendliness in the youth group, and the social side has an important place. Apart from the specially arranged dances and social evenings, any Fellowship programme needs its quota of jolly evenings, with games, competitions, impromptu concerts, limerick evenings and Christmas parties. A summer holiday camp may also be mentioned here.

The running of sports clubs is not without its difficulty. Canon Green has said : " I know no branch of club work at once so difficult and in its results so unsatisfactory, as the managing of a boys' cricket or football team." [2] Other experts say that this is not generally true, but those who do meet this difficulty can find it heart-breaking.

> *Youth's Job in the Parish*, A.Y.P.A., pp. 33, 34, 67–76.
> *Christian Leadership in the Service of Youth*, S.C.M., pp. 13–15.
> G. Fallows and S. Lord, *Youth Fellowship Programmes*, 1945, pp. 31–54.
> *Programme Possibilities for Church Youth Groups*, 1945, pp. 45–52.

---

[1] See below, Chapter XIX, § 3 (*b*).
[2] Peter Green, *How to Deal with Lads*, 1910, p. 86. (See also his following pages.)

H. C. Warner, *Christian Youth Leadership*, p. 94.

S. G. Hedges, *Club Games and Activities*, and other books. (National Sunday School Union.)

§ 5. PARTNERS IN THE WORK

(a) *In the Church*. The Church of England Youth Council was constituted in 1942 by the Church Assembly, and entrusted with the guidance, co-ordination and extension of all types of youth work in the Church of England. It works to strengthen and extend the Church's own youth work, and, because of its concern for the great number of young people who are not in touch with any religious body, it co-operates with other bodies in the country concerned with youth work as a whole.[1] Incumbents and Youth Leaders can be kept in touch with the latest books, information and general matters affecting youth, through the *Review* published by the C.E.Y.C., 69, Great Peter Street, Westminster, S.W.1.

Most Dioceses have now a Diocesan Youth Organizer or a Bishop's Chaplain for Youth and a Diocesan Youth Council which should be concerned with all sides of Youth work. The parish should be in touch with its Diocesan Council, and as far as possible join in any of the activities which it promotes. Some Dioceses have formed a Diocesan Youth Assembly or a Diocesan Youth Fellowship, the latter often suggesting a rule of life for its members.

(b) *The Government Service of Youth*. The voluntary youth organizations by their many years of hard work brought the State to recognize the gap in the social services of the nation, which until 1939 made little provision for youth outside the secondary schools and evening institutes. By the issue of Circular 1486 in November, 1939, the State came into partnership with the voluntary organizations in order to provide an adequate youth service as part of the educational system of the country. The State is now giving grants on a generous scale to voluntary youth organizations which are concerned with all sides of youth work—*i.e.*, with the physical, mental and spiritual needs of boys and girls. Most Local Education Authorities generally recognize that if the needs of youth are to be adequately met, youth work should be concerned equally with the spiritual as well as with the physical and mental development of young people. They are very conscious of their inability to use techniques which will help forward the spiritual development of the young people, and they are looking to the Church for a lead. Goodwill exists almost everywhere, and there is a real desire to co-operate.

[1] See *A New Generation for Christ, passim.*

Grants are given to Church Clubs for equipment, maintenance and Leaders, as well as to other voluntary organizations. Application must be made to the Local Education Authority, so the Youth Secretary for the area should always be consulted for advice and directions on procedure. The parochial youth organizations should be linked to the local Youth Committee, and the parish priest should co-operate with it, in any way in which he is asked.

A parish priest might well consider if his ordinary parochial organizations are making sufficient provision for the youth of his neighbourhood. If the Church has adequate premises, it can run its own Youth Centre, and provide the management committee, though difficulties arise if the premises are also needed for general parochial purposes; then a Community Centre is really required.[1] If the Church does run a Centre, trained Christian leadership is essential, and not easy to find. The clergy cannot undertake the burden of management unless a curate is on the staff for that purpose, though they must direct the religious activity. Alternatively, the parish priest might stimulate local voluntary interest for the formation of a centre apart from Church premises, and work in co-operation with local Free Church ministers.[2] If the Local Authority has its own Youth Centre in the neighbourhood, the clergy should be ready to co-operate in it in any possible way.

If the parish priest and his assistants are in any way responsible for the conduct of a Youth Centre, there are many books to help them. Besides those mentioned under separate heads in § 4 above, the following are worthy of particular note:

D. Edwards-Rees, *The Service of Youth Book*, 1943.
J. M. Brews, *In the Service of Youth*, 1943.
H. C. Warner, *Youth in Action*, pp. 136–162.
H. C. Warner, *Christian Youth Leadership*, 1942, pp. 30–63.
Christian Leadership in the Service of Youth, S.C.M., 1943
Peter Green, *How to Deal with Lads*, 1922.
William Temple, *Social Witness and Evangelism*, 1943. Appendix A.
L. J. Barnes, *Youth Service in an English County*.
Youth's Opportunity, H.M.S.O., 1945 (Further Education in County Colleges).

(c) *Pre-Service Training Organizations.* The Sea Cadets, the Air Training Corps, the Army Cadets and the Girls' Training Corps have absorbed a considerable number of young people. They are

---

[1] See *Community Centres*, H.M.S.O., 1945.
[2] See below, Chapter XX, § 2 (d).

naturally organized normally outside the sphere of parish work, and, like the fighting services, are undenominational, but with provision for all denominations to minister to their own members. Some parish priests may be appointed Hon. Chaplains to one or another of these organizations, and they will have the help of the Diocesan Adviser for pre-service training units, and from him the parish priest interested will obtain the information which he needs. The Church of England Youth Council has given valuable help in its *Notes for Cadet Chaplains*, 1943, which contains notes on the Pre-Service Training Units, suggestions for the padre in his opportunities and difficulties, and suggestions for Orders of Services for use at church parades and on other occasions.

SELECT BIBLIOGRAPHY

Books on the subject are now legion. Those below marked * contain classified bibliographies and information on: Periodicals, General Books, Addresses to Youth, Art and Music, Bible, Biography, Civics and Sociology, Doctrine, Drama, First Aid, Games and Physical Education, Hobbies and Handicrafts, International, Missionary, Prayer and Worship, Psychology, Sex and Health.

A. P. Jephcott, *Girls Growing Up*, 1942.
J. Macalister Brew, **In the Service of Youth*, 1943.
D. Edwards-Rees, **The Service of Youth Book*, 1943.
A. P. Jephcott, *Clubs for Girls*.
Basil Henriques, *Club Leadership*.
H. C. Warner, **Christian Youth Leadership*, 1942.
H. C. Warner (Editor), **Youth in Action*, 1939.
*Youth in the Church (C.E.Y.C.), 1937.
*Youth's Job in the Parish (A.Y.P.A.), 1939.
G. Fallows and S. Lord, **Youth Fellowship Programmes*, 1945.
*Programme Possibilities for Church Youth Groups, S.C.M., 1944.
Douglas Cooke, ** Youth Organizations of Great Britain*.
*Christian Leadership in the Service of Youth, 1942.
J. Singleton, *Epilogues for Youth*, 1943.
G. S. Pain and E. H. Hayes, **Senior Lessons Handbook*.
R. G. Martin, **Talking Things Over*, 1942.
Peter Green, *Teaching for Lads*, 1923.
Percy Dearmer, *Lessons on the Way*, 5 vols., 1921–25.
Unto a Full Grown Man, A.Y.P.A. Series.
Sid G. Hedges, *Club Games and Activities*, &c.
Peter Green, *How to Deal with Lads*, 1922.
Lambeth Report, 1930, Section V.
Leslie L. Keating, *Sex Education in the Club*, 1945.
D. Carroll and A. Thomas, *Drama and Youth*, 1945.
L. S. Hunter, *A Parson's Job*, 1931, Chapter X.
J. B. Goodliffe, *A Parson and his Problems*, Chapter II.
D. Edwards-Rees, *A Rural Youth Service*, 1944.
Youth in the Country, 1945 (Report of a Commission of the C.E.Y.C.).
Evangelism and Youth, C.E.Y.C., 1945.
The New Generation and Sex Relationships, C.E.Y.C.
Sex Education in Schools and Youth Organisations, H.M.S.O.
The Youth Service after the War, Youth Advisory Council Report, 1943.
The Purpose and Content of the Youth Service, Youth Advisory Council Report, 1945.

CHAPTER XVII

THE CHURCH'S WORK AMONGST ADULTS

§ 1. THE PURPOSE

MANY lay people are content to feel that ordinary church attendance and private prayer are sufficient both to fulfil their duty to God and to satisfy their own needs. Certainly, without these stalwarts, Sunday worship would be sadly depleted. Among them can be found many of the quiet, modest Christians who do much good without fuss and without limelight, and often these are those who most appreciate the ministrations of the clergy. Yet they are always in danger of getting into a rut: their spiritual life is apt to stagnate and the Church is denied much good service they could render.

Recent years have seen a development in weekday activities for adults, and the life of the parishes has been strengthened thereby. The purpose of such activities is to deepen devotion and fellowship and to promote education and service. Though much of this work is of earlier origin than that for Youth, it can be regarded to-day as a continuation of the work which the various organizations try to do for the young people. These adult organizations make their influence felt in many ways. They do draw in people who can ultimately be passed on to the congregation as full members, and they also give scope to the keenest church people to exercise in work and service the love which they feel towards their church. These keen people form the inner circle, and the foundations of their faith and devotion are strengthened by their meeting together in fellowship. Further, Christianity is effectively brought into weekdays, and is regarded less as only a Sunday affair. Moreover, here lies the basis of parochial Evangelism, for the real way of bringing men and women to Christ and enlarging the borders of the church is through such groups of lay people, though it is true that many groups fail to reach this higher objective.

One great fact to be recognized is the woeful ignorance amongst the adults of to-day in matters concerning the Church and Christianity. Although great strides have been taken in education as a whole, the Church has failed to keep pace, and the future presents many dangers. This is recognized in the Report of the Arch-bishops' Commission on *Training for the Ministry*,[1] which says: " It is clear that after the war there will be great developments in edu-cation generally, not least in adult education. It is of the first importance that the Church should be equipped to take a vigorous part in these developments . . ." The Report goes on to suggest how the clergy of the future can be trained for this task. But the teaching given must be in accordance with modern methods.

> " In church and school the teaching has been line upon line, precept upon precept. We have been content to pour teaching (of a sort) over the people in copious floods. Catholicism, in particular, has been afraid of self-expression in lay people. Only a small amount of what is poured is absorbed, unless the listener is at the same time provoked to ask and seek." [2]

Sermons obviously are not enough. The Church must bring to its aid in teaching all the methods of discussions, free inquiry and corporate study, and this is the purpose of the weekday adult groups.[3] Canon Pym expressly urges that such teaching should be courageously positive, and that facts should be boldly faced.[4]

Again, adult education is an important objective of the Church not only for the benefit of the adults themselves but also because this is a way of training the parents of the next generation. Parents are too ready to push off their responsibilities on to the Day and Sunday Schools when it is they themselves who really hold the place of supreme importance in the religious training of their children.

> " All mothers and fathers ought to be made aware that their way of life is more influential during the infancy of their children than any oral teaching. Deep-seated emotional tendencies and moral attitudes are engendered in the earliest years of a child's life by its daily experience of sympathy and love or antagonism and fear in its simplest and most necessary relationships with its father and mother. The first introduc-tion to worship and to the Bible should be given, wherever possible, by the parents. We need to remember that parents cannot accomplish this task satisfactorily without preparation and help. The work of parent education through voluntary organizations is a powerful agency or ally of the Church." [5]

[1] 1944, p. 66.
[2] L. S. Hunter, *A Parson's Job*, p. 77.
[3] See Edward S. G. Wickham, *Parson and People*, Chapter III.
[4] T. W. Pym, *A Parson's Dilemmas*, 1930, Chapter III.
[5] *The Churches Survey their Task*, 1937, pp. 150, 151. Partly quoted in E. F. Braley, *A Policy in Religious Education*, 1941, p. 158. Chapter 8 of this book gives a fuller discussion of the subject.

More than ever before, Christians must emphasize the fundamental importance of the home, and the Church must be prepared to help parents to realize their great privilege.

§ 2. For Women

(a) *The Mothers' Union.* The most powerful organization for women in the Church of England has for its central objects:

    i. To uphold the sanctity of marriage.

    ii. To awaken in all mothers a sense of their great responsibility in the training of their boys and girls—the fathers and mothers of the future.

    iii. To organize in every place a band of mothers who will unite in prayer, and seek by their own example to lead their families in purity and holiness of life.

By the Constitution, all official workers and speakers must be members of the Church of England or of a Church in communion therewith, and a Parochial Branch may only be begun with the consent of the incumbent and must be carried on in accordance with his wishes. So the M.U. is definitely a Church organization and the incumbent's position is safeguarded. More often than not the parson's wife is enrolling member. Membership is not restricted to members of the Church of England. Ordinary membership is open to married women, who:—

    i. Have been baptized, affirm their belief in the principle of infant baptism, and undertake to bring their children (if any) to Holy Baptism.

    ii. Accept the teaching contained in the Apostles' Creed.

    iii. Are faithful to their marriage vows.

    iv. Declare their adherence to the three Central Objects.

Associate membership is for single women who are interested.

Membership is received through an admission ceremony, which should be held in church and made solemn and impressive. At this ceremony the member receives a card that sets out the objectives and gives the M.U. prayer. Membership should be carefully guarded. Often the M.U. is regarded as a kind of women's meeting attached to a church, to which all women are invited to come.

The first objective, " to uphold the sanctity of marriage," implies the Christian principle of the permanence of the relationship between husband and wife. Consequently any divorced person, whether ' innocent ' or not, or any woman who marries a divorced man, is ineligible for membership. The Union is right in maintaining a rigid rule, for it exists to stress the lifelong tie of marriage, and it believes that this insistence only will preserve Christian home life. This must be accepted by any incumbent who may otherwise feel that in certain conditions there can be re-marriage after divorce, or who feels that those who have been so married may be admitted to Holy Communion. The Mothers' Union is not a Society for church women as such with this particular rule added as something of minor importance: the rigid rule is the *raison d'être* of the Union. Any sympathy that may rightly be felt for those whose married life has gone wrong must be expressed through different channels.

Nevertheless, for parochial purposes it is the other objects rather than the first which count for most—the training of parents for their great task and the creation of a fellowship of mothers to unite them in prayer and practice. The typical M.U. branch holds regular services and meetings, either devotional, instructive or educational. Visiting speakers are the rule, but rarely do they follow a regular syllabus, except of some short-term nature. More imaginative use of this opportunity could make the M.U. meetings more effective educationally, and " thus avoid the lack of system that seems to prevail at present of having to accept anyone whose chief qualification is a willingness to speak." [1]

Very often in the eyes of the parish priest the value of the M.U. is the fellowship it creates among the women, the opportunity it gives him of some devotional teaching, and the important work the branch can do for the support of the Church.

One difficulty experienced by the average branch is the winning of the younger mothers. The Fellowship of Marriage is an associated society which tries to do this, but even when it does succeed it does not always achieve the further success of passing on its members to the M.U. at the right time. The Mothers' Union so often tends to be a Grandmothers' Union, and talks on the training of children become somewhat out of place. A very determined effort to counteract this difficulty has been made by the M.U. in its Younger Wives Campaign.

The Mothers' Union as a central body has considerable influence, and while it supports its primary objective it uses its influence rightly. In some other matters where Church opinion is divided, as in religious education and the maintenance of the dual system, central action by the M.U. is often an embarrassment to an incumbent who has a branch in his parish, but who may perhaps disagree

[1] E. F. Braley, *A Policy in Religious Education*, 1941, p. 159.

with the central pronouncement. For this reason every incumbent must keep in touch with the policy of the M.U. by following the Journal or the Workers' Paper.

(b) *The Women's Meeting.* From the parochial point of view, much of the good work done by the M.U. could be achieved by a Women's Meeting.[1] With weekly meetings, in talks given by the clergy, an instructional scheme can be given more easily. The needs of the women in devotion and in service can similarly be satisfied. Such an organization lacks the admission ceremony and the world-wide associations, and has no one objective above all others.

Canon Peter Green[2] advocates a weekly meeting for women and a quarterly meeting for the M.U., restricting membership of the latter to communicants. This is going beyond the requirements of the constitution of the Union, but it does lead many mothers to think seriously of Confirmation, although it must be said that any women's organization is a fruitful source of candidates for Confirmation.

Whatever organizations a parish may have, provision should be made for weekday celebrations of the Holy Communion for mothers, many of whom cannot attend on Sundays. Canon Green[3] suggests 9.30 a.m. on Mondays as against any other day of the week, since Sunday provides a suitable preparation; but in many areas Monday is washing day. Local conditions must decide. Mothers' Union branches often have a monthly corporate Communion; some priests would urge that a weekly regular day is more easily remembered.

(c) *Fellowship and Service.* Apart from the devotional and educational needs in every parish, there is a place for women's work run solely for their own fellowship and for the benefit of the Church. Sewing and working parties, which in industrial areas prepare for the Bazaar, and in other parishes do work for the hospitals and the poor, have their own particular procedure. In some parishes parochial teas are an institution, and some women caterers in church work would be a credit to big business firms. It must, however, be acknowledged that these working parties are frequently a source of parish quarrels and petty jealousies—in fact, most parish worries of this kind originate from them. They need to be led by women of real Christian character and handled with tact by the parish priest. Concerts and parties are open to the same difficulties. Casting

[1] They have their dangers, perhaps more at one time than now. See: C. F. Rogers, *Principles in Parish Work*, pp. 183–185.
[2] Peter Green, *The Town Parson*, 1919, pp. 199, 200.
[3] *Ibid.*, p. 198.

for parts is a delicate business, and running amusements for women is an exacting one—those tasks often fall to the lot of the parson's wife. Mothers' Outings are another source both of fellowship and of difficulties. Careful planning of rail and 'bus facilities and catering arrangements can all be spoilt by those who fail to catch trains and buses and delay the whole party. If it were not for the fact that the women's annual outing is the only chance that some of the working-class mothers have of getting away from their homes,[1] these affairs would be best left alone.

Some provision ought to be made also for older girls, for whom marriage becomes increasingly unlikely, and who ought not to remain in the junior organizations, like the G.F.S.[2] They need some kind of Guild to keep them together for service, doing needlework for the church, for bazaars, or for Rescue Homes, or a Circle for study and prayer, or the Sanctuary Guild to band them together for the care of the church.

§ 3. FOR MEN

(a) *A Parochial Men's Society.* The churchwardens, sidesmen and men of the Church Council can form the nucleus of a useful Men's Society to which other men attached to the church may be invited. Adult confirmation candidates usually become enthusiastic members. The aims of such a society would be the creation of fellowship among the men of the church, the study of subjects connected with Christian faith and life, and the giving of service to the church in all possible ways. On the whole, men are better at discussion than women, and the views they express at meetings can help the incumbent to obtain a deep insight into the minds of the ordinary laymen. Subjects that have been found to interest the men are as varied as Gambling, Divorce, Church and State, Social Credit, the Atonement, and Worship. Meetings can be monthly during the winter. A line of study on sociology, guided by some of the papers issued by the I.C.F., can give an objective and prevent the discussions from being merely discursive.

For service the members can be called upon to do any useful job for the church, such as putting up bazaar stalls, removing furniture, or undertaking the heavy side of church spring cleaning, as well as work of an evangelistic nature. In those parts of the country where the social instinct is strong—for instance, in the West Riding—some men like to run a ' Tea and Concert ' as an all-male affair.

---

[1] J. B. Goodliffe, *The Parson and his Problems*, 1933, p. 72.
[2] See above, Chapter XVI, § 3 (b).

(b) *The Church of England Men's Society.* The well-known C.E.M.S. can supply the organization needed in the parish for a Men's Society. It is a Fellowship of Communicant Churchmen linked together by prayer, worship and study for winning men to Christ. Thus it is definitely evangelistic in aim, but for the most part a parochial branch is run very much as the Society described above. The C.E.M.S. has the advantage of being organized into Federations for the purposes of mutual help, instruction and guidance, so the weak parochial groups are strengthened by the strong. The Federations form a Diocesan Union which can undertake work, especially of an evangelistic nature, for the benefit of the Diocese. But the C.E.M.S. must be kept to its task; it is easy to degenerate into second best.

(c) *Men's Services and Brotherhoods.* These special ways of meeting the needs of men are not now so prominent as they were a few years ago. They were usually timed for Sunday afternoon, and were of a P.S.A. or popular type, easy to attend, at which the address was the main attraction. They tended to become ends in themselves, for very few of those attracted to them were afterwards led on to the regular services and to Confirmation. They are neither evangelistic nor do they offer training for the faithful.

> " It is not unfair to say that free-and-easy assemblies and popular gatherings, with bands, solos and straight talks . . . from which the sober restraints of ordered worship are absent, are an unsatisfactory substitute for the regular use by men of the Prayer Book with their wives and children at their side." [1]

But in former years Bishop Watts Ditchfield did some wonderful work with men in these and in other ways. [2]

(d) *Institutes and Sports.* These are often thorny subjects in parochial politics.

> " Clubs and guilds are valuable adjuncts of work among men on two conditions: that they are under really Christian leaders, and that their membership is the privilege of the insider and not a bait to catch those who stand aloof from the Church's general life." [3]

The difficulty is that these two conditions are hard to attain. Institutes usually begin with good intentions, but those who desire the amenities without the obligations somehow creep in; by being

---

[1] R. C. Joynt, *The Church's real Work*, 1934, p. 59.
[2] J. E. Watts Ditchfield, *The Church in Action* (Lecture IV), and also *Fishers of Men.*
[3] R. C. Joynt, *The Church's real Work*, p. 63.

good billiard-players or good footballers they become important committee men, and the interests of the church are placed on one side.   Similar difficulties were noticed in the work of running boys' clubs,[1] but with men's institutes safeguards are harder to maintain. The billiard table never leads to the Lord's Table; the institute is a discredited method of Evangelism.   Billiard tables are best off church premises, unless they are distinctly a very minor part of the programme of a Men's Society.   Clubs for outdoor sports, if they are not merely for the adolescents, are best independent of the church, financially separate, paying for the use of rooms like any other hirers.

§ 4. General Activities

(a) *Educational*.   The most thoroughgoing method is that provided by the Church Tutorial Classes Association.   Its aim is :—

> " to provide opportunities for the continuous and thorough study, under competent guidance, of the fundamental principles of Christian faith and practice; of the Bible; of the nature and history of the Church; the origin and growth of its constitution, its creeds and its worship; of the work of the Church overseas; of the relation of religion to science; of Christian ethics and the application of Christ's teaching to the life of to-day; and of other religious subjects." [2]

There are three types of Church Tutorial Classes—Three-Year, Sessional and Terminal—which have to satisfy certain conditions to be recognized.   The C.T.C.A. is willing to give advice, and has published some useful literature.   An advantage of the C.T.C.A. method is that the members pledge themselves to come regularly, and the standard of study is very high.   But it must be admitted that the Tutorial Class is a method for the few.

> " Nevertheless, those to whom it will appeal are people whom it is immensely worth while to serve. Although they may not be numerous, they are not so few as clergy are disposed to think—the thoughtful layman and laywoman have often given up the clergy in despair, so that they do not know each other." [3]

A most comprehensive book for parochial educational purposes is *The Teaching Church*, with the sub-title *A Handbook of Adult Religious Education*, edited by Canon Woodard, on behalf of the Bishop of Manchester's Education Group in 1928, when Dr. Temple

---

[1] See above, Chapter XVI, § 4 (*e*).
[2] From the Statement of the C.T.C.A.
[3] L. S. Hunter, *A Parson's Job*, p. 83.

was Bishop of Manchester. The book considers the subject from all angles, and gives much useful information about books, libraries, organization and kindred matters. The same group inspired a new and excellent publication, *The Teaching Church Review*. More up-to-date information is given in the Livingstone Report, 1944, and in *Re-Educating Adults*, 1945, by R. E. Parsons.

Even if the full Tutorial Class is not possible, some educational work is a necessity if the Church is to deepen its life. Study circles for both men and women can be formed on a short-term basis for the study of various subjects, as suggested by the C.T.C.A., or by the I.C.F., or by the Religion and Life Week movement. Classes for Bible Study in connection with the Bible Reading Fellowship can discuss the questions provided on the monthly reading notes, and Missionary study is another possibility. Dr. Hunter recommends week-end conferences in which a group of people go away for a week-end with the priest if possible, or have the conference conducted at home.[1]

Other opportunities for study are presented by Lent and Advent. A School of Bible Study can run on the discussion group method, or a similar Missionary School or School of Sociology can occupy four or six weeks.

Now that the Cinema has become a normal part of English life, it is obvious that the medium of the film can be used more profitably both for devotion and education. Indeed, it is safe to say that, in future, few parishes will be able to neglect the film. But this does not mean that other methods of 'visual aids' have been entirely superseded. For convenience, 'visual aids' for the screen fall into five classes: the sound film, the silent film, the film strip, the lantern slide, and book illustrations, maps, small objects, etc., for use with the epidiascope. Advice in all these five methods can be obtained from the Church of England Films Commission, which was set up, at the request of the late Archbishop William Temple, to act as the official centre for the Anglican Church in all matters connected with films.

For the sound film the apparatus is expensive, but the cost of sound-projectors is likely to be reduced, and a constant use of films should make this method universally practicable in most parishes. It will be many years before religious films (other than a few 'freaks') will be shown on the commercial screen. There are already in existence a number of religious films of the type known technically as 'Documentary' and 'Interest' films. Many

[1] L. S. Hunter, *A Parson's Job*, Chapter VI.

Q

more are likely to be produced. Films of this kind are most suitable for use in schools, for adult education, and for general meetings. The silent film continues to be essential for some teaching purposes. It has the advantage of enabling the teacher to elaborate his own commentary. Particularly when children and young people are concerned, the ability to assimilate varies greatly from parish to parish and from group to group, and no sound commentary can be quite as effective as the specially prepared commentary of the priest or teacher on the spot.

Neither has the sound film done away with the need for the illustrated lecture by the use of still pictures. The film strip is likely to replace the lantern slide and to hold the field in the future. Film strips are more easily transported, more convenient to handle, and less fragile than slides. The lantern-slide department of the Church Assembly Press and Publications Board has many interesting sets on various subjects of Church interest. The S.P.C.K. and the Church Army can also supply sets of slides; and certain firms, such as Newtons, have excellent material, though naturally, as these are commercial firms, their charge for hire is higher than those of the Church organizations. The publicity departments of such undertakings as railways have also sets useful for meetings of more general interest. The epidiascope will also commend itself to the lecturer who tries to illustrate his subject from books and photographs of his own choice.

The Films Commission has set up an Information Department to deal with inquiries of all kinds. In particular, the department is able to advise clergy, educationists, leaders of youth organizations and others on: (a) methods of using films in religious work, (b) the choice of films, (c) the choice and installation of projectors and equipment. The Commission also issues classified lists of religious films and others suitable for religious work, and it has a film-booking department. The Commission, which has its headquarters at S.P.C.K. House, has wider plans for research, demonstration and production.

(b) *Devotional.* Meetings of a devotional kind are naturally associated with those of an educational nature. As already indicated, films and lantern slides can provide devotional help as well as give instruction. Most devotional opportunities, however, will be provided by the services of the church in the daily or weekly celebrations, in the daily offices, in the observance of Saints' Days, and in the mid-week choral Evensong. Those who give addresses at these should clearly recognize that only the very keen come.

" On Saints' Days it is assumed that the audience will consist of the very best people in the parish. There are subjects that are specially suited to them, and it is a pity when their time is wasted by the effort to construct a sermon of the life of a saint of whom we know little or nothing." [1]

There are various guilds and societies for clergy and laity which exist for the cultivation of the spiritual lives of their members, as well as having other specific objectives. [2]

Prayer meetings are by no means out of date, though they can be very dull unless the leader is himself well prepared, and also ready to prevent long and rambling efforts of others. Intercession services of a more formal character help to deepen the spiritual lives of those who come. Ember seasons, rogationtide and the seasons associated with overseas missions can all be observed with profit.

(c) *Evangelistic.* The great possibilities before the lay folk in Evangelism have already been discussed. [3] It is not necessary to repeat the description of teams of speakers, visiting campaigns and other methods, but it should be emphasized that these have their proper place in a list of the adult activities of the church.

(d) *Service and Fellowship.* Many of the keenest members of the church will naturally become its officials, and their particular jobs will be their official work. The Church Council and the various committees will claim others, and the choir should not be forgotten as an important sphere of adult service. The time given by devoted people in the service of their church is worth far more than material gifts, and the more responsibility that can be shared with officials, the greater the fellowship between clergy and laity. In planning adult work allowance should be made for the time of the lay people already absorbed in their official duties.

Other adult activities are mainly for the cultivation of fellowship among the church members, but, indirectly, they usually bring financial benefit to the church. Under this head can be classed the various socials and dances, the concerts, and the work of the dramatic and operatic societies. These last are sometimes faced with the dangers that so easily beset sports clubs. They can become ends in themselves, and people are brought in for their talent, and not for their churchmanship. Societies like these should be suppressed before such a state of affairs is reached. But it must be

---

[1] H. L. Goudge, *Christian Teaching and the Christian Year*, 1937, p. 14.
[2] A list with addresses can be found in the *Church of England Year Book*.
[3] See above, Chapter XIV, § 2 (*b*) and (*c*); § 3 (*c*).

admitted that these societies can bring Christian people together in
happy fellowship.[1]

§ 5. ORGANIZATION

If societies and organizations, whether for children, adults or
young people, are to be run successfully, they should be as far as
possible decentralized. Of some the clergy will naturally be the
Leaders, but while the incumbent always must know all that is
going on, most organizations are best left to keen and competent lay
people. The list of officials for each will vary according to requirements; there will generally be a Leader or Chairman, a secretary
and a treasurer, and, if necessary, a committee. All officials should
be confirmed members of the church.

Each society should be taught to keep records, in the form of
minutes or a log book, and to keep strict accounts, which must be
audited. Each organization should have its annual meeting, at
which accounts are read before all the members, reports made and
officials and committees elected. These meetings should take place
before the Annual Parochial Church Meeting, so that opportunity
may be given to all sections of parochial interest to make nominations for the Church Council elections. The accounts of the
organizations should also be presented or lie on the table at the
Annual Parochial Meeting, so that everyone can see that all
accounts are in order.[2]

From time to time the incumbent should review the work of the
various parochial activities and consider possible improvements.
Each in turn can be investigated with the Committee concerned.
It may sometimes happen that the organization is ceasing to fulfil
the purpose for which it began, and the time may have come for
its formal extinction.

In the incumbent's filing system should be folders for each of
the organizations. The folders should contain brief records of the
meetings and activities, lists of members, lists of speakers, future
plans and programmes. The literature issued by the Central
Societies should be filed, whether there is a branch in the parish or
not; such information may be of value in another parish. All
records can be useful—e.g., for Annual Outings, a single sheet can
record the numbers present; times of trains or buses; hours of
meals, menus, where taken, the cost, and any comments made at
the time. The following year plans may be made in much less time.

[1] See also above, Chapter XII, § 3 (a).
[2] See above, Chapter VIII, § 4 (b); Chapter X, § 3 (a).

In a numbered indexing system each society will have its sub-sections—*e.g.*, Mothers' Union: Central information; Our Branch, officials and members; Records of meetings, including Annual Meetings; Programmes and speakers; Missionary Share Plan; Concert records; Annual Outings.

SELECT BIBLIOGRAPHY

A. L. Woodard (Editor), *The Teaching Church*, 1928.
L. S. Hunter, *A Parson's Job*, 1931, Chapter VI.
E. S. G. Wickham, *Parson and People*, 1931, Chapter III.
T. W. Pym, *A Parson's Dilemmas*, 1930, Chapter III.
R. C. Joynt, *The Church's real Work*, 1934, Chapter IX.
J. E. Watts Ditchfield, *The Church in Action*, 1913, Chapter IV.
A. L. Preston, *The Parish Priest in his Parish*, 1933, Chapter VII.
R. E. Parsons, *Re-Educating Adults*, 1945.
Towards the Conversion of England, 1945, pp. 127-134.
The Church and Adult Education, C.A. 772 (A). A Report of the Adult Section of the National Society's Education Committee. (Chairman, Sir Richard Livingstone), 1944.
M. Francis, *The Family Club*, 1946.
The Church's Guide to Films for Religious Use (The Church of England Films Commission), 1946.

CHAPTER XVIII

THE PARISH MAGAZINE

§ 1. The Importance of the Magazine

" Almost every priest has a monthly opportunity of exercising part of his ministry in his parish magazine. Without being unduly critical, it must be owned that the opportunity is usually lost." [1] It would be too easy to heap quotation upon quotation about the pathetic ineffectiveness of the average parish magazine. Many charges are brought against this unhappy little parish paper. Its technique is out of date, the parochial matter usually called the Vicar's Letter is dull and dismal, the inset is ' churchy sentimentalism,' and the cover inartistic. It is held up to ridicule by the few educated people who venture to open it.

> " The Parish Magazine is too frequently a puerile performance. The inset is exclusively ecclesiastical and goody-goody. The vicar's letter is often querulous and a disguised complaint, or a summary of petty little parochial treats and events described with a sad effort at feeble humour." [2]

In his very useful little book on *The Parish Magazine,* Canon Swift [3] confirms this view by giving the attitude of the world as shown in the *Report on the British Press* issued by Political and Economic Planning (P.E.P.), which says : " A further host of small sectional periodicals, mainly parish magazines, have not been considered of sufficient importance to be included." Yet among those which are included are School magazines and the local time-table.

In 1942 an exhibition of parish magazines was held at Cambridge, and some 150 magazines were shown representing the many types of parishes both in town and country. A review of the exhibition states : " Many editors seemed to have considered neither aims nor technique; their scrupulous avoidance of uniformity or attention to modern journalistic methods was unfortunate, almost impious." [4] Yet even technique is less important than the aims of the magazine :

[1] A. W. Hopkinson, *Pastor's Progress,* p. 171.
[2] J. B. Goodliffe, *The Parson and His Problems,* p. 116.
[3] J. M. Swift, *The Parish Magazine,* 1939, p. 11.
[4] Alan Webster in *Theology,* July 1943, pp. 156 ff.

226

" The Church is surrounded by an environment that is either hostile or indifferent. . . . In the present situation the aim of a parish magazine should be to teach both Christians and others." [1]

This is by no means an over-ambitious aim, for actually the circulation of parish magazines taken together is enormous. " In 1936 . . . 11,085 parish magazines had a monthly circulation of 2,763,000." [2] This circulation is higher than the daily sales of some of the popular newspapers, and runs very close to the most popular Sunday newspapers. Parish magazines are to be found in all sorts of houses, and are often left lying about on the table, and thus catch the interest of casual visitors. They are certainly taken and read by very many who never come to church services; indeed, " It is not generally recognized how widely they are read by many people who do not come to Church." [3] Clearly the Church has no better medium for publicity than its parish magazines, but unfortunately it must depend on its 11,085 different editors, who have various ideas about their job, or none at all.

The printed word is a powerful force to-day, still more powerful than the wireless and the cinema, certainly far more powerful than the spoken word of the pulpit. Yet there is no comparison between the amount of preparation the average parson will give to his sermon and that which he will devote to his magazine. More often than not, the latter is dashed off against time, and its hasty preparation is easily seen by the reader; yet it is at least as important as preaching, if not for the good, then certainly for the harm it can do to the Gospel, when it is ill-prepared and puerile. To-day the magazine is almost the only weapon for counteracting very harmful influences from the secular Press. Not infrequently in the popular Press there is misrepresentation of the church and the clergy, and occasionally direct or veiled attacks on organized Christianity. Very rarely do the ordinary people trouble to read the great dailies, and hardly ever the Church weekly Press. Only the parish magazine can attempt to keep the man in the pew informed correctly in these public controversies. Nor need the magazine keep only to the defensive, but can go over directly to the attack. It should show the aim and purpose of the Gospel.

It cannot be said that the continual complaint, and inevitable appeal, and the occasional bun-fight report, give any adequate

[1] Alan Webster in *Theology*, July 1943, pp. 156 ff.
[2] J. M. Swift, *The Parish Magazine*, p. 12.
[3] *Putting our House in Order*, p. 47.

presentation of Christianity. Something better can be expected of men who in the pulpit can prove themselves capable both of preaching and teaching the Gospel. At any rate, the common pitfalls can be avoided. " To use a parish magazine to propagate inaccurate astrology is possibly no more harmful than to fill the vicar's letter with complaints of overwork and underpayment." [1] Yet samples of both appeared, apparently, in the Cambridge Exhibition.

So much depends on the parish priest. He may with some truth say that he has not received a journalistic training, nor has he the gifts of an editor, just as he will say that he has no financial ability and no knowledge of ancient buildings. But whatever else he may do, he must make some attempt to produce his parish magazine, just because it is part of his work for the proclamation of the Gospel. Just as he must learn the art of preaching, so he must learn the art of writing and editing the parish magazine. " The parish magazine may be made one of the best media of evangelism." [2]

§ 2. THE CONTENTS OF THE MAGAZINE

(a) *The Local Matter.* Whatever else the magazine may contain by the way of insets, the local matter prepared by the parson is the most important part. It is described as ' local ' because it is printed locally, and not because it is concerned only with local matters. If the magazine is read at all, certainly this part is, even by those who consider the insets sentimental and useless. Thus its methods of presentation deserves some thought. In by far the great majority of magazines the local matter takes the form of the ' Vicar's Letter,' followed, as some say appropriately enough, by a list of funerals. The letter is not the best form of presentation of all the matter of the magazine. Canon Swift argues for an editorial rather than a personal letter, as the general medium of presentation, abolishing needless addresses and other appendages of the letter. The personal letter strikes with more force when it is used occasionally.[3] The argument is strong, but many readers look for a letter, though they ask for a letter that is both ' chatty ' in form and has a Christian message. Weak personal comments on the political situation, or the common war-note in war-time, are not desired, but the Christian viewpoint on Education, Industry, and similar topics can be made the subjects of good articles. The best method is to have a short personal letter concerned with a Christian topic, and

---

[1] Alan Webster in *Theology*, July 1943, p. 158.
[2] J. M. Swift, *The Parish Magazine*, p. 18. Cf. above, Chapter XIV, § 2 (c) iii.
[3] *Ibid.*, pp. 20, 21.

just occasionally with the parochial need of the moment, and leave the rest of the space for news and articles.

The parochial notes and news receive many sneers, but they are necessary for the circulation of the magazine. The readers look for them. The popular newspapers have such features, and their editors are experts in gauging public sentiments. In the first place, the magazine is expected to give notice of events for the month, and this is done through the Calendar, an important feature, and short descriptive notes to indicate the purpose and nature of the services and functions. In the second place, the magazine is a record, and thus eventually a source of historical information, and the results of events are news. The church people really do wish to know the final result of the Gift Day. The same is true of the Parish Register, regarded by some as unnecessary. Advertisers know the value of the spaces opposite this page.

> " A well-kept register appearing each month has considerable local interest. Not only do relatives look for such a feature and preserve the magazine in which the family name appears, but many parishioners, especially the women, turn to the register first of all." [1]

To these must be added other routine items, the sidesmen's rota, the flower list, and other useful reminders.

It adds to the interest of the magazine if news can be exclusive, for the first notice of the prospective visit of the Bishop to preach at church should not be seen in the local Press, but in the magazine. Space should be provided for the organizations, and their leaders invited to contribute news of their activities; a place set aside for Youth Notes, and, if possible, a children's corner, add to the interest of the magazine and increase its circulation. As a rule parochial notes should be arranged together, set out with headings and appropriate sub-divisions. Further:

> " In those parishes where sermons are planned well ahead due notice of the courses can be given in the Magazine. A list of books to be read in conjunction can help to attract the interest of the more intellectually minded of the congregation." [2]

Nevertheless the magazine should not be narrowly parochial, and a good proportion of the space must be reserved for more general matter. There is often a need for a series of articles popularizing Church institutions, such as the " Church Officials," the " Diocesan Quota," " What We Do in Church and Why." There is even more

[1] J. M. Swift, *The Parish Magazine*, pp. 29 f.
[2] C. F. Rogers, *Pastoral Theology and the Modern World*, 1920, p. 29.

need for real Christian teaching on doctrinal and devotional subjects, as " Does God answer prayer ? ", " How to meditate on the Bible," and " God and Industry ". In the Cambridge Exhibition, " of the 150 exhibits about thirty aimed at teaching their readers, and about fifteen of these contained articles intelligible to non-Christians, too low a proportion if it is remembered how many read the magazine, yet never attend church ".[1] The treatment in the daily Press of the Report of the Commission on Doctrine in the Church of England showed how much ought to be done to keep the people well-informed about the work and teaching of the Church. The task is not easy, indeed many parsons may feel that they are not capable of writing such articles. If so, perhaps there is the possibility here for communal effort. Where a group of specialist clergy are at work, one " might concentrate on the intelligent presentation and defence of the faith. With the goodwill of the clergy he might even use parish magazines for this purpose." [2]

But more parish priests could write the necessary articles themselves if they took the trouble to be correct in their information. There is much to help them. News Letters, Church weeklies and bulletins are issued, and often extracts from these can be used as they stand without further editing.[3] Possible information, as it arrives, should be kept together in a folder marked ' Magazine—Current Number,' so that an abundant wealth of material gradually accumulates ready for use on the editing day.[4]

(b) *The Insets*. Equally with the local matter the inset receives its share of criticism. It appeals more to the working classes than to the educated, and the sentimental serial is followed by many readers. On the whole, this is not so bad as the rest of the average magazine. Canon Swift suggests the use of two insets, distinguished by different colours on the magazine cover, so that people can have the inset of their choice, which is not always the same as the priest's preference. When Canon Swift says that some people buy both issues, he indicates the popular view about the inset.[5]

In addition to the inset, the Missionary Societies, the C.M.S. and the S.P.G. provide quarterly notes free of charge, and these are valuable. Many magazines include also the Diocesan Leaflet. This paper is open to the same accusations as the parish magazine, and usually it is not clear whether it is a circular from the Bishop to

---

[1] Alan Webster in *Theology*, July 1943, p. 156.
[2] *Putting our House in Order*, 1941, pp. 46, 47.
[3] The Press Bureau of the Church Assembly issues useful articles.
[4] See below, § 4 (d).
[5] J. M. Swift, *The Parish Magazine*, p. 45.

the clergy or a leaflet of diocesan news for the laity. It ought to be exclusively the latter,[1] with additional articles of general Church interest, and should grasp further opportunities of Christian teaching. Reviews of books suitable for the laity make an excellent feature.

§ 3. PRODUCTION AND PRINTING

(a) *Production.* The first thing to strike the eye of the reader of a periodical is its cover, and the cover of a parish magazine is not as a rule a good introduction. In the Cambridge Exhibition, " frequently the covers contained many of the worst features of Victorian stained-glass windows ".[2] A poor photograph on a worn block printed on the wrong kind of paper is the general impression of a cover. Covers can be artistically designed, or excellent photographs can be used with advantage, to give the magazine an attractive and striking appearance which few could forget. Canon Swift suggests a periodical change of cover, and a special design for very important occasions such as the Jubilee of the Church.[3]

The good impression created by the cover should be maintained by the lay-out inside. Advertisements can be artistic, and blocks can relieve a page of heavy-type advertisements. There should never be a blank space on an advertisement page, for such space can be used to announce the times of Church services, the Bazaars, or the Free-Will offering scheme. Even worse is the blank space in the local matter; whereas the former space shows lack of initiative, the latter space denotes poverty of mind.

The local space itself should be carefully arranged, with headings and sub-divisions to help the readers. If a regular order is followed people will know where to look for their favourite feature. Good type and paper add to the beauty of the page, and ' drop letters ' and small line-blocks for headings are inexpensive and add further to the appearance of the magazine.

(b) *Printing.* Often the printer is not a matter of choice. There may be a vested interest of long standing, and careful negotiation is needed. Yet the printer himself must be considered. His expenses are high, and it would be very wrong if the Church were to seem to encourage poor craftsmanship, at cut prices, for the sake of a small saving. Where possible, a local printer should be employed, so that the editor may confer with him about production. Usually it is best to ask for quotations—and specimens—from several firms.

[1] See below, Chapter XX, § 5 (c).
[2] Alan Webster in *Theology*, July 1943, p. 158.
[3] J. M. Swift, *The Parish Magazine*, p. 14.

The printer will always appreciate the Editor's consideration, if he helps by sending the ' copy ' in good time, well written if not typed. Proofs should be accurately corrected; there are no such things as printer's errors, as it is the business of the proof reader to see that all is correct. The proper signs and marks should always be made.[1]

§ 4. THE BUSINESS SIDE

(a) *Circulation*. Nothing shows the parish priest as a man of many occupations more than the parish magazine, for not only must he edit it, but he must also arrange for its production and distribution; he must increase its circulation, or at any rate maintain it; he must generally attend to its finances; and he must be his own advertising agent. The great newspapers depend on their circulation for their stability, and little can be said of the magazine as an evangelistic or teaching agency if it has a poor circulation.

In most parishes it is quite easy to increase the circulation. The clergy are continually making new contacts, through the occasional services, and through Sunday School scholars. Most people contacted in this way will take the parish magazine. At the foot of the Baptism application form, parents can be asked to say if they would like the magazine; a large proportion do ask for it, though some give up soon afterwards. There is a tradition about taking magazines: " My mother used to take one, so perhaps I ought to."

A good plan is to increase steadily each year by adding fifty or a hundred each January. A steady increase helps the planning of the distribution. One or two weeks' visiting with this as a subsidiary purpose will soon obtain the required extra numbers, as well as meeting the inevitable decreases of the end of the year. People who move away are often glad to stay on the subscription list and receive copies by post. There should always be some available at the church for casual purchases.

(b) *Distribution*. Like most other work in the parish, the distribution of the magazine is as good or as bad as voluntary work can make it. The magazine distributors are a heroic band who must turn out in all weathers, try to collect subscriptions (not an easy task in some areas), and sometimes find themselves out of pocket because they are too shy to ask for arrears. No small wonder if some of them get rather late sometimes and do not always remember, when they are ill or on holiday, that the work has still to be done.

---

[1] J. M. Swift, *The Parish Magazine*, p. 31. A list of the correct signs.

The distributors should be helped as much as possible, first by the regular appearance of the magazine.[1] It is not always the distributors' fault when the magazine is late in arriving. The rule of publication on the Friday before the last Sunday of the month, or whatever it is, should be rigidly observed. They must be ready for a distributors' meeting at a regular time.

The distributors should also have easy geographical areas, and every list needs annual revision. New cards or books written by the secretary should be ready each January. Usually every distributor has a few friends outside her area; these addresses are always a source of perplexity when the cards are rewritten. Magazine distributors should have a proper status as members of the church voluntary staff, and can also help in many other ways, as district visitors, by reporting sickness or other needs to the clergy.

(c) *Finance.* Because of its aim and purpose, a magazine is worth while, even if it is not a sound financial proposition, but there is no reason why the magazine should not pay its way, and there is every reason why it should make a profit. The finances of the magazine are not complicated. The expenses are simply the cost of printing, the expense of the insets, and a few sundries such as bank charges, stationery and postages. The income is from two sources: the sales of the magazines and the payments for advertisements. The magazine will make a good profit if the cost of printing is reasonable, the circulation good, and the advertisements managed in a business-like way.

A layman who does the advertising side saves the priest much work, but in some parishes in a priest's ministry this work will certainly be left to him. It is quite valuable for the parish priest to see the advertisers himself. It takes him round to see the business people and shopkeepers of his parish at least once a year, and they are usually pleased to see him. The advertisements should be on a business footing, the rates rising and falling with the circulation, and not on a charity, help-the-church, basis. There are always some grumblers, some who say it does them no good, but who never withdraw their advertisements, and some people think they ought to be the only people of their trade in the magazine. The majority value the publicity it gives them, and are ready to receive suggestions for the better display of their matter.

A more exhaustive estimate of the financial value of the magazine is given by Canon Swift, and he is certainly right when he says:

[1] C. E. Russell, *The Priest and Business*, p. 46.

" Often I have had reason to be thankful for the profit made by the magazine." [1]

There is, however, another point of view—namely, that, if the magazine is a good method of Evangelism, it should be distributed free to every house in the parish.

> " If it is properly circulated, the magazine should take a message, and give information about the Church, to every house in the parish. It may be a real evangelistic agency of surprising value. There are lots of parishioners who like to know what is going on, who feel interest, and some sympathy, even if they never attend services. The aim, therefore, should be to have the magazine paid for out of church funds, as a necessary and vital agency in parochial work, and delivered free to every house in the parish." [2]

The aim is certainly good, but free literature is rarely valued.

(d) *Filing*. The publishing of a magazine is a business, and must be handled in a business-like way. Every year copies of the magazine should be bound for permanent use at the vicarage or in the parish office. In addition, a priest can keep in his own filing cabinet the local matter, which, detached from the cover and advertisements, takes very little space. Former years can be put together in one folder, last year's issues and this year's numbers in two separate folders. Folders may also be used for the current number; for ideas often culled from other magazines; for finances, quotations of costs, and accounts; and for the method of distribution.[3] In this latter a complete list of all customers can be a valuable aid to visiting.

[1] J. M. Swift, *The Parish Magazine*, pp. 39–48.
[2] A. W. Hopkinson, *Pastor's Progress*, p. 171.
[3] See above, Chapter II, § 4.

SELECT BIBLIOGRAPHY

J. M. Swift, *The Parish Magazine*, 1939.
J. M. Swift, *Editing a Parish Magazine*, 1946.

CHAPTER XIX

FOR THE WIDER WORLD

§ 1. THE MISSIONARY COMMITTEE

(a) *Its Important Work.* It has already been shown that the primary duty of the Church Council has a direct bearing on Parochial Evangelism,[1] but it is not limited to that. The actual wording of the Powers Measure is:

> " It shall be the primary duty of the Council in every parish to co-operate with the incumbent in the initiation, conduct, and development of Church work both within the parish and outside." [2]

Clearly there is a wide field for Evangelism outside the parish, for it extends throughout the whole world. Missionary work is of supreme importance to all Christians because it is fulfilling our Lord's command to preach the Gospel to all the world. The Bible is a missionary book and the Christian Church is a missionary Church. This is enough to require that organization in support of Home and Overseas Missions should be an integral part of parochial administration.

It is also true to add that the parish that neglects missions is not only false to the Gospel of Christ, but suffers from the dangers of narrow parochialism. Dr. Hensley Henson has testified to the value, in the parish, of live missionary interest:

> " I was always astonished at the amount of money which was contributed to the Church Missionary Society from the diocese during a period of extraordinary economic distress. This active concern for world evangelization did undoubtedly tend to widen the outlook of many religious people. . . ." [3]

When interest is turned inwards, life becomes stunted, if not dead. On the other hand, missionary interest in a parish is a tremendous stimulus to the spiritual life of the parish. Far from it being dangerous to parochial finances to give liberally to outside objectives, it has been demonstrated many times over that when people are taught to give generously to missions, they learn at the same time to be generous at home.

[1] See above, Chapter XIV, § 1 (c).
[2] The Parochial Church Councils (Powers) Measure, 1921, § 2.
[3] H. Hensley Henson, *Retrospect of an Unimportant Life*, Vol. II, 1943, p. 393.

Yet, unless the parish has had a long missionary tradition, there is usually some opposition to a missionary policy from many of the laity, and not least from the Church Councillors.

> " The average layman does not go so far as to disparage world evangelization: he believes in missions, in their proper place. But that place is not always with him first, or even a prominent place." [1]

Often the parish priest has to work away at missionary interest by himself, or, at best, with the help of a small band of keen workers. Nevertheless, whether the lay people who are keen be few or many, the priest must always be keen. The missionary interest of a parish is more than anything else a true measure of his own work and enthusiasm. It is sad but true that sudden fluctuations in annual parochial contributions are due very largely to changes in incumbents. The people can tell if missions are ' dragged in ' or form part of the whole message.

> " The flock must see by unmistakable signs that their shepherd counts the making known of the salvation of God in Christ a primary obligation, binding on every Christian according to his powers and opportunities." [2]

Missionary education is important enough, therefore, to be given a recognized place in Pastoralia. Very few books on the subject mention Overseas missions at length. Archdeacon Joynt's book already quoted is one exception, but the Report of the Archbishops' Commission on the *Training for the Ministry* [3] emphasizes the great importance of the various means in which the vision of the Church's wide task may be stimulated amongst ordinands:

> " Pre-ordination residence in a missionary school or college overseas may be invaluable: a course of ' parochialia ' should include the study of ways of missionary education in parishes: ordinands may in vacation help in missionary campaigns or corporately visit some overseas Church. . . ."

If all the clergy are trained along these suggested lines, the laity would soon realize that missionary zeal is not merely a hobby of a few incumbents who have a kink in that direction.

(b) *Its Constitution*. While it is true that the creation and maintenance of missionary interest in a parish rest largely upon the parish priest, a properly constituted Missionary Committee can render valuable service, and can also provide for a continuance of the work during an interregnum between two incumbents. The

[1] R. C. Joynt, *The Church's real Work*, 1934, p. 117.
[2] *Ibid.*, p. 111.   [3] 1944, pp. 60, 61.

existence of a Missionary Committee also prevents this activity from being regarded as a hobby of the parson, and shows that it is the concern of the laity as well. This Committee should be one of the committees of the Church Council, so that the Council can have direct reports on its work, and generally so that it can be the conscience of the Council in regard to its primary duty. A certain number of members should be appointed by the Council, and they should co-opt others to represent the various organizations and sections in the parish—*e.g.*, from the Mothers' Union, the G.F.S., the Sunday School Departments. The parochial secretaries of the various missionary and charitable societies, as Missions to Seamen, Missionary Service League, King's Messengers, Waifs and Strays, A.C.S., Ladies' Home Mission Union, should also be on the Committee.

The Committee will appoint its own officers, chairman, secretary and treasurer. The duties of the Committee will include the cultivation of interest in missions through Education, Intercessions, and Witness, and the stimulation of giving and working for missions. It may undertake particular activity for raising funds, such as Garden Parties, Sales of Work, and Missionary Evenings. It can prepare a parochial missionary budget, and can allocate money given for unspecified objects (as through the Duplex scheme) to particular societies.

It is good to put the activities for Home Missions and charitable Societies under this Committee, for these are associated branches of the same kind of work, and no sense of conflict or competition is desired. It might even be deemed advisable that the Missionary Committee and the Evangelistic Committee [1] should be one and the same, for they exist for similar purposes—the fulfilling of the primary duty of the Church Council, the one outside and the other within the parish. If it is desirable that they should be separate, there should be some form of *liaison* between the two.

§ 2. THE FIVE POINTS FOR MISSIONARY SUPPORT

Whether he works through a Missionary Committee, or whether he is his own executive in this department, the parish priest must observe the balance between the five points for missionary support. It is not enough to ask for collections and contributions and send them in to some missionary society. Missionary interest is created first by a knowledge of the facts, of the extent, growth, place and

[1] See above, Chapter XIV, § 1 (c).

R

needs of the mission fields. If the first cardinal point is learning, the second is prayer. Prayer cannot be first, for intelligent prayer needs information, but once the facts are known, prayer becomes necessary, that God may be thanked for the success of past work, and asked to give the spiritual power needed for the work of the moment. True prayer seeks to express itself in action, strong in the new realization of God's will for the world. Action can be expressed in three ways: in giving financially for the missionary work, in working for it in various ways at home, and also in witnessing for it, by interesting others in this great work of the Church. The five cardinal points for missionary support are, then: Learning, Praying, Giving, Working, Witnessing.

(a) *Learning*. It is necessary to know something of those parts of the world where missionaries are at work, something of the geography of the land, of the history, customs, life and religions of the people who live in them. Then something must be known of the history of the missions to those people, of their failures and successes, of the difficulties and advantages, and particularly of their needs of the moment. It is also necessary to understand the present-day policy of missions, their relevance to political, economic and social factors in the world, and their place in world-wide missionary statesmanship.

How is this to be done? The time-honoured system of Anniversary sermons has its value, but also its dangers. It does secure at least once a year a reference to the work overseas, and perhaps an appeal for the funds, but it is obviously inadequate as a means of missionary education. " The annual sermon for missions ought to be dethroned from the lonely pedestal of isolation on which it often stands." [1] Sermons on the work can be given in suitable seasons, and missionary illustrations are often apt in other sermons.

But real missionary education demands greater effort, by way either of a Missionary School, or of a Missionary Teaching Week-end. The former will arrange for weekly meetings over a period of about six weeks, each run on the discussion group method; the latter has a week-end scheme of meetings arranged round the Sunday, so that the sermons are included in the teaching scheme. Each method follows a set syllabus, such as that issued by the Church of England Missionary Council, called *The Christian Fellowship*, and known as M.113, published in 1944 as the successor to the original M.13. Such schemes aim at reaching the many;

---

[1] R. C. Joynt, *The Church's real Work*, 1934, p. 111.

other schemes of missionary education reach only the few. Study Circles can attract a dozen to a score for intensive study, using either a book or some study outlines put out by the missionary societies. Individuals can be encouraged to read books, either by buying some at missionary gatherings or by borrowing from a circulating library, of a missionary society.[1] Most societies publish very interesting and well-arranged annual reports, missionary magazines and pamphlets of various kinds. The C.M.S. has a Readers' Club, through which, for a small annual subscription, all pamphlets are sent to members. The other method of encouraging individual reading is for the parish to have its own missionary library, which could occupy a shelf in the church or school. A secretary is needed to keep trace of books, and the same person could see to the circulation of missionary magazines.

(b) *Prayer*. It is the parish priest's duty to see that there is proper provision for corporate prayer for missions. Every Sunday prayers may be said at one or more services, and biddings made at the celebrations from time to time. At the weekday services this aspect of the work of the Church should have its share of the intercessions. It is a helpful custom to observe the special seasons for missionary intercessions, the festivals of the Conversion of St. Paul, St. Peter (S.P.G.), St. Matthew (C.M.S.), St. Luke (Medical Missions) and St. Andrew. Every year the Missionary Council publishes special forms for prayer and thanksgiving for use at St. Andrewstide, and copies are sent to all incumbents; these are also useful at other times, and should be filed away.

Corporate intercession can be strengthened by the making of a Missionary Corner [2] or Chapel in the church. There should be in it a map of the world, preferably one showing the Anglican Dioceses, and on it can be marked the places of special interest to the parish—*e.g.*, where missionaries from the parish or the Diocese are working, or where the parish has its shares under the Mission Share Plan, and where the various deputations coming to the parish have been stationed. In the corner can be missionary books and magazines, books and cards of missionary prayers, and photographs of missionaries and mission stations. The care of these should be the responsibility of one member of the committee.

Individuals should be helped to include missionary intercessions in their own prayers. Topics for prayer appear in missionary magazines; the societies publish periodical prayer papers, and

---

[1] The C.M.S., S.P.G. and U.M.C.A. all have excellent libraries.
[2] See the *S.P.G. Handbook*, 1931, p. 63.

Q.I.P. (the *Quarterly Intercession Paper*) [1] has a good circulation. Keen people can be taught to find their own topics for prayer from the books they read, or by using a map and their knowledge of the distribution of mission stations. Invalids can do a wonderful work of intercession for missions.

(c) *Giving*. When a person knows about the work, and prays about the work, it will not be very long before he gives for the work. There are various ways of giving, just as there are various ways of maintaining the Church at home.[2] Direct giving is the biggest support of overseas work. Annual donations or subscriptions of a certain fixed figure secure regular income, and for these the donor can become an accepted member of the society concerned. Under the covenant subscription scheme, under certain conditions, income tax can be reclaimed; the societies will readily give information about this. Most of the parishioners will give either through the Duplex scheme or through missionary boxes. The Duplex scheme encourages regular giving both for home and overseas work; its danger is that it is nobody's job to obtain new members and the income gradually diminishes, and the missionary contributions suffer in the long run. The missionary box is still the mainstay of the parochial income. The societies nowadays supply fascinating boxes of various shapes with different appeals. Many people will take them, if asked, and missionary meetings, exhibitions, schools, etc., all give opportunity for producing them. A most successful way is to invite Confirmation candidates to take them for a year, after speaking of the importance of the world-wide Church; most of them continue to use them after the first year, and each year's batch of candidates provides for a continual increase in income.

Direct interest can be secured by the Mission Share Plan, or the 'Own Missionary' system of the C.M.S., or the 'Underwriting' or 'Share' systems of the S.P.G. The Mothers' Union, Sunday School and Young People can all promise to raise a certain sum every year, and thus have a real share in the work.

Church collections can also be allocated for missions, there will be the 'Anniversary' collection, perhaps an allocation from the Communion alms, and collections at special services. Collapsible Lenten boxes for receiving the fruits of self-denial are very productive, and are issued both by the C.M.S. and the S.P.G. A Day of Prayer and Gifts can combine the two big ways of supporting the work of Church extension.

---

[1] Obtainable from the Editor, *Q.I.P.*, Church House, Wakefield.
[2] See above, Chapter X, § 2 (*b*).

The direct giving can be augmented by indirect methods, such as Garden Parties, Sales of Work, Exhibitions, Missionary Plays, some of which can also give an opportunity for missionary teaching. Some parishes may prefer to give a grant from the annual Bazaar, or to provide for a missionary stall from it.

The income for missionary work may thus be very varied; a correct record should be kept of all sources of income, and information supplied to the societies when requested.[1] Missionary money should be remitted to the proper society as soon as possible; it should not be kept with Church money.[2]

(d) *Working.* There are two ways of working for missions, and the first is for the working parties to make articles to send overseas. Equipment for hospitals and schools is always needed, or articles for outfits for missionaries about to set sail. It is necessary to be in touch with the 'Wants' departments of the society supported, so that the right things can be made—that is, those most needed—and made in the right way. Working parties can be very happy gatherings. The other way of working for Missions is to make things to sell, either at a sale of work, or privately, the proceeds going to the missions fund. There is, of course, no difference between this and the work for a parochial sale of work, unless the workers are connected together in some form or union that also meets for prayer and study.

(e) *Witnessing.* If the work is to continue, the interest of others must be gained; indeed, the very nature of the objective of missionary work makes it imperative that all others must be made to be interested in it. The Missionary Committee must have its propaganda department or Ministry of Information. The various ideas already mentioned for stimulating learning and giving are the very things to use to gain new members.

Exhibitions with displays of articles, curios, photographs, in a certain scheme, with courts and stewards, together with speakers, or lantern lectures or films or plays, are all good propaganda. The S.P.G. and the C.M.S. have well-organized departments for the supply of all these things. Some are suitable for parochial purposes, some exhibitions are much larger, and should be used in a large hall, and supported by a number of parishes. Missionary Evenings of a varied and interesting nature can be built up by keen adults or children. A country may be chosen, and games, talks or songs connected with that country will provide entertainment as well as instruction. Imitation Broadcasts are an up-to-

---

[1] See above, Chapter II, § 3 (*b*).   [2] See above, Chapter X, § 3 (*a*).

date feature, or a voyage round the world visiting the districts where the parish ' holds its Shares ',[1] with living pictures on the stage, can add novelty to teaching.

§ 3. Methods of Organization

(a) *Children.* The work among children is most important for two reasons: first and foremost, it gives them the necessary missionary education, which will bear fruit in later life, and secondly (a reason not to be despised), the contributions from the children provide a valuable source of income for missionary work. If no special organization is desired, then all existing organizations in the parish can be connected up with missionary work. The C.L.B., the Scouts and Guides can be registered or linked through the Societies; the missionary lessons for children for the year can be taken, and contact made with opposite numbers in other lands. The Sunday Schools should certainly take part in the education of the children, the lesson book should have at least four missionary lessons, and a special interest ought to be maintained with a selected part of the mission field through a ' Share '. Schools can also be affiliated to the societies. In senior departments where *Plans, Projects and Propositions* are used, it will be noticed that several in that series lead up to a missionary project, such as a pageant, an exhibition, or a series of plays.[2]

But missionary education is best given in a purely missionary organization. It might be difficult to introduce another when many organizations already exist in the parish, but it can sometimes be introduced as a club for younger boys and girls, which can centre its games, activities and learning round the great objective, the spread of the Church. The King's Messengers of the S.P.G. and the C.M.S. Discoverers of the Way provide such organizations. They are very similar in structure, and their work covers all the Five Points. A graded syllabus for study is issued each year (or those issued by the Edinburgh House Press are used), and there is an examination held just before Easter for those who wish to take it. Prayer forms an important part; the children are encouraged to give in some way, and they can work by making little things to send overseas. After a period of probation, the children can be admitted members, and allowed to, wear a badge.

The departments at the headquarters of the societies will supply all the information required. The Edinburgh House Press also

---

[1] See (c) above.   [2] See above, Chapter XV, § 3 (b).

issues some valuable teaching material in *Learning by Doing, Learning by Acting* and *Practical Books,* which have been prepared on each country. Useful practical handiwork books published by the C.M.S. are *Things to Make* and *Hands at Work*; these are things to sell, not articles to send overseas. Two delightful magazines for children are published, *The Round World* by the C.M.S., and *The King's Messengers* by the S.P.G. The Eagle stories are excellent little books about missionaries, and will thrill any child.

(b) *Youth.* Missionary education should have its established place in the programme of any Young People's Fellowship.[1] The members at Confirmation should be encouraged to take missionary boxes, and the proceeds put together and allocated to their ' Youth Own Missionary '. The keener members may be gathered into a study circle, encouraged to attend area ' Youth Week-Ends ' or to go to the Summer Schools of the Societies. The C.M.S. has a useful Youth Service Bureau, which supplies good information for use in work among young people.

Young people like large crowds, and it is more inspiring to them if parishes co-operate. The Youth Committee of the Diocesan Missionary Council, or of the Local Association of one of the missionary societies, can organize joint rallies, speaking teams, teams giving plays and week-ends. The members usually return from these joint affairs ready to bring new life into the parish.

Those of the young people who become really very keen are the most likely people to offer their services for the mission field itself. Their sense of vocation can be fostered through the ' Companions of the Way ' of the C.M.S., or the ' Missionary Preparation Union ' of the S.P.G.; in these no pledge is given on either side. When the call to serve overseas becomes more definite, direct contact can be made with the Candidates' Departments of the societies, which will give information about training according to the qualifications of the candidates. It is an important part of the priest's duty to watch for possible missionary candidates as well as for possible ordinands. The importance of the necessary qualifications must be stressed from the beginning, as well as the higher importance of the spiritual life, to prevent deep disappointment if the offer cannot be accepted.

(c) *Adults.* As it is for children, so it is for adults; the missionary interest can be gained through the means of existing organizations or through a definite missionary association. Missionary speakers can be provided for the organizations, and they can be encouraged

[1] See above, Chapter XVI, § 4 (a).

to give good support in contributions and work. However, a missionary fellowship of some kind is the best way to create a missionary-hearted nucleus in the parish. The 'Missionary Service League' of the C.M.S. definitely follows the five-point programme, and the 'King's Workers' of the S.P.G. are a similar body. Study outlines are provided for members, suggestions for work are given, as prayer, giving and witnessing all naturally come into the programme. For the keener lay people who wish to feel more in the missionary fellowship, the societies provide Laymen's Associations, and there is always work which the laity can do for the local Missionary Associations.

(d) *Literature.* A further word is needed about the supply of books. Missionary books were once rather despised, but now they reach a high standard. This is largely due to the productions of the Edinburgh House Press, formerly the United Council of Missionary Education, in which all missionary societies, Anglican and Free Church, co-operate. Each year a subject or country is chosen, and a series of books in various grades for all interests and ages is planned.[1] There are books for study, introductory, intermediate and advanced for adults; background books for adults and children; teaching books on modern lines for each grade of children; the 'Hero Stories', 'Yarns' books, and various kinds of practical books; and there are various reading books for all ages.

The missionary societies themselves also have good publishing departments, and augment the supply of books from the Edinburgh House, maintaining where necessary their own angle of approach. The Annual Reports are usually more than just mere reports; they are good literary productions.

§ 4. THE SOCIETIES

The different parishes have customarily associated themselves with certain of the various missionary societies of the Church. Choice is coloured, no doubt, by churchmanship and tradition, and it is not always wise, from the point of view of missionary interest, to make any change of society in a parish of long tradition. There is a considerable and weighty logical argument that the Church should be its own missionary society, and that increased powers and authority should be given to the Missionary Council to organize the work. But the society method is the traditional Anglican method. The societies are more than associations for

---

[1] An interesting account in the S.P.G. Handbook, 1931, *Home Work*, pp. 38–47.

finding money for overseas work: they are fellowships, communities of keen, like-minded people associated for a purpose and united by that purpose in prayer and in action, some overseas and many more at home. It has been well argued that communities within the community of the Church have existed throughout the ages for the purposes of effecting special work.[1]

For the time being, however, the Church of England does its missionary work through the missionary societies, and every parish priest should be a member of a society and bring in the support of his parish with his own interest. Besides ensuring that he has made an adequate place for missionary interest in his parish, he should play his part in the wider organization of his society. These organizations follow the lines of the Dioceses, Archdeaconries and Deaneries; there are official organizing secretaries working for the societies in each area, and the local associations have their own honorary officials, who, with their committees, are responsible for co-ordinated activities. Anniversary Week-Ends are often planned by them, and every incumbent of the parishes co-operating should help by giving prompt and cordial answers to correspondence.[2]

Furthermore, co-ordination between the societies is also necessary, in the Church and in each Diocese. The Missionary Council of the Church of England and the several Diocesan Missionary Councils have done much to stimulate a more general interest in missions in the parishes. The *World Call* reports, and the *Unified Statements*, exercised considerable influence, even if the financial response was thought disappointing. Every incumbent should keep in touch with his D.M.C. and invite its officials or other representatives to address the Parochial Missionary Fellowship from time to time.

Another means of co-operation between the clergy supporting different societies is to be found in the recently formed Younger Clergy Missionary Fellowship. Its activity for the time being is principally confined to the Northern Province, and for the most part it is sponsored by the various Diocesan Missionary Councils. Membership is only for the younger men; no one over forty can be an official, and the objects of the Fellowship are missionary study, prayer and support. As the missionary interest in the parishes depends largely on the clergy, the importance of this method of training the junior clergy cannot be under-estimated.[3]

All such methods of co-operating between the various missionary

---

[1] An interesting exposition of the argument for the Societies is given by M. A. C. Warren, in *The Calling of God*, 1944.
[2] See above, Chapter III, § 3 (*a*) ii, and below, Chapter XX, § 6 (*a*).
[3] Cf. Archbishops' Report, *Training for the Ministry*, § 123.

interests are good, but every parish will have the main society of
its own choice, though few will reserve their interests only to one.
The main societies recognized by the Missionary Council of the
Church Assembly are, with the dates of foundation: Society for
Promoting Christian Knowledge (1698/9); Society for the Propaga-
tion of the Gospel in Foreign Parts (1701); Church Missionary
Society (1799); Church Missions to Jews (1807); Colonial and
Continental Church Society (1823); South American Missionary
Society (1844); Melanesian Mission (1849); The Missions to Sea-
men (1856); Universities' Mission to Central Africa (1858);
Church of England Zenana Missionary Society (1880); Jerusalem
and the East Mission (1888); Bible Churchmen's Missionary
Society (1922). Various Associations and Auxiliaries are also
recognized, including many Diocesan Associations through which
some parishes prefer to work. Inter-denominational societies are
listed as Associates, and of them the most important is the British
and Foreign Bible Society.[1]

In its allocation of money not earmarked the parochial Missionary
Committee should consider the needs of the various aspects of the
work of missions, as represented in the various societies. Medical
work, Christian literature, distribution of Bibles, work among Jews
and among our own people overseas, should all have some small
claim, even if the larger proportion goes to a more general society.

The parochial Missionary Committee may also be charged with
the work of organizing the support in the parish for Home Missions
and general charities. Contributions for the C.P.A.S. or the
A.C.S., and for such things as the Waifs and Strays Society, Earl
Haig's Poppy Fund, Diocesan Rescue Homes, etc., can be raised
in similar ways as for Overseas Missions, through church collections,
donations, collecting boxes, and Sales of Work. These methods
should never become just means of raising money, but the direct
interest in the work should also be cultivated.[2]

[1] See *Partners*, the last pre-war Unified Statement, 1939, pp. 115–117.
[2] Information about the work of the various societies working at home and
overseas, with the addresses of their headquarters, can be obtained from the
Official Year Book of the Church of England.

SELECT BIBLIOGRAPHY

R. C. Joynt, *The Church's real Work*, 1934, Chapter XIV.
A. L. Preston, *The Parish Priest in His Parish*, 1933, Chapter V, pp. 77–84.

Publications of the Missionary Council of the Church Assembly, and of the
various Missionary Societies.

CHAPTER XX

BEYOND THE CONGREGATION

§ 1. Outside Contacts

It has already been said that in large town parishes the dangers of narrow parochialism have become rather the dangers of narrow congregationalism, and that this state of affairs is not surprising in view of the demands made upon a single-handed priest, if he is doing his best to shepherd his flock and to care for individual needs.[1] But such narrow congregationalism is neither good for the parson nor for his people. The Anglican parson is still the person of the parish, and he is not bounded by the limits of his congregation; nor can he regard the rest of his parish merely as a collection of individuals needing conversion. He has important work within his parish, outside his congregation, with various groups of people, if he wishes to develop contacts with them. His primary purpose in these outside contacts will be evangelism in one or other of its forms.

However, in the affairs of the world at large the ecclesiastical parish is no longer the unit. Outside contacts will thus be partly within the bounds of the parish, but some will take him outside, and there he will work in co-operation with his brother clergy. In various proposals for reconstruction within the Church in some large towns the union of several parishes together has been visualized, so that a staff of priests could be maintained, some of whom would have special qualifications for making these outside contacts.[2] Such development would certainly make this kind of work easier, but until the time when such reconstruction has been achieved every parish priest must consider how much responsibility rests upon him for undertaking the different opportunities which his parish presents.

There is a further sphere of activity that will take the priest beyond his parish boundaries, and that is in the work which his Diocese or the various Church Societies will call upon him to do. This is work of a different nature, but it also helps the parson and his flock to see beyond the congregation.

[1] See above, Chapter VIII, § 1.
[2] *Putting our House in Order*, 1941, p. 45.

247

§ 2. THE FREE CHURCHES

(a) *Purpose*. The most important groups in the parish outside the congregation will be the other bodies of Christian people. The parish priest can either offer his co-operation or refuse it, but he cannot ignore the fact that the other churches are there. The past fifty years have seen a growing feeling of the need for unity. Many lay people attend services of different denominations quite impartially, and though they may have a preference for one kind of worship, they are quite tolerant of others. The practical advantages of union between the churches are increasingly seen by the layfolk, and some people realize the more important fact of the deep sin of disunion in the Church of Christ.

> " The world is partly restive, and partly scornful, at the lack of unity, the lack of fellowship between Christians. And something more than restiveness, something more than disappointment, weighs often on the souls of Christians themselves. Indeed our divisions have the nature of tragedy." [1]

The pathway to union may be that pursued at present—that is the way of the scholars seeking for the right formula of unity, or it may be as others press, the way of people seeking to live together in unity, as the will of God requires; unity may come in response to efforts in both directions. There is thus a need for each parish to seek for that sense of community among the churches within the parish. So the purpose of contacts with the Free Churches is to develop the growing spirit of unity, understanding and fellowship, and further to give Christian witness on such issues where there is a common mind.

Attempts to reach this community spirit must be tentative. Those tried already may not be on the right lines, but attempts must be made. Some writers deprecate these efforts; " Amateur attempts to stitch together the torn fragments have sometimes more good will than good sense." [2] Yet explorations must be made so that the parish can take its small share in the wide Œcumenical movement proceeding in the world at large.[3] Even if there is no attempt at co-operation, the work of other churches cannot be ignored. Time and energy can be wasted by covering common ground, by petty competition, and by becoming a prey to exploitation by tramps seeking relief and by children seeking treats.[4]

---

[1] G. K. A. Bell, *The Modern Parson*, 1928, p. 63.
[2] R. C. Joynt, *The Church's Real Work*, p. 124.
[3] See *A Christian Year Book*, S.C.M., for a review of various movements.
[4] C. F. Rogers, *Principles of Parish Work*, 1905, pp. 101, 102.

" The mentality of the small tradesman who regards every other tradesman as a competitor for the custom of the community is an unlovely thing when transferred to the business of the churches." [1]

(b) *Fellowship.* The clergy of various denominations ought to have some form of fellowship, and a Ministers' Fraternal is the usual practice. Some parishes are large enough to form a unit, otherwise the unit must be an area embracing a group of parishes. If it meets often enough, the Fraternal can undertake a course of study designed particularly so that members can come to understand the position of the various churches, and it can also arrange for the united work of the churches in the district. There is no doubt that:

> " The initiative in creating and maintaining such relationships rests with the Anglican clergy, and among them pre-eminently with the vicar of the mother-church of a town. It does not require in the smallest degree a compromise of any principles of churchmanship, but only a tactful avoidance of patronage and tolerant, friendly, straightforward dealing." [2]

The attitude of approach is certainly of importance; too often in the past there has been an assumption of superiority on the part of the priest and a natural sensitiveness on the part of the minister. All should approach each other in a frame of mind which recognizes equality, humbly acknowledges good work, and offers real friendliness. In an individual way, this friendliness can also be offered to the Roman Catholic clergy, although there is not much contact in the strictly ecclesiastical sphere. It leads " more often than we sometimes imagine to practical, even if not official, co-operation in social service." [3]

The cultivation of fellowship among the laity is also necessary, and can be developed through joint meetings of adult organizations or youth fellowships, or from visiting speakers who come to describe the work and doctrine of their church again for the purpose of mutual understanding. But the best means of creating fellowship lies in the active co-operation in Christian worship and work.

(c) *Worship.* There are various national and local occasions which demand a United Service. Such a service will naturally be in the parish Church in some parishes, while in others it will be held in the various denominational buildings, according to local circumstances. Often the practice is for the preacher on such

[1] L. S. Hunter, *A Parson's Job*, 1931, p. 199.
[2] *Ibid.*, pp. 198, 199.
[3] G. K. A. Bell, *The Modern Parson*, pp. 61, 62.

occasions to be of the visiting denomination; the service is of a
' free ' rather than of a ' liturgical ' nature. Dr. Bell suggests
" some authorized form of united common prayer which could be
used on special occasions outside and apart from our traditional
liturgical services ".[1]

Interchange of pulpits is permitted under certain conditions by
permission of the Bishop; it has its greatest value in non-liturgical
services which are devoted to intercessions for unity; occasions do
sometimes arise when a nonconformist could fittingly speak at a
statutory service.[2] Dr. Hunter especially presses for the mother-
church of an ancient parish to have an inclusive spirit which looks
back to the time when " the whole community used to meet there
to worship God, and the worship was a consummation of the
common life " [3] and which points forward to such a time returning
again. Of other forms of worship, prayer meetings and intercessions present excellent opportunities for co-operation.

(d) *Evangelistic and Social Witness*. Some of the clergy of the
Church of England who would hesitate to enter into an interchange of pulpits are certainly ready for co-operation in Evangelism, suggestions for which have already been mentioned.[4] The
parish can also enter wholeheartedly into any wider campaign
or crusade, such as those sponsored by the Religion and Life
Movement (The British Council of Churches).[5] Often this joint
work leads to the establishment of a Christian Council of Social
Service (or Local Councils of Churches) which can bring to bear
the whole weight of the Christian Conscience on civic affairs, by
resolution or deputation on such important matters as Public
Health, Housing, Juvenile Crime, the Drink Menace, Gambling
and general moral problems. The danger of these Councils is
their tendency to be negative rather than positive, to make more
fuss about Sunday games than bad housing.

Unless the parish is large and approximates to the local government area, such a Council cannot be regarded as a parochial
activity. The local Fraternal can, however, undertake some
specified social work, such as the running of a Youth Centre.[6]
They are usually too large an undertaking for one church to face,

[1] G. K. A. Bell, *The Modern Parson*, p. 65.
[2] The Diocesan must be consulted before a nonconformist is invited to preach
in church.
[3] L. S. Hunter, *A Parson's Job*, p. 201.
[4] See above, Chapter XIV, § 3 (b) and (d). See also *Towards the Conversion of
England*, pp. 96–99.
[5] 56, Bloomsbury Street, London, W.C.1.
[6] See above, Chapter XVI, § 5 (b).

but co-operating churches in an area can share both the financial administration and the spiritual oversight of an important social service.

§ 3. CIVIC OBLIGATIONS

(a) *Public Life.* Dr. Bell in his advice to ordinands emphasizes the duty of co-operation within the parish.

> " Whether the community be large or small, in country or town, there are certain activities in which it is engaged, certain public services by which it benefits. Get to know your town, your village—as a community, with body, mind and spirit." [1]

He means that the clergy should understand the life of the people, their habits and circumstances, and the vital statistics. The keen seeker will soon be brought into contact with local government, and such contacts are of great value.

The connection of an incumbent with public life will depend on the type of his parish and the area of local government. Small townships which are urban districts or municipal boroughs have often the same boundary as the parish, and then the parson has a public position, and is often invited to share in the social functions of local government. In larger municipalities it is not quite the same.

> " So far as City interests are concerned the link between the Town Hall and the Church is the Vicar of the town, if there is one parish recognized as the mother-church, but in a big city his work and influence need to be supported and supplemented." [2]

Whatever the local government, contact should be established through the permanent officials, the Town Clerk, the Chief Constable, the Director of Housing and the Medical Officer of Health. Now that the social work of the Church has passed wholly into the hands of local government, much of the work of ordinary officials in municipal departments is pastoral in character. " Officials, whether they be policemen or sanitary inspectors or hospital almoners, find part of their work consists in sorting out tangled personal relationships." [3]

In a small town the parson may find it fairly easy to co-operate; in the city various clergy may be asked to undertake various tasks appropriate to their knowledge and experience.[4] At the least the

[1] G. K. A. Bell, *The Modern Parson*, p. 51.
[2] *Putting our House in Order*, p. 45.
[3] *Ibid.*, p. 47.   [4] *Ibid.*, pp. 48, 49.

parson should know the public workers within his parish: police, relieving officers, district nurses, and if possible even rent and rate collectors.[1] He should also know something of the public services, and this knowledge is best gained, if at all possible, before ordination.

> "We do not agree that the winning of such experience can be properly postponed until after ordination, and that a man may reasonably be expected to pick up all that he need know in the course of his work. He ought to be prepared to know what to look for, to have some acquaintance with the agencies concerned in social welfare and some conception of the part which the clergy can play in co-operating with them." [2]

The machinery of the social services is still increasing, in fact the greatest problem is keeping up-to-date,[3] but the clergy can do much, as the Archbishops' Commission points out, to keep " in the foreground the human objects for which the machinery exists." [4]

But the parish priest has a wider task than just co-operating with the social services; he must also be ready to voice the Christian witness in social affairs. This task is not now his alone. The keeping of the public conscience is better shared with the Free Church bodies; indeed, much of the public work mentioned could be shared with them, as this co-operative approach is in keeping with the national temper to-day.[5]

(b) *Civic Services.* It is now almost a general custom for a newly elected Mayor and Corporation to observe a Civic Sunday, in some areas always in the parish church. Civic Services can be an important factor in the life of the community, but they cannot be regarded as sufficient evidence that the community is wholly Christian. The danger of complacency in this respect has been well expressed:

> "Men are quick to say that Christianity must either baptize modern society or be buried in it, and then by the way of a baptismal office plan a series of civic, or semi-civic services . . . such occasions are not without value and some contact is made, but it can be compared with the contact made with

[1] C. F. Rogers, *Principles of Parish Work*, pp. 102–110.
[2] Archbishops' Commission's Report on *Training for the Ministry*, 1944, p. 56.
[3] Cf. G. K. A. Bell, *The Modern Parson*, p. 53. He mentions *Public Social Service, a Handbook of Information*, published by the National Council of Social Service. There is also a publication of the Charity Organization Society, *How to help Cases of Distress*, issued annually, and the *Annual Charities Register and Digest.*
    Other books of reference: J. J. Clarke, *The Local Government of the United Kingdom*, 1927; W. Blackshaw, *The Community and Social Service*, 1939.
[4] *Training for the Ministry*, p. 56. (See § 115, 116.)
[5] Cf. L. S. Hunter, *A Parson's Job*, 181–189.

many parishioners who bring their child to the parish church to be baptized and do not come again. Attempts to baptize modern society which consist of big meetings and special services leave no lasting mark on its daily life." [1]

The Civic Service itself calls for the careful planning that all services need, entrances and exits and other movements requiring special attention. [2]

(c) *Local Government.* " There are ordained men who because of their special gifts can easily take a place on County, or Borough, or other Councils." [3] The question is, as Archdeacon Joynt points out, whether any priest has time for such work. In the country it is possible that a priest can serve with good purpose on the Urban District or the Rural District Council, [4] but it is more difficult in a busy town parish. There is the added difficulty that in the city it is not easy to secure election without the support of a political party, and a priest may not wish to pledge himself in any way.

§ 4. GENERAL CONTACTS

(a) *Hospitals.* [5] A hospital in the parish cannot be ignored by the parish priest, nor can it be jealously guarded as a private possession. Some hospitals have chaplains or part-time chaplains; a large municipal hospital without a chaplain will need more care than a parish priest can possibly give. For the larger hospitals several clergy can share the work; it is better for each to do a period of ward duty, including celebrations, rather than for each to pay intermittent visits. A smaller hospital may well be the concern of the parish priest, and certainly he should see that the staff, both nursing and domestic, has its due share of pastoral oversight. Celebrations and services for the staff should be arranged at times convenient for their difficult hours, at the parish church, if there is no hospital chapel.

(b) *Schools.* Though for a city an educational expert in touch with the local education authority is desirable, [6] each parson should contact the school in his parish. [7] Friendly relations can be culti-

[1] *Putting our House in Order*, p. 45.
[2] P. Dearmer and F. R. Barry, *Westminster Prayers*, 1936, p. 44, " A Civic Service ".
[3] R. C. Joynt, *The Church's real Work*, p. 126.
[4] Cf. J. W. Parker, *The Rural Priesthood*, 1939, Chapter VII.
[5] See also below, Chapter XXI, § 5 (e).
[6] *Putting our House in Order*, p. 45.
[7] C. F. Rogers, *Principles of Parish Work*, p. 106.

S

vated with the teaching staff, interest can be taken in the Speech
Days and Sports Days, and there is always a possibility of an
Annual School service or a school-leaving service. In some areas
the incumbent may be elected or co-opted to the Board of
Governors.

Evening Institutes are not so plentiful, but they can often be
connected with the parochial Youth Work, and there is a possible
opening for the S.C.M.

(c) *Men.* Various ways of meeting people, especially men, outside the ordinary range of congregational activity, are possible,
and are extremely valuable for the parson. They will help him
to know men and keep in touch with their ideas and thinking,
and this is undoubtedly part of the exercise of his ministry. The
Friendly Societies,[1] Rotary, the British Legion, and even clubs and
pubs, offer wide possibilities to a priest with ability to use them.[2]

(d) *Industry.* Another cross-section of society is determined by
the way people earn their livelihood; the industrial life of the
people counts for much in the make-up of character and personality. The lay missioners of the Industrial Christian Fellowship
are particularly concerned with this aspect of people's lives, and a
city might well have several experts in this work. But the factories
of the parish are the care of the parson, and he should try to contact both masters and men. Big firms to-day have welfare departments through which lies an obvious line of approach. With the
consent of both management and workers, services can be arranged
in the dinner hours, or, better still, just straightforward addresses
can be given. Such diverse places of employment as post offices,
railway and transport stations, hotels and big stores must be
included.[3]

But first " the Vicar should . . . set himself . . . to understand
the industrial life of his parish. He should try to realize the conditions of work in the district, and their effect on character ".[4]
Some preliminary training before ordination is as necessary in
this as in the knowledge of social services;[5] indeed, the two go
together. *Training for the Ministry* envisages " some weeks spent in
vacation in a factory, on the land or in a large parish ", but a
strong recommendation is made that special institutions should
give the necessary training to ordinands, provide courses for older

[1] C. F. Rogers, *Principles of Parish Work*, p. 109.
[2] See also above, Chapter XVII, § 3.
[3] *Putting our House in Order*, p. 51.
[4] C. F. Rogers, *Principles of Parish Work*, p. 103.
[5] See above, § 3 (*a*).

clergy, and act as research centres for the Church in social affairs.[1]
Such centres would prove invaluable. The parish priest's own
relations with the folk of his parish would be vastly improved if
he could gain a deeper insight into the conditions of their work
and its effect upon them and upon the whole district.

§ 5. DIOCESAN OBLIGATIONS

(a) *The Parish.* Some priests and their congregations may not
be very aware of civic obligations inside and outside their parishes,
but they can hardly ignore the outside claims of the church to
which their own small community belongs. Every parish has its
diocesan obligations, and so has the parish priest. This is no
doubt partly recognized when the Bishop comes to confirm, and
perhaps more so when he comes to institute a new incumbent;
but the sense of obligation is most felt in the parish when it learns
to pay its diocesan quota.[2] The parish priest will try to persuade
his Church Council to pay its quota in full, but he should also
see that the people understand the purpose of the quota, and
how, through it, the parish shares in the work of the Diocese.

> "We are Churchmen, and for the sake of both the Church
> and of our own souls should welcome the opportunity of
> paying our contribution to the work of the Church as a whole.
> We may realize our own difficulties vividly, but almost cer-
> tainly other parishes are harder pressed than we are."[3]

From the study of the Diocesan Budget the parish priest can
explain how each £1 of the quota is proportionately spent in
diocesan activity, evangelistic or educational, in maintenance or
building, and so on. The parish should also be encouraged to
share in any special diocesan appeal, and where possible, to join
in any celebrations and services of a diocesan nature in the Cathedral
or elsewhere.

(b) *The Priest.* For his own sake the parish priest should not
keep himself to himself, and deceive himself that he is keeping all
his time for his flock.

> "It is a grave mistake, from every point of view, very
> starving for themselves and unjust to the Diocese, for the
> clergy never to move outside the immediate circle of their

[1] *Training for the Ministry*, 1944, pp. 56, 66. See also *Towards the Conversion of England*, 1945, pp. 64, 65.
[2] See also above, Chapter II, § 3 (b); Chapter III, § 3 (a) ii; and Chapter X, § 2 (a).
[3] W. K. Lowther Clarke, *Almsgiving*, 1936, p. 116.

parish. . . . Don't, for heaven's sake, shut yourself up into the parish, without a window looking into the larger world." [1]

For the priest himself there is the very grave danger of loneliness.

" There is no escaping the fact that the man who tries to live independent of his fellows is condemning himself to a life that is less than human, and to a mental condition that is less than sane." [2]

But apart from himself he has a duty to others, and to the Church at large; he has a contribution to make to help others, even if he imagines that others do not help him. He may even appear to waste time at committees, yet " most of the business of the world is carried on by means of committees, and . . . what often appears nothing but waste of time is, in reality, work of greatest importance ".[3] It is seldom true that the parson never gains fresh ideas and new inspiration in his meetings with others, for he usually returns to his own work with renewed vigour.

" In practical work attendance at committees is necessary if for no other reason, because from the companionship of fellow-workers enthusiasm becomes contagious, and we learn again to believe in our cause." [4]

For such reasons Dr. Henson gave his ordination candidates this advice: " Throw yourself frankly into the life of the diocese."[5] Attendance is a matter of obligation at certain meetings, such as the Deanery Clergy chapter, and the Ruri-Decanal Conference. These meetings sometimes undertake study or arrange discussions, but generally other meetings of clerical groups for study (of a theological, pastoral, or missionary character) can be joined.[6] These gatherings have been highly commended: " The meetings of clerical societies, which are fortunately common, are, we believe, often of the greatest value and deserve every encouragement." [7] Helpful syllabuses are published by various agencies.[8]

In a different plane is the Bishop's or Archdeacon's Visitation, the former usually attracting more interest than the latter, which has almost shrunk to nothing more than the legal admission of churchwardens. The Diocesan Conference is usually well attended

[1] G. K. A. Bell, *The Modern Parson*, p. 60.
[2] A. W. Hopkinson, *Pastor's Psychology*, 1944, p. 74.
[3] C. F. Rogers, *Principles of Parish Work*, 1905, p. 55.
[4] C. F. Rogers, *Pastoral Theology*, 1912, p. 127.
[5] H. Hensley Henson, *Ad Clerum*, 1937, p. 197.
[6] R. C. Joynt, *The Church's real Work*, p. 129.
[7] *Training for the Ministry*, 1944, p. 68 note.
[8] *E.g.*, Society of Sacred Study, Way of Renewal. Cf. Chapter IV, § 1 (*d*).

by all the clergy, and a good percentage of the lay representatives make their appearance. It is an excellent opportunity for the country clergy to come to one of the larger cities or towns of the Diocese, and their wives are often very conveniently the lay representatives of their parish. The Diocesan Conference does not seem to confer with ease, and often becomes merely a sounding-board for episcopal utterances. The parish priest should be sufficiently interested to know the way in which the Conference is constituted, and the extent and importance of its powers.[1]

Some of the clergy will be called upon to serve the Diocese by becoming members of diocesan committees, or of the Diocesan Board of Finance. Such work should not be undertaken lightly; meetings should be attended regularly, and afterwards notices of agenda filed away with added notes on the business transacted. It need not be said that membership of committees should not be regarded as an opportunity to gain benefits for the member's own parish; rather, he must cultivate a diocesan outlook. Some priests will be further required as chairmen and secretaries of such committees; others to act as Rural Deans [2] and Chapter Clerks. All should do their duties faithfully and in a business-like way. The Church owes much to these many and varied voluntary officials.

(c) *The Bishop and the Clergy.* The smooth working of the Church as a whole depends very much on the relations between the Bishop and his clergy. Prof. Rogers has said, " The Bishop's first duty is to his clergy ",[3] and the clergy need not fear to turn to the Bishop for advice. Dr. Bell advises:

> " Do not hesitate to look upon him as your friend, or to go to him in case of difficulty; I do not mean for trifling affairs. . . . He is the father of the family, not an inaccessible potentate, and believe me, he welcomes personal relations, and personal dealings." [4]

There is no straightforward way in which the Bishop can admonish his clergy as a whole; addresses on clerical failings seem out of place in diocesan conferences, and a diocesan letter meant for the lay-folk does not lend itself to the purpose of providing hints to the clergy on worship and prayer. It helps when the Bishop's regulations and rulings for the clergy are available in handy form and frequently revised. When a Bishop issues a personal circular

---

[1] Representation of the Laity Measure, 1929, and Diocesan Conferences Regulations, 1935. See *Opinions of the Legal Board*, 1939, pp. 49 f., 110 f.
[2] R. C. Joynt, *The Church's real Work*, p. 100.
[3] C. F. Rogers, *Principles of Parish Work*, 1905, p. 114.
[4] G. K. A. Bell, *The Modern Parson*, 1928, p. 61.

letter on a new and urgent matter, it should command the immediate attention of all his clergy.

§ 6. THE VOLUNTARY SOCIETIES

(a) *The Church's Agencies.* The Church of England is peculiar in that it does much of its important work through the agency of voluntary societies. This was seen particularly in the matter of overseas missions, and it is also true of Home Missions and Charities. The Assistant Curates Society, the Church Pastoral Aid Society, the Industrial Christian Fellowship, the Waifs and Strays Society, are but some of the great societies that do important work for the Church.

To the work of some of these societies the parish will probably contribute, and the parochial support may be organized by the Missionary Committee.[1] But, quite apart from financial interest, every parish priest should take a real interest in the work, and keep in his filing cabinet up-to-date information about most of these societies. Most of the societies send out free literature from time to time; the Industrial Christian Fellowship sends out admirable pamphlets for a small annual fee. Brief information about the societies will be found in the *Church of England Year Book,* which gives the addresses of the head offices.

(b) *Sectional Societies.* The personal interests of the parson will draw him into connection with societies with a narrower aim in view. The party organizations have an important part in the Church of England, and, though the parish priest should not meet exclusively those of his own way of thinking, he should belong to his own section of the comprehensive Church. It is through these sectional groups, which consist of members sufficiently like-minded to get something done, that the most zealous work is done for overseas missions, home evangelism and the training of the ministry. Other sectional interests have a temporary objective to achieve, as the Life and Liberty Movement; the Men, Money and the Ministry Group; the Clergy Defence Society; the Church Day School Managers' Association; and others of like nature. It is good for the whole Church to have groups within it that are pressing for particular objectives or that further some specific form of churchmanship; it is not good for the members of any particular group to think that they are the only people in the Church.

(c) *Voluntary Work.* In connection with the various diocesan

[1] See above, Chapter XIX, § 4.

committees and the voluntary and sectional societies, almost every parish priest is called upon to do a voluntary organizing job, and it will naturally be in accordance with his chief interest. Whether he be the honorary secretary of a diocesan committee, or an area honorary secretary of a society, the priest should see that the work is done thoroughly and efficiently, or he will bring his cause into disrepute.

He must organize his own committee, issue notices of agenda in good time, keep careful minutes and be up-to-date in his correspondence. In arranging meetings he must secure his halls in good time, and book his speakers well in advance. Some societies have an annual Sunday that involves the arrangements of deputations and an interchange of pulpits, perhaps with the provision of hospitality. Records of everything done should be filed and so easily transferred to, and understood by, a new secretary.

The chief trial of the honorary secretary is the brother parson who does not answer letters, who loses correspondence, finds occasions for finicky criticism and is slack in support.

> " Now the great burden of administrative work of a diocese falls on too few people, and of them a good proportion are already overworked parish priests. . . . Some of them have been carrying these burdens a long time, and with sometimes scanty appreciation from some of their brethren who live on such a high spiritual level that they neglect to answer letters and to keep appointments, such courtesies and obligations being too secular for their attention. That humbug causes serious addition to the labours of those who are bearing the burden and heat of the day; and they are too few." [1]

There is, of course, a danger of devoting too much time to these outside affairs; " I know that one can commit the grave fault of never being in one's parish ",[2] says Dr. Bell, while urging the importance of diocesan claims. Archdeacon Joynt also emphasizes this:

> " Neglecting his own vineyard to till others is a misappropriation of a sacred trust, however excellent the purpose may be. It is a bad sign when a man has a higher repute for devotion and pastoral efficiency outside than inside his own parish boundaries." [3]

It is a matter for the priest to make his time-table to allow for sufficient outside work, but not for too much of it.

[1] *Putting our House in Order*, pp. 43, 44.
[2] G. K. A. Bell, *The Modern Parson*, p. 60.
[3] R. C. Joynt, *The Church's Real Work*, p. 128.

§ 7. Beyond the Diocese

The parish priest's interests should not stop at the Diocese, but should go beyond, as it naturally does, to the work of the whole Church of England and the Anglican Communion. The proceedings of Convocation and the Church Assembly should be keenly followed. Some may be content with the reports in the Church papers, others may prefer to read the official proceedings. The Church Assembly Measures and Reports are obtainable from the Press and Publications Board, and by payment of a small sum from time to time as needed, all Measures and Reports are forwarded as issued. History is made as we live, and the main framework of the history of the Church to-day is to be seen in the work of the Church Assembly. Some few priests will develop this interest particularly, and seek to be elected as proctors to Convocation and the Assembly.[1]

[1] Cf. *The Church Assembly and the Church,* 1930.

SELECT BIBLIOGRAPHY

L. S. Hunter, *A Parson's Job,* 1931, Chapters XII and XIII.
G. K. A. Bell, *The Modern Parson,* 1928, Chapter III.
C. F. Rogers, *Principles of Parish Work,* 1905, Chapter IV.
Putting our House in Order, 1941, Chapter IV.
J. J. Clarke, *The Local Government of the United Kingdom,* 1927.
W. Blackshaw, *The Community and Social Service,* 1939.
Public Social Service, a Handbook of Information.
Annual Charities Register and Digest.
How to Help Cases of Distress (Annual).
L. S. Hunter, *Let us Go Forward,* 1944, Chapter VI.
C. H. Cleal, *The Chaplain in the Factory,* 1945.
Towards the Conversion of England, 1945.
The Church and Local Life (The British Council of Churches).

Part IV
THE MINISTRY TO THE INDIVIDUAL

CHAPTER XXI

VISITING

§ 1. THE PURPOSE OF VISITING

So far the main consideration of parochial activity has been from
the angle of corporate life, although even in that corporate life the
part of each individual presents no small problem. But the parish
priest has a very important duty to each individual, and though
the ministry to the individual is indissolubly connected with the
wider life of the Church as a whole, it is in itself a major concern
of the parson. Moreover, the foundation of the ministry to the
individual undoubtedly rests upon visiting, though this is often
derided by some incumbents, and frequently performed by others,
without a real appreciation of its purpose. Purposeless visiting
does not lead very far. On the other hand, a sense of purpose in
visiting helps to create a definite method, enables visiting to be
planned, and thus increases its value.

(a) *Knowing the People*. The Good Shepherd Himself gives the
hallmark of a true pastor. " I know my sheep, and am known of
mine." The first purpose of visiting is to get to know the people.
Without that knowledge it is impossible to help them or to minister
to them. This is part of the object of the social functions of the
Church, which enable the clergy to meet the people, but this is
nothing compared to meeting them in their own homes and by
their own fireplaces. The priest must see the background of the
lives of his people, of his men and women, of his boys and girls,
if he is going to preach to them, if he is to guide them in any way,
if he is to unite them in organizations, and if he is to lead them
to work together. As he gets to know the people, they will get to
know him. Very few people come to the parson for advice until
they know him, but when the priest has visited a house once or
twice, he is felt to be an old friend, and it is to him that the people
will turn in time of need.

There are two indirect results of getting to know the flock. It
gives an inspiration to preaching and provides an unfailing supply
of sermon topics. There is more than a sense of reality about a
sermon when the preacher has had personal contact with his

hearers. But the very first thing which is learnt about one's fellow-creatures in visiting is their unreasonableness, and it can be very disheartening. Canon Green warns the beginner: " Only very young men will expect their fellow-creatures to display reason, and the unreasonableness of others is no excuse for neglecting one's own duty." [1]

(b) *Pastoral Objectives.* However, the parish priest has more to do than just to get to know his people; indeed, that very knowledge will lead to the further exercise of his ministry. As he discovers their needs he will find himself shepherding the faithful, strengthening the weak, and ministering to the sick, the infirm and the aged. These are all pastoral duties which will occupy much of the time which can be spared for visiting. It is in this sphere that it is true in the long run that " a house-going parson makes a church-going people ", but it takes a very long time to prove this.

The sick and the weak, or possible backsliders, certainly need care, but the faithful often look for more attention than is their rightful due. As they get to know the clergy they expect fairly regular visits, and in fact the clergy are tempted to yield to this demand, for visiting these pillars of the church is very pleasant. But if visiting time is limited, these are the first visits to cut out.

(c) *Evangelistic Objectives.* It is unfortunate that so much visiting is concerned only with pastoral care, and stops short of evangelistic effort, difficult as the latter may seem. In addition to the shepherding of the faithful and the strengthening of the weak, there is also the duty of recovering the lapsed and the seeking of the lost. The Good Shepherd is not content with the sheep that know His voice and follow Him, but He goes to save the sheep that is lost.

Visiting can be the highway of evangelism. Whatever other evangelistic methods may be adopted, none of them can bring such a close individual contact.

" It is easy to forget that visiting ought to have a definite spiritual aim, and that the shepherd of the flock is always and everywhere the ambassador of his Master, and as such he will be watchful for every open door for bearing direct personal witness for Him." [2]

Visiting clergy are not merely social callers, ready to exchange the time of the day and discuss the quality of the weather; they have a weightier task to perform, though it is not easy to take the

[1] Peter Green, *The Town Parson*, p. 36.
[2] R. C. Joynt, *The Church's real Work*, p. 54.

opportunity when it comes, and it needs experience to know the right thing to say.

(d) *The Value of Visiting.* It is no easy matter to assess the results of visiting; it certainly cannot be done in the way an insurance agent or canvasser of vacuum cleaners would calculate his results. Perhaps some of the value is negative. The clergy are expected to visit, and it is felt to be their job.[1] Thus the omission of visiting alienates the people and hinders the parson's work.

It is when visiting is performed without purpose that no results can be seen, and this is the logical outcome. An insurance agent knows what he wants, and he knows whether he gets it or not. In a way his task is like the parson's in being twofold: he has to collect premiums from old customers and he has to gain new business, so it is both pastoral and evangelistic. If the pastor went visiting with a purpose, with the directness of an insurance agent, then perhaps he would produce more results.

Visiting has another value when it is performed in the true spirit, for it is a great tonic, and often when the study depresses a few visits restore humanity. It certainly is the source of much amusement; quaint things are said, though sometimes they are sad. An unfailing sense of humour is an important weapon of the visitor.

Yet it must not be thought that visiting is easy, and that it needs no training. " The need of definite training under the guidance of an experienced teacher extends to every part of the priest's office, but in nothing is it more exigent than in house to house visiting." [2] Priests help their assistants least in this of all ministerial duties.

> " One needs all the help of a right method and point of view. Yet many clergy have no instruction in the matter and no help. They are just pitchforked into a district and told to visit it." [3]

Visiting makes the greatest demand upon personality, just because it is so individual. This is especially so of evangelistic visiting, for the parson never knows what to expect, and his mind must be on the alert and ready for any opportunity, and at the same time be prepared for ill-natured rebuffs and unpleasant insinuations. It is not to be wondered that there is " constant

[1] Cf. Peter Green, *The Town Parson*, p. 35; J. B. Goodliffe, *The Parson and his Problems*, p. 80; and H. E. Savage, *Pastoral Visitation*, 1909, p. 6; for agreement. C. F. Rogers, *Principles of Parish Work*, pp. 188 and 194, strongly disagrees.

[2] H. E. Savage, *Pastoral Visitation*, p. 32.

[3] Peter Green, *The Town Parson*, p. 37.

temptation to neglect it." [1] Often the priest will feel towards this task a reluctance to begin, and a shrinking from it altogether, which is partly due to the reserve which every Englishman feels towards the task of talking about spiritual things to other people. But it is a task in which perseverance is needed. " Too many of the clergy give up long before they have made a fair attempt to become competent visitors." [2]

In the end the real value of visiting is known only to the Master Himself. Canon Goodliffe sums up wisely:

"But sincerity, naturalness, and a sense of humour will at least make their own impression in God's good time, and in His way, and perhaps we must to-day realize our best sermons will not be those of the pulpit, but the impromptu talks, the explanations, and the dispelling of crude theories met in the drawing-rooms and kitchens of our parish." [3]

§ 2. PLANNING THE VISITATION

In a small town parish or in a country parish the task of visiting may be comparatively simple, but in a large town parish some kind of method and an attempt at planning is essential. It is true that the card-index parson is often derided, as by Mr. L. B. Cross, when speaking of the Christian home as becoming a thing of the past:

"Many circumstances have contributed to this; not the least of these is the Church's failure during the past half-century to maintain an intimate relationship with the family. I know that most modern parishes are organized on the card-index system, but they seldom get far beyond the system, and after all, it is the personal contact and direct sympathy, not office efficiency, which in the long run count. The magnification of the altar has led to the neglect of the hearth. The present-day incumbent, especially in our large cities and in the suburbs, is far too much the imitation business man." [4]

Of course, a visiting method which does not lead to visiting defeats its own end, but granted the aim of true visiting, a lack of system brings grave dangers. It is so easy to give too much attention to one set, and thus fall " into the growing danger of over-visiting the sheep and neglecting the goats ". [5] A lack of records can engender a false sense of achievement, but system shows how

[1] H. E. Savage, *Pastoral Visitation*, p. 160 (see Chapter VII).
[2] L. S. Hunter, *A Parson's Job*, p. 203.
[3] J. B. Goodliffe, *The Parson and his Problems*, p. 88.
[4] *The Modern Churchman*, Vol. XXXIII, p. 162.
[5] Peter Green, *The Town Parson*, p. 57.

little is actually done, and is an ever-present reminder of a vast field still to cover. Just as the lack of a time-table can lead a priest to fritter away his time meant for study and prayer, so the lack of a visiting method will easily make a priest give up visiting altogether as a hopeless task.

(a) *Methods.* When he first comes to a parish, a new incumbent or a new curate should follow a definite line of attack. It is important to know the church officials, the regular church members, and their families, and these should be visited first, with a second visit soon after. The next line of attack is to visit the homes of the children in the Sunday Schools and in the parochial organizations. Here is a link between the pastoral and the evangelistic visiting, for many of the parents seen are not church people, but most have a certain amount of interest. These visits are some of the most profitable that can be paid. When these homes have been visited twice, the next stage is reached—the continuing of the work. All the time could be devoted to periodical visitation of those already seen, which means practically complete preoccupation with his own connection. In the second stage the known are best left alone, although they will complain, apart from the needs of special circumstances, unless a revision campaign is conducted, say once in three years, and every house on the list is visited in a short space of time, in a succession of quick five-minute calls. Or a periodical circular can keep people in touch as the next stage is essayed.

The final stage, which is never complete, is that of extension— the visiting of houses where there is no connection. House-to-house [1] campaigns are often described as a waste of time, but they ought to be undertaken from time to time. The purpose is to seek for the lapsed, especially for churchpeople who have moved into the district and have not troubled to go anywhere since, and to awaken some kind of response in those who go nowhere. Roman Catholics and Nonconformists should be greeted courteously and visited occasionally as time permits. Children can be gathered for the Sunday School; frequently a real link with the house can be obtained by an invitation to take the parish magazine. In time of trouble people will remember and turn to the parson whose name comes before them once a month.

New housing estates must be tackled in this way. In any type of town parish one district tackled thoroughly is better than trying odd streets here and there. Opinions differ about consecutive

[1] See H. E. Savage, *Pastoral Visitation*, 1909, Chapter II.

visiting, house by house, street by street; Canon Green [1] advises it, but Archdeacon Joynt and Bishop Watts Ditchfield say not.[2] Each priest will decide for himself. The amount of visiting varies enormously. Solid visiting usually achieves ten to fifteen houses in an afternoon, and two hundred a month is suggested as a minimum.[3] A quick revision campaign should include up to thirty in an afternoon, and about four hundred a month.

(b) *Information and Records.* Before all the churchpeople can be visited in the first stage, the information about them must be gathered together. The best way is to compile a street book,[4] one which is convenient for carrying round. It can be loose-leaf, or the usual " Where is it? " alphabetical index book. Each street should have a page or more, and the numbers noted down the page for easy reference, odds and evens separate if that is easier for visiting. Information from all the lists available should then be inserted, for example, from all the lists of names and addresses of the Mothers' Union, all other organizations, the Electoral Roll, Communicants List, Magazine Homes, Sunday and Day School Registers, and perhaps also from the Confirmation and Baptisms Registers. Thus against each number of the street, where there is a Church family, the members connected with the church will be noted. Some members of the congregation are difficult to trace, and for these forms may be given out in church asking for names and addresses. Such information can also be inserted in the street book. The book can be carried round, the right houses visited, and Mrs. Smith can be asked, how she likes the M.U., if Tom is regular at Sunday School, and if Mary is a good Guide. Further information gleaned can be added to the book.

A page of the street book would be like this; the italic entries are added later in the house to house visiting:

RAWSON STREET

1. Mason, Mrs., Com. Mary, G.F.S.
3. *Sharpe*, R.C.
5. *Johnson*, Noncon. Call occ.
7. Jones, Mr., P.C.C. Mrs., M.U. John, S.S.
9. Harris, Mag.
11. Brown. Thomas, S.S.
13. *Robinson. Young family. Prom. S.S.?*

---

[1] Peter Green, *The Town Parson*, p. 43.
[2] R. C. Joynt, *The Church's real Work*, p. 55; J. E. Watts Ditchfield, *The Church in Action*, 1913, p. 61.
[3] Cf. J. T. Inskip, *The Pastoral Idea*, pp. 241, 242; H. E. Savage, *Pastoral Visitation*, p. 62 suggests six a day for five days.
[4] Cf. J. T. Inskip, *The Pastoral Idea*, pp. 239, 241.

Besides the street book which travels with the visitor, the incumbent needs in his study a card index or loose-leaf file containing an alphabetical list of families, a card or page for each. On each card is entered all information gathered in the visits, and set out · in more extended form than in the street book. Different-coloured cards may be used to mark different classes, churchpeople on white cards, non-conformists on blue cards, and so on according to need. If the ages of children are required, a note of the date of birth is the only method always up-to-date. Plain blank cards, 5 × 3, are a convenient size, the information is typed or written, and they are filed alphabetically.[1] For example:

```
HARRISON                          21 Rawson Street.
Mr.  Com., E.R.
Mrs.  Com., M.U., E.R., P.C.C.
Miss Mary.  S.S.T., Com., E.R.
Miss Ethel.  Mag. Dis. (5.6.28).
John.  S.S. (8.11.33).  Slack.
```

Some prefer to have cards printed to their own design, and then filled in as required, e.g.:

```
Name.......................... Address............................
      Birth.  Bap.  Conf.  Organizations.  Mag.  Remarks.
```

These records have many obvious uses. The address of any family can be quickly found, circular addressing is simple, even if the circular is intended for a certain section, such as communicants. Strictly speaking, there is no need for separate lists of communicants, members of organizations, etc.; as far as the parish priest is concerned, all his information is contained in the one system. The value of these records is increased if the date of each visit is recorded. It can be done on the back, or at the foot, of the cards, or the dates can be inserted in the street book. The second way helps as a guide to visiting when actually in the street, and provides a ready answer to those who say "We never see the clergy". The first way provides a more permanent record, and the visits of all the staff can be recorded on the same cards, with each date initialled.

A real difficulty is keeping the records up-to-date, for removals, deaths, and weddings are constantly occurring. If the card index is all-embracing, the same alteration has not to be made in several

[1] Cf. C. E. Russell, *The Priest and Business*, pp. 21, 22.

T

lists. If possible, when church families move away, they should be commended to their new priest; the card from the index can be sent to him, or some of the information from it. The clergy are often blamed for not making commendations, but it is often difficult to do so. Some families go without notice, and even when an address is given, it is not easy to discover in which parish the new house is.

Another way of filing is provided by the Unicard system, which is interesting but over-elaborate.[1] It has excellent ways of arranging for the increasing ages of children and for developing the Electoral Roll. It provides a number of area cards instead of a street book. The cards are not of a standard index size—a needless inconvenience.

(c) *Planning the Visitation.* "Nothing can be effectively done without a fixed plan of action."[2] A good map of the parish which shows all streets and yards is necessary. A walk round the parish will discover the arrangements of numbers in the streets.[3] The whole parish should then be divided into areas, according chiefly to geographical convenience. Five large areas, A, B, C, D, E, each subdivided into four, marked A1, A2, A3, A4; B1, B2, B3, B4, etc., give a permanent system useful for many purposes. These can be the same areas for magazine distribution, or provide a system for circular distribution by Scouts, Guides or others. For visiting purposes there is an area for each of five days a week, and a sub-division for each of four weeks of a month, leaving some days in a short fifth week for making adjustments. Sick visits or other special visiting can determine the order of areas in any one week, so area A, say, is not always taken on Wednesday. The scheme one month may work like this (allowing for the day off):

	1st week.	2nd week.	3rd week.	4th week.
Tuesday	A1	B2	C3	A4
Wednesday	B1	A2	A3	B4
Thursday	C1	C2	D3	C4
Friday	D1	D2	B3	E4
Saturday	E1	E2	E3	D4

This method saves much time and energy, and each part of the parish gets its regular share of visiting. For a staff of clergy the division of labour can be worked in this way. But it must be remembered that any such scheme must be very elastic, as there is always much to interrupt, such as weddings and funerals. The

[1] Obtainable through S.P.C.K. or Mowbrays.
[2] H. E. Savage, *Pastoral Visitation*, p. 175 (see pp. 175–178).
[3] Peter Green, *The Town Parson*, p. 41.

demands of special visiting often push out any routine work, but the framework method can always be available when time permits. For a quick revision campaign the areas provide an easy way of tackling it.

§ 3. PARTICULAR VISITATION

Somewhere between the pastoral visitation to all churchpeople to get to know them better, and the distinct evangelistic house-to-house visiting to gain new people, there is a wide field of particular visiting,[1] which is part pastoral and part evangelistic in purpose.

(a) *Business Visits.* Perhaps such visits are neither pastoral nor evangelistic, although calls of this kind help to establish a definite link between pastor and flock. These visits are really concerned with the administrative detail of the parish, and cover such diverse purposes as calls on the churchwardens about money, or on some secretary about meetings; visits to individuals to invite them to take up certain church work, such as magazine distributing or Sunday School teaching; visits to open missionary boxes or collect delayed Duplex envelopes; or a call or two to obtain new magazine customers or magazine advertisements. There is a surprising number of these necessary visits, but, strangely enough, because these are calls with a business purpose, they are not counted by the people called upon as true ' visits '.

(b) *Special Purposes.* This is the best way to follow up first visits in which some special interest of the household was observed. The purpose in view may be just an invitation to the services of the church, or suggestions for joining the Mothers' Union or Sewing Parties or Men's Gatherings, or definite invitation to possible Confirmation candidates.[2] The special purposes may also be of a ' shepherding ' nature, seeking up men and boys for their classes, or giving reminders of meetings of the C.E.M.S. or the Club,[3] in a way which indicates that the members are really wanted by the pastor. A very important special purpose is the visiting of the homes of the Sunday School scholars, not only to interest the children, but also the parents, who can be persuaded sometimes by the argument that it is not much use sending the children unless the parents come to church too. Interest in the children creates a very favourable evangelistic atmosphere among parents.

[1] C. F. Rogers, *Principles of Parish Work*, p. 186. This is the only kind of visiting recommended by Prof. Rogers.
[2] Peter Green, *The Town Parson*, pp. 54–57.
[3] *Ibid.*, pp. 50–54.

(c) *Pastoral Care.* The most important particular visiting is concerned with pastoral care; one section alone—the visiting of the sick—takes so large a share of the priest's time that it is reserved for fuller treatment.[1] Other personal circumstances require visits from the clergy. Baptism, for instance, really necessitates visits to parents beforehand to speak about the services and make sure that the requirements for God-parents are understood, and later follow-up visits are needed to keep contact with the family; a good way is for the deaconess to take the baptism cards to the houses afterwards. Again, marriages require visits to check the addresses given for banns, and visits afterwards to the new home to see the young couple. Funerals need a visit beforehand to express sympathy, and maybe to offer a prayer, as well as to discuss some detail of the funeral service; later other visits can help the bereaved through the period of loneliness which follows.

An extension of this pastoral care is the visiting on the anniversary of births, marriages and deaths, to express congratulations or to renew sympathy just when it is most needed. Such visits are greatly valued. But if done at all, it should not be reserved for a few, and in consequence some system is essential. Memory ticklers must be consulted, and a good way is to make 366 pages in a book with a plain date at the head of each page; enter the event as it happens on the appropriate date with a note of the year; red ink can be used for marriages, black ink for funerals.[2] A card index can, of course, be used for the same method, which can easily be combined with the monthly reminder scheme (explained in Chapter III, § 2 (*b*)), so that one set of cards can cover reminders of both business and pastoral events. The following up of this practice can grow to large proportions, and its value must be considered in relation to other demands upon visiting time.

(d) *Social Visits.* Another range of visits, small or large according to the parish, covers such things as sewing-parties and teas at various homes. These are in a way corporate visits; the contact is maintained with sections of the church community in the warming atmosphere of a meal. To a certain extent going out to meals with church officials (or entertaining them at the vicarage) can be counted as excellent visits, as they allow for time to cultivate the acquaintance of the most important men and women of the church.[3]

[1] See below, § 5.
[2] The Unicard system has a similar scheme.
[3] R. C. Joynt, *The Church's real Work*, p. 57. See also above, Chapter VIII, § 3 (*b*).

§ 4. PAYING THE VISIT

After such a theoretical discussion of the kinds of visiting, it is
necessary to recollect the warning given by Mr. Cross that the
card-index system seldom gets beyond the system.[1] The whole
method depends, after all, on the visits, and paying the visit is
much harder than keeping a record of it. Very little is done by
incumbents to teach their curates how to visit.[2] Like the preacher,
the visitor should know the technique of his job, even though he may
be a born visitor.

(a) *Times and Manner.* When should visits be paid? Afternoons
are the traditional time, but it depends very much on the neighbourhood. Many closed doors indicate that women as well as
men are at work. Evenings are necessary to find them at home,
though mornings are sometimes satisfactory. Men and boys can
be seen only in the evening, or round about tea-time. Local
circumstances will determine the best times for visiting, and will
also prescribe something of the etiquette of paying the visit, of the
method of knocking and other matters, and the clergy should be
on the watch for things of this kind.

Visiting should always be done in a courteous spirit. " The
poorer the home the more call there is for this." [3] The patronizing
attitude is intolerable and very much resented, and it is often
suspected of being there when actually it is not. " In parochial
visiting it is essential to cultivate a sensitive courtesy; and to set
an example of quiet self-control and unfailing regard for the feelings of others." [4] The young priest must learn to go in all humility
to keep the necessary genial friendliness from becoming patronizing.
That tact is needed goes without saying, and a touch of humour
is expected in the modern parson. Visiting requires a ready
adjustment to the circumstances of different houses, for the rich
and the poor must be visited without discrimination. Yet perhaps
the worst fault the priest can have is that of being tongue-tied.
Small talk is quite innocuous and must be cultivated. A tongue-
tied canvasser would soon be unemployed. The aim of a visit,
no doubt, is spiritual, but conversation usually must begin from
the ordinary and normal, and only a fund of small talk can get
the ball of conversation rolling. If the priest does his visiting in
the spirit of friendliness, showing by word and action that he is

[1] See above, § 2.
[2] Cf. Peter Green, *The Town Parson*, p. 37.
[3] R. C. Joynt, *The Church's real Work*, p. 55.
[4] H. E. Savage, *Pastoral Visitation*, p. 44.

more than interested in his people, and indeed is anxious to love and to serve them, then that visiting will produce much fruit. But one thing he has to watch: he must refuse to share in gossip.[1]

(b) *Church People.* First visits should be carefully prepared. Information about the family should be culled from all possible sources. A woman whose children attend regularly at Sunday School will not be pleased if she is asked if her children go any-where.[2] Knowing the name and the interests of the family soon breaks the ice and prepares for quick friendliness with the house-hold. But opportunities should be taken to discover the names of other members of the family, and if they have any connection with the church. Some little conversation may establish some mutual interest, as being born in neighbouring counties,[3] knowing other clergy or parishes, or being married on the same day, for people always treasure such connections. They are also always very proud if they have a relative who is a minister.

The first visit establishes, as it were, a bridgehead, and a second visit should follow soon to consolidate the position. It is surpris-ing how readily the priest is received on his second visit, and, indeed, he may well sometimes wonder if it is the same house. The second and later visits should not be content with this standard of relationship, but should quickly lead to conversation connected with Church and the spiritual life. Each individual has to be considered separately, in order to see how best to stimulate church-manship. A challenge to a higher standard should be given, leading occasional attenders to be regular members, regular members to Confirmation, confirmed members to regular and frequent acts of communion; on parallel lines a challenge should be given in spiritual life. A later visit which does not lead to a talk on spiritual things is in danger of proving a failure and a waste of time.

The wise priest will think of certain kinds of visiting as giving him the opportunity he cannot have in the modern pulpit. For in the pulpit he has to generalize, and deal hastily and super-ficially with the themes of the Christian religion, because sermons have to be short and preaching has to consider the most ignorant of the congregation. In visiting almost alone can the priest give his message thoroughly. Visiting will therefore sometimes be the most profound expression of his own reading and meditation, and he will not be the giver only.

[1] H. E. Savage, *Pastoral Visitation*, p. 46.
[2] Peter Green, *The Town Parson*, p. 42.　　　　[3] *Ibid.*, p. 45.

Special purpose visits to churchpeople of course can go straight to the point and lead up to the intention in hand.

(c) *House-to-House Visiting.* Here the procedure is quite different. The first objective is to get inside the house, and the second to discover the religious position of the family. This must be done with tact, although people are usually willing to say where they belong and express a vague feeling that they ought to go more. Interest in other members of the family is soon satisfied. To those who are attached to other places of worship a word of encouragement is given; to those who go nowhere or who call themselves Church of England without attending, an invitation to come can be given (a card setting out the time of services and meetings can be left) [1]; where there are children an attempt should be made to get the parents to send them to Sunday School; to lapsed communicants should be given a strong plea to begin again. Notes can be taken in the street book, either in the house or afterwards; especially the lapsed communicants should be noticed, so that their names can be added to the list for Easter Cards. Where interest has been aroused, second visits can be paid soon after to remind people of promises made. The parochial organizations can be suggested to which various members of the family could belong.

Reactions from the people will vary tremendously. Some will be mildly interested, many indifferent, some few hostile. Some will be concerned with excuses for not attending church; they either have no clothes, or they cannot understand the service, or they are afraid of being suspected by their neighbours of going to get something. [2] Strange misrepresentations and superstitions will be discovered by the diligent visitor, and he has achieved something if he tries to put these right. [3] Others will be encountered of an anti-church type, who have many complaints about the clergy or the universe; others will be aggrieved over the action of particular parsons. Some have pet subjects which come out at the first opportunity, as social credit or spiritualism; others seek only to shock the visitor, or to get him talking on a side-issue. [4] The way our Lord talked to the woman of Samaria by the well gives an excellent illustration of keeping the conversation to the point, in spite of several attempts at evasion by the woman ' visited '.

(d) *The Place of Prayer.* To pray with all Christian people

[1] Peter Green, *The Town Parson*, p. 75.
[2] J. B. Goodliffe, *The Parson and His Problems*, pp. 80, 81.
[3] *Ibid.*, pp. 81, 82.
[4] *Ibid.*, pp. 83–87.

visited ought to be natural, but has become the exception rather than the rule. Prayer comes into its rightful place on the special pastoral visits; everyone expects a prayer for the sick, so the priest ought to pray with the bereaved, and also with the young married couple in their new home, or for the newly baptized baby. In the social visit prayer would be out of place, but when the conversation in a visit has led to problems of faith and conduct, or to new resolves of service and dedication, then prayer should be made for grace and guidance.

English people are reserved in this matter, and the clergy also share that reserve, yet the people think it is the work of the parson that he should pray. Perhaps people expect prayer more often than the parson thinks. Every time will not be convenient, as when the people of the house are at tea, or bustling round, or visitors are coming and going. Other times may be doubtful. Canon Green urges: " Seize every opportunity for prayer and when in doubt as whether or not to suggest prayer, always make the suggestion." [1] But this must be made a practice from the very first setting foot in the parish.

Visiting should always begin with prayer, either at home or, preferably, with the whole parochial staff at church. The latter course is not always possible, as the staff may have many and varied duties which begin at different times. The priest who has to set out alone is well advised to make the church his first port of call, in order to offer his afternoon's visiting with his mind on those whom he hopes to see, and upon the tasks, often perplexing, that he has to perform. If he does so, he will often find that the church is also his last stopping-place on his way home, to offer thanks and to ask forgiveness. And, quite apart from the spiritual value of such a practice to himself, these frequent visits to the church cannot fail to have an effect upon his parishioners.

§ 5. SICK VISITING

In some ways the visiting of the sick is the hardest and yet the easiest of all visiting. [2] It is easy because it has the tremendous advantage of a definite objective, and the people always expect the clergy to visit the sick. But it is also hard because it is a responsible task, and good results can only be obtained if the visit-

---

[1] *The Town Parson*, p. 49. Cf. J. B. Goodliffe, *The Parson and his Problems*, p. 86; R. C. Joynt, *The Church's real Work*, p. 55; J. T. Inskip, *The Pastoral Idea*, p. 256.
[2] See H. E. Savage, *Pastoral Visitation*, Chapter III; and Peter Green, *The Town Parson*, pp. 58–71.

ing is rightly undertaken. That it is one of the duties a pastor should undertake is certainly made clear in the Book of Common Prayer, which provides an office for the Visitation of the Sick.

In the first rubric of this office it says that the Minister of the Parish shall come when notice has been given. Who is to give this notice? If people called their parish priest when they sent for the doctor, much recrimination would be saved and much good work could be done. Yet the people expect the priest to know when someone is sick. The priest must make the best of this difficult situation. Some families will send for the priest, other churchpeople sometimes report cases, but otherwise the priest must rely on casual conversation for information. He must be alert, too, for the slightest mention of an illness in a conversation is meant to be an invitation to come to the patient.

The Office in the Prayer Book is hardly suitable for these days, as Canon Green says,[1] yet it contains much that can be used.[2] The 1928 Prayer Book has it set out in a much more convenient form, and in this Book there are also other suggestions for readings and prayers. The priest must always be ready for extempore prayer, but he is well advised to make his own pocket prayer book for sick visiting, and have a marked Bible for suitable passages.[3] Prayers and passages will be used according to the circumstances of the illness and the stage which it has reached. The suggestions in the 1928 Book are classified. The different classes of illness need separate treatment.

(a) *The Dying.* When the priest is called to visit the sick, it is very often a call to a person who is dying. There is a superstition about this, as some people like to feel that this is the right thing to do just before death. Usually the call comes too late to do very much, as the sick person may already be unconscious. Even then prayer should be said, because it is *for* the sick man, and not to him, and even if he seems unconscious, frequently the repetition of the familiar words of the Lord's Prayer gains response. If the patient is some way off death, and is still mentally capable, then more can be done. Other sick-room visitors should be asked to leave, so that the talk can be private and an opportunity be given to the patient to ease his conscience as the Prayer Book

[1] Peter Green, *The Town Parson*, p. 61.
[2] F. G. Belton, *A Manual for Confessors*, 1936, p. 261; Cf. J. T. Inskip, *The Pastoral Idea*, p. 245; and J. E. Watts Ditchfield, *The Church in Action*, p. 70.
[3] W. Walsham How, *Pastor in Parochia*, was very popular at one time for this purpose. The Guild of St. Raphael has recently produced a *Priest's Vade Mecum*, devoted entirely to sick visiting and its needs. It is published by S.P.C.K.

directs. The visit of the priest has not primarily a healing purpose: " Our Lord is a Saviour first of all, and then a Healer." [1] Some schools of thought would press strongly for confession just at this point, if the patient can be brought to it, but the solace of reconciliation to God can often be brought to him in other ways.[2]

If the patient is a regular communicant, then he can be better prepared for the passing from this life. The difficulty here is usually the reluctance of the doctor or the family to allow the patient to be told that the end is near. Even with the best of churchpeople prejudice and suspicion are very strong, yet so much can be done to strengthen the soul through the dark valley of the shadow. There should be simple confession and absolution, the Holy Communion given, then prayers of preparation and commendation to the life to come. Priests of differing churchmanship will of course follow differing methods, but all should read, whether they follow it or not, the helpful discussion of the value of reservation for the administration of Communion to the Sick, and the administration of Extreme Unction, by Canon F. G. Belton.[3]

Some illnesses bring near the danger of death, though they are nothing more than short severe illnesses. A few calls and inquiries, perhaps daily at the height, and a few short words of prayer are all that are required. The priest may be gifted to take a more active share in the Ministry of Healing; in this he must co-operate with the doctor. This opens a wide subject which must be studied at length elsewhere.[4]

(b) *Long Illnesses*. Very useful work can be done with those who have a long spell of sickness, either that which is eventually fatal, or that which eventually leads to recovery. There is time to give definite teaching and to develop prayer and Bible Reading with the patient. The aim is to get to know the patient well and to be able to help him with his spiritual difficulties. If recovery is impossible, there is time to lead gradually to the preparation for the end; if recovery is in any way probable, plans can be made for a better use of life when health returns.

(c) *Chronic Cases*. Regular routine visiting must be devoted to bed-ridden and paralysed people and to the aged. The Holy Communion must be arranged for them at regular intervals, and those who are not confirmed can be prepared for Confirmation, which the Bishop will readily take at the patient's home. Invalids

[1] R. C. Joynt, *The Church's real Work*, p. 57.
[2] Peter Green, *The Town Parson*, pp. 43, 44.
[3] F. G. Belton, *A Manual for Confessors*, 1936, pp. 279–320.
[4] *The Ministry of Healing*, S.P.C.K.

should be encouraged to pray for others, and some can come to understand the great task of intercession for missionary work and for individuals.   The idea that all prayers said by them and with them must be for their own recovery must be overcome.

(d) *Infectious Cases*.   These will mostly be in the isolation hospitals, and they are equally the concern of the priest.   Proper precautions should be taken, for obvious reasons; the administration of the sacrament in such cases needs great care.   Useful information is given by Canon F. G. Belton.[1]

(e) *Hospitals*.   Some hospitals have regular chaplains, but, whether they have chaplains or not, the priest must visit the sick from his own parish and congregation.   Visiting days should be avoided, and every courtesy shown to the nursing staff.   Reports of patients are appreciated by their families, especially in infectious cases.   Where the local hospital has no chaplain, the clergy should make some routine among themselves so that the sick can be regularly visited.[2]   Prayer is no more out of place in the hospital than in the home.   In hospital work the public institutions for the aged should be counted as an integral part.[2]

(f) *Records*.   A record of the sick should be kept, either at the end of the street visiting book, or in a separate ' sick ' book.   The patients should be graded according to their needs, those to be visited quarterly, or monthly, or weekly; those in various hospitals, and in which ward; and add a separate page for those who will not need visits for long.   Dates of visits should be entered, and a note when the Sacrament is taken to them.   These records will be the natural basis of the lists of sick people for whom prayers are bidden at the Holy Communion.

[1] F. G. Belton, *A Manual for Confessors*, pp. 250–255; cf. J. T. Inskip, *The Pastoral Idea*, pp. 260, 261 ; and H. E. Savage, *Pastoral Visitation*, p. 96.
[2] See H. E. Savage, *Pastoral Visitation*, Chapter V.

SELECT BIBLIOGRAPHY

H. E. Savage, *Pastoral Visitation*, 1909.
Peter Green, *The Town Parson*, 1919, Chapter II.
R. C. Joynt, *The Church's real Work*, 1934, Chapter VIII.
A. L. Preston, *The Parish Priest in His Parish*, 1933, Chapter I.
J. B. Goodliffe, *The Parson and His Problems*, 1933, Chapters VII, VIII.
J. T. Inskip, *The Pastoral Idea*, 1905, Chapter VIII.
J. E. Watts Ditchfield, *The Church in Action*, 1913, Lecture III.
F. G. Belton, *A Manual for Confessors*, 1936, Part VI.
The Ministry of Healing, S.P.C.K.
T. W. Crafer, *The Priest's Vade Mecum*, 1945.

CHAPTER XXII

CONFIRMATION

§ 1. PRELIMINARIES

SOME of the most valuable individual work that the parish priest can do is in the preparation of candidates for Confirmation. This is, above all else, the Church's own Youth Work, and is the main aim behind all the various Youth activities described in an earlier chapter. At first sight the preparation for Confirmation has the appearance of a corporate activity, but in reality it is distinctly individual. It is true that most instruction is given in classes, but there should be no illusion that this is another series of sermons; individuals must be considered and their needs met, especially through the interviews. As is the case in many other functions of the ministry, the method of preparing for Confirmation is not so much studied as picked up from older priests.

> " In a well-organized parish it is common for the cleric in his first year to attend the Confirmation instructions given by some other able member of the staff, and in this fashion to get the experience he needs for the time when he too must start to instruct." [1]

But even this method, as the writer quoted points out, is not possible for private interviews; the whole approach to Confirmation requires study and application.

The practical approach is the chief concern here, but it should have a sound historical and doctrinal background. Valuable studies are provided by the first volume of *Confirmation* by various writers,[2] and also in the first three chapters of *Confirmation To-day*,[3] which includes a masterly examination of the present situation.

A number of preliminary matters call for first attention:

(a) *Age of Candidates.* A long tradition in England has been that the middle ' teens ' is the most suitable age for Confirmation. In recent years psychologists have taught that the adolescent is just at the wrong age. The difficulty arises because Confirmation

---

[1] *Confirmation*, by various writers, S.P.C.K., Vol. II, 1927, p. 163.
[2] S.P.C.K., 1926.
[3] The schedule attached to the Interim Reports of the Joint Committees on Confirmation, October, 1944.

is a combination of two things—the gift of grace with admission to Holy Communion, and intellectual understanding with a renewal of vows. According to psychologists, the former is better before adolescence and the latter should be postponed until afterwards.[1] As, however, Confirmation is still one and indivisible, in actual practice an insistence on the earlier age is made at the expense of deeper teaching.[2] Dr. Dearmer argued that our Prayer Book intended an early age by the phrase ' years of discretion ', but adds, " Many of the most experienced and successful parsons consider that better permanent results are secured by not having young people confirmed too early." [3] It must also be remembered that there is often a considerable difference between the development of town and country children of the same age. There are certainly no statistics to show that those who are confirmed young make better churchmen, or are more persistent, than those confirmed in the late teens, but it is also arguable that postponement owing to age often means never.

No definite decision was reached in *Confirmation To-day*, where, in Chapter IV, there is a full discussion of the age question, and in Chapter V a consideration of the separation of the various elements involved in Confirmation.

(b) *Source of Candidates.* In the majority of parishes the Sunday School, the Youth Fellowship and the junior organizations will supply most of the candidates. Some children of church families may escape this net and be drawn in through church attendance. A sermon on the subject annually is recommended by Archeacon Joynt, who complains of the guilty silence of the clergy,[4] but even more preparation of the parish than this is needed if the parish is to be Confirmation-conscious.[5]

The priest's share will be to notice those in the congregation who do not communicate, and discover in his visiting if they are not confirmed. A list of possible candidates from all sources ought to be compiled during the year, and when the time comes they can be invited to the classes. A circular letter or form can be used, such as the various forms printed by the S.P.C.K.,[6] or a personal visit can be made, or a personal letter sent. The last method, though very arduous, is by far the most successful—" The influence

---

[1] *Confirmation*, Vol. II, pp. 1–11, 112–114.
[2] Cf. J. B. Goodliffe, *The Parson and his Problems*, pp. 31 ff.
[3] Percy Dearmer, *The Parson's Handbook*, 1940, p. 397.
[4] R. C. Joynt, *The Church's real Work*, p. 67.
[5] *Confirmation*, Vol. II, pp. 116–120.
[6] *Ibid.*, " Some Illustrations ", pp. 14–16.

of the notice board is very small, and the power of the personal touch is very great ".[1]

(c) *Records of Candidates.* Two sets of records are necessary, one of attendances at the classes, and the other the permanent record of those confirmed. A record of attendance is necessary, and to this should be added, as obtained for each candidate, the full name, address, date of birth and date and place of baptism. This information can be obtained at the third or fourth class, or at the first interview, preferably on forms prepared for the purpose.[2] If the use of Baptism cards were universal, much time would be saved; as it is, nearly every date of baptism has to be investigated. It should be noticed that the baptism of such other denominations as baptize with water in the name of the Holy Trinity is valid, but if no record has been kept, or if there is any doubt, conditional baptism should be given. The Salvation Army and the Quakers do not baptize, the Baptists only use a dedication service for infants, and the Roman Catholics do not usually answer letters on the subject. All inquiries made should be accompanied by a stamp for reply. A form must be completed for the Bishop giving all the information listed above.[3]

After Confirmation the information must be entered in a Confirmation Register. Some churches do not seem to possess this important record. It is useful to put on record the information gleaned about baptism, but it is necessary to record the place and date of Confirmation and the name and title of the Bishop confirming.[4] Space for the record of the first Communion, and a column for notes about departures, lapses or deaths, is also useful.

§ 2. THE CLASSES

(a) *The Aim.* Some priests make the aim of their classes the presentation of a complete scheme of instruction in the Faith, others the teaching of a complete outline of Christian morals, while others regard the classes as a preparation for conversion.[5] There are some priests who see the value of these three different aims, and in trying to achieve all three, get themselves confused about the purpose of their classes. But these aims, though good, are not really suitable for Confirmation classes. For in a course of some

---

[1] R. C. Joynt, *The Church's real Work*, p. 67. For the value of the personal letter, cf. Bertram Pollock, *A Twentieth-Century Bishop*, 1944, Chapter XXIV.
[2] *Confirmation*, Vol. II, " Some Illustrations ", pp. 17–25.
[3] See above, Chapter II, § 3 (*b*).
[4] Peter Green, *The Man of God*, p. 221.
[5] *Confirmation*, Vol. II, pp. 158–160.

dozen or so short talks instruction of any kind is necessarily limited, and any comprehensive scheme is out of question; as for the third aim, conversion cannot be so surely planned that it should come exactly at the moment of Confirmation, though it is true that Confirmation should be presented as a time of decision. Rather, the classes should be a training ground for Christian practices, prayer and Bible-reading, worship and Sacrament, and so the instruction in Christian faith and conduct should be used to illustrate and explain the meaning of these practices.

With this aim in view, it can be seen that the classes should be formed, not with the idea of giving a certain number of talks to as many as possible, but with the plan of helping individuals to their best advantage. Candidates will be grouped according to age, or sex, or training, as need requires, sometimes all meeting together. The free time of young people to-day is very limited, and this may often affect the formation of classes, but as far as possible different groups should be graded, and the talks adapted to their circumstances.[1]

(b) *The Subjects of the Talks.* It is a great temptation to try to do too much, for the range of possible subjects is very wide. " One may be tempted to get as much as possible into the golden period of preparation, but it is a temptation to be resisted." [2] Various experiments have been tried in recent years, some of them spreading the Confirmation course over nine or twelve months. This is good if it replaces the normal weekly instruction and is not in addition to it. The Confirmation School has a similar scheme, according to which the doctrinal and moral teaching is taught in the course of two or three years, and the Confirmation classes simply aim at combining preparation for Confirmation and Holy Communion.[3] There must be some well-grounded instruction in some such department of the Sunday School, but some form of direct Confirmation instruction is certainly necessary, but of not too long duration. If the classes are extra to the ordinary times of instruction, fourteen or fifteen weeks should be the limit, or the candidates will lose their enthusiasm. That there should be special training is in accordance with the general practice of most priests, and this seems to be in keeping with human nature, which is pre-

[1] *Confirmation*, Vol. II, pp. 162, 163.
[2] J. T. Inskip, *The Pastoral Idea*, p. 231.
[3] See above, Chapter XV, § 3 (*b*). The scheme is worked out in A. R. Browne-Wilkinson, *The Confirmation School*, 1930; and in A. R. Browne-Wilkinson, *Pastoral Work among Children*, 1934, Chapters IX and X, the latter chapter describing the actual confirmation preparation that is necessary.

pared to accept special training for things deemed important, just as crews train for a boat race, and the Commandos trained in time of war.

An alternative method of training is that suggested in the Book of Common Prayer, where the catechizing of children is ordered at Evening Prayer. There is a good argument for having one sermon each Sunday morning with catechizing in the evening. The other members of the congregation learn from the instruction given to the children. Yet, generally speaking, this seems to be an attempt to revive a method of a bygone age which is not suitable for the present time. The members of the congregation do not readily take to this method, and, curiously enough, suspect the parish priest who does it of being lazy.[1]

The majority of priests adopt the short-range plan, which is the best at the present time if the aim given is remembered. The Catechism is usually made the basis of the subjects for instruction, and several helpful books have been published following the conventional lines.[2] The subjects generally cover: the Purpose of Life, Belief in God and in Christ, the Challenge of Christ, the Bible, Worship and Prayer, Christian Conduct and Service, and the Sacraments, Baptism, Confirmation and the Holy Communion. To this list some would add Almsgiving, Social Service and Sex. It is important to keep these subjects connected with the practices of the Church.

Each year the priest will have a new selection of candidates, and to them the talks will be fresh, but they will not be fresh for the priest. It is a good plan for the priest, while keeping the main points the same each year, to arrange the subjects round a new theme every year or so, and thus avoid the danger of the talks becoming stale. The general theme could be called, " The Confirmation Time ", or, " The Friends of God ", or " Church Membership ", very much as titles are given to Sunday School lesson books. To give an instance, the talks in the first series would include, " A Time to Pray " (Prayer), " A Time to Read " (The Bible), " A Time to Repent " (Sin and Forgiveness), " A Time to Receive " (Holy Communion), and so on.

A scheme like this helps to create cohesion between the talks, but it is even better to base the whole instruction on the Communion Service.[3] In this plan most of the subjects fall into their rightful

[1] Percy Dearmer, *The Parson's Handbook*, pp. 246, 391.
[2] *Confirmation*, Vol. II. Excellent outlines are given, pp. 35–83.
[3] See above, Chapter XIII, § 3 (a).

place, and they are connected with an act for which the classes are
training the candidates. Two or three hurried classes are not
sufficient for instruction on this Service, but when the instruction
requires that the Holy Communion Service should be inspected at
every class, and each subject is definitely connected with some
place in the service, with the movement of the service explained as
the classes proceed, then by the end of the course the candidates
will at any rate know where the Service is in the Prayer Book and
have an idea of its unity and purpose. This is an excellent way of
making the classes a training-ground for Christian practices. It
will be remembered that the Creed, the Lord's Prayer and the
Ten Commandments are all to be found in this service, the Bible
is encountered in the Epistles and Gospels, the Christian Year in
the Collects, Almsgiving at the Offertory; Sin, Confession and
Absolution come in their natural places; sacramental teaching
comes in various places, especially in the Prayer of Consecration;
teaching on Service, the Church, and Thanksgiving is connected
with the Post-Communion. All that it is necessary to add is teaching on Baptism and Confirmation, and they can be described as
the essential preliminaries to Holy Communion, and the scheme is
complete. During the instruction it is essential to teach the
practical details of the reception.

> " These little details seem fussy, but they are of tremendous
> importance. There are very many men and women who have
> not made their Communion for years because of an embarrass-
> ment they felt at Holy Communion in adolescence through
> incomplete instruction." [1]

The curious thing about Confirmation classes is that good
Sunday School method often seems to be forgotten. Again, it
should be emphasized that the classes are not just for mere talks.
Teaching can be improved by asking questions to stimulate thought
among the younger candidates, by provoking discussions among
the older adolescents, or by encouraging the taking of notes on the
talks. But the notebook-and-pencil method is beyond the reach
of the majority of confirmees. It is considered by some to help if
a summary of the talks can be given to each candidate, either the
priest's own notes duplicated, or the printed stock summaries
which can be obtained from S.P.C.K. and other sources. [2]

(c) *Sex Instruction.* Recent years have seen the necessity of sex

---

[1] A. R. Browne-Wilkinson, *Pastoral Work among Children*, 1934, pp. 209, 210; cf.
Percy Dearmer, *The Parson's Handbook*, 1940, pp. 272, 273.
[2] *Confirmation*, Vol. II, pp. 30, 31.

U

instruction more widely recognized in secular educational circles. Many priests have long included this subject in their Confirmation talks, and, though ideally such instruction is best given by parents, while they remain reluctant to do it there is much to be gained if it is given in teaching with a firm Christian basis. Undoubtedly the best way is to let the subject come in naturally in the course, with no appearance of an awkward interloper, but as a subject part and parcel with the whole scheme. Obviously it comes under moral conduct, and if each commandment is inspected, the necessary peg is provided by the seventh. It is doubtful if indirect reference to keeping the body under control and the necessity of keeping pure really cuts any ice, or helps the candidates in any way; this only increases the mystery. It is useless to assume that they know the facts, and give only the Christian principles in sexual conduct. They do know a certain amount, but usually their sources of information leave much to be desired, and most of them are worried because they are not sure if they know all they ought to know. A simple but clear statement of the basis of sex, with some mention of the moral dangers, is necessary, due regard being given to the ages of the candidates. For girls a lady doctor can do this well, or the woman worker on the staff. The parish priest himself can talk to the boys, but the subject needs clear thought and careful handling.

Not all are agreed that the subject should be included. So important an authority as *Confirmation To-day* says:

"There is probably more to be said against than for the practice of including sex instruction in the preparation for Confirmation, as it can be better given at other times, and indeed should be imparted in gradual stages from earliest childhood as the right opportunities occur." [1]

On the other hand, many priests are genuinely anxious to tackle this task, but do not quite know how to do it. There are various books and pamphlets that can help them. In *Confirmation*, Vol. II, there is an article on "Adolescence and Sex Instruction", but it is concerned rather with the psychology of the adolescent than with his instruction. [2] The British Council of Churches issued a very helpful leaflet in 1944 entitled *Aids to Sex Instruction,* and it gives an excellent list of recommended pamphlets. *The New Generation and Sex Relationships* is a pamphlet published in 1944 by the Church of England Youth Council in consultation with the Church of England

---

[1] *Confirmation To-day,* 1944, p. 53.
[2] *Confirmation,* Vol. II, pp. 93–115.

Moral Welfare Council. It gives a suggested course of talks on sex relationships which can be given in Youth Clubs.[1]

(d) *Devotion.* Canon Green said long ago, " The Class is for Instruction and not for Worship," [2] and the candidates should be told that their devotional preparation should be in their private prayers and in regular attendance at church. Regular attendance at worship must be regarded as an essential part of the preparation for Holy Communion; some make the excellent suggestion that the Parish Communion should be attended.[3] The candidates should be told which prayers to use, and instruction in joining in the Church's worship will naturally come in the training course. The Confirmation prayer, " Defend, O Lord . . .", adapted, can be suggested, and other prayers from the usual sources.[4] But the Confirmation classes themselves will have very little devotion; merely short prayers at the beginning and at the end. Towards the end of the course a quiet afternoon for preparation conducted in the church can be very helpful, or some longer form of retreat can be provided if circumstances permit.

(e) *Adult Candidates.* Most of the discussion on Confirmation preparation is mainly concerned with the needs of the young people, but there are some adult candidates almost every year to consider. Much of what has been said will be applicable to adults, but they must have separate classes, and the instruction will differ to a certain extent. Many adult candidates have been brought up in other denominations, and the church's services must be explained to them. Otherwise the adult classes give a golden opportunity for the discussion of many aspects of the faith, and they can give the parish priest some of the most interesting work he will be called upon to do. Some endeavour should be made to find the newly confirmed adults a definite piece of work in the church.

§ 3. INDIVIDUAL INTERVIEWS

(a) *Preliminaries.* It has already been insisted that preparation for Confirmation is important work among individuals, and, however well the classes may be planned for individual needs, they are not sufficient in themselves. The candidates are all different, and there is certain to be a special word of help which the priest can give to each one, and it must be given alone. It is thus necessary

---

[1] See also above, Chapter XVI, § 4 (c).
[2] Peter Green, *How to Deal with Lads*, p. 113.
[3] E. S. G. Wickham, *Parson and People*, 1931, p. 39.
[4] *Confirmation*, Vol. II, pp. 31–34.

to have a succession of private interviews with all the candidates.
In some parishes it may be important to disarm misunderstanding
beforehand, for anything which might look like confession is suspect;
but, whatever the difficulties, the step must be taken.

The practical considerations are formidable. The priest may
have a large number of candidates, and planning the times in
order to see them all is no mean undertaking. Every odd opportunity has to be taken. One interview is barely sufficient; it has
been urged that each candidate should be seen at least three times—
at the beginning, just before Confirmation, and during the course.

(b) *The Purpose.* The real purpose is to get to know them in
order to help them in their spiritual lives. This is not easy in a
short interview, and supplies the reason why more than one is
usually necessary. A private interview with the parish priest
will be rather overwhelming for most of the candidates, and their
mental processes will be somewhat inhibited by the circumstances.
This can partly be overcome by the arrangement of the room, some
flowers to be seen and mentioned, or a kitten around to create
naturalness. Something in the room can give a lead to conversation, for the first objective is to get the candidate to talk. It is far
more important for the candidate to talk than the priest, who has
his chance in the class, but the conversation must be skilfully
guided, by means of questions and comments, to the things that
matter. Somehow the difficulties which the candidate feels about
life and about the Church's practices must be brought to light and
put straight. They are never really very difficult, though serious
enough for him.

One interview must be concerned with prayer and Bible-reading.
What does the candidate actually do about it? Suggestions for
better practice can be given. Some priests may use the interview
for a few words on purity. The last interview can stress the importance of the moment of Confirmation, the need for decision and
the place of vocation in life.[1] Possible candidates for the ministry
may be discovered in this way.

The importance of the private interview is thus summed up by
Dr. Inskip:

" Have a private interview with each, and press upon each
the necessity of decision for Christ before being able to give
the answer ' I do ' to the solemn question of the Bishop. Note
down each year any points on which you want to speak

[1] See *Confirmation To-day*, 1944, Chapter III, " Confirmation and the Christian
Calling ".

privately to the candidates. Do not crowd too much on them at a private interview, but some of the following may be touched upon: decision for Christ, private prayer, knowledge of Catechism, reading of Bible, regularity at Holy Communion, interest in Missions, definite work for God." [1]

(c) *Confession.* Many priests will emphasize the importance of Confession, if not in open class, perhaps in the private interview. The Anglican Church does not compel it, but certainly offers it. Canon Green says that attention should be drawn to the offer, and his advice and experience in this matter are worth consulting. [2] Priests in a parish with ' evangelical traditions ' will most likely not mention it, but be content with the interview in its place. The subject belongs rather to the general attitude of the priest and his parish to spiritual direction, which is considered later. [3]

(d) *Presentation.* It must be made clear from the beginning of the classes that the priest is under no obligation to present to the Bishop for Confirmation every candidate who cares to come to the class, just as the act of coming to the classes does not imply the candidate's final decision that he wishes to be confirmed. Sooner or later the priest must decide which candidates he can present and those which he cannot. It will be in the last private interview that his decision will be made known, and to those to whom a negative answer is given an explanation must be made. Usually no refusal is absolute; generally the candidate is asked to wait another year.

The refusal to present to the Bishop is a very serious decision to make, and must be made on good ground. Those who have attended very irregularly can hardly be called prepared, but they usually disappear of their own accord. Late comers are a problem of their own, and should not be accepted unless they are prepared to cover the instruction. Moral fitness and suitability will be weighed, but those who attend regularly and show a reasonable interest, if not real keenness, should be presented. It is difficult to decide which are the best candidates: some of those who appear uninterested often make the best churchmen. Unless there is a very clear wrong motive, the weakest of candidates must be given the benefit of the doubt. [4]

---

[1] J. T. Inskip, *The Pastoral Idea*, p. 230.
[2] Peter Green, *How to Deal with Lads*, pp. 116–130.
[3] See below, Chapter XXIV, § 4. Cf. *Confirmation To-day*, pp. 53, 54. (Many priests will not go as far as this.)
[4] For interviews as a whole, see *Confirmation*, Vol. II, pp. 133–137, 151–155, 163–168.

§ 4. The Service

The great care which the priest has devoted to the preparation of his candidates is often spoilt by the service itself. If he has to take his candidates to a neighbouring church—and this will often happen—there is little he can do about it, but when the service is in his own church, then every detail must be given careful thought.

(a) *Preparation of Church and People*. The churchwardens are important people at a Confirmation, as the duty of allocation of seats belongs to them, and often they act as stewards directing the candidates in their coming up to the Bishop. So the wardens should be told the number of candidates from each church, and must reserve enough seats to give them plenty of room. Reserved seats may be marked with the names of the visiting churches. Some seats may be reserved for sponsors, one or two to each candidate, and admission to these seats may be by ticket, but this often creates difficulties in families that do not like to be divided. Sidesmen should be on duty to make sure that no one intrudes into the reserved seats. Each time a Confirmation is to be held at the church—and it may not happen every year—the wardens may rehearse the method of bringing out the candidates in the way best suited to the church. The Bishop's instructions cover this point, and the idea behind them is to ensure that returning candidates do not stumble over others already kneeling.

The choir is also important in the service, and it requires instruction in details. Attention should be paid to the place of the hymns, and how hymns should be sung; mention is necessary of the versicles and responses, so that the choir is ready for them; the importance of silence before and after the service must also be stressed.

The congregation also needs help. On the previous Sunday some instruction can be given about Confirmation, and a request be made for silence before the service. Before the actual Confirmation service begins, the parish priest can describe from the pulpit the part of the congregation in the service, when they are to kneel, when to pray silently for the candidates, and how they should remain at the end until the candidates have left the church. If the Bishop so desires, it can also be announced that the Bishop wishes to speak to the parents and sponsors after the service.

(b) *Preparation of the Candidates*. Some time early in the course of teaching the girls should be told about their dress, and it is only fair to tell them in good time. It is generally necessary to warn them against extravagance and adornments, and to tell them about veils, if the parish does not do its duty in providing them. The meaning of Confirmation and the two parts of the service will also naturally be mentioned early in the course, but in the last class before the Confirmation itself the service should be carefully explained with practical details; as, the times to come, where the girls will prepare (ten minutes is the maximum time for any candidate to be in church beforehand); tickets should be issued then, if that is the practice of the church,[1] and they should be told what to do before the service and during the quiet times of the service. The candidates may be given copies of the service with suitable devotions added,[2] or a list of suitable hymns for use may be given to them. For example, the following hymns can be suggested from Ancient and Modern: before the service, 470; in the time for quiet prayer, 349; after the laying on of hands, 541, 542; and after the Blessing, 778. A valuable guide, "How to spend the time during your Confirmation," is printed in *Pastoral Work among Children.*[3]

Some candidates will be nervous about the coming up to the Bishop, so the way this is done should be explained to them, and they may be told that stewards will direct them so that they will make no mistakes. They must be put at ease in this way, so that the service can be of the greatest spiritual help to them. The candidates need also to be told what to do at the end of the service and how to leave the church, and it may be suggested that the rest of the day should be spent quietly, avoiding the excitement of such things as dances.

(c) *The Service.* The Bishop will decide how the service will be ordered, and his instructions should be well studied. Recent years have fortunately brought more simplicity into the service, and the accretions of hymns and addresses have been pruned. More has been made to emphasize the unity of the service and the importance of the gift of God, instead of the old over-emphasis on the renewal of vows with the inevitable last hymn, " O Jesus, I have promised ". All that is needed in the service is an opening hymn; the 1928 Preface; an address by the Bishop, brief and to the point, giving something the candidates will readily remember; then, either before or after the Promise, a hymn to the Holy Ghost, sung quietly while the candidates are kneeling; next, the rest of the office as it stands, with a hymn before the Blessing. The service can be complete in an hour with a hundred candidates.[4]

---

[1] Percy Dearmer, *The Parson's Handbook*, p. 398.
[2] *E.g., My Confirmation Day*, published by S.P.C.K.
[3] A. R. Browne-Wilkinson, pp. 211, 212.
[4] *Confirmation*, Vol. II, p. 89.

Dr. Dearmer recommends a steward in robes to take the place
of the churchwardens in ordering the outcoming of the candidates,
and he would have the further duty of giving stage directions where
necessary to the candidates, which might be a help to weak
memories.[1] Further consideration of the details of the service,
which really concern the Bishop, will be found in Percy Dearmer's
The Parson's Handbook, pp. 396–408; and in *Confirmation*, Vol. II,
pp. 84–89 and 228–242. Some interesting liturgical suggestions
for use if the various parts of Confirmation are separated are made
in *Confirmation To-Day*, Appendix II.

§ 5. THE YOUNG COMMUNICANT

" After-Care " is the usual word which would have been used to
head this section, but, like " Follow-Up ", it is not the best of words
for the purpose. It tends to suggest that the important event has
happened, instead of emphasizing that the Confirmation candidates
are now the young communicants with a future before them. They
do indeed need care, and while much that is done for them will
come under the usual activities for young people, special care is
required to help them to keep their communicant status. The
problem is a serious one. Archdeacon Joynt gives figures[2] that
show a regular regrettable falling away of many who are confirmed.
In *Confirmation To-day* is given[3] a Percentage Table, to show the
approximate constant average for the years 1913–36:—

Of every 100 children born,

> 67 are baptized at Church of England fonts,
> 34 join Church of England Sunday Schools, etc.
> 26 are confirmed,
> 17 lapse after Confirmation,
> 9 continue as Easter Communicants.

These figures reveal a grave pastoral weakness, but there is a
consolation in the fact that though some who have been confirmed
subsequently lapse, at a crisis of life it may be possible to recall
them to Holy Communion.[4]

(a) *The First Communion.* At Confirmation the candidate receives the status of a communicant, and so the first Communion is

---

[1] P. Dearmer, *The Parson's Handbook*, p. 402.
[2] R. C. Joynt, *The Church's real Work*, p. 73.
[3] *Confirmation To-day*, pp. 57, 58; see also pp. 21, 22.
[4] J. B. Goodliffe, *The Parson and his Problems*, p. 33.

next in importance to Confirmation, and the priest's Confirmation work is not done until all his candidates are begun in their communicant life. So the first Communion must be well planned.[1] The day should be fixed well ahead, so that parents and sponsors can be present. If the young communicants are encouraged to make a monthly rule, the first Communion can be arranged to fall on the right Sunday for the month. Some priests are inclined to arrange a first Communion on a week-day or on a Sunday when there will not be many other communicants, in order that it may be clearly a first Communion, and such priests have been known to secure some dignitary—even the Bishop himself—to celebrate on this occasion. It is more than doubtful whether this is so effective and edifying as arranging that the first Communion should be made at an ordinary Parish Communion that is well attended. Some prefer the first Communion to be on a great Feast, perhaps even at Easter; so that impressionable young people may see something of the strength of the congregation, and men as well as women going to the altar.

A personal letter or a circular can be sent to those who have been confirmed in previous years, reminding them of their own first Communion, and inviting them to be present. The tradition of the parish will determine the type of service, and perhaps its time, but it should be remembered that music helps tremendously with the young people, who will find the waiting during the administration a little tedious at first.

Some priests like their newly confirmed members to sit together; this maintains the corporate spirit of the Confirmation class, and it helps to make sure that all are present. Others prefer that they should come with their families and sit with them. This is how it should be in later Communions, and it helps at the first Communion because the candidate will not be so nervous when kneeling at the rail with an experienced communicant. The group way represents an end, but the family party represents the new beginning. It is worth while repeating that candidates should be well instructed in the way to receive the elements, and how to come up and when to leave the rail.

(b) *Later Communions.* Though it sometimes happens that a confirmee does not come to the first Communion, this is very rare if proper care is taken.[2] The real difficulty is the building up of

---

[1] J. B. Goodliffe, *The Parson and his Problems*, p. 38. Cf. Peter Green, *How to Deal with Lads*, pp. 131–143.
[2] But see Peter Green, *The Man of God*, pp. 133–134.

a communicant life. One way is to provide adult help. It must be said that the slackness of the adults is a real deterrent to the young people, who can hardly fail to wonder where the older people are when they first begin coming to Communion. The idea of sponsors at the Confirmation service is partly to make provision for someone to come with the young communicant to the celebrations. It is important that the Confirmation candidates should have sponsors, and these need not be the same as the Baptismal Godparents. If a candidate has no sponsors, perhaps an older person will be willing to be responsible for seeing that he comes to Communion, calling for him at his home if that be necessary.

It is a common custom to give manuals or 'companions' to the newly confirmed. These are definitely treasured, and are a great help to them in their private prayers as well as at the Communion services. Many of them have no other books of prayers. Churchmanship will again decide which manuals to give.

(c) *Shepherding*.[1] Neither sponsors nor manuals will take the place of the real shepherd. It is a great task for the parish priest to keep in touch with his young communicants, but it is a highly profitable task if he can perform it. There are three different aspects of this work.

The first is by direct contact. Frequent personal letters to all may be impossible, but they can be used with great effect with the backsliders. Yet even a printed postcard reminder of a monthly corporate Communion is by no means worthless; the parents see it, too, and not only value the parson's interest in their sons and daughters, but are themselves reminded to help them to get up on Sunday morning. The special occasion and anniversaries can be marked with a circular letter; anything that comes by post is valued in the working-class homes.

Communications by post are not the only ways of keeping up a personal touch. Occasional conversations, walks or cycling, or with some a chat in the priest's study, can often strengthen the wavering at just the right moment.[2]

The strengthening of the spiritual life of the young communicant is a difficult problem. Communicant Guilds very rarely attract; at best the Bible Class or Young People's Fellowship will retain a hold on some, and further spiritual help can be given here. Churchmanship of one kind probably keeps some hold through the Sacrament of Penance. The reason for the lapse of so many communi-

[1] *Confirmation*, Vol. II, p. 91.
[2] *Ibid*. (R. C. Joynt), pp. 263–279.

cants is the fact that training in churchmanship is so difficult once the Confirmation classes are over.[1]

The corporate aspect of the life of the young people should not be neglected. Clubs for Boys and Girls, and the various Youth Organizations definitely keep the young people linked to the Church. If they do lapse for a time, they are always there to be recalled to their duties. Lapsed communicants not belonging to such organizations usually disappear more easily. In the essay on " After-Care " contributed by Archdeacon Lovell Clarke, this kind of work among young people is very strongly pressed.[2]

There is a danger in merely trying to cultivate habits without at the same time giving a width of outlook. The best way of helping the young communicant is to give him the vision of God's purpose for the world, and inspire him to help to work for it; he will soon see the need for grace to do this work for Christ.

> " In the after-care of the confirmed, there has been perhaps too much concentration on the formation of pious habits, and a failure to inspire young people with such a programme of Christian *action* as would challenge them to ' go out into all the world ' for Christ, and thus bring them to realize how greatly they need constant renewal by the grace of God, given through Word and Sacrament in the fellowship of the Church."[3]

(d) *School Confirmations*. The preparation of candidates for Confirmation at school is a subject in itself.[4] The parish priest, however, is only concerned about those boys and girls from his parish who are confirmed at school. Generally speaking, he will find that they are well prepared, but his difficulty will be to fit them into the family life of the parish church. Close co-operation is needed between the school, the home and the church.[5] If the family is a good church family, the priest will know of the coming event. He should take an interest in the Confirmation of his young parishioners at school, writing a little personal note on the eve of the service if he cannot be present in person. He should try to see them during vacations, enter their names in his Confirmation Register and Communicants List, and let them have copies of any circulars or notices which are suitable for them.[6]

[1] *Confirmation*, Vol. II (W. P. T. Atkinson), pp. 280–301.
[2] *Ibid.* (H. Lovell Clark), pp. 243–262.
[3] *Confirmation To-day*, p. 56.
[4] *Confirmation*, Vol. II, pp. 175–227.
[5] *Confirmation To-day*, pp. 54, 55.
[6] R. C. Joynt, *The Church's real Work*, p. 80.

SELECT BIBLIOGRAPHY

Confirmation (S.P.C.K.), Vol. I, 1926; Vol. II, 1927.
Confirmation To-day (Convocations' Report), 1944.
A. R. Browne-Wilkinson, *Pastoral Work Among Children*, 1934, Chapters IX and X.
A. R. Browne-Wilkinson, *The Confirmation School*, 1930.
R. C. Joynt, *The Church's Real Work*, 1934, Chapters X and XI.
J. B. Goodliffe, *The Parson and his Problems*, 1933, Chapter III.
A. L. Preston, *The Parish Priest in his Parish*, 1933, Chapter IV.
Peter Green, *How to Deal with Lads*, 1922.
Peter Green, *Teaching for Lads*, 1923.
Percy Dearmer, *The Parson's Handbook*, 1940, Chapter XIV.
E. S. G. Wickham, *Parson and People*, 1931, Chapter VI.
R. W. Howard, *Talks in Preparation for Confirmation*, 1941.*
The Author of ' *The Way* ', *A Preparation for Confirmation*.
H. C. Libbey, *Confirmation Talks on Church Teaching*.
Talks on Preparation for Confirmation (I.C.F.).
H. E. Crewsdon, *Your Confirmation*.
Leslie E. Keating, *Sex Education in the Club*, 1945.
The New Generation and Sex Relationships, 1944, C.E.Y.C.
Christian Sex Education, 1946, The British Council of Churches.
Preparation for Confirmation (A book for instructors with special reference to the place of sex in Christian Life), 1937, S.P.C.K.

* Contains suggestions for Manuals and other literature for the Candidates.

CHAPTER XXIII

THE OCCASIONAL SERVICES

§ 1. A TRULY PERSONAL MINISTRY

THERE are many times when a town priest feels like complaining about the manifold duties connected with the occasional services of the Church. They make such a big demand upon the time of the clergy, and mostly for people who have very little connection with the Church. It is quite a common quip to speak of those who only come to church in a carriage—the perambulator, the wedding-taxi and the hearse; or of those whose only connection with the church is at the times when they are hatched, matched and dispatched. So often little good seems to come from such dreary affairs. Yet it is very unwise to complain; rather, indeed, is there cause for thankfulness that the Church still touches the lives of so many at such vital moments. It may be a matter of convention and habit, but the Church would be in a sorry state if it did not maintain these last links with the masses of the population.

The occasional services really give the priest an opportunity for the exercise of a truly personal ministry. The people have an obvious need, and they come to the church to satisfy it; what is said or done in such circumstances can make a lasting impression. Because of this the occasional services present great opportunities of Evangelism, which until recent years have been sadly neglected. It is important to recognize that, whatever may be said, how the priest takes the service makes its own impression. His manner may be just casual and careless, or it may be reverent and dignified. Kneeling before a service is not affectation, but a sign to the people of the need for reverence in the church.[1]

§ 2. BAPTISMS AND CHURCHINGS

(a) *Preliminaries.* Generally speaking, the days are gone when the priest was in church at certain stated times and baptized all who came. For some years an increasing insistence on due notice, with a proper form, has gone home to people, who have on the whole accepted the higher standard of requirements, as in keeping

[1] J. B. Goodliffe, *The Parson and his Problems*, p. 66.

297

with the ceremony. Often now notice is considerable, both parents
are anxious to be present, and God-parents are well provided.
Patience, prudence, and persuasion of the people have gradually
won the day. Baptisms are no longer, as a rule, haphazard,
though they are still to some extent indiscriminate.[1]

Notice of Baptism should always be required; the Canterbury
Recommendations suggest a week's notice as the norm.[2] A form
should be given to the parents when notice is given and the time
fixed; the form should be returned in a day or two. Particulars
as required for the Baptismal Register should be entered on the
form. Various sample forms have been issued.[3] If the form is
eventually returned to the parents as a signed record of the Baptism,
the back of the form may be used for a letter to parents.[4] Usually
the form gets dirty, and a better plan is to issue a form with notes
for parents at the foot on a portion made detachable by a per-
forated division. Parents should be instructed to detach the notes.
A Baptism Card given at the service becomes the permanent
record for the parents to keep.

The week's notice gives time for a possible visit to the parents
and God-parents to talk about their duties at the service and to
explain the meaning of the rite.[5] Both parents should be persuaded to come; it might well be made a rule.[6] If possible,
God-parents should be communicants; they must be baptized.
In some districts they are difficult to obtain, and the parish priest
should help in finding them.[7] The verger should not be parish
God-father, and if a group of parish sponsors is maintained, the
list should be long enough to prevent each having an absurd
number of God-children.[8] An alternative way of trying to bring
home to people the importance of the rite is to issue a printed
letter saying that parents will be required to sign at the church
that they will send the child to a Church of England Sunday
School. This may be going beyond the powers of the incumbent,
but it certainly has the right aim in view.

The visit to the house will also give an opportunity to suggest in

---

[1] For Recommendations for modern practice, see the *Convocation of Canterbury,
Report of the Joint Committee on the Administration of the Sacrament of Holy Baptism*, 1940.
[2] Canterbury Recommendations, p. 5, No. 1.
[3] *Ibid.*, p. 8; C. E. Russell, *The Priest and Business*, p. 33; C. F. Rogers, *Principles
of Parish Work*, p. 289. See end of this chapter.
[4] The Unicard system has such a form.
[5] C. F. Rogers, *Principles of Parish Work*, pp. 133 ff.
[6] J. B. Goodliffe, *The Parson and his Problems*, p. 63.
[7] Canterbury Recommendations, p. 5, No. 2.
[8] Peter Green, *The Town Parson*, p. 103.

a tactful way that the suggested name might not be suitable. Strange names are sometimes proposed.[1] Children are now normally registered by name before they are a week old. The registered name can be legally changed or added to at Baptism, and a certificate, signed by the clergyman who performs the rite of Baptism, can be taken to the registrar of births, for the purpose of having the entry of birth amended. This must be done within twelve months from registration. Forms can be obtained gratuitously by clergymen on application to the Registrar-General.[2]

Application is sometimes made by parents living outside the parish boundaries. The Canterbury Recommendations deprecate this.[3] The applicants are usually those who have a sentimental attachment to the church, or else they do not care for the churchmanship of their parish church. It must be recognized that parish boundaries mean very little to-day. The fact that non-parishioners can be entered on the Electoral Roll under certain conditions recognizes this. Moreover, it is often good for a young couple to bring their child to be baptized where they were married. Many priests must have experienced the fact that in the first few years of married life of people in a certain class many moves from house to house are often made, so that their old parish church is their only spiritual centre for a number of years. It is best to have no hard-and-fast rule, but to consider each application on its own merits, though babies of families definitely settled miles away from the parish should not be accepted.

(b) *The Service.* The Prayer Book requires that Baptism should be administered on Sundays or Holy Days, after the Second Lesson at Matins or Evensong. This is exceptional rather than the rule, and where it is practised it is considered an innovation. It would be practically impossible in town parishes to do this for all babies, but some endeavour should be made to have a congregation present. A Baptism at Evensong is good for the worshippers at times; perhaps it might be possible to have four fixed Sundays in the year when public Baptism is administered at Evensong.[4] Children's Services could be used more frequently; the afternoon is obviously the best time for babies.[5]

" There is need for reform in the general surroundings of the

---

[1] Peter Green, *The Town Parson*, p. 105.
[2] *Suggestions for the Guidance of the Clergy, with Reference to the Marriage and Registration Acts*, 1928, pp. 16, 17, 34.
[3] Canterbury Recommendations, p. 6, No. 8.
[4] Peter Green, *The Town Parson*, p. 103.
[5] Canterbury Recommendations, p. 5, No. 4.

font." [1] Some modern churches have a proper baptistry; other
churches could make the font the centre of the Children's Corner,
or at any rate hang suitable pictures on the walls nearby. Whatever is done, the font must still appear to have a place in the
church comparable to the position of the high altar. The tradition
of the Church of England is that the font should be near the main
door of the church.

The service is " too long and too difficult for simple people to
follow and understand ", and " is probably the most difficult
theologically in the Prayer Book ". [2] Instructions to the God-
parents can be given briefly before the service begins, otherwise
they rarely will join in the service. It is helpful to the congregation if the minister makes a change of voice and posture to indicate
the different parts of the service. The practical points of holding
the baby and doing the Baptism should be taught by the incumbent to his deacon. [3] Considerable dignity can be given to the
service if it is taken during Evensong, and a procession made in due
form to the font. [4] A talk can be given on the meaning of Baptism
and the duties of the God-parents, either before the promises or at
the end. If a visit has been made beforehand, this is not necessary.

In large parishes a considerable number of babies may be baptized at one service. Some people have suggested a separate
service for each child. [5] This is impracticable in a busy parish;
it savours, moreover, of snobbishness and makes the service more
private than ever. An alms-dish may be at hand for the offerings
which most people wish to make on this occasion. Some priests
devote this to work overseas. Others use it for a very necessary
Vicar's Discretion Fund, and from it purchase Baptism Cards,
Confirmation Manuals, vestry requisites, and similar useful items.

(c) *Maintaining Contact.* Some attempt should be made to keep
in contact with the babies and their parents. [6] Baptism Cards [7]
should be given at the end of the service, or they may be taken to
the house on a visit afterwards. Names should be entered on the
Baptismal Roll under the birthday dates. A Sunday School
teacher attached to the kindergarten is a good person to have in
charge of this Roll, and she will send out birthday cards each year

[1] Canterbury Recommendations, p. 5, No. 6.
[2] *Ibid.*, p. 4.
[3] Peter Green, *The Town Parson,* p. 106.
[4] Percy Dearmer, *The Parson's Handbook*, pp. 380–386.
[5] J. B. Goodliffe, *The Parson and his Problems*, p. 63.
[6] Canterbury Recommendations, p. 5, No. 7.
[7] See above, Chapter VI, § 1 (*b*).

until the child is old enough to come to Sunday School. The Roll must be checked from time to time owing to the many moves young parents make; occasionally the child dies, and a careful note must be made, for then it is very painful for the parents to receive a birth-day card. The Canterbury Recommendations suggest an annual visit by the incumbent—a rather difficult task in a town parish.

Various other ways can be used for keeping a link with the house. The Mothers' Union can have a baby party annually for mothers and the babies baptized during the previous year. Inci-dentally, this is a good recruiting ground for members of the Union. A Mothers' Union member might be present at every baptism, ready to make contact with the mothers. An annual service for parents and babies is not impossible, but not easy to conduct.

(d) *Churchings.* The little rite [1] can be made beautiful as a service of thanksgiving for fathers and mothers who readily appre-ciate the invitation to come to the altar rail to give thanks to ·God. Too often, however, it is just a superstitious custom for many working-class mothers—something that must be done as soon as possible to make them clean. One of the prayers added in the 1928 Book is for use when the child has died. Special care should be taken for parents who have lost the child, even to the extent of arranging for a different time apart from the more fortunate parents.

(e) *Private Baptisms.* When a child is in danger of dying, or is to undergo an operation, it must be baptized at home. [2] A basin borrowed from the house is sufficient for the font, but care should be taken to empty it after use. In some districts the water is regarded somewhat superstitiously. The service will be shortened if necessary to the bare minimum of words. Care should be taken to enter the particulars in the Baptismal Register, with a further note when either the child dies or is received into the Church. The second necessary ceremony if the child lives is often neglected. When a child is dangerously ill and a priest is unobtainable, Lay Baptism is permissible. This can be made clear to Confirmation candidates—and to others when instruction on Baptism is given— telling them how it should be done with water and the correct words, and how the parish priest should subsequently be notified with particulars.

(f) *Adult Baptisms.* Almost every Confirmation class produces a candidate not already baptized. His preparation for Baptism

[1] Cf. J. B. Goodliffe, *The Parson and his Problems*, p. 64; Peter Green, *The Town Parson*, pp. 106, 107; and Percy Dearmer, *The Parson's Handbook*, pp. 423–425.
[2] Percy Dearmer, *The Parson's Handbook*, p. 387.

X

will be covered mainly in the Confirmation classes. The service
for those of Riper Years should be taken for all who have reached
the age for Confirmation. A priest, not a deacon, should take the
service.[1] Sometimes an adult comes to ask for Baptism, perhaps
at the Baptism of an infant relative, and expects to be baptized
on the spot. There must always be preparation; indeed, notice
of an adult baptism should be given to the Bishop. Adults should
not be baptized unless they genuinely desire to come into full
Church membership, and a refusal to go on to Confirmation
would be a sufficient indication of their lack of real intention,
provided the connection between Baptism and Confirmation had
been explained to them.

§ 3. MARRIAGES

(a) *Legal Preliminaries.* The interest of the Church in marriage
is primarily spiritual, but the position the Church of England
occupies in law in the celebration of marriage from a legal point
of view makes it imperative that every priest should know the
legal requirements for marriage, and see that they are always
satisfied. The *Diocesan Year Book* generally contains a good summary of the legal details.[2]

For the publishing of the banns of marriage the incumbent can
require seven days notice, so that he can check the information
given, if he so desires. It is his responsibility to see that the conditions of residence are fulfilled, and that the other particulars are
correct. He is wise if he asks for written consent for minors from
their parents or guardians, though this is only legally required for
the issue of a licence. For exceptional circumstances, as when one
of the parties lives outside England, he should consult his Year
Book, or the Bishop's Legal Secretary, and not trust to memory
or guess. The banns must be read in each church concerned on
the required three Sundays;[3] the membership of the Electoral
Roll of a parish does not dispense with the reading in the parish
of residence. Certificates of reading the banns should be issued
to the officiating minister, and must be in his hands before the
ceremony can take place.[4] It is worth while asking for certificates

---

[1] Percy Dearmer, *The Parson's Handbook*, pp. 388, 389.
[2] See also, *Opinions of the Legal Board*, 1939, pp. 174–179.
[3] For the correct way of reading, see P. Dearmer, *A Short Handbook of Public
Worship*, 1931, p. 59; *The Parson's Handbook*, 1940, pp. 323, 324. Notice that the
banns need not necessarily be read on consecutive Sundays, and they need not
necessarily be read on the same Sundays in each of the churches where they are
published.
[4] See also above, Chapter VI, § 1 (b).

to be delivered a day or two beforehand. Grave inconveniences can be caused if the legal requirements are not correctly observed. No risks should be taken in circumstances of doubt. Certificates of banns should be inspected to make sure that the particulars agree. If the priest has forgotten to enter the banns in time, or has made a mistake for which he is personally responsible, he should secure a licence for the couple at his own expense.

When parishes are united under law, care should be taken to see that the churches are all licensed for weddings before a ceremony is performed. Also, during times of temporary closing of a church for repairs due regard should be paid to the conditions of the official licence for closing; services held outside the church without a proper licence will invalidate all banns read at them. If a deacon solemnizes a marriage it is not invalid, but inasmuch as there are blessings to be pronounced, such a marriage is irregular, and should only take place under abnormal conditions of exceptional urgency when a priest is not present and is unobtainable. Marriage can take place in church by Bishop's licence, and the responsibility for the licence rests upon the Surrogate or the Diocesan Registrar who issues it. The incumbent acts upon the licence, but should he discover any inaccuracy in it he should report to the person who issued it. Licences should be kept at the church for a period, say two years; a banns book kept for about five when full.

The marriage of a divorced person whose former spouse is living is valid in law, but no clergyman can be compelled to solemnize the marriage or to permit any such marriage to be solemnized in his church. Most bishops require that any such applications should be referred to them. There are differing opinions on this subject, which bristles with difficulties. The parish priest must think them out for himself in his study of Christian Ethics. A practical solution is a civil marriage at a Registry Office, and, if the parties so desire, prayers afterwards at the church. The applicants should always be courteously received and their difficulties sympathetically considered, as the practice of the Church is explained. The admission to Holy Communion of people married after divorce is another question, and the Bishop's advice should be sought.[1]

[1] Besides books on Christian Ethics which discuss the subject theoretically, the practical problem as it faces the parish priest is well considered in the Report of the Joint Committee of Convocations, *The Church and Marriage*, 1935. There is a minority report. In some important particulars the law has changed since this report was issued.

(b) *Personal Preliminaries.* It is to be hoped that the days when the parties saw the parish clerk or verger to put in the banns, and met the parish priest for the first time at the wedding, are now over. This is an intensely personal affair, which needs the personal attention of the parish priest all through. Marriage is a lesser sacrament of the Church, and Canon Pym has well argued that, compared with the preparation devoted to other lesser sacraments, like Confirmation and Holy Orders, matrimony has been much neglected.[1] The least the priest can do is to see the couple when they come to give notice of banns. He will first enter the appropriate particulars on a printed form,[2] arrange the day and time and book it in his diary, explain about fees, the organ, music and hymns. He should then go further, and suggest that the couple should come and see him again and talk about the ceremony and about marriage. The parish priest in this has an important duty. The Bishops at the Lambeth Conference of 1930 pointed the way: " The Conference urges the need of some further preparation for those members of the Church who are about to marry ".[3]

Certainly some preparation for marriage is needed.[4] The Church's concern about divorce is looking at the problem from the wrong end, and " adequate preparation for marriage could surprisingly lessen the number of divorces ".[5] Such preparation, the experts insist, should include preparation on the physical side, since many marriages go wrong because of sexual maladjustment. Canon Pym urges that the preparation should be given by clergy, and not by doctors, for the question is not one of physiological facts, but of the art of sexual relations in marriage, and this should only be given by married priests. He recommends that possibly one or more experts could be trained in each Rural Deanery so that couples could be sent to them for this instruction. It is obvious, however, that the priest who is going to celebrate the marriage is the best person to do this, if he can, and many more could be proficient with a little training. Many priests hesitate to try, but almost without exception young couples are willing to be advised.

The preparation should include three parts: the spiritual, the common sense, and the physical. It is as well to begin with the

[1] T. W. Pym, *Our Personal Ministry*, 1935, p.101.
[2] See C. E. Russell, *The Priest and Business*, p. 34; C. F. Rogers, *Principles of Parish Work*, p. 291 ; see end of this chapter.
[3] *Report of the Lambeth Conference*, 1930, p. 43.
[4] *The Church and Marriage*, pp. 26, 27.
[5] T. W. Pym, *Our Personal Ministry*, p. 105.

physical, though it is never merely physical, because the young couple will be expecting this to come. The matter should be made quite plain, in ordinary language which the couple can understand, and not hinted at mysteriously in roundabout words. It is necessary to mention the emotional differences between a man and a woman, and how this affects sexual relationships; this is very important, but great care is needed when this is explained to young couples, and the young priest must study some of the books on the subject before he does so. It is sometimes necessary to explain that the promise to obey does not mean that the man can demand sexual relationship just as he wishes against the women's inclination.

Such preparation will vary according to the district of the parish and the circumstances of the people. In some districts marriage is often anticipated during engagement, and this is a possible factor to keep in mind when interviewing the man and woman. Circumstances also will prescribe how often the priest will be able to interview the couple, and if it is possible to see either alone.

The common-sense point of view is the giving of a few illustrations of the need for co-operation in all things in married life, not speaking of ' give and take ', but of each giving to the full as the foundation of a happy marriage. The spiritual part of the preparation will follow on this, in the stressing of the truly religious basis of marriage, the religious atmosphere in the home in the training of children, the right use of Sunday and the need of prayer together. There should be no mention of divorce, nor even of the indissolubility of marriage, but rather the assumption all through of the permanence of marriage. Nor should there be any need to mention the subject of birth-control, unless the couple speak of delaying the arrival of the first child. If the priest does the preparation well, the couple will return later to ask him about this.

These three parts of the preparation can be built round the marriage service, the reading of which together forms a natural procedure, and an easy introduction to the various points made. The natural interest of the couple in the ceremonial can be turned to good account, and the marriage will be made a happier and a more spiritual ceremony. The completion of the marriage service with a celebration of the Holy Communion is difficult under modern conditions, but in the interview the priest can help them to decide to which Communion service they will go after the wedding. This will arise at the appropriate rubric in the Prayer Book.

In his interviews the parish priest will need much help, but recent years have seen a considerable literature on this subject, and there are many books designed to assist the parson.[1]

(c) *The Service*. Different districts vary remarkably in the way in which there is a natural atmosphere of reverence about a wedding. In some areas it is necessary for the priest to go into church early and, by his presence, kneeling, at the altar or in his prayer-desk, recall the people to a sense of the presence of God. Intoxicants are not used quite so much before the service as formerly, and generally speaking the service is not quite so much an occasion for wit as once it was.[2] Music creates a right atmosphere, and certainly the talks or rehearsal with the bridal couple help tremendously. Very young pages and bridesmaids, and photographers who walk round in the service, should be discouraged.

Before the service the bridegroom and best man should be seen in the vestry and the particulars of the register checked, the fees settled, and a last reminder of a few small details to put them at their ease as they return to their places to wait. When the bride arrives, the priest comes to the chancel step, or enters his stall, and reads the exhortation, from the 1928 Book for preference, and this should be read as carefully as any other part of the service. The service is taken with a continual running commentary to the bridal couple in a low voice, directing their actions, especially making sure that they face each other for the plighting of troth and the giving and receiving of the ring. The 'father' should be told what to do, " Give the bride's right hand to me ", or " Say ' I do ' ", otherwise there is an awkward pause or fumbling actions. The congregation should be asked to stand while the couple kneel to join hands and to receive the first blessing. The couple only are led to the altar during the psalm, and the prayers are taken, the priest facing west. A very short talk can be given to the couple before the final blessing, and if they have been properly prepared, this can be simply about spiritual matters.[3] Both the 1662 Book of Common Prayer and the Revised Book of 1928 speak of a sermon " declaring the duties of man and wife ". For the bridal couple this has been done in the interviews beforehand. Some priests interpret the rubric to mean that a brief address

[1] See Bibliography at the end of this chapter.
[2] Peter Green, *The Town Parson*, p. 108.
[3] *Ibid.*, p. 112, a sample address; J. B. Goodliffe, *The Parson and his Problems*, p. 61, no address recommended.

should be given to the congregation on the meaning of the ceremony which it has just witnessed. This is certainly better than a long whispered talk to the bridal couple during which the congregation will get very restless. Hymns can help the service, one or more at the various suitable places; and prayers may be added, as a blessing for the ring, and a prayer for the future home. Various helpful details for the conduct of the ceremony may be studied in:

> Percy Dearmer, *The Parson's Handbook*, 1940, pp. 409–414.
> Peter Green, *The Town Parson*, pp. 109–114.
> H. I. Smith, *Anglican Weddings*, pp. 40–47.

(d) *The Registers*. The registers in the vestry should be prepared as far as possible beforehand. Such things as a supply of pen-nibs, stamps and blotting-paper are a matter of proper care of the vestry. Some people recommend the signing of the registers in church during the singing of a hymn or music after the first part of the ceremony; [1] then, after the final blessing, the bridal procession leaves the chancel while the wedding march is being played. But many working-class people find writing laborious, and they need to be watched as they sign to make sure both books are alike. The officiating priest should sign in their presence.

In the rare circumstances of a correction in the registers being necessary afterwards, the incumbent should first make sure of the facts and then write to inform the Registrar-General, who will instruct him on procedure. The correct completion of the registers is a matter of some importance, and a pamphlet giving helpful details is issued by the Registrar-General, and is supplied on request. Quarterly returns are made to the local Registrar on demand, and this routine work must always be promptly done.

(e) *Maintaining Contact*. After so much trouble taken for the bridal couple, it is a great pity if the priest does not keep in touch with them afterwards. Their future address should be duly noted, and a visit paid soon afterwards and a prayer said for their new home. Encouragement and help should be given them in church attendance. At the anniversary of the occasion [2] a further visit may be paid, or a personal letter of good wishes sent, suggesting that the occasion be marked by attendance at Holy Communion. Some churches arrange an annual service to which all couples married at the church are invited to come.

[1] J. B. Goodliffe, *The Parson and his Problems*, p. 62.
[2] See scheme explained in Chapter XXI, § 3 (c). The Unicard system has special cards.

§ 4. BURIALS

(a) *Preliminaries.* In a town parish the preliminaries are very
few. A message from the undertaker will give the particulars,
and with him the times will be fixed. This will depend partly on
the circumstances of the cemetery authorities and of the taxi
services. The interment will be at the cemetery, and for many
parishioners the service will be in the cemetery chapel. Those
with a closer connection with the church will ask for a service
there, and this should be encouraged, rather than, say, restricted
only to communicants.[1] It should be made clear to the undertaker that no times should be fixed without consulting the incumbent, especially for a service in the church, and that as long a
notice as possible should be given. The parish priest then has
time to call at the house and offer consolation to the bereaved and
help them with prayer.

In country parishes, and in parishes on the borders of towns
where there are churchyards, the procedure is more prolonged.[2]
All parishioners have the right of the burial service, except the
unbaptized, the excommunicate and the suicides. The choice of
place where the grave is to be dug and its depth rests entirely with
the incumbent. It is customary to observe family sentiment and to
keep graves for family use, but this is entirely at the incumbent's
discretion. Fees must be in accordance with custom or those
fixed by lawful authority, now the Ecclesiastical Commissioners.
Non-parishioners have no right of burial, but the Church Council
can give permission and with the incumbent fix a special fee.
The cost of digging and making the grave or vault must be
borne by the relatives concerned. They must provide the grave-
digger, though they are bound to employ the sexton if there is
one.

The difference between public cemeteries and churchyards has
led to much confusion. In public cemeteries grave-spaces are
purchased outright, but this cannot be done in a churchyard, and
payment to the incumbent cannot reserve any space unless it is
confirmed by faculty.

Before reading the Burial Service, the officiating minister should
have the Registrar's certificate, and the detachable part should be
completed and returned after the service. Notes on this are given

---

[1] Peter Green, *The Town Parson*, p. 115.
[2] A. L. Harriss, *Concerning Churchyards*, 1938, pp. 7–26. Relevant facts are
usually given in Diocesan Year Books. See also *Opinions of the Legal Board*, 1939,
pp. 131–133.

in the Registrar-General's pamphlet on Registration. Canon law requires the incumbent to record the names of those interred with the day and the year.

(b) *The Service.* In some parts of the North of England pre-liminary prayers are expected to be said at the house before the *cortège* leaves. Though at first sight this appears to be spiritually desirable, actually it makes the whole procedure unduly prolonged and drawn-out, and the edge is taken off the service proper. Where the custom does obtain, people are very conservative, and very sentimental about it, and the time for change is not yet. All that need be said in such areas is a prayer or two for the faithful departed, one for the mourners, extempore if desired, with the Lord's Prayer and the Grace. If some of the relatives are too old or ill to leave the house, then a psalm and a short lesson can also be said. Some desire to have the whole service, as they call it, at the house, and so proceed direct to the graveside. This is much to be deprecated, for it is not in accordance with the Prayer Book, and appears to be due either to laziness or to a desire to get it over quickly.

The service in church can be made a very dignified ceremony, especially in the country, where there is a lych gate and a church-yard.[1] Even in the town the service in church need not be dreary, but should strike the note of triumphant hope. The 1928 Book helps to do this. Music also helps, if obtainable, and even hymns said quietly add a homely and familiar note for the mourners. A few words after the lesson are welcomed by working folk; again the note of Christian hope should be foremost—sympathy, not sentimentality, is required. Only rarely should the virtues of the deceased be mentioned, but a tribute to a loyal church worker is surely fitting.

When the interment is at the cemetery, an unfortunate break comes with the journey. Nothing need be said at the graveside except the committal; everything else is said beforehand. Dr. Dearmer advocates that only a few representatives of the family should go to the graveside;[2] an excellent suggestion not yet practicable.

Some people find it a comfort to have the body of a relative resting in church overnight as a fitting preparation to its final disposal. Indeed, it may happen that the only alternative to this is that the body should pass the night in an undertaker's mortuary.

[1] Percy Dearmer, *The Parson's Handbook*, pp. 427–437.
[2] Percy Dearmer, *A Short Handbook of Public Worship*, p. 65.

The body should be received at the church by the priest in the way set out in the Burial Office; the sentences are said as the body is brought to its resting-place, and then one of the psalms from the Office and a collect can be said, concluding with the Grace. The body can rest on a catafalque or bier at the chancel step before the high altar, or it may be necessary, for practical reasons, for it to be placed before a side altar. The Burial Office will begin next day with one of the psalms.

Whether the body is brought into church overnight or not, a service of Holy Communion for the mourners on the morning of the funeral can bring great comfort to them. This may take all the bitterness out of the funeral service, as they are brought to understand the union of the Church Militant with the Church Expectant in the Holy Communion.

Cremation has much to commend it, not the least for the less trying circumstances of the committal, and an Archbishop of Canterbury has now been cremated. There are two possible orders. The usual way is for the cremation to follow the church service, the committal to the flames taking the place of the committal to the ground. A little explanation of the words of the committal ' to the refining fire ' will help the mourners; they are apt to misunderstand it as ' the everlasting fire '. Some people do not find this order very pleasant. The alternative is for the cremation to take place first, attended by one or two male mourners and the priest, and then the ashes to be brought into church for the funeral service with a committal to the ground following. One difficulty of this method is that there is no really dignified method of carrying a small casket of ashes in and out of church. Again the procedure may be tediously long if the ashes are to be buried at a distant cemetery.

Sometimes a priest must take a turn at cemetery duty. If this continues for a lengthy period it can be very trying. A few words may be said to each party with the hope that something may reach home. An attempt to locate them can be made, and a commendation to their parish priest sent afterwards. Results must be weighed carefully against the exacting amount of time required for this.

(c) *Maintaining Contact*. In some parts the family will ask for a memorial service, by which they mean a Sunday service appointed for the purpose. They will turn up as arranged, and be glad to have a prayer for the departed and for mourners. A special address should be given sparingly, and also the granting of special hymns, or the congregation will grow tired of singing "Abide with me" every other Sunday.

Soon after the funeral a visit to the house is very welcome, but the number of funerals may well limit this. If practicable, a visit can be paid on the anniversary [1] of the death—not of the funeral—and the right day must be noted. The opportunities of contact through bereavement are immense. Working-class people, though reserved, are deeply sentimental about death, and the priest's kindly help and words at such a time are never forgotten. Sometimes a whole family may be recalled to the Church. Undoubtedly the occasional services are opportunities for Evangelism.

[1] See scheme explained in Chapter XXI, § 3 (c).

SELECT BIBLIOGRAPHY

Convocation of Canterbury, Report of the Joint Committee on the Administration of the Sacrament of Holy Baptism, 1940.

J. B. Goodliffe, *The Parson and his Problems*, 1933, Chapter V.

P. M. Barry, *A Present for the Vicar*, 1945, Chapter III.

Peter Green, *The Town Parson*, 1919, Chapter III.

A. L. Preston, *The Parish Priest in his Parish*, 1933, Chapter II.

Percy Dearmer, *The Parson's Handbook*, 1940, Chapters XIII (Baptism), XV (Matrimony), XVI (Churching), XVII (Burials).

Suggestions for the Guidance of The Clergy with Reference to the Marriage and Registration Acts. (Issued free by the Registrar-General.)

A. S. May, *Handbook on Marriage in Church, Chapel, and Registry Office.*

The Church and Marriage, 1935, Report of Joint Committee of Convocations.

T. W. Pym, *Our Personal Ministry*, 1935, Chapters X and XI.

A. S. Nash (Editor), *Education for Christian Marriage*, 1939,* (especially Chapters XII, XIII, XIV).

H. I. Smith, *Anglican Weddings*, 1939.

Pastoral Preparation for Marriage, The Blackburn Moral Problems Group.

The Threshold of Marriage, Church of England Moral Welfare Council. (Copies to be given to couples.)

A. H. Gray, *Successful Marriage*, 1941.

Lindsay Dewar, and others, *An Introduction to Pastoral Theology*, 1937. Part III, Chapter IV.

A. L. Harriss, *Concerning Churchyards*, 1938.

* Useful Bibliography in this book.

ST. JOHN'S CHURCH, BRADFIELD
APPLICATION FORM FOR INFANT BAPTISM

Child's CHRISTIAN Name...

Date of Child's Birth...

Father's Name in Full..

Mother's Name in Full...

Address...

Father's Profession or Work...

Names and Addresses of Godparents. (Are they baptized and Confirmed?)

    1. ....

    2. ....

    3. ....

Date arranged for Baptism........................at.........p.m.

Is the service of Churching required?........................

Please return this form at least THREE days before Day of Baptism.

Would you like to receive a copy of the Parish Magazine each month?...............

Parents please tear off this portion and keep.

Date arranged for Baptism...at...............p.m.
The Vicar expects BOTH PARENTS to be present on this solemn occasion, when their child is admitted into the Church of Christ.

It is the duty of Parents and Godparents :—

1. To see that the child is taught to say prayers morning and evening, and to worship God in Church.
2. To see that the child is taught the Christian Faith and brought up as a member of the Church of England and sent to Sunday School.
3. To take care that the child is brought to the Bishop to be confirmed when the time comes.
4. To pray for the child.

A baby boy should have two Godfathers and one Godmother, and a baby girl two Godmothers and one Godfather. The parents may be Godparents if they wish. Godparents should be confirmed, and must be baptized.

The usual time for Baptism at St. John's Church is 3.15 p.m. on the First and Third Sundays each month. Other times are arranged in exceptional circumstances.

"Churching" (or "Thanksgiving after Childbirth") is held after Baptism or before any service as desired.

There is no fee for Baptism or Churchings, but thank offerings may be placed in the box by the font.

ST. JOHN'S CHURCH, BRADFIELD
NOTICE OF BANNS AND OF MARRIAGE

Particulars required.	Bridegroom.	Bride.
Names in Full.		
Ages.		
Condition.	B. W.	S. W.
Occupation.	\	
Residence.		
Parish.		
Father's Name.		
Is he living?		
His occupation.		'

Licence or Banns. Date of first publication............................:...
For Marriage at St. John's:—

      Date.................. Time..................
      Is the organ required?..................
      Any hymns required?..................
      Appointment for Interview.
            Date..................Time...............Place..................

Future Permanent Address...
....
Signatures of applicants..

The priest who sees the couple should take the particulars (assuring himself, if necessary, that they have not been divorced), telling them the fees, explaining that a certificate of banns is required from the other parish, and that parents' consent is required for minors.

When completed the couple should be asked to read it, and then sign the form.

CHAPTER XXIV

THE NEEDS OF INDIVIDUALS

§ 1. The Shepherd of Souls

BEHIND the manifold activities of the parson lies the shepherd's real work—his ministry to the individual. This is the part of the parish priest's work which is always in danger of being squeezed out by too much organization. " All organization, all arranging, and ordering have to do with things." [1] Yet the real concern of the priest is with persons, and as the neglect of the personal factor has been a general characteristic of the present age, so the parson has to watch to see that he does not share that failing.

> " In an age dominated by science, which deals with objects and with persons only so far as they can be treated as objects, it is well to remind ourselves that the texture of our experiences is determined more deeply by our relation to persons than by our relation to things." [2]

In his little book, *Real Life is Meeting*, Dr. J. H. Oldham, building his theme on the work of Professor John Macmurray and of Martin Buber in *I and Thou*, lays great emphasis upon the importance of the personal factor, and how life is built up by personal encounters. " It is through our response to other persons that we become persons. . . . *All real life is meeting.*" [3]

The individual work of a parson is thus of twofold importance. In his personal encounter with another person he can do far more to bring that person to an awareness of God than all his planning and preaching can do. But also in that same personal encounter he himself becomes a stronger and more defined personality with a greater understanding of God. Canon Pym [4] is speaking about particular interviews when he says, " The practice is to regard with an air of expectancy everyone who ever comes to one, as a person who shall teach us something fresh about God ", but this attitude should apply to all individuals with whom the priest comes into contact, especially to all those who come knocking at the vicarage door. The truth brought out by Tolstoy in his fine

---

[1] J. H. Oldham, *Real Life is Meeting*, 1942, p. 30.   [2] *Ibid.*, p. 16.
    [3] *Ibid.*, p. 31.   [4] T. W. Pym, *Our Personal Ministry*, p. 41.

story, *Where Love is God is,* applies to all people, but especially to ministers. The priest expects to meet his Master in his prayers; no less should he expect to find Him among the many who come to the vicarage door for help and advice.

§ 2. OFFICE CALLERS

(a) *Office Hours.* Most of those who come to the vicarage door do not come seeking spiritual advice, but though he will not succeed with all, he is a poor parson who allows everyone to go away without spiritual help of some kind. Again, it is the impression which people receive at the vicarage door that will be the prevalent impression of the priest and his wife in the parish. All men and women have souls to save, but some are hindered on the pathway to salvation by a discourteous and autocratic parson. Courtesy to all is essential, even to those to whom relief must be refused.[1]

Much of the trouble is caused through the priest being disturbed in important work, in preparing a sermon or some other detail that needs concentration. Regular office hours have much to be said in their favour, especially if the parochial staff is more than one. If the suggestion of an office at church or school is adopted, the method is quite easy. A notice is put up showing the hours the clergy are in attendance one or two mornings and one or two evenings a week.[2]

The difficulty is that even such an allowance of time will not be suitable for everyone. In the long run more time is saved by allowing people to come when they will, though they should be asked to wait while a meal is in progress. The single-handed incumbent should let it be known that a certain day is his free day, and that callers are not welcomed on that day. Nothing should be done to give any impression that the priest is not available outside office hours for matters of urgency. These remarks refer to the routine office callers, not to those seeking definite spiritual help; for these latter it is often more advisable to provide special times.

(b) *Different Callers.* In the ordinary town parish there will be many who will call simply to give notice of Baptism or of banns of marriage, and these will be interviewed as described elsewhere.[3] Undertakers may call with particulars of a funeral, or district visitors will call with information about the sick; the information

---

[1] Peter Green, *The Man of God,* p. 122. Cf. above, Chapter VII, § 2 (*c*).
[2] C. E. Russell, *The Priest and Business,* pp. 11, 12.
[3] See last chapter.

will be noted and a word of thanks given. There will also be numerous church workers who will call with some church business to discuss, if the parish priest is not too busy, and the priest should be ready to notice if, as sometimes happens, the visitor has some other subject to discuss, which is the real reason for his call.

Other callers are those who have papers to sign. The regulations on the paper should always be read and observed very strictly; many who bring them do not trouble to read them carefully. Some of the papers can only be signed if the priest has a personal knowledge of the caller, others only require a witness to the signature. A signature already written cannot be witnessed, and it should be noticed that often the purpose of the witnessing is to make sure that the person in question is living. Papers must not be signed beforehand and brought by a relative to be witnessed.[1] A passport application should not be signed on the strength of a mere nodding acquaintance, though some young students will bring passport applications to the clergy on the grounds that a maiden aunt comes to church. A minister of religion cannot sign a vaccination paper, or witness any statutory declaration.

Testimonials are often sought, not only by the members of the congregation and the older scholars, but often by people living in the parish whom the priest has never seen before. The unknown applicant should always be politely refused, though a new incumbent in a parish must take pains to find out which inquirers are genuine. A reference should be given only for a definite purpose, and dated; it should say how long the person has been known, and how well known. It is useful to state the part the person takes in the church, and if confirmed and a regular communicant. Every reference should be a real guide to the person to whom it is addressed.[2]

Another class of callers consists of beggars, some of whom, though not all, are professional cadgers and twisters.[3] Callers asking for some kind of help create the most exacting of interviews. Everyone must be seen, some kind of judgement made on the circumstances, and help given or refused. Every parson will be mistaken sometimes; the parson who boasts that he is never taken in probably has the wrong rule of helping none. It is never advisable to give money direct to the casual caller, though food

---

[1] C. E. Russell, *The Priest and Business*, p. 14.
[2] *Ibid.*, p. 13. Cf. E. S. G. Wickham, *Parson and People*, pp. 48, 49.
[3] T. P. Stevens, *Rogues*, 1944. A small pamphlet giving excellent and amusing illustrations.

can always be offered, even if they are obvious impostors. In general practice it is better to help parishioners, and refer travellers on the road to the relieving officer, or to send them with a note to the Church Army [1] or Salvation Army Hostel.

A common request of the casual caller is for money to pay his fare to some place where he has obtained work; the obvious safeguard is to take the beggar to the station, buy him a ticket and put him on the train. Those who claim to live in the parish, but who are not recognized, should be visited before anything else is done. (This rule is disconcerting to travellers who have given a local address, especially when the priest prepares to go 'home' with them forthwith.) In helping the poor parishioners, opinion is divided on the question whether money should be given direct, or if an arrangement should be made with local tradesmen for the delivery of goods on a note from the incumbent, the cost being settled later. Often those who most need help do not ask for it, and the priest's knowledge from his visiting will tell him where help would be appreciated; money should be given in these circumstances. Accidents, especially, put people in pecuniary difficulties.[2]

Some callers in distress really need to be put in touch with the right Charitable Society. Many exist in these days for all kinds of classes, and the parish poor fund, usually small, should not be drained to help those who can be better assisted through the appropriate channels. In fact, the parson's chief duty is to pass people on to the right place, and this applies not only to those who need financial aid, but also to those who need information. The parish priest must have a store of general information to help callers who wish to know something. Perhaps it is about the Rates, or Relief, or Hospitals, or Pensions. These people are really wanting someone to help them to get their just dues. An invaluable book for useful information is *The Annual Charities Register and Digest*, and its companion annual, *How to Help Cases of Distress*. If the information in these is not sufficiently clear, the inquirer should be sent to the Citizens Advice Bureau, if there is one locally.[3]

[1] The Church Army provides the clergy with slips requesting a night's lodging for the bearer.
[2] Cf. C. F. Rogers, *Principles in Parish Work*, pp. 148–150. Prof. Rogers summed up his methods in his book *Charitable Relief*, an excellent book in its time, but now out of date in view of modern legislation.
[3] See also above, Chapter XX, § 3 (a). An interesting book in this connection is, J. C. Pringle, *Social Work of the London Churches*, 1937.

Y

Court troubles sometimes come the parson's way, and these may mean visits to the local courts. Magistrates are always willing to listen to the clergy, and take their witness to character into careful consideration. It is vital that such evidence should be rigorously objective and effusiveness avoided. Matrimonial difficulties also come along; a young couple may be more than ready to come and ask the parish priest for advice, especially if he has given them an interview before they were married. The possible saving of a home may be the result of such a call.

Other callers are organizing secretaries for societies, and they do not wait for office hours. Some are brother clergy, and some are lay men or women. They all, of course, are seeking to create more interest in the society they represent, and wisely they try to do so by offering help to the parish priest. But there are a multitude of societies, and all secretaries cannot be equally welcome; a frank statement of the activities of the parish is the best way to meet them. Some representatives are only to be seen when a flag day is in prospect. So numerous are the requests in town parishes for help on flag days, all for good causes, that in self-defence a parish priest must restrict his interest to two or three a year, and plainly make this known to others.

SELECT BIBLIOGRAPHY

The Annual Charities Register and Digest.
How to Help Cases of Distress, A Year Book of Information.
J. C. Pringle, *Social Work of the London Churches*, 1937.
T. P. Stevens, *Rogues*, 1944 (from S.P.C.K.).
H. E. Savage, *Pastoral Visitation*, 1909, Chapter IV.
C. F. Rogers, *Charitable Relief.*

§ 3. THE PERSONAL MINISTRY

(a) *Place and Time.* Quite apart from those who wish to see the incumbent for some matter of office routine, there are always some who wish to come for spiritual help, and there would be many more if facilities were given. Some are hesitant to make an approach to the parish priest, some think he is too busy, and others do not know how to come.[1] Consequently the priest must be accessible at home and available at the church; for the one he must be ready at all times to receive the genuine inquirers, and for the other he needs to be about the church after services, and not always in the vestry or at the main entrance. But these two possibilities are not usually enough. Canon Pym advocates

[1] E. S. G. Wickham, *Parson and People*, p. 49 (see all his Chapter VII).

very strongly that the parish priest should devote certain advertised times to being available in some definite place.[1]

Some people prefer to talk in the study, and a way of direct access to it is valuable.[2] Others prefer to be in church, when the' priest will wear a cassock and be more impersonal. A notice can indicate the times when he will be at the vicarage or at the church for such a purpose. The times must be suitable for the type of people the parson expects to come; lunch hour in the centre of a city, evenings in the suburban and working-class areas, and after-noons in the more residential districts. If nobody comes, the times allocated need not be wasted, but may be used for study or for meditation.[3] People may not make use of the opportunity at all, or be slow to do so—much may depend on the priest himself; but when they do come, various kinds of questions will be put forward, either intellectual or moral, or merely requests for information on religious and Church matters. Such questions may lead on to other things. A priest may not be able to meet all the inquiries himself, but " he must look upon the whole thing as an opportunity for making other men, better than himself, available ".[4] It must be made clear that, whatever the question or difficulty brought to him, the priest hears it in strict confidence, and will never refer to it again unless requested.

(b) *Technique*. Whatever may be the range of the psychological expert, the average parson must be content with trying to help the normal person. In fact, it could be argued that too much thought has been devoted to psychological aberrations, and not enough attention given to normal spiritual needs. A priest will develop his own simple technique for giving help in interviews. A primary need is to be a good listener, a hardship for many parsons.[5] He has to find out exactly what it is that is troubling his questioner, and this is not always self-evident in the subject the inquirer first introduces. Patient listening will gradually discover the real difficulty, though questions can be used to draw out the person and at the same time develop in the questioner's mind an idea of the inquirer's home and family life. If a person is a known member of the church, the questioning will be easier still. There should be no sense of hurry or of boredom, but only of sympathetic interest indicating a readiness to help.[6] The process is so slow that further interviews may be required.

[1] T. W. Pym, *Our Personal Ministry*, pp. 7–31.
[2] *Ibid.*, p. 23.
[3] *Ibid.*, p. 24. Cf. Peter Green, *The Town Parson*, p. 223.
[4] *Ibid.*, p. 28.   [5] *Ibid.*, pp. 32–42.   [6] *Ibid.*, p. 41.

It is important that the adviser should be unemotional in the sense of not being shocked at anything told to him, or his judgement will be emotionally clouded, nor should he be over-interested in any particular problem, or he may invest it with exaggerated importance. Particularly the adviser must be unemotional in sexual problems, and not by any nervousness of his own create an unnatural atmosphere.[1] Not only in this, but in all his work, the parish priest should realize the difference in the emotional make-up of women and men. In his work as an adviser he should be on his guard against ' transference ', and the fixing of a woman's affections upon the director.[2] A priest must discourage any over-attention in any form from any particular woman. The complementary relation of the sexes both makes it possible for a clergyman to give great help to women, and at the same time creates a source of possible danger.[3]

The priest will naturally find psychology of great help to him in this kind of work, so long as he does not tend to regard people who come " as cases and types, rather than as individual fellow-human beings to be loved and helped ".[4] Many are frightened by psychology because it seems so concerned with pathological conditions, but it should be remembered that it has much to teach about the " mechanism of ordinary human nature ",[5] provided that it is expressed in " terms of our own religious faith, of our experience of God, and of human life ".[6] With ordinary sane people it is best to call sin by its name, and not dress it up in pathological terms.

(c) *Direction.* It is not the purpose of the adviser to solve other people's problems for them; indeed, he cannot do it, but he should try to help them to solve them for themselves. He can help them to see all the facts and separate them into *pros* and *cons*; he can supply them with information that bears on the problem; he can make the points at issue clear; he can show where the decision is needed, but the decision itself should be made as a general rule by the person concerned. The aim must be to help people to do without assistance.

" Their religion must be their own and not mine; they must learn how to distinguish right from wrong in general,

[1] T. W. Pym, *Our Personal Ministry*, pp. 43–52.
[2] *Ibid.*, p. 53. Cf. *Introduction to Pastoral Psychology*, pp. 258–265.
[3] T. W. Pym, *Our Personal Ministry*, pp. 55–57.
[4] T. W. Pym, *Spiritual Direction*, 1928, p. 60.
[5] *Ibid.*, p. 61.
[6] *Ibid.*, p. 62.

and which is the right thing to do in their particular circumstance. They must learn *how to think Christianity*, and not depend on someone else to do their thinking for them." [1]

On the same theme, Mr. A. W. Hopkinson writes, "Advice should be given sparingly, after the example of Christ." [2]

But even then the person will need help, and there is an art in turning the conversation along the right lines by suitable questions, which will help the inquirer to decide smaller points for himself.[3] The director must watch himself, for dominance is a real danger in direction; some people are very suggestible and are ready to take orders and advice. There are others who go on asking for advice till they get what satisfies them, and there are others again who often ask for advice but never act upon it. Indeed, it has been said, " The people who come most often for advice are those who are least ready to act upon it." [4]

People will need direction for different reasons. Some will come who find it difficult to make a big decision in life, as in a matter of vocation; others will come because they desire to be better men and women, yet, seeing their failings, cannot be freed from them. These in particular need to be shown how bad habits, specially in such things as ill-temper and laziness (often blamed upon heredity), can be overcome in the grace of God. So the moral life must be shown to be based upon the spiritual life, and inquirers must be taught to see how God can be a reality in their lives; they must be taught how to pray, how to concentrate in prayer, and, further, how to use and enjoy the Sacraments. A positive view of life must be given, not merely an answer to any particular problem of the moment.[5] The director's real aim is to help people to a Christian attitude to life with faith in Christ and a sense of dependence on God; so his work is then primarily to help those who come to him in the developing of their spiritual lives. No priest should be content with just telling people to go and pray about their problems; they need real guidance in that very thing.

(d) *Moral Disease.* The average parson will desire to help the normal person, but not all people who come to him will be normal—

[1] T. W. Pym, *Our Personal Ministry*, p. 59.
[2] A. W. Hopkinson, *Pastor's Psychology*, 1944, p. 92.
[3] T. W. Pym, *Spiritual Direction*, pp. 64–84.
[4] A. W. Hopkinson, *Pastor's Psychology*, p. 91.
[5] T. W. Pym, *Our Personal Ministry*, pp. 69–88, 125–155. Cf. T. W. Pym, *Spiritual Direction*, pp. 110–145, 168–201, and also T. W. Pym, *A Parson's Dilemmas*, pp. 51–70, 108–126.

in fact, some abnormal people are likely to be attracted by the advertised accessibility of the parson. Some people's troubles spring from physical diseases, and they should be advised to see a doctor. Other troubles can be classed as moral diseases, and it is not quite sufficient to hand the sufferer over to the psychotherapist. A priest of the right kind is the best man for him to see. The parish priest may begin the investigation. "But if the clergy are to rise to meet their responsibilities in this respect, they must be more than well-intentioned amateurs, and they must make a careful and scientific study of the problems of the soul." [1]

The task of the spiritual physician who treats with moral disease is concerned with those who are—"under the influence of unconscious forces. It is the interplay of these forces with his environment which leads to those states which we rightly call morbid." [2] The two causes of psychological disease are the internal pride or self-love, and the unfavourable outward circumstances. "A neurotic is one whose pride or self-love has come into serious collision with the circumstances of life." [3] The average priest, however, will not get very far in the treatment of such diseases; he must content himself with being able to spot abnormal conditions, and know something of the symptoms of such things as recidivism, scrupulosity, pathological lying, anxiety-states, and sexual aberrations. These really difficult diseases should be passed along to those who know the right method of treatment.[4]

§ 4. THE MINISTRY OF RECONCILIATION

(a) *The Position in the Church of England.* To some it may appear that to write of spiritual direction before speaking of confession is to put the cart before the horse. Yet this is necessary because of the different attitudes in the Anglican Church towards confession. All priests will practise some kind of spiritual direction, and the laity of every different shade of ecclesiastical outlook will seek for such help at times, but there are many different opinions among priests about the way confession should be used, and there are deep prejudices among many of the laity about the whole practice. The official attitude of the Church is to be found in the Book of

---

[1] Dewar and Hudson, *A Manual of Pastoral Psychology*, p. 159.
[2] H. Balmforth and others, *An Introduction to Pastoral Theology*, p. 214.
[3] *Ibid.*, p. 215.
[4] A fuller description of moral disease and its treatment is given in *A Manual of Pastoral Psychology*, Chapters VI and VII, and in *An Introduction to Pastoral Theology*, Part III.

Common Prayer, at the end of the first exhortation in the Communion Service:

> "Therefore if there be any of you, who by this means cannot quiet his own conscience herein, but requireth further comfort or counsel, let him come to me, or to some other discreet and learned Minister of God's Word, and open his grief; that by the ministry of God's holy Word he may receive the benefit of absolution, together with ghostly counsel and advice, to the quieting of his conscience, and avoiding of all scruple and doubtfulness."

As the exhortations are very rarely read, these words are seldom heard by the lay people, and nothing is substituted in any other place. There is also in the Prayer Book the "Order for the Visitation of the Sick", and in this natural provision is made for confession and absolution, and incidentally this service provides the only direct form of absolution in the Prayer Book.

Thus the Church of England makes provision for private confession, and there has been a tradition of its practice in some sections of the Church ever since the Reformation.[1] But there is no compulsion in any way comparable with the Paschal custom of the Roman Church. Some priests of the Anglican Communion would by no means be content to speak of the Sacrament of Penance as being voluntary, which they would say gives a false impression.[2] But the Anglican position is undoubtedly, "all may, some should, none must".[3]

Another wing of the Church would be very reluctant to grant so much, but some of the Evangelical tradition would to-day be prepared to agree with Canon Pym's summing up:

> "There are at least three conditions of mind which seem to demand this ministry for the soul's health. . . . 1. There are people who need assurance of God's forgiveness, and cannot obtain that assurance in any other way. 2. Confession is often the only solution for the man who is not conscious of any special need of forgiveness because he does not recognize sin in himself for what it really is. 3. It is this formality, the emphasis placed on the office of the confessor rather than on his personality which alone makes it possible for many people to obtain advice which they feel conscious of needing, and to unburden themselves to anyone at all."[4]

[1] H. Balmforth and others, *An Introduction to Pastoral Theology*, p. 106.
[2] F. G. Belton, *A Manual for Confessors*, 1936, pp. 8–11.
[3] H. S. Box, *Spiritual Direction*, 1937, p. 27. Cf., M. A. C. Warren, *Strange Victory*, 1946, p. 65.
[4] T. W. Pym, *Spiritual Direction*, pp. 32–37.

(b) *Procedure.* That school of thought which emphasizes confession has its own ways of training priests in the right procedure. There are many other priests who would agree that confession is necessary for some and offered to all who wish for it, who would be at a loss to know how to proceed should their ghostly counsel be sought in confession.

> " At least all clergy should be competent, if called upon, to perform this ministry properly; there is also urgent need for many more competent priests who do not press Confession as the duty on all and sundry, but who willingly and ably help in that way those who need it." [1]

It is not enough for a priest to hear what the penitent has to say, and then pronounce absolution. All priests should be familiar with the traditional procedure, even if they do not wish to follow it in full detail. If a priest wishes to follow his own methods, he should at least know exactly what he wants. [2]

First the priest should be clear about the nature of the Sacrament of Penance, and its theological exposition. Further he must also know about the essential parts of the Sacrament—contrition, confession, and penance. He must understand the theology of sin and guilt, the distinctions between venial and mortal sin, and between material and formal sin. To turn theory into practice, he must be ready to help a penitent to prepare for confession, to distinguish between temptation and sin, to recognize the various occasions of sin; and the priest must also know how to hear confessions, when to give counsel and advice, when to ask questions, when to give absolution, and when it should be deferred. [3] For all these points there are several brief but excellent helps for confessors. [4] There is nothing mechanical in the procedure when properly performed. In the confessional the priest acts as a spiritual father, a director of souls, a spiritual physician and a spiritual judge. [5]

The technical side of the confessor's work should be learnt from books or from competent instructors. It may not be amiss to add here some commonsense points to observe in the hearing of

---

[1] T. W. Pym, *Our Personal Ministry*, 1935, p. 89. Cf. Kenneth Mackenzie, *The Priest and Penance*, 1943, pp. 7–10.

[2] T. W. Pym, *Our Personal Ministry*, p. 94.

[3] F. G. Belton, *A Manual for Confessors*, 1936. Traditional methods.

[4] F. G. Belton, above mentioned. A useful simple guide is, Kenneth Mackenzie, *The Priest and Penance*, 1943. Cf. H. Balmforth and others, *An Introduction to Pastoral Theology*, pp. 135–163; T. W. Pym, *Spiritual Direction*, pp. 85–133; T. W. Pym, *Our Personal Ministry*, pp. 89–100.

[5] Belton, Part IV. Mackenzie, p. 60.

confessions, even at the cost of repeating some of the observations made on the general direction of souls. Canon Belton speaks of the importance of deportment;[1] the priest should be dignified, yet without presumption; he should be correct in his choice of words, avoiding slang expressions, and he should be impersonal, avoiding familiarity. Yet the priest should also have a personal interest in each individual as a true spiritual father,[2] never giving the impression of being too busy to listen, or of being in a hurry. He will never show that he is shocked, and he must try to give the impression that he expects the best from his penitents.

Commonsense is needed in many ways, so that there is no scandal and the Church brought into disrepute. The priest should never make a mystery of confession by clearing the church and locking the door.[3] In a parish where confession is not usual, the wise priest will arrange for someone else to be in church when he hears the confession of a woman, so long as strict privacy is maintained; certainly he will not shut himself up in the vestry with a female penitent.[4] There is always more danger of familiarity and pleasantness in confession with a woman than with a man; some women will try to prolong the confession if they can because they enjoy talking of their spiritual difficulties.[5] To avoid the danger of familiarity, Canon Pym suggests that the penitent should kneel at right angles to the confessor, not opposite to him, so that there is no need even to meet his eye.[6] Pym also says that lately ordained priests are not the best people to hear the confession of girls and young women.[7] One other caution comes from Canon Belton, who says that it is not generally wise to hear the confessions of one's own domestic servants, or of one's personal friends,[8] and the same caution should apply to one's parochial staff.

Care is also needed to see that the seal of confession, which is the obligation imposed upon a priest to keep secret everything known to him in sacramental confession, is never unwittingly broken. No priest would deliberately do so, but precautions are necessary to see that it is not done inadvertently.[9] This may be done in speaking in a loud voice at confession; in speaking in

[1] F. G. Belton, *A Manual for Confessors*, 1936, pp. 175–178.
[2] H. Balmforth and others, *An Introduction to Pastoral Theology*, pp. 135–138.
[3] Kenneth Mackenzie, *The Priest and Penance*, 1943, p. 25.
[4] *Ibid.*, p. 26; Cf. F. G. Belton, *A Manual for Confessors*, 1936, p. 109.
[5] *Ibid.*, p. 109.
[6] T. W. Pym, *Our Personal Ministry*, 1935, p. 94.
[7] T. W. Pym, *Spiritual Direction*, 1929, p. 107.
[8] F. G. Belton, *A Manual for Confessors*, 1936, p. 183.
[9] *Ibid.*, pp. 96–99.

sermons of sins heard in confession in a way likely to lead to identi-
fication, especially when it is done by a priest who has heard few
confessions, or who has few penitents; by change of conduct
towards a penitent; by injudiciously warning parents about their
children; by speaking to penitents about their confessions unless
invited to do so.

(c) *Penance and Direction.* The giving of a penance has always
been part of the Sacrament of Penance, and indeed gives it its
name. " The idea of penance is that we must do something to
express our sorrow; but the experience of the Church has been
that it is best to make this act as light as possible." [1] The traditional teaching has been questioned.

> " There is a certain air of unreality in the teaching of moral
> theology regarding ' satisfaction ', or the doing of penance
> after confession. The word ' satisfaction ' is indeed un-
> fortunate, and may well be dropped in this connection. The
> only satisfaction for sin is the sacrifice of the Cross, and peni-
> tents should often be reminded of this, and that nothing that
> they themselves can do is of any avail by itself." [2]

A penance, if given, should be regarded only as a sacramental
admission that a sinner deserves punishment. Too often it may
be that the penance is regarded as the end of the matter, but
though forgiveness is freely given for those who are penitent, the
real outcome of forgiveness should be newness of life. " The
grace of forgiveness is dynamic." [3] A true act of penance should
be an expression of this new life.

The place of spiritual direction in the ministry of reconciliation
is by this made plain. The true confessor is a spiritual physician
and director of souls whose aim it is to lead his penitents on to
newness of life.

[1] Kenneth Mackenzie, *The Priest and Penance,* p. 31.
[2] H. Balmforth and others, *An Introduction to Pastoral Theology,* p. 150.
[3] T. W. Pym, *Spiritual Direction,* p. 94.

SELECT BIBLIOGRAPHY

T. W. Pym, *Our Personal Ministry,* 1935.
T. W. Pym, *Spiritual Direction,* 1928.
A. W. Hopkinson, *Pastor's Psychology,* 1944.
E. S. G. Wickham, *Parson and People,* 1931, Chapter VII.
L. D. Weatherhead, *Psychology in the Service of the Soul.*
L. Dewar and C. E. Hudson, *A Manual of Pastoral Psychology,* 1932.
H. Balmforth and others, *An Introduction to Pastoral Theology,* 1937.
F. G. Belton, *A Manual for Confessors* (Revised Edition), 1936.

Kenneth Mackenzie, *The Priest and Penance*, 1943.*
H. S. Box, *Spiritual Direction*, 1938.*
O. Hardman, *The Christian Life* (Two volumes).
K. E. Kirk, *Some Principles of Moral Theology*, 1920.*
L. Dewar (Ed.), *Training in Prayer*, 1939.
F. P. Harton, *The Elements of Spiritual Life*, 1932.
H. S. Box (Ed.), *The Theory and Practice of Penance*, 1935.
H. S. Box (Ed.), *Priesthood*, 1937, Chapter VII.*
K. E. Kirk, *Conscience and Its Problems*, 1933.
H. E. Fosdick, *On Being a Real Person*, 1943.
E. S. Waterhouse, *Psychology and Pastoral Work*, 1939.
L. Dewar and C. E. Hudson, *Christian Morals*, 1946.

* These books contain useful bibliographies to the subjects in the wide range of study opened up in this chapter.

.

Part V
PERSONAL CONSIDERATIONS

CHAPTER XXV

THE BENEFICE AND THE VICARAGE

§ 1. THE PARSON'S FREEHOLD

(a) *The Legal Position.* Every incumbent must have some
knowledge of the law, not only concerning his Church Council and
churchwardens and Church matters in general, but also concerning
his own special position. Like the Crown, the Public Trustee and
the Postmaster-General, and in common with most holders of
ecclesiastical positions, with the exception of the unbeneficed, he is a
Corporation Sole. That is to say, certain rights and properties are
vested in the corporation as distinct from the individual who happens
to hold the office for the time being. To quote the *Official Year Book* :

" The residence house and glebe are vested in him as owner,
upon whatever tenure they are held. The Church and churchyard are ordinarily, unless there be a lay rector, the Incumbent's freehold, subject to the rights of the parishioners, and
the jurisdiction of the Ordinary. But in respect of all these
freehold rights, the Incumbent for the time being is a limited
owner—for his incumbency only—and is subject to restrictions
as to his dealings with the properties. He is instituted or
licensed to a benefice, and on his admission thereto becomes
entitled to hold it for a freehold estate for life, or until he
resigns, or is deprived by lawful authority ".[1]

The parson thus holds a well-nigh unassailable position.

" Whether he be conscientious, hardworking, and respected,
or indifferent, idle, and despised, his income is secure so long
as he avoids conduct which shocks the public conscience and
compels episcopal action." [2]

But lawful authority makes very little demand upon him; the
minimum duties required are very light, the requirements of residence
are very mild, and the possible moral and legal offences, though
grave, are very few.[3]

[1] *Official Year Book of the Church of England.* See under " Parson " in the " Summary of Legal Information ".
[2] H. Hensley Henson, *The Church of England,* 1939, p. 170.
[3] A summary of the various Acts of Parliament under which action against
Incumbents can be taken is given in *Thy Household the Church* (V. A. Demant, and
others), 1943, pp. 89–93. Cf. *Putting our House in Order,* 1941, pp. 91–94.

331

(b) *Advantages and Disadvantages*. The existence of the parson's freehold is not without effect on the parson's ministerial life. The advantages have been strongly pressed throughout the centuries.

> " The parson's freehold enables the incumbent to act without fear or favour, and he may speak his mind and follow the dictates of his conscience. Neither malice nor antagonism can dispossess him. He is not removable by disfavour in high places, nor by some passing whim of his patron or parishioners."[1]

An incumbent is free from economic pressure, as far as his livelihood is concerned, from the rich families of his parish, though these families can show their displeasure by the withdrawal of their subscriptions towards church funds. The intention of the freehold is to secure that the prophet shall be free to prophesy.

Just as he has security to speak, he has also security to plan. Knowing that progress is slow, and that often much conservatism has to be overcome, he can afford to wait for his plans to mature. Plans are worth while because he has security to see them through. This is not only true of the parish, but it is also true of the priest's own life. He is granted economic security for which men crave. In the lives of most men the twin evils of sickness and unemployment rear their ugly heads. The incumbent is able to plan for the future of his family, take thought for the education of his children, and make provision for the future from an income which is certain, though it may be small. There are also subtler points to consider. The freehold encourages the initiative of the leader of men; the creation of a system of salaried employees of a soulless central machine would create a red-tape administration, and give the clergy a civil service mentality.[2]

But the parson's freehold is not without its dangers. Because his position is so strong, he is at once open to grave temptations, of which mere laziness is the least. The fact that unprofessional behaviour is difficult to rebuke and punish is made worse because it involves a minister of Christ. Ordinary lay-folk do not approve the parson's economic security, which is denied to them; they regard it not as security to speak boldly, but as security to live without worry. There is also the danger of the man who stays too long, of the " square peg in the round hole ", and of the aged and infirm incumbents. But these last difficulties are not so much the results of the existence of the parson's freehold as the fault of the system, which fails to move men along at the right time, to

---

[1] *Putting our House in Order*, p. 82.
[2] *Thy Household the Church*, p. 85.

put the right man in the right place, and to make adequate provision for the aged and infirm.[1]

On the whole, some modification of the freehold is inevitable, for there is a growing opinion that pastoral efficiency would be increased thereby. Legislation is being enacted by the Church Assembly, to replace the Benefices (Ecclesiastical Duties) Measure of 1926, which proved to be unsatisfactory and became a dead letter.

(c) *The Incumbent's Responsibility.* Just because he is in such a position of privilege, the incumbent has a greater responsibility. As a man of God he must recognize the obligations of his position, and frame his time-table to fulfil all his duties adequately. Because of the peculiar temptations of his position, he must be on his guard more than ever against the misuse of time. There is no fear of dismissal if he should become slack, so he should be doubly sure that he does not.

Again, his income is secure; he has no danger of unemployment, and generally speaking he will not face a drop in income, so there is no excuse for him to get into debt. He knows his income; he should live within it.

Since he shares this privileged position, he should strive to see that it is not abused by others as well as by himself. By influence he should help to secure a standard of professional conduct among his brother clergy. He should try, too, to help to secure an improvement in the legal position by constitutional means.

§ 2. THE BENEFICE INCOME

(a) *Sources.* One of the trials of the incumbent is the lack of a systematic regular income, owing to the fact that there are so many possible sources of income, which produce their payments at different times. It is regrettable that when a priest is considering an offer of a benefice he has not only to ask its value, but to investigate the sources of the income. " . . . The incomes of benefices come from many and varying sources, and . . . in the case of older benefices, hardly two incomes are made up from the same set of sources." [2]

The main sources of income are the investments held in trust by the Ecclesiastical Commissioners and Queen Anne's Bounty. These now include the securities that produce the income of the old tithe-rent charge. Changes during the past few years have provided the convenient arrangement whereby the income from

---

[1] *Putting our House in Order*, pp. 82–94.   [2] *Ibid.*, p. 75.

z

these sources is paid quarterly. Some benefices will have other invested capital under other trusts, mostly local in character, some connected with charities, and thus subject to certain conditions and under the ęye of the Charity Commissioners. Other secured income may come from such sources as rent of glebe-lands, houses and other property. That these sources of income are widespread is seen in the difficulties that confront those who advocate reforms through the pooling of benefice incomes.

> " These (various sources) could in time, following patient inquiry and probably some litigation, be taken over and administered through the Commissioners . . . but it would be a prolonged task even if the work of unravelling the mysterious sources of many benefice-incomes were delegated to local or diocesan commissioners." [1]

Other income is unsecured, and is thus subject to much variation, sometimes considerable. There are fees (for weddings, funerals, churchyard charges, research certificates), the Easter offerings, pew rents, parochial augmentations, and voluntary subscriptions. In those parishes where the unsecured income is a large proportion of the total income, the value of the freehold becomes negligible. In some parishes the incumbent might find himself under the obligation of working to raise his own stipend, particularly where the parochial augmentation comes from a Bazaar. Pew rents are also a source of friction and sometimes anxiety. These unsecured sources of income present a real problem to those reformers who seek to equalize incomes.

However, the majority of incumbents will receive their quarterly cheques from the Commissioners or the Bounty Office, and these organizations also enter into the lives of all incumbents in various ways. Their nature, history and responsibilities should be understood by all parsons. Short accounts will be found in the *Official Year Book of the Church of England*, and a brief account, with some criticisms of their method of work, in Chapter VIII of *Putting our House in Order*. [2]

(b) *Calculation.* Not only are there many possible sources of income, but there are considerable differences in income between the different parishes, a fact which provokes the indignation of the *Men, Money and the Ministry* Group. More irritating still is the fact that the method of calculation of income is also subject to variations,

[1] *Putting our House in Order*, p. 75.
[2] Cf. George Middleton, *The Resources of the Church*, and J. R. Brown, *Number One Millbank*, 1944.

and unless this is understood there may be much disappointment and heartburning after a benefice has been accepted.

In order to assess the value of a benefice, it is not only necessary to discover the various sources of income, but also to know the various parochial allowances (if any) and the various permanent outgoings. The rateable value of the vicarage has also to be taken into consideration in several ways. *Crockford's Clerical Directory* is a useful guide, and generally gives gross and net incomes where these are not the same; but, as the figures are voluntarily supplied, they are not completely reliable, and are often not up-to-date. The Church of England Pensions Board has the most reliable figures, and these appear to be used by the Commissioners and the Bounty Office. The form for the annual return supplied by the Pensions Board is in itself a useful summary of the sources of income on the one hand, and of the permanent outgoings on the other. It is worth while noticing that until the full effect of the last Tithe Bill is felt—that is, when all life interests have passed away—it will be impossible to know from official lists whether the figures given for tithe rent charge are on the old level or the new, and inquiry must be made. In the gross figure of income the following items are not usually taken into account: the annual rent value of the vicarage, and the payments by the parish for dilapidations, rates on the vicarage, and pensions premiums, although all these are counted in the pensions calculation.

The outgoings which must be deducted from the gross figure to arrive at the net income include: ecclesiastical dues, land tax, curate's stipend (where compulsory), the cost of collection of pew rents and fees, charges of administration. But these do not include dilapidations assessment, rates on the vicarage, and the 'expenses of office' as allowed by the Income Tax authorities, though these are allowed in the pension calculation.

It will be noticed that the value of the benefice is for Income Tax purposes and for the Pensions Board purposes different from its value for ordinary reference purposes. The incumbent might well wonder what his income is, for the figures given to him when he is offered a benefice, and as generally understood in the parish, have something of a fictitious character. This difficulty has been recognized officially. A Church Assembly Committee in its Report, C.A. 771, says:

> " A newly appointed incumbent often has real difficulty in discovering what the income of his office is, and often fails to know whether the endowment income is secure or likely to

change owing to the fluctuations of investments or other causes. It is no one's business to keep a full and up-to-date record." [1]

In Part III of its Report the Committee proposed that the Assembly should take measures to establish a Register of Benefice Incomes.

(c) *Expenses*. The least satisfactory aspect of the calculation in the figures is the place of the item ' expenses of office allowed by the Income Tax authorities '. It is a valuable consideration that the justice of this item should be recognized by the Income Tax authorities in the calculation of Income Tax, but this figure is not reckoned in the calculation of the net income. Why should a clergyman be supposed to receive a certain income, and yet have to pay his expenses of office out of it? Indeed, part of these expenses are, strictly speaking, expenses for which the parish should pay, such as postages, stationery, travelling expenses and perhaps others. In some few parishes these things are provided by the parish; they ought to be in all. If the priest wishes to give to the parish, he should do it through the usual channels. But he ought not to be under the necessity of asking for such payments; every parochial treasurer, or the Church Council itself, ought to see that the petty cash payments of the clergy are adequately covered, for they are often considerable. [2]

§ 3. THE BENEFICE PROPERTY

(a) *The Parsonage*. To the pastor whose sole desire is to minister to his people, the house in which he is expected to live presents an unexpected and disconcerting problem. Unless it is one of the few modern houses, it will almost certainly be too large, too inconvenient, too cold, too expensive and too nerve-racking to the incumbent and his wife.

> " Far too many parsonage houses are larger than the income and the needs of a benefice warrant. They lack the labour-saving mechanism and the conveniences of a modern house. They exact a lot of wear and tear, emotional as well as physical, on the part of the vicar and wife, from which the parish derives little benefit." [3]

Yet it is in this house that the incumbent must reside by law, unless permission for him to live elsewhere is granted by the Bishop. [4]

[1] C.A., 771, 1945, p. 13.
[2] Cf. C. F. Rogers, *Pastoral Theology and the Modern World*, 1920, pp. 36, 37.
[3] *Putting our House in Order*, p. 109.
[4] There are some people who enjoy living in a large house. Cf. H. Hensley Henson, *Retrospect of an Unimportant Life*, Vol. II, p. 67.

There is much to be said for a house of residence for the parish priest. In these days of housing shortage, much time and trouble are saved by its existence, and it is by no means certain that the right house would be found in the parish, especially in central town areas, if no house were provided. The priest's work is such that he should live reasonably near his church. Part of the difficulty is the variation in the sizes of clerical families; the house has to be large enough to accommodate the larger families. Then there must be a room in the house for an adequate study, until the day comes when a single study-office is provided in the parochial buildings.

The repairs and upkeep of the parsonage are to some extent provided by the dilapidations payment, but in so large a house there is always a succession of minor repairs, decorations are constantly required, adequate heating is a problem, and the cleaning requires domestic help. The modern parson's wife is not afraid of domestic work, but she usually yearns for a small compact house where it could be done in reasonable time. It is clear that when a benefice is offered, not only must the income be investigated, but the house must be inspected. A call to a parish should scarcely depend on the kind of parsonage, yet if it really is unsatisfactory, the pastoral work can be gravely hindered.

Possible steps can be taken to counter the problem. The house can be sold, but purchasers are not easy to find, and the process is complicated. Mr. Joseph McCulloch describes his own experiences in this respect; he was fortunate in forcing the pace, although he had been assured that it would take half a life-time to sell one vicarage and build another.[1] It is now possible, under the Parsonages Measure, 1939, to rebuild or recondition the house from part of the endowment capital. The loss of income is often more than offset by the saving in maintenance expense. The building of new parsonages must be approved by the Bounty Office. It has been questioned whether the present regulations are the best. Although it is true that a pokey house is not desirable, the standard size still assumes that the priest will need and have a maid. Parsonages, like churches, are still planned on a too solid and permanent basis.[2] Such is the speed of progress that houses are out-of-date in a very short time. Modern estates of houses are built on a short-term plan.

Again, the house may be fairly satisfactory, though a little out-

[1] Joseph McCulloch, *We have our Orders*, 1943, pp. 69–71.
[2] *Putting our House in Order*, p. 111.

of-date. An interregnum is a time for some possible improvements and repairs. New kitchen ranges, baths, water-supply, central heating systems, might possibly be needed and installed. The present survey system could be modified with good effect to ensure an inspection as soon as the house is empty. Such improvements cost money. If the cost is small, it may be met from the dilapidations fund as an interim repair. If the cost is large, one method is to obtain a loan from Q.A.B. and mortgage the income; another is to ask the parish to raise some of the money, and ask help from the Diocesan Dilapidations Board. It is a mistake for the incumbent to try to shoulder all the expenses himself, or even to saddle his parish with them. The secretary of the Diocesan Dilapidations Board should be seen, and his help and advice secured. If each incumbent did his share in tackling the problem, in the course of time a better standard of parsonages would be attained.

The parsonage is part of the parson's plant. It is possible to make it a parochial home, a place for meetings and classes, for small social gatherings, and, in the country perhaps, for a garden party. To do this invites all kinds of difficulties, and sometimes leads to unfortunate wear and tear, yet it does help to display to the parish the Christian family ideal.

(b) *Dilapidations*. The present way of providing for the repairs of the vicarage and the other benefice property is a big advance on previous methods. The quinquennial inspection by the Diocesan Surveyor is followed by a report with instructions on the immediate repairs, future repairs, and an order for the assessment for the next five years. Legally the incumbent is responsible for the payment of the assessment, but many parishes to-day undertake this responsibility. It covers fire insurance and the cost of administration.

When the repairs fall due at the end of a five-year period, there is generally enough in hand to cover their cost, unless interim repairs have been heavy. If there is a balance after repairs have been met, it may be returned proportionately to those who made the payments. If the amount is insufficient, the incumbent is liable for the deficiency, though the Church Council may pay it for him, or he may obtain assistance from the Diocesan Dilapidations Board, or from the Bounty Office, or the work can be done on a mortgage loan. It is worth the incumbent's trouble to ask for separate contracts with the various tradespeople, joiner, mason, painter and plumber, instead of giving the full contract to one man. The surveyors are usually considerate and understanding men, but there is provision for lodging objections to the repairs ordered, and for appeals against the assessment's rate. Every help is given by the Bounty Office, which continually supplies a printed sheet of information, which should be closely studied by all incumbents. A copy appears in the *Official Year Book of the Church of England*, and another copy, with additional notes, is given in *Opinions of the Legal Board*.[1]

At the time of the quinquennial survey the fixtures belonging to the benefice are checked. A copy of the list is supplied afterwards for the church chest. The incumbent may be unfortunate enough to have a parsonage where some of the fixtures pass by sale from one priest to the next. He should watch his legal position carefully. All such fixtures ought to be acquired by the Church Council for the benefice.

(c) *Rates.* Owing to its size and often to its position, the rateable value of a parsonage is often a considerable item for the incumbent to face. It is sometimes possible, for an appeal for reduction in the rateable value to be granted on the grounds that the incumbent is forced to live in the house, or if he is granted leave of absence the house can only be let under limited conditions. In one appeal it was decided that the rent which an incumbent could reasonably be expected to pay was about one-seventh of the gross annual value of the living. Any incumbent who feels that his assessment is too high is advised to investigate the matter. Nor is it only a question of the amount of the rates. Two other advantages arise when the assessment is reduced, for a reduction also takes place in the Schedule A Income Tax assessment, and in the assessment for the Clergy Pension premium.

(d) *The Glebe.* Though this is the concern mostly of the country parson, all incumbents should know something about it, for many town parsons find their way later into the country. The parson generally knows little or nothing about agriculture; for him the glebe is an unnecessary burden. Once it may have been true that the care of the glebe and the farm property kept the parson in touch with the soil, and so with his parishioners, but such an argument has not much weight to-day. There is always the temptation—" to treat the gross income from his glebe as net, and to spend too little on its proper upkeep. The fact that his ownership is temporary tempts him the more to improvident landlordism." [2] Incumbents of those country parishes that have glebe

[1] 1939, pp. 144-153.   [2] *Putting our House in Order*, p. 106.

land, farms and buildings are advised to study the proper ways of caring for such property. Careful administration can improve the benefice income in the course of time. But surely the day should soon come when the parish priest, even in the country, should be relieved of such a care. In some dioceses Diocesan Committees have been set up to advise incumbents about their glebe.

The parsonage garden is usually more than ample to keep the priest in touch with the soil. A small garden and lawn can be a joy to a man who makes gardening a hobby and an exercise. Even then in a town some parishioners grumble that their priest is more a gardener than a shepherd. In the country the parson who gardens has a real link with his people. Generally, however, the gardens are so vast that they discourage work, and few incomes to-day allow for a paid gardener. " Thus vicarage gardens grow unkempt and look, as indeed many are, uncared for." [1] Sometimes it is the trees in the garden which become untidy and need attention, but it must be noticed that all timber on the benefice property is under the direction of the Diocesan Dilapidations Board.[2]

§·4. Patronage and Appointment

(a) *Method.* The appointment of priests to parishes is known as presentation to benefices, and the rights of presentation are in the hands of patrons, who may be either private or public. Private patronage, including that of Patronage Trusts, amounts to slightly more than half of the total.[3] The Public Patronage includes that· of the Crown, the various Church authorities and the Universities and Colleges. This patronage system has an age-long historical origin, and is subject to much criticism to-day. Some argue that all patronage should be ecclesiastical and under Diocesan Patronage Boards, and that private patronage works unjustly.[4] Others declare, " that the most conscientious of patrons are either Deans and Chapters and College bodies, or private patrons, in that they were more likely to consider the needs of Mr. and Mrs. Bull before anything else." [5] Mr. Joseph McCulloch adds: " My informant assured me that Bishops were the most injudicious of patrons and Party Trusts the most unscrupulous." [6] Yet others would say that

[1] *Putting our House in Order*, p. 105.
[2] *Opinions of the Legal Board*, pp. 207–213.
[3] For figures see G. K. A. Bell, *A Brief Sketch of the Church of England*, p. 100; and *Putting our House in Order*, p. 60. Both quote C.A. 128.
[4] *Putting our House in Order*, pp. 59–60.
[5] Joseph McCulloch, *We have our Orders*, p. 63.
[6] *Ibid.*, p. 64.

Bishops and Party Trusts exercise great care over their appointments. The truth would seem to be that, quite indifferently, all classes of patrons make both good and bad appointments.

But the problem facing any particular priest is that of knowing how God's call is to come to him. All ministers, will believe in their call to the work, but the way in which the call comes for some particular sphere of work is so uncertain and unsystematic that it appears that the machinations of men often nullify the guidance of God. Hard-working priests with good qualifications are often left forgotten, while others whose only claim to distinction is that they have failed in one parish, receive preferment. The uncertainty of patronage and the variations of benefice incomes make the movements of clergy difficult, and often a source of needless anxiety to them.

Yet every priest must wait until preferment comes his way. " It is the tradition in the Church that no priest make personal application for preferment." [1] The Bishop of Barking in his advice to candidates for the ministry says, " Make up your minds never to apply directly or indirectly for the incumbency of a parish, unless reasons of health necessitate your seeking a lighter charge." [2] He gives as his reasons that such a priest if appointed will not feel it to be a call from God; that he will feel under an obligation to the patron and the parish, and that, when difficulties come, he will feel that they are of his own making. Yet ordinands are advised by the Bishop of Barking to seek their own first parish and to make a wise choice. [3] It is now frequently said that the tradition in not making application is being more and more ignored, and in point of fact it always has been ignored in the sense that there has been much indirect wire-pulling. [4]

It is now becoming a practice to invite application for some important posts connected with the Church Assembly, and of the Church Societies. Some reformers urge that a similar method should be adopted for benefice appointments. From the information submitted a short list could be compiled, and a final appointment made after an interview. A priest could then apply for the kind of parish for which he felt himself called to work, and whatever the result of the competitive considerations, he could accept it as the guidance of God. He could not then feel that his name was forgotten or overlooked.

---

[1] Joseph McCulloch, *We have our Orders*, p. 64.
[2] J. T. Inskip, *The Pastoral Idea*, p. 141.
[3] *Ibid.*, p. 142.   [4] Joseph McCulloch, *We have our Orders*, p. 64.

It is worth remembering that it was by indirect personal application that Charles Simeon became Vicar of Holy Trinity, Cambridge.
He saw God's plan for himself, and he was right.

> " I had often when passing Trinity Church, which stands in
> the heart of Cambridge, and is one of the largest in the town,
> said within myself, ' How I should rejoice if God were to
> give me that Church, that I might preach his Gospel there
> and be a herald for Him in the midst of the University '. But
> as to the possession of it, I had no more prospect of attaining
> it than of being exalted to the See of Canterbury.   It so
> happened, however, that the incumbent of it (Mr. Therold)
> died just at this time, and that the only bishop with whom
> my father had the smallest acquaintance had recently been
> translated to the See of Ely.   I therefore sent off instantly to
> my father to desire him to make application to the bishop
> for the living on my behalf. This my father immediately
> did." [1]

But how many priests could claim to have the spiritual discernment of Charles Simeon?   It is said that where the personal
application system has been adopted the results have been far from
satisfactory.   The present patronage system of the Church of
England may not seem to work to everyone's satisfaction, but it
does provide a method whereby a priest receives a call to a sphere
of work, the initiative in the matter not being taken by himself.
This is certainly the happiest method as far as he himself is
concerned.

(b) *The Church Council.* By a Measure of the Church Assembly
passed in 1931, the Church Council has now a say in the appointment of a new incumbent.[2] Under the Measure the Council
must be notified of the vacancy; it may make representations to
the patron on the kind of incumbent desired, and can elect to
proceed under the Measure. Before making the presentation the
patron must then have the consent of the churchwardens acting on
behalf of the Church Council. If consent is refused, a system of
appeals can come into operation.

Though it is only right that the Church Council representing
the people should have a say in the matter, the procedure has to
be considered seriously by the would-be incumbent. No one
desires the odium of being turned down. Some priests, when this
has happened to them, have requested the patron to appeal, and
when their personal character has been vindicated, they have

---

[1] Quoted in Charles Smyth, *Simeon and Church Order*, 1940, p. 37.
[2] *Opinions of the Legal Board*, p. 188.   See also pp. 195–198.

withdrawn. It can hardly be wise to proceed against the wishes of the people and to begin a ministry where confidence is lacking. The churchwardens must be seen beforehand, and the priest will use great discretion in the interview.

(c) *The Offer.* Every offer of an appointment or benefice must be seriously considered as a possible call, and a spirit of prayer for guidance should prevail throughout the whole consideration. Some would go as far as to say that every offer should be accepted, unless there is a duty to the position already held. Has the work there been completed and a well-thought-out plan of action succeeded? A short stay in a parish can often achieve much, but too speedy moves are not always good for parish or priest, and a greater danger is that of staying too long. Apart from special circumstances, the future work of the priest should be considered, and his experience should be broadened by different spheres of work. In a first parish, where so many mistakes are often made, five to eight years give a reasonable limit; in later parishes a reasonable average is eight to ten years, but it is not always the priest's fault if he stays over his time. Work in the ministry to-day moves at a much more breakneck speed than formerly, so that the leisurely stay of twenty to thirty years belongs to a by-gone age.

If it is permissible to leave the present parish, the next consideration, unfortunately, for the majority of priests has to be financial. Work can only be undertaken if it can be afforded. Wise words are said by Bishop Henson:

> " It was, I thought, clearly my duty, in the interest of the cause for which I had contended, to accept a Bishopric, provided that I could afford to do so, and that I could reasonably believe that my strength was equal to the work. I would not accept any position which I could not afford to hold, nor any for which my physical strength was inadequate." [1]

Yet surely financial considerations cannot be the sole reason for accepting or rejecting an offer.

> " The right consideration, be it noted, is—Is a man, with such and such gifts and views, the man for the job, which requires and can fully use a man with those particular gifts and views? Only too often a decision to move or not to move is determined by the size and ages of a man's family, or by the parsonage house, vis-à-vis the stipend." [2]

[1] H. H. Henson, *Retrospect of an Unimportant Life*, Vol. I, 1942, p. 212.
[2] *Putting our House in Order*, pp. 62–63.

There are times when a call has to be taken in a spirit of sacrifice and adventure, but this is senseless when the need for that sacrifice is occasioned by an inefficient system of Church finance. As things are, a priest must not decide solely because the income is large and the house good; on the other hand, he must be reluctant to accept even an attractive sphere of work if it will obviously bring him into financial difficulties and worries. It is thus necessary, when an offer is made, that the income should be checked and the vicarage duly inspected.[1]

The next step is to consider the suggested parish and its needs in relation to the priest's own gifts and capacity. Is it town or country? What is its type of congregation and organizations? What is its type of churchmanship and the prevailing kind of activity? Are there special needs, schools, hospitals? Are there any financial worries? Then the church itself should be seen and the contents inspected. The last incumbent may be willing to give his impressions. The spiritual possibilities and difficulties can be assessed, and the strength of the call tested before God in prayer.

The stage has then been reached when the advice of friends can be sought. The various impressions received should be explained to them with a description of the reactions experienced when considering the possibilities and difficulties. If possible, at least one friend should be consulted who knows the parish proposed.

Finally, if conviction is growing that it is the right parish, the churchwardens can be seen. The priest will find out more about the parish from them. He will ask about the parochial finances, and if there are any debts. He will be wise to inspect previous balance-sheets for himself; the way some people present figures can be so misleading. To prevent later heart-burnings, the exact extent of the obligations which the parish undertakes should be made clear—*e.g.*, payments of dilapidations, incumbent's expenses of office, rates and so on. If the Church Council contemplates dropping any of the augmentations paid to previous incumbents, this should be made perfectly clear. The priest must make no conditions or promises; to accept a benefice in that way is possibly simony. The wardens act for the Church Council, but they have no right to ask questions designed to enable them to report what the candidate would do if he were made incumbent.

This final interview with the wardens should bring all factors to light, and a decision should then be possible.

---

[1] See above, § 2 and 3.

SELECT BIBLIOGRAPHY

Official Year Book of the Church of England.

Opinions of the Legal Board, 1939.

Kenneth M. Macmorran, *Cripps on the Law Relating to the Church and Clergy,* 8th Edition, 1937.

G. K. A. Bell, *A Brief Sketch of the Church of England,* 1929, Chapter VII.

Putting our House in Order, 1941.

Thy Household the Church, 1943.

George Middleton, *The Resources of the Church.*

J. B. Brown, *Number One Millbank,* 1944.

The Diocesan Year Book or *Diocesan Directory* of the Diocese in which the priest is beneficed.

H. Hensley Henson, *The Church of England,* 1939, Chapters VI and VII.

CHAPTER XXVI

TAKING CHARGE OF A PARISH

§ 1. The Arrival

(a) *Preliminaries.* When the offer of a benefice has been accepted, much investigation about the parish has already been done in the necessary consideration of the offer. The general nature of the parish will thus be known, and the personal side connected with the vicarage and the income thoroughly understood. The patron no doubt will inform the Bishop, but the incumbent-designate will also write a courtesy note if he has not already consulted him about acceptance. In due course the Bishop will fix the date of the institution. Meanwhile preparations for coming into residence can be made. While the vicarage is empty, any necessary repairs, decorations and cleaning can be done, and this is an opportune time for the renewal or modernization of any of the fittings.

This moving into a vicarage is all very expensive. There is help for this when a priest goes to his first benefice. The Ecclesiastical Commissioners will pay him " on his institution an addition to the income for the first difficult year ".[1]

During the interregnum the new parish should be left severely alone. A wise priest will not interfere in any matters, and unless absolutely necessary, he will not preach or take any occasional offices. The time is useful, on the other hand, for learning as much as possible about the parish, its history and its routine. Once the incumbent is instituted and inducted, he is responsible for his new parish. It is of great benefit to have a settled procedure in taking charge. After the first sole charge the method becomes a habit and part of a routine, but a priest taking charge for the first time should give some consideration to each step. A false move in his first few months may give a serious setback to his ministry in his first parish, and thus perhaps to his whole ministry. " His difficulties will commonly have their origin in his own unwisdom and lack of consideration." [2]

(b) *Institution and Induction.* Besides writing to inform the Bishop

---

[1] J. B. Brown, *Number One Millbank*, 1944, p. 35. Application must be made within twelve months of institution.
[2] H. Hensley Henson, *The Church of England*, 1939, p. 170.

of the acceptance of the patron's offer, a letter should be also sent to the Bishop's legal secretary, asking for instructions about the legal documents required and the fees payable. If a priest is moving to a new Diocese, he should at once obtain a copy of the Diocesan Year Book, Calendar or Directory, which will give him the necessary addresses and other useful information. The Bishop will fix the date of the institution and arrange for the induction. In many Dioceses a combined service of institution by the Bishop and induction by the Archdeacon and Rural Dean is held in the parish church, and a fixed form of service is used. This is a very effective way of introducing the new parish priest to his people, and it is a service the people can take part in with understanding.

A service of this kind, when several dignitaries are present, needs careful arrangement. It is the duty of the churchwardens to prepare for it, but tactfulness on the part of the incumbent-designate can help to avoid any scrappiness in preparation. Invitations should be sent to all neighbouring clergy, irrespective of ' colour '. Adequate arrangements should be made for the robing and seating of the dignitaries taking part in the service, and also for the robing and seating of the visiting clergy. Small vestries usually necessitate the robing of the clergy in other buildings, so sidesmen should be appointed to attend to the clergy and marshal them in procession at the right time. The exit from the church should be prepared in as much detail as the entry, so that unseemly nodding is avoided and the processions leave without appearing to be a flock of scattered sheep.

During the induction ceremony there is often a short procession to various parts of the church; everything should be mapped out to avoid awkward corners, overhead obstacles and incorrect stations. If the institution [1] takes place in church, a convenient table with writing requisites should be provided and a seat available for the Registrar. The newly instituted incumbent is required to read the Thirty-Nine Articles publicly in the parish church on the first Sunday on which he officiates, or on some other occasion approved by the Ordinary. [2]

(c) *Parochial Welcome.* " In the majority of parishes, a new incumbent can count upon a friendly welcome from the parishioners. They will regard him with goodwill, and be ready to give him their confidence." [3] Many parishes provide some sort of social function a day or two after the institution to give expression to this welcome.

[1] A short note on the declarations and oaths is given in *A Brief Sketch of the Church of England*, G. A. K. Bell, 1929, pp. 101, 102.
[2] Clerical Subscription Act, 1865.
[3] H. H. Henson, *The Church of England*, 1939, p. 170.

It is a good way for the parish priest to meet the people, and after the lay officials have said their say, the new incumbent can briefly indicate his general line of ministerial work. On the first Sunday the communicants should be encouraged to come together at a celebration of the Eucharist by their new parish priest. It is natural that many people, some of them only very occasional church-goers, may attend a new incumbent's first service, simply in order to see what kind of preacher he is. The wise priest will try to turn this to advantage—but not by trying to show-off.

(d) *The Sequestration.* During the interregnum, sequestrators, usually the two churchwardens, or sometimes one or two of them with the Rural Dean, are appointed by the Bishop to be in charge of the temporalities of the benefice. They have to provide for the church services during the interregnum, and, if need be, to care for the vicarage property, and pay the necessary expenses from the income from the benefice which will be paid to them.[1] Any funds outstanding after such provisions belong to the new incumbent. As soon as possible after the institution, the sequestrators should give a report of their stewardship, presenting an account of income and expenditure, and handing over the balance. A copy of the account will be needed by the Income Tax authorities. Some sequestrators, not knowing the position, are reluctant to give the balance to the incumbent. It is a curious arrangement, arising from the circumstances of the freehold, but it is a useful way of providing for the fees of institution, the cost of moving and the expenses of cleaning and decoration, which are often considerable and sometimes amount to more than the sequestration balance.

§ 2. BEGINNING THE MINISTERIAL WORK

(a) *Spiritual Emphasis.* First impressions count for much, and the new incumbent's first actions should be to emphasize the spiritual nature of his calling and method of work. On the first Sunday, not only the message of the sermon, but also the prayers and every detail of the services should be carefully prepared. Actually the priest is on strange ground, and nothing ludicrous, even if forgivable, should mar the first day. As the ministerial work develops in preaching, visiting, evangelism, Sunday School and Youth work, and in every department of parish life, it is essential to aim at a high spiritual standard. Spiritual levels tend, unfortunately, to drop, as the

[1] Article on " Sequestration " in " Legal Information " in the *Official Year Book of the Church of England.* Also some particular details in *Opinions of the Legal Board,* p. 202 ; reprinted in a pamphlet of the Church Assembly, L.C. 42.